contents

Letter from the Editors 4

Eat Healthy—For Life! 5

   Defy Your Risks 6
   Know Your Dietary Challenge 7
   Attack Fat and Cholesterol 8
   What's Your Blood Pressure? 12
   How Much Should You Weigh? 13
   Set Goals for a Healthy Lifetime 14
   Start Exercising—Today! 16

Appetizers & Beverages 17

Breads 57

Desserts 105

Fish & Shellfish 161

Grains & Pasta 211

Meatless Main Dishes 243

Meats 273

Poultry 319

Salads 365

Sandwiches & Soups 403

Side Dishes 443

Index 487

Dear Friends,

If you have heart disease or believe you are at risk, our goal is to give you hope and power to improve or maintain your heart's health. Each recipe in *501 Delicious Heart Healthy Recipes* includes detailed **nutrient information** so you'll know which recipes are best for you. You'll get **per-serving counts for calories, fat, cholesterol, and sodium.** And since some of you may have diabetes, too, we've included **carbohydrate counts** and **diabetic exchange values.**

We know what it's like to be pressed for time to cook. So we have identified **"Super Quick"** recipes that can be prepared and on the table in 15 minutes or less and **"Make Ahead"** recipes that allow you to get started ahead of time so that last minute meal preparation is easier.

♥ **501 recipes—chosen because they taste so good and they're good for your heart, too!**

In the next few pages, you'll find facts about **how the food you eat affects your heart,** why **sodium** and **saturated fat** are factors in heart disease, whether or not you need to take **vitamin supplements,** and why **exercise** is critical. Refer to these pages often—and if you have questions, ask your doctor or other health-care provider.

We hope this book makes your journey toward a healthier lifestyle easier and more enjoyable.

The Editors

501 Delicious
HEART
HEALTHY
RECIPES

compiled and edited by
Susan M. McIntosh, M.S., R.D.

Oxmoor
HOUSE.

Library of Congress Control Number: 2001-132271
ISBN: 0-8487-2499-2
Printed in the United States of America
First Printing 2001

Be sure to check with your health-care provider before
making any changes in your diet.

Editor-in-Chief: Nancy Fitzpatrick Wyatt
Senior Foods Editor: Katherine M. Eakin
Senior Editor, Copy and Homes: Olivia Kindig Wells
Art Director: James Boone

501 Delicious Heart Healthy Recipes

Editor: Susan M. McIntosh, M.S., R.D.
Associate Art Director: Cynthia R. Cooper
Designer: Carol Damsky
Copy Editor: Jacqueline Giovanelli
Contributing Copy Editor: Dolores Hydock
Editorial Assistant: Jane Lorberau
Contributing Indexer: Mary Ann Laurens
Director, Test Kitchens: Elizabeth Tyler Luckett
Assistant Director, Test Kitchens: Julie Christopher
Recipe Editor: Gayle Hays Sadler
Test Kitchens Staff: Jennifer Cofield;
  Gretchen Feldtman, R.D.; David Gallent;
  Ana Kelly; Jan A. Smith
Senior Photographer: Jim Bathie
Photographer: Brit Huckabay
Senior Photo Stylist: Kay E. Clarke
Director, Production and Distribution: Phillip Lee
Books Production Manager: Theresa L. Beste
Production Assistant: Faye Porter Bonner

We're Here for You!

We at Oxmoor House are
dedicated to serving you
with reliable information
that expands your imagina-
tion and enriches your life.
We welcome your comments
and suggestions.
Please write us at:

**Oxmoor House, Inc.
Editor, *501 Delicious Heart
Healthy Recipes*
2100 Lakeshore Drive
Birmingham, AL 35209**

**For more books to enrich
your life, visit
oxmoorhouse.com**

Eat Healthy—For Life!

Eat Healthy—
For Life!

*Whether you've been told you have heart disease
or you're the picture of perfect health,
heart-healthy eating makes good sense.*

Defy Your Risks

Your risk of developing heart disease increases as you age, is greater for men than women, and tends to run in families. You're more likely to have heart disease if you're a smoker, are overweight, or have diabetes. **You can't do a thing about your age, gender, or family history. But you may be able to improve or control many of the other risk factors by making certain lifestyle changes.**

HOW TO IMPROVE RISK FACTORS

• **Quit smoking.** A smoker has more than twice the risk of having a heart attack as a nonsmoker.

• **Lower your blood cholesterol.** High levels of blood cholesterol make you more likely to develop heart disease.

• **Lower your blood pressure.** High blood pressure increases your risk for having strokes and heart attacks.

• **Get some exercise.** A lack of physical exercise makes you more susceptible to heart disease.

• **Lose weight.** People who are overweight or obese tend to have higher than desired blood pressure and blood cholesterol.

• **Check your blood sugar.** People who have diabetes are more likely to develop heart disease than people who do not have diabetes.

Know Your Dietary Challenge

Use *501 Delicious Heart Healthy Recipes* as your guidebook to good heart health. It follows the American Heart Association's (AHA) guidelines for heart-healthy eating.

SIX HEALTHY HEART GUIDELINES

• **Total fat** should be no more than 30% of total calories.
• **Saturated fatty acid** and **trans fatty acid** intake should be less than 10% of total calories (less than 7% if you have heart disease, have had a heart attack, or have high cholesterol).
• **Polyunsaturated fatty acid** intake should be 8 to 10% of total calories.
• **Monounsaturated fatty acids** should provide about 10 to 15% of total calories.
• **Cholesterol** intake should be less than 300 milligrams per day.
• **Sodium** intake should be no more than 2,400 milligrams per day.
(Growing children, teenagers, and pregnant or breast-feeding women have needs that may exceed these restrictions.)

The recipes have been especially chosen because they meet the AHA guidelines, they're good for your heart, and they taste delicious. You'll find tempting appetizers like Mediterranean Nachos (page 35) and luscious desserts, including Chocolate Cream Pie on page 138. Vegetarians will enjoy many meatless entrées such as Vegetable Lasagna (page 255), while meat-lovers will delight in seeing more than 40 pages devoted to meat, including such delicacies as Port Marinated Steaks on page 282.

If you've been diagnosed with heart disease and are following a specific fat or sodium level, choose recipes that fit your diet plan. And if you have questions, check with a registered dietitian or your health-care provider.

♥ Women are at Risk, too

Women, especially before menopause, have a lower risk of developing heart disease than men. **But after menopause, a woman's risk of heart disease increases** and she's less likely than a man to survive a first heart attack.

In the past, a woman's risk of developing heart disease was underestimated. We now know that many women, especially after menopause, are at risk.

Lowering cholesterol levels can be quite effective in decreasing a woman's risk of heart attack and stroke. It's critical that women with high levels of blood cholesterol do all they can to lower their blood cholesterol.

Attack Fat and Cholesterol

One of the primary signs of heart disease is a high level of blood cholesterol. There's cholesterol in everyone's blood—in fact, the body makes some cholesterol itself. But when the cholesterol in your blood gets too high, it collects on the walls of arteries and blood vessels, causing a condition called atherosclerosis, which is a symptom of heart disease.

Cholesterol travels through the blood in packages called lipoproteins. **The type of lipoprotein package determines whether the cholesterol is "good" or "bad."** "Good" cholesterol (**HDL cholesterol**) travels on high-density lipoproteins which remove cholesterol from the arteries. "Bad" cholesterol (**LDL cholesterol**) travels on low-density lipoproteins which deposit cholesterol on artery walls.

What should your blood cholesterol be? To find out, check the chart below:

Cholesterol (mg/dl)	Desirable	Borderline high-risk	High-risk
Total cholesterol	under 200	200-239	240 or higher
LDL	under 130	130-159	160 or higher
HDL	35 or higher	under 35	under 35

While a high level of blood cholesterol increases your risk of developing heart disease, you can lower your risk by decreasing the level of total cholesterol and LDL cholesterol in your blood. **Cutting back on the fat in your diet can help lower blood cholesterol.** In fact, a healthy meal plan includes no more than 30 percent of total daily calories as fat. Here's how this translates to grams of fat per day:

If you eat	You can have
1200 calories/day	up to 40 grams of fat/day
1600 calories/day	up to 53 grams of fat/day
2000 calories/day	up to 67 grams of fat/day
2200 calories/day	up to 73 grams of fat/day

This recommendation doesn't mean that every food you eat has to fall under the 30 percent level. For example, Maple-Glazed Salmon on page 184 provides 41 percent of calories as fat because salmon is a fatty type of fish. But when you eat the salmon in a meal with low-fat rice or pasta and vegetables, the fat percentage for the whole meal will be less than 30 percent.

The amount of fat is not all that's important—consider the type of fat, too. Fat in food is made up of units called fatty acids. These are classified as **monounsaturated, polyunsaturated, saturated,** and **trans fatty acids.** Different fatty acids affect health by raising or lowering blood cholesterol.

Type of fatty acid	Effect on cholesterol	Where it's found	Recommended amount
Monounsaturated	Lowers "bad" Raises "good"	Avocados, peanuts, and peanut, canola, and olive oils	10 to 15 percent of total calories
Polyunsaturated	Lowers "bad"	Vegetable oils (such as sunflower, corn, and safflower), nuts, and sunflower seeds	10 percent of total calories
Saturated	Raises "bad"	Animal fats (butter, whole milk, ice cream, meat, and poultry skin) and coconut, palm, and palm kernel oil	Less than 10 percent of total calories
Trans	Raises "bad" Lowers "good"	Hydrogenated vegetable fats (shortening and stick margarine), and commercially fried foods and baked goods	Minimal

Since one goal of a heart-healthy diet is to lower blood cholesterol, **it's wise to limit the cholesterol that you eat.** If you eat fewer foods from animal sources, you will eat less cholesterol. The AHA recommends that healthy individuals should limit cholesterol to less than 300 milligrams per day. If you already have heart disease, the recommendation is to stay under 200 milligrams.

Get the Upper Hand on Trans Fats

Trans fats raise "bad" (LDL) cholesterol about as much as saturated fats do. To make matters worse, trans fats actually lower "good" (HDL) cholesterol, too. Trans fats are formed when hydrogen is added to an oil to make it firm, as in margarine or vegetable shortening. Trans fats are also high in commercially baked cookies, pastries, and fried foods.

Heart-Smart Shopping
A variety of reduced-fat margarine and butter products are now available for heart-healthy cooking and eating:

• Regular **margarine** is made with vegetable oil. Regular margarine (without any kind of "light" descriptor) must be at least 80% fat; the other 20% is water, coloring, flavoring, and additives.
• **Reduced-fat, reduced-calorie,** or **diet margarine** has no more than 60% oil, with 25% less fat and calories than regular margarine.
• **Light** or **lower-fat margarine** contains no more than 40% oil and has at least 50% less fat than regular margarine.
• **Fat-free margarine** must have virtually no fat—less than 0.5 grams of fat per tablespoon.
• **Vegetable oil spreads** do not meet the criteria for regular margarine, but are not low enough in fat to fit into one of the modified margarine categories. These spreads may be as high as 79% oil, or as low as 0%.
• **Butter** is at least 80% milk fat and up to 20% water and milk solids.
• **Light butter** has about half the fat of regular butter because water, fat-free milk, and gelatin are added.
• **Whipped butter** or **margarine**, with air beaten into it, has a better consistency for spreading than cold stick butter or margarine.

So what's the best product to buy? The type depends on how it will be used. Note the percentage of oil on the label, and use these tips as a guide:

Butter or Margarine?

Since many margarines contain trans fats, some food experts say that butter is better for you than margarine. But butter has saturated fat, which raises blood cholesterol, just as margarine (with trans fats) does. While the debate continues, the best advice is to eat less of both.

• **90% oil**—Use for baked products such as pie crusts when an exact amount of fat is necessary. Also use for most cookies and cakes.
• **60 to 90% oil**—Use almost anywhere that butter or margarine is specified. Do not use for baked goods such as pie crusts that require an exact amount of fat and moisture.
• **50 to 60% oil**—Use for most cooking, sautéing, topping, and spreading. Do not use for baking, unless the recipe calls for reduced-calorie margarine.
• **49% or less oil**—Use only for spreading, topping, and adding flavor to recipes that already have a significant amount of moisture. Do not use for baking.

Heart-Smart Cooking

The step-by-step instructions in *501 Delicious Heart Healthy Recipes* make it easier to create light, fresh, heart-healthy meals. You can use these methods to modify your own recipes, as well.

- **Bake, broil, roast, steam, sauté, or poach** foods in nonstick cookware.
- **Roast meats and poultry** on a rack so that fat drips away.
- **Serve more vegetable dishes** and smaller amounts of meat.
- **Remove poultry skin and meat fat** before or after cooking.
- **Limit your intake of organ meats** like liver.
- **Cut cholesterol** by eating no more than 4 egg yolks per week.
- **Use egg whites or egg substitute** instead of whole eggs.
- **Choose fat-free dairy products** like fat-free milk and yogurt.
- **Buy light, lower-fat, or fat-free margarines** for spreading. Choose one with no more than 2 grams of saturated and trans fats combined.
- **Look for margarine products made with "liquid" oil** rather than "hydrogenated" oil or "vegetable shortening." When you see the word hydrogenated, the product is higher in trans fats.
- **Use less margarine or butter** of any kind.

Do You Need Vitamins?

For years, research has looked at how vitamins and minerals affect our health. Those that may play a role in decreasing the risk for developing heart disease include beta carotene, vitamin C, vitamin E, and certain B vitamins, including folic acid.

The best way to get needed vitamins and minerals is to eat healthy food—especially fruit, vegetables, and whole grains. If you don't eat nutritiously or have special needs, you may be wise to take a multivitamin/mineral pill. Older adults might consider a vitamin B12 supplement and most adults should consider a calcium supplement. However, taking a supplement does not mean you can ignore eating healthy food. **Supplements may provide certain nutrients, but they don't provide fiber and other disease-fighting substances found in food.**

What's Your Blood Pressure?

Knowing whether or not you have hypertension (high blood pressure) is critical to protecting your heart since hypertension increases the risk of heart disease and strokes. **There are often no warning signs—you may not know your blood pressure is high until you have a blood pressure test.**

This chart shows the categories of blood pressure. Even normal and high normal blood pressure levels increase your risk of stroke and should be lowered to the optimal level, if possible.

Blood pressure (mm/Hg)	Optimal	Normal	High Normal	High Blood Pressure
Systolic (top number)	less than 120	less than 130	130–139	140 or higher
Diastolic (bottom number)	less than 80	less than 85	85–89	90 or higher

If you have high blood pressure, your doctor will probably tell you to reduce the sodium you eat, lose weight, increase physical activity, and limit alcohol. Even if your blood pressure is normal, it's wise to cut back on the sodium you eat. The average American eats more than 4,000 milligrams of sodium a day, and excess sodium today may increase your blood pressure in years to come. **The AHA recommends that healthy people consume under 2,400 milligrams of sodium daily—less if your blood pressure is high.**

Ways to Cut Back on Sodium

- **Gradually use less salt** (a teaspoon contains about 2,300 milligrams sodium) to give your tastebuds time to adjust.
- **Use herbs and spices** to add flavor without salt.
- **Avoid high-salt seasonings** such as garlic salt, seasoned salt, and monosodium glutamate (MSG).
- **Buy no-salt-added canned soups** and vegetables and packaged mixes.
- **Eat reduced-sodium chips** and crackers instead of salted snacks.
- **Check the sodium on labels** of packaged and processed foods. High-sodium foods don't always taste salty.
- **Limit high-sodium condiments** like soy sauce, ketchup, mustard, salad dressings, pickles, and olives.
- **Some medicines are high in sodium.** Check labels and ask your pharmacist if you have questions.

How Much Should You Weigh?

Being overweight or obese is another risk factor you can control.
The **Body Mass Index** (BMI) measures your weight relative to your height and is considered a more accurate measurement of body fat than former "ideal" weight charts.

To use the BMI table below:

1. Find your height in inches on the left side of the table.
2. On the row corresponding to your height, find your current weight.
3. Look at the numbers at the top of the column to find your BMI.
4. Once you've found your BMI, use the health risk chart to determine if you are overweight or obese. If you are, turn the page for tips on how to get your weight under control.

BODY MASS INDEX TABLE

BMI	19	21	23	25	27	30	32	34	36	38
Height				Weight (pounds)						
58"	91	100	110	119	129	143	152	162	172	181
59"	94	104	114	124	134	149	159	169	179	188
60"	97	107	117	127	138	153	163	173	183	194
61"	101	111	122	132	143	159	169	180	191	201
62"	103	114	125	136	147	163	174	185	196	206
63"	107	119	130	141	152	169	181	192	203	214
64"	111	123	135	146	158	176	187	199	211	223
65"	114	126	138	150	162	180	192	204	216	228
66"	118	131	143	156	168	187	199	212	224	236
67"	121	134	147	159	172	191	204	217	229	242
68"	125	139	152	165	178	198	211	224	238	251
69"	128	142	155	169	182	203	216	230	243	257
70"	133	147	161	175	189	210	224	237	251	265
71"	136	150	164	179	193	214	229	243	257	271
72"	140	155	170	185	199	221	236	251	266	281
73"	143	158	174	189	204	226	241	257	272	287
74"	148	164	179	195	210	234	249	265	281	296

BMI AND HEALTH RISK

Below 18.5 = Underweight
18.5 to 24.9 = Healthy Weight
25.0 to 29.9 = Overweight
30+   = Obese

If you are 5 feet 7 inches (67") and weigh 147 pounds, your BMI is 23. This means that you have a low risk of developing a weight-related disease, such as heart disease or Type 2 diabetes.

Set Goals for a Healthy Lifetime

Here are the basic principles to remember:

• **Reach and maintain a healthy weight.** If you determine that you need to lose weight, start by setting reasonable goals that will last a lifetime. There are two ways to lose weight: eat fewer calories than your body needs for energy, or burn extra calories by increasing your level of activity. To lose one pound a week, cut back or burn 500 calories a day (3,500 calories equal 1 pound). Combine walking or another type of aerobic activity with a cutback in calories and gradual weight loss should result.

• **Eat a variety of foods that are low in fat.** Different foods contain different amounts of vitamins, minerals, and other nutrients. For instance, fruit provides vitamin C, but no protein; meat provides protein but no vitamin C. Since we need some of each of the nutrients to stay healthy, it's wise to eat a variety of foods from each of the main food groups. Here are the recommended servings:

Basic Food Group	Recommended Servings
Breads, cereal, pasta, & starchy vegetables	6 or more per day
Vegetables & fruit	5 or more per day
Lean meat, poultry, & fish	About 6 ounces (cooked) per day
Eggs	No more than 4 yolks per week. (egg whites are not limited)
Fat-free or low-fat milk & dairy products	2 to 4 per day
Fats, oils, nuts, seeds, & sweets	Use sparingly

• **Eat more foods rich in fiber,** such as whole grain breads and cereals, legumes, vegetables, and fruit. A healthy diet contains 25 to 30 grams of fiber a day. Pork-and-Black Bean Chili (page 437) is just one of many high-fiber recipes in this book.

• **Limit the cholesterol you eat.** Cholesterol is found in meat, poultry, fish, dairy products (except those that are fat-free), and eggs. Mexican-Style Poached Eggs on page 270 shows a healthy way to prepare eggs for breakfast or brunch, while other recipes on pages 271 and 272 demonstrate the use of egg substitute in meatless entrées.

• **Keep an eye on the amount of sodium you eat.** Throughout the book you'll find recipes that use herbs and spices and reduced-sodium products to add flavor. The recipe for Orange-Spiced Carrots (page 460) is a great example of how to use fruit and spices instead of salt. **If you have high blood pressure, congestive heart failure, or edema, your prescribed sodium level may be very low. Before preparing a recipe, make sure the sodium content fits your restrictions.** We limited salt and other high-sodium ingredients, yet some recipes do include these ingredients. Omit these as your tastebuds become accustomed to less salt.

• **Use nutrient information in recipes to make sure you eat a healthy diet.** Each recipe provides easy-to-read information about key nutrients important in the prevention of heart disease. No more confusion about whether a recipe fits your diet plan. For example, you'll find this valuable information next to the recipe for Crispy Oven-Fried Chicken on page 324:

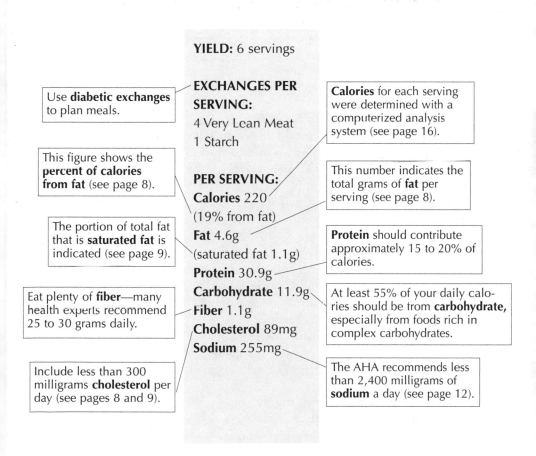

YIELD: 6 servings

Use **diabetic exchanges** to plan meals.

EXCHANGES PER SERVING:
4 Very Lean Meat
1 Starch

Calories for each serving were determined with a computerized analysis system (see page 16).

This figure shows the **percent of calories from fat** (see page 8).

PER SERVING:
Calories 220
(19% from fat)

This number indicates the total grams of **fat** per serving (see page 8).

The portion of total fat that is **saturated fat** is indicated (see page 9).

Fat 4.6g
(saturated fat 1.1g)
Protein 30.9g

Protein should contribute approximately 15 to 20% of calories.

Eat plenty of **fiber**—many health experts recommend 25 to 30 grams daily.

Carbohydrate 11.9g
Fiber 1.1g
Cholesterol 89mg
Sodium 255mg

At least 55% of your daily calories should be from **carbohydrate,** especially from foods rich in complex carbohydrates.

Include less than 300 milligrams **cholesterol** per day (see pages 8 and 9).

The AHA recommends less than 2,400 milligrams of **sodium** a day (see page 12).

Start Exercising—Today!

A regular exercise program is critical to keeping your blood cholesterol normal and increasing your level of HDL "good" cholesterol. It can also help you control high blood pressure and lose or maintain weight. Any regular exercise of moderate intensity is helpful, although more intense exercise is better. Aerobic exercise has long been promoted for heart health, but we now know that resistance exercise (such as lifting weights to build body strength) is valuable, too. Resistance exercise increases metabolic rate, increases levels of HDL "good" cholesterol, and decreases LDL "bad" cholesterol. (Resistance exercise is not recommended for those with angina, congestive heart failure, or valve disease.)

About Our Recipe Analyses

Each recipe in *501 Delicious Heart Healthy Recipes* has been kitchen-tested by a staff of qualified food professionals. Registered dietitians have determined the nutrient information using a computer system that analyzes every ingredient. The testing ensures the success of the recipes; the analysis helps you fit them into your menu plans.

The nutrient information that appears with each recipe is explained on page 15. Values are as accurate as possible and are based on these assumptions:

• When the recipe calls for cooked pasta, rice, or noodles, we base the analysis on cooking without additional salt or fat.
• The calculations indicate that meat and poultry are trimmed of fat and skin before cooking.
• Only the amount of marinade absorbed by the food is calculated.
• Garnishes and other optional ingredients are not calculated.
• Some of the alcohol calories evaporate during heating, and only those remaining are calculated.
• When a range is given for an ingredient (2 to 2½ cups, for instance), we calculate using the lesser amount.
• Fruits and vegetables in the ingredients are not peeled, unless specified.

appetizers & beverages

YIELD: 32 servings

EXCHANGES PER SERVING:
1 Fruit
½ Fat

PER SERVING:
Calories 92
(28% from fat)
Fat 2.9g
(saturated fat 1.8g)
Protein 0.8g
Carbohydrate 16.9g
Fiber 1.4g
Cholesterol 8mg
Sodium 51mg

Make Ahead
TOFFEE DIP WITH APPLES

¾ cup packed brown sugar
½ cup powdered sugar
1 teaspoon vanilla extract
1 (8-ounce) block ⅓-less-fat cream cheese, softened
¾ cup toffee bits (such as Skor) (about 4 ounces)
1 cup pineapple juice
6 Red Delicious apples, each cored and cut into 8 wedges
6 Granny Smith apples, each cored and cut into 8 wedges

1. Combine first 4 ingredients in a bowl; beat at medium speed of a mixer until smooth. Add toffee bits, and mix well. Cover and chill.

2. Combine juice and apples in a bowl; toss well. Drain apples; serve with dip. **Yield:** 2 cups (serving size: 1 tablespoon dip and 3 apple wedges).

Make Ahead
FRUIT KABOBS
WITH COCONUT DRESSING

*Three simple ingredients create a complex, creamy,
marmalade-kissed dressing.*

1 1/2 cups vanilla low-fat yogurt
1 1/2 tablespoons flaked coconut
1 1/2 tablespoons low-sugar orange marmalade
  1 medium-size Red Delicious apple
  1 medium pear
  1 tablespoon lemon juice
 20 (1-inch) fresh pineapple chunks
 20 seedless green or red grapes
 20 fresh strawberries, capped

1. Combine first 3 ingredients; cover and chill.

2. Core apple and pear; cut each into 20 bite-size
pieces. Toss apple and pear pieces with lemon juice.

3. Thread fruit alternately onto 20 (6-inch) wooden
skewers. Serve kabobs with coconut dressing. **Yield:**
20 servings (serving size: 1 kabob and 1½ tablespoons dressing).

♥ *Since coconut is a plant food, it contains no cholesterol.
However, coconut is very high in fat, and the fat is mostly
saturated, which increases blood cholesterol. If you're a
coconut lover, don't give it up altogether; enjoy it in very
small amounts as in the recipe above.*

YIELD: 20 servings

**EXCHANGE PER
SERVING:**
1/2 Fruit

PER SERVING:
Calories 43
(13% from fat)
Fat 0.6g
(saturated fat 0.3g)
Protein 1.1g
Carbohydrate 9.2g
Fiber 1.2g
Cholesterol 1mg
Sodium 13mg

GAZPACHO DIP

YIELD: 80 servings

EXCHANGE PER SERVING:
Free
(up to 3 tablespoons)

PER SERVING:
Calories 7
(51% from fat)
Fat 0.4g
(saturated fat 0.1g)
Protein 0.1g
Carbohydrate 0.7g
Fiber 0.2g
Cholesterol 0mg
Sodium 8mg

To serve this dip as a salad, spoon the mixture over shredded lettuce, and top with shredded reduced-fat Cheddar cheese and fat-free sour cream.

- 8 green onions, thinly sliced
- 2 large tomatoes, chopped
- 1 firm avocado, chopped
- ½ cup diced green bell pepper
- 1 (4.5-ounce) can chopped green chiles, undrained
- ½ (4.5-ounce) can chopped ripe olives, drained
- 2 garlic cloves, minced
- 3 tablespoons apple cider vinegar
- ¼ teaspoon pepper
  Lime slices (optional)

1. Combine all ingredients except lime slices, tossing gently.

2. Cover and chill up to 4 hours. Garnish with lime slices, if desired. Serve dip with baked tortilla chips. **Yield:** 5 cups (serving size: 1 tablespoon).

♥ *More than half the fat in an avocado is monounsaturated—making it a high-fat food that's actually good for your heart. Use it in your favorite Mexican dish or thinly slice one for a quick sandwich.*

Super Quick
BLACK BEAN DIP

1 (15-ounce) can black beans, drained
1 (8-ounce) can no-salt-added tomato sauce
½ cup (2 ounces) shredded reduced-fat sharp
    Cheddar cheese
1 teaspoon chili powder

1. Combine beans and tomato sauce in a small saucepan; bring to a boil over medium heat, stirring occasionally. Remove from heat.

2. Mash beans with a potato masher or back of a spoon. Add cheese and chili powder; cook, stirring constantly, until cheese melts. Serve dip warm with toasted pita triangles and fresh vegetables. **Yield:** 2 cups (serving size: 1 tablespoon).

YIELD: 32 servings

EXCHANGE PER SERVING:
Free (1 tablespoon)

PER SERVING:
Calories 19
(19% from fat)
Fat 0.4g
(saturated fat 0.2g)
Protein 1.3g
Carbohydrate 2.6g
Fiber 0.5g
Cholesterol 1mg
Sodium 37mg

Make Ahead
WHITE BEAN DIP

1 (15.8-ounce) can Great Northern beans,
    drained
2 teaspoons minced fresh thyme or ½
    teaspoon dried thyme
2 teaspoons balsamic or red wine vinegar
1 teaspoon olive oil
½ teaspoon dry mustard
½ teaspoon pepper
¼ teaspoon salt
2 tablespoons minced fresh parsley

1. Combine first 7 ingredients in a medium bowl. Mash until mixture is smooth, using a potato masher; stir in parsley. Transfer to a small serving bowl; cover and chill at least 1 hour. Serve with fat-free pita chips or raw vegetables. **Yield:** 1¼ cups (serving size: 1 tablespoon).

YIELD: 20 servings

EXCHANGE PER SERVING:
Free (1 tablespoon)

PER SERVING:
Calories 16
(17% from fat)
Fat 0.3g
(saturated fat 0.1g)
Protein 1g
Carbohydrate 2.6g
Fiber 0.5g
Cholesterol 0mg
Sodium 62mg

**EXCHANGE PER
SERVING:**
Free (1 tablespoon)

PER SERVING:
Calories 17
(21% from fat)
Fat 0.4g
(saturated fat 0.3g)
Protein 1g
Carbohydrate 2.1g
Fiber 0.3g
Cholesterol 1mg
Sodium 52mg

Super Quick
BLUE CHEESE-BEAN DIP

⅓ cup evaporated fat-free milk
½ teaspoon dried thyme
½ teaspoon freshly ground black pepper
¼ teaspoon ground sage
¼ teaspoon salt
2 (15-ounce) cans cannellini beans, rinsed
    and drained
2 garlic cloves, sliced
2 ounces crumbled blue cheese
1 tablespoon grated Parmesan cheese
  Cooking spray
½ cup soft breadcrumbs, toasted
2 tablespoons chopped fresh parsley

1. Position knife blade in food processor bowl; add first 7 ingredients. Process until smooth; stir in cheeses.

2. Spoon bean mixture into a shallow 1-quart baking dish coated with cooking spray. Cover with heavy-duty plastic wrap, and vent; microwave at HIGH 6 minutes, stirring every 2 minutes.

3. Combine breadcrumbs and parsley; sprinkle over bean mixture. Serve dip with Melba toast rounds, pita wedges, or no-oil-baked tortilla chips. **Yield:** 3 cups (serving size: 1 tablespoon).

Note: Make ½ cup soft breadcrumbs by tearing 1 slice of fresh or slightly stale sandwich bread into small pieces. To toast breadcrumbs for this recipe, place them on a baking sheet; broil 2 minutes, stirring occasionally.

HUMMUS WITH RASPBERRY VINEGAR

Raspberry vinegar gives this hummus a little kick, but you can use any kind of vinegar you have on hand.

> 1 tablespoon olive oil
> 1½ cups diced onion
> 2 tablespoons raspberry vinegar
> 1 (15½-ounce) can chickpeas (garbanzo beans), undrained
> 1 tablespoon chopped fresh cilantro
> ½ teaspoon ground cumin
> ½ teaspoon coarsely ground black pepper
> ¼ teaspoon salt
> Cilantro sprigs (optional)

1. Heat oil in a nonstick skillet over medium-high heat. Add onion, and sauté 5 minutes or until onion begins to brown. Add vinegar; bring to a boil, and cook 2 minutes or until vinegar evaporates. Cool to room temperature.

2. Drain chickpeas through a sieve over a bowl, reserving ¼ cup liquid. Place chickpeas and chopped cilantro in a food processor, and process until mixture resembles coarse meal. Add onion mixture, ¼ cup reserved liquid, cumin, pepper, and salt, and process until smooth. Garnish with cilantro sprigs, if desired. **Yield:** 2 cups (serving size: 2 tablespoons).

YIELD: 16 servings

EXCHANGE PER SERVING:
½ Starch

PER SERVING:
Calories 44
(27% from fat)
Fat 1.3g
(saturated fat 0.2g)
Protein 1.9g
Carbohydrate 6.6g
Fiber 1g
Cholesterol 0mg
Sodium 75mg

Super Quick
WHITE-BEAN HUMMUS DIP

¼ cup chopped green onions
2 tablespoons fresh lemon juice
2 tablespoons tahini (sesame-seed paste)
½ teaspoon dried oregano
¼ teaspoon ground cumin
⅛ teaspoon salt
⅛ teaspoon black pepper
1 (19-ounce) can cannellini beans or other
  white beans, rinsed and drained
1 garlic clove, peeled

1. Combine all ingredients in a food processor, and process until mixture is smooth. **Yield:** 1¾ cups (serving size: 2 tablespoons).

Make Ahead
CLASSIC ONION DIP

Serve this dip with assorted raw fresh vegetables, Melba toast rounds, or reduced-fat crackers for a healthy snack.

1 (8-ounce) carton fat-free sour cream
½ cup finely chopped onion
2 teaspoons low-sodium soy sauce
¼ teaspoon garlic pepper

1. Combine all ingredients in a medium bowl; stir well. Cover and chill 1 hour. **Yield:** 1 cup (serving size: 1 tablespoon).

ROASTED RED PEPPER AND ONION DIP

1½ cups sliced red onion (about 1½ red onions)
2 garlic cloves
1 (12-ounce) jar roasted red bell peppers, drained and coarsely chopped (or 3 large roasted red bell peppers, chopped)
¼ cup fine, dry breadcrumbs
3 tablespoons plain fat-free yogurt
1 tablespoon red wine vinegar
1 teaspoon olive oil
¼ teaspoon salt
⅛ teaspoon hot sauce

1. Preheat broiler.

2. Place onion and garlic on an aluminum foil-lined baking sheet; broil 5½ inches from heat 10 minutes. Let stand 5 minutes.

3. Position knife blade in food processor bowl; add onion, garlic, and chopped red bell pepper. Process mixture until finely chopped. Add breadcrumbs and remaining ingredients to processor bowl; process until smooth. Serve with pita wedges, reduced-fat crackers, or raw fresh vegetables. **Yield:** 2 cups (serving size: 1 tablespoon).

YIELD: 32 servings

EXCHANGE PER SERVING:
Free (1 tablespoon)

PER SERVING:
Calories 12
(23% from fat)
Fat 0.3g
(saturated fat 0g)
Protein 0.4g
Carbohydrate 2.1g
Fiber 0.3g
Cholesterol 0mg
Sodium 28mg

Super Quick
MOCK PEA GUACAMOLE

EXCHANGE PER
SERVING:
Free (1 tablespoon)

PER SERVING:
Calories 11
(0% from fat)
Fat 0g
(saturated fat 0g)
Protein 0.7g
Carbohydrate 1.9g
Fiber 0.6g
Cholesterol 0mg
Sodium 44mg

    2 cups frozen English peas, thawed
  1/2 cup sliced green onions (about 2 onions)
    2 tablespoons chopped fresh cilantro
 1 1/2 tablespoons fresh lime juice
    1 tablespoon salsa
  1/4 teaspoon salt
  1/4 teaspoon hot sauce

1. Position knife blade in food processor bowl. Add first 4 ingredients; process 30 seconds or until smooth, stopping once to scrape down sides. Add salsa and remaining ingredients; stir well. Serve with fat-free tortilla chips or raw vegetables. **Yield:** 1 1/2 cups (serving size: 1 tablespoon).

Make Ahead
VEGETABLE-CHEESE SPREAD

YIELD: 48 servings

EXCHANGE PER
SERVING:
Free
(up to 3 tablespoons)

PER SERVING:
Calories 7
(12% from fat)
Fat 0.1g
(saturated fat 0.1g)
Protein 1g
Carbohydrate 0.5g
Fiber 0.1g
Cholesterol 0g
Sodium 29mg

This thick and chunky mixture is perfect for spreading on crisp breads, crackers, or Melba toast. You can also stuff it into a juicy summer tomato.

  1/2 cup seeded, diced tomato
  1/2 cup chopped cucumber
  1/2 cup chopped green bell pepper
  1/3 cup shredded carrot
  1/4 cup sliced green onions
    1 tablespoon red wine vinegar
    1 teaspoon dried savory
    1 (12-ounce) container 1% low-fat cottage
         cheese

1. Combine all ingredients; cover and chill. **Yield:** 3 cups (serving size: 1 tablespoon).

Make Ahead
TUNA SALAD BITES

For an attractive touch to these appetizers, score the peel of each cucumber lengthwise with fork tines before slicing the cucumber.

1 (6-ounce) can low-sodium chunk white tuna in water, drained
½ cup finely chopped carrot
⅓ cup thinly sliced green onions
¼ cup sliced pimiento-stuffed olives
¼ cup low-fat mayonnaise
3 tablespoons minced fresh parsley
1 tablespoon lemon juice
½ teaspoon black pepper
2 medium cucumbers, cut into ½-inch slices

1. Combine first 8 ingredients in a medium bowl, stirring well. Cover and chill at least 1 hour.

2. Scoop out a hollow space in center of one side of each cucumber slice, using a ½-teaspoon circular measuring spoon or a small melon baller. Fill centers of cucumber slices with tuna mixture. Serve immediately. **Yield:** 12 servings (serving size: 1 appetizer).

YIELD: 12 servings

EXCHANGE PER SERVING:
½ Lean Meat

PER SERVING:
Calories 31
(20% from fat)
Fat 0.7g
(saturated fat 0.1g)
Protein 3.3g
Carbohydrate 3.3g
Fiber 0.7g
Cholesterol 5mg
Sodium 79mg

EXCHANGE PER SERVING:
Free
(up to 2 tablespoons)

PER SERVING:
Calories 11
(16% from fat)
Fat 0.2g
(saturated fat 0.1g)
Protein 1.7g
Carbohydrate 0.5g
Fiber 0g
Cholesterol 3mg
Sodium 45mg

Make Ahead
CURRIED CHICKEN MOUSSE

Curry powder blends 20 spices, herbs, and seeds into a potent seasoning secret. Teamed with tender chunks of chicken, it creates a make-ahead mousse that is nothing short of marvelous.

1 envelope unflavored gelatin
1 cup cold water, divided
2 teaspoons chicken-flavored bouillon granules
¼ teaspoon ground red pepper
1 teaspoon curry powder
2 teaspoons minced onion
1¼ cups finely chopped cooked chicken breast (skinned before cooking and cooked without salt)
¼ cup finely chopped celery
1 (2-ounce) jar diced pimiento, drained
1 tablespoon chopped fresh parsley
1 (8-ounce) carton fat-free sour cream
Cooking spray

1. Sprinkle gelatin over ½ cup cold water in a small saucepan; let stand 1 minute. Cook over low heat, stirring until gelatin dissolves (about 2 minutes).

2. Add bouillon granules, red pepper, and curry powder, stirring until bouillon granules dissolve; remove from heat. Add remaining ½ cup cold water and minced onion, stirring well; chill until consistency of unbeaten egg white.

3. Stir in chicken and next 4 ingredients; spoon mixture into a 4-cup mold coated with cooking spray. Cover and chill at least 8 hours. Unmold and serve with reduced-fat crackers. **Yield:** 2¾ cups (serving size: 1 tablespoon).

Super Quick
ONE-MINUTE SALSA

YIELD: 48 servings

Got a minute? Then you have time to make this spunky salsa. Four ingredients and a blender are all it takes.

1 (10-ounce) can diced tomatoes and green chiles, undrained
1 (14½-ounce) can no-salt-added stewed tomatoes, undrained
1 teaspoon pepper
1 garlic clove, minced

1. Combine all ingredients in container of an electric blender; process 30 seconds, stopping once to scrape down sides. Serve with baked tortilla chips. **Yield:** 3 cups (serving size: 1 tablespoon).

EXCHANGE PER SERVING:
Free
(up to 3 tablespoons)

PER SERVING:
Calories 3
(0% from fat)
Fat 0g
(saturated fat 0g)
Protein 0.1g
Carbohydrate 0.8g
Fiber 0.1g
Cholesterol 0mg
Sodium 21mg

Make Ahead
FRESH TOMATO SALSA

YIELD: 32 servings

Seeding the tomatoes prevents the salsa from being watery. To seed a tomato, cut it in half horizontally and scoop out the seeds with a spoon.

3 cups tomato, seeded and diced (about 3 large)
½ cup diced red onion
3 tablespoons chopped fresh cilantro
3 tablespoons fresh lime juice
½ teaspoon salt
2 garlic cloves, minced
1 jalapeño pepper, seeded and diced

1. Combine all ingredients in a medium bowl. Let stand 30 minutes before serving. **Yield:** 2 cups (serving size: 1 tablespoon).

EXCHANGE PER SERVING:
Free
(up to 3 tablespoons)

PER SERVING:
Calories 4
(0% from fat)
Fat 0g
(saturated fat 0g)
Protein 0.2g
Carbohydrate 0.9g
Fiber 0.2g
Cholesterol 0mg
Sodium 38mg

EXCHANGE PER SERVING:
Free
(up to 3 tablespoons)

PER SERVING:
Calories 5
(36% from fat)
Fat 0.2g
(saturated fat 0g)
Protein 0.1g
Carbohydrate 0.9g
Fiber 0.2g
Cholesterol 0mg
Sodium 45mg

Make Ahead
FIESTA ONION SALSA

The playful flavors of sweet onion, green chiles, and peppery cumin create a zesty party starter.

1	cup chopped sweet onion
3/4	cup chopped tomato
1	(4.5-ounce) can chopped green chiles, drained
3	tablespoons sliced ripe olives
2	tablespoons white wine vinegar
1/4	teaspoon salt
1/4	teaspoon Worcestershire sauce
1/8	teaspoon ground cumin
1/8	teaspoon pepper
1/8	teaspoon hot sauce

1. Combine all ingredients; cover and chill at least 2 hours. Serve salsa with no-oil–baked tortilla chips. **Yield:** 2 cups (serving size: 1 tablespoon).

♥ *The monounsaturated fats found in foods like olives, canola oil, and avocados can actually lower blood cholesterol. But remember that total fat still counts. All fats—polys, monos, and otherwise—are concentrated sources of calories and should be controlled if you're concerned about your weight.*

ROASTED CORN SALSA

Plum tomatoes are a good substitute if you don't have ripe summer tomatoes.

  5 ears yellow corn
    Cooking spray
  2 cups diced seeded tomato (about 2 small)
½ cup finely chopped green bell pepper
½ cup finely chopped red bell pepper
⅓ cup diced peeled jícama
¼ cup peeled diced avocado
⅓ cup finely chopped red onion
  3 tablespoons finely chopped fresh cilantro
  1 garlic clove, minced
  1 jalapeño pepper, seeded and minced
  2 tablespoons fresh lime juice
2½ teaspoons extra-virgin olive oil

1. Preheat oven to 475°.

2. Remove husks from corn. Scrub silks from corn.

3. Cut kernels from ears of corn. Place corn in a single layer on a jelly-roll pan coated with cooking spray. Bake at 475° for 15 minutes or until slightly charred, stirring every 5 minutes. Remove corn from pan; let cool.

4. Combine corn, tomato, and remaining ingredients, stirring well. **Yield:** 4½ cups (serving size: 1 tablespoon).

YIELD: 72 servings

EXCHANGE PER SERVING:
Free
(up to 2 tablespoons)

PER SERVING:
Calories 10
(27% from fat)
Fat 0.3g
(saturated fat 0g)
Protein 0.3g
Carbohydrate 1.9g
Fiber 0.4g
Cholesterol 0mg
Sodium 2mg

EXCHANGE PER
SERVING:
½ Starch

PER SERVING:
Calories 42
(39% from fat)
Fat 1.8g
(saturated fat 0.8g)
Protein 3.8g
Carbohydrate 3.2g
Fiber 1.2g
Cholesterol 4mg
Sodium 94mg

CHEESE TARTLETS

8 slices reduced-calorie wheat bread
¾ cup (3 ounces) shredded reduced-fat
     Swiss cheese
¼ cup grated Parmesan cheese
1 tablespoon minced fresh parsley
1 teaspoon Dijon mustard
⅛ teaspoon garlic powder
     Dash of hot sauce
3 large egg whites
2 tablespoons diced pimiento, drained

1. Preheat oven to 400°.

2. Trim crusts from bread slices. Cut each bread
slice into 4 squares; gently press each square into
ungreased miniature (1½-inch) muffin pans. Bake
at 400° for 3 to 4 minutes or until lightly browned.
Set aside.

3. Combine Swiss cheese and next 5 ingredients;
set aside.

4. Beat egg whites in a large mixing bowl at high
speed of an electric mixer until stiff; fold in cheese
mixture. Spoon 1 teaspoon mixture into each
bread shell. Bake at 400° for 6 to 8 minutes or
until filling is slightly puffed.

5. Remove tartlets from pans; top evenly with
diced pimiento. Serve immediately. **Yield:** 16
servings (serving size: 2 tartlets).

SPINACH-STUFFED MUSHROOMS

1 (10-ounce) package frozen chopped
    spinach, thawed
20 large fresh mushrooms
    Cooking spray
1/3 cup plain fat-free yogurt
1/4 cup grated Parmesan cheese
1/4 cup diced onion
1/4 cup (1 ounce) shredded reduced-fat
    Cheddar cheese
1/4 cup (1 ounce) shredded reduced-fat
    Monterey Jack cheese
1 tablespoon sherry
1/4 teaspoon salt
1/4 teaspoon garlic powder
1/4 teaspoon dried oregano
1 tablespoon grated Parmesan cheese

1. Preheat broiler.

2. Drain spinach, and press between layers of paper towels until barely moist; set aside. Clean mushrooms with damp paper towels; remove stems. Finely chop stems; set aside.

3. Coat a large nonstick skillet with cooking spray; place over medium-high heat until hot. Add mushroom caps; cook, stirring constantly, 5 minutes. Drain. Place caps on rack of a broiler pan, stem sides up; set aside.

4. Combine spinach, chopped stems, yogurt, and next 8 ingredients; spoon evenly into mushroom caps. Sprinkle evenly with 1 tablespoon Parmesan cheese. Broil 5½ inches from heat 5 minutes or until thoroughly heated. Serve immediately. **Yield:** 20 servings (serving size: 1 stuffed mushroom).

YIELD: 20 servings

EXCHANGE PER SERVING:
1 Vegetable

PER SERVING:
Calories 32
(31% from fat)
Fat 1.1g
(saturated fat 0.6g)
Protein 2.8g
Carbohydrate 3g
Fiber 1g
Cholesterol 3mg
Sodium 87mg

YIELD: 15 servings

EXCHANGE PER SERVING:
½ Starch

PER SERVING:
Calories 52
(28% from fat)
Fat 1.6g
(saturated fat 0.9g)
Protein 2.2g
Carbohydrate 7.3g
Fiber 0.5g
Cholesterol 5mg
Sodium 122mg

ROASTED GARLIC AND PORTOBELLO CROSTINI

- 2 whole garlic heads
- 1 (6-ounce) package presliced portobello mushrooms
- 2 tablespoons balsamic vinegar
  Olive oil-flavored cooking spray
- 15 (½-inch-thick) slices French bread baguette (about 5 ounces)
- ¾ cup (3 ounces) crumbled goat cheese

1. Preheat oven to 350°.

2. Remove white papery skin from garlic heads (do not peel or separate cloves). Wrap each head separately in foil. Bake at 350° for 1 hour; let cool 10 minutes. Separate cloves; squeeze to extract garlic pulp. Discard skins. Set pulp aside.

3. Combine mushrooms and balsamic vinegar in a shallow dish, turning mushrooms to coat. Let stand 15 minutes.

4. Coat a large nonstick skillet with cooking spray; place over medium-high heat until hot. Add mushroom and vinegar mixture; cook 5 minutes or until mushrooms are tender, stirring occasionally.

5. Preheat broiler.

6. Spread roasted garlic pulp on 1 side of each bread slice; divide mushrooms evenly among bread slices. Spoon 2 teaspoons cheese onto each crostino. Place crostini on a baking sheet; broil 2 minutes or until toasted. Serve immediately. **Yield:** 15 servings (serving size: 1 crostino).

MEDITERRANEAN NACHOS

The easiest way to cut pita bread into wedges is with a pizza cutter or kitchen shears.

- 2 (6-inch) pita bread rounds
  Cooking spray
- 1/4 teaspoon salt
- 1 (15 1/2-ounce) can chickpeas (garbanzo beans), drained
- 1/4 cup sliced green onions (about 2 green onions)
- 2 tablespoons lemon juice
- 1 tablespoon fat-free milk
- 1 teaspoon olive oil
- 2 garlic cloves
- 1 cup chopped tomato (about 1 medium tomato)
- 3 tablespoons chopped ripe olives

1. Preheat oven to 450°.

2. Separate each pita bread round into 2 rounds; cut each round into 6 wedges. Place wedges on a large baking sheet; coat wedges with cooking spray, and sprinkle evenly with salt. Bake at 450° for 5 minutes or until lightly browned.

3. Meanwhile, position knife blade in food processor bowl; add chickpeas and next 5 ingredients. Process until smooth, stopping once to scrape down sides.

4. Spread 2 teaspoons bean mixture over each pita wedge; sprinkle wedges evenly with chopped tomato and olives. Serve nachos immediately.
Yield: 24 servings (serving size: 1 nacho).

YIELD: 24 servings

EXCHANGE PER SERVING:
1/2 Starch

PER SERVING:
Calories 32
(17% from fat)
Fat 0.6g
(saturated fat 0.1g)
Protein 1g
Carbohydrate 5.7g
Fiber 1.4g
Cholesterol 0mg
Sodium 76mg

CHICKEN NACHO WEDGES

EXCHANGES PER
SERVING:
½ Starch
½ Very Lean Meat

PER SERVING:
Calories 57
(22% from fat)
Fat 1.4g
(saturated fat 0.6g)
Protein 5.2g
Carbohydrate 5.9g
Fiber 0.4g
Cholesterol 11mg
Sodium 138mg

4 (8-inch) fat-free flour tortillas
  Cooking spray
1 cup finely chopped green bell pepper
¾ cup finely chopped red onion
1½ teaspoons ground cumin
1 (14½-ounce) can Mexican-style stewed
  tomatoes, undrained and chopped
1½ cups chopped cooked chicken breast
¼ cup minced fresh cilantro
1 cup (4 ounces) shredded reduced-fat
  Monterey Jack cheese

1. Preheat oven to 375°.

2. Arrange tortillas on a large baking sheet coated with cooking spray; set aside.

3. Coat a large nonstick skillet with cooking spray; place over medium heat until hot. Add bell pepper and onion, and cook 5 minutes or until tender, stirring often. Add cumin, and cook 1 minute. Add tomato; cook 3 minutes, stirring occasionally.

4. Spoon tomato mixture evenly over tortillas; top with chicken and cilantro. Sprinkle cheese evenly over chicken. Bake at 375° for 8 minutes or until tortillas are crisp. Cut each tortilla into 6 wedges. Serve immediately. **Yield:** 24 servings (serving size: 1 wedge).

MINIATURE CHICKEN TOSTADAS

YIELD: 20 servings

1   cup finely chopped cooked chicken breast
      (skinned before cooking and cooked
      without salt)
1/2 cup finely chopped jícama
1/2 cup (2 ounces) shredded reduced-fat
      Cheddar cheese
1/4 cup light mayonnaise
1   tablespoon drained diced pimiento
1   (4.5-ounce) can chopped green chiles,
      drained
8   (6-inch) corn tortillas

1. Preheat oven to 350°.

2. Combine first 6 ingredients; set aside.

3. Cut each tortilla into 5 rounds, using a 2-inch
biscuit cutter. Place rounds on a large baking sheet;
bake at 350° for 6 minutes. Turn chips, and bake 2
to 3 additional minutes or until crisp.

4. Preheat broiler.

5. Spread chicken mixture over chips (about 1 tablespoon per chip). Broil 5½ inches from heat 3
minutes or until mixture is hot and bubbly. Serve
immediately. **Yield:** 20 servings (serving size: 2
tostadas).

**EXCHANGES PER
SERVING:**
1/2 Starch
1/2 Lean Meat

PER SERVING:
Calories 50
(22% from fat)
Fat 1.2g
(saturated fat 0.4g)
Protein 4.2g
Carbohydrate 6g
Fiber 0.6g
Cholesterol 10mg
Sodium 104mg

PITA CHIPS

YIELD: 16 servings

EXCHANGE PER SERVING:
1/2 Starch

PER SERVING:
Calories 33
(11% from fat)
Fat 0.4g
(saturated fat 0g)
Protein 1.2g
Carbohydrate 6.8g
Fiber 0.9g
Cholesterol 0mg
Sodium 100mg

You can indulge guilt free with these lemon-garlic pita chips.

3 (6-inch) whole wheat pita bread rounds
  Butter-flavored cooking spray
3 1/2 teaspoons lemon juice
1 garlic clove, pressed
1 tablespoon minced fresh parsley
1 1/2 teaspoons minced fresh chives
1/4 teaspoon salt
1/8 teaspoon pepper

1. Preheat oven to 350°.

2. Separate each pita bread round into 2 rounds; cut each round into 8 wedges. Arrange wedges, cut sides up, in a single layer on a large baking sheet. Coat wedges with cooking spray.

3. Combine lemon juice and garlic; lightly brush over wedges. Combine parsley and remaining 3 ingredients; sprinkle mixture evenly over wedges.

4. Bake at 350° for 12 minutes or until lightly browned. Transfer chips to wire racks; cool completely. Store in an airtight container. **Yield:** 4 dozen (serving size: 3 chips).

Make Ahead
CARAMEL CORN CRUNCH

1 (3-ounce) package reduced-fat microwave popcorn (such as Orville Redenbacher's Smart Pop)
2/3 cup packed brown sugar
6 tablespoons reduced-calorie stick margarine
6 tablespoons reduced-calorie maple-flavored syrup
1 teaspoon vanilla extract
1/4 teaspoon baking soda
Cooking spray

1. Preheat oven to 250°.

2. Cook popcorn according to package directions. Place popped corn in a large bowl; set aside.

3. Combine sugar, margarine, and syrup in a 2-quart saucepan; place over medium heat. Bring to a boil, stirring constantly. Cook 5 minutes, without stirring, or until candy thermometer registers 250°. Remove from heat; stir in vanilla and baking soda.

4. Pour syrup mixture over popcorn; stir until evenly coated.

5. Spread mixture onto 2 jelly-roll pans coated with cooking spray. Bake at 250° for 20 to 25 minutes or until mixture is crisp. Cool in pans on wire racks; break into small pieces. Store in an airtight container. **Yield:** 14 cups (serving size: 1 cup).

YIELD: 14 servings

EXCHANGES PER SERVING:
1 Starch
1/2 Fat

PER SERVING:
Calories 89
(32% from fat)
Fat 3.2g
(saturated fat 0.4g)
Protein 0.8g
Carbohydrate 15.8g
Fiber 0g
Cholesterol 0mg
Sodium 123mg

Make Ahead

MAPLE AND PEANUT BUTTER GRANOLA

Stir some granola into low-fat vanilla yogurt for a quick but hearty breakfast.

3 tablespoons crunchy reduced-fat peanut butter
½ cup pure maple syrup
3 tablespoons water
1 teaspoon ground cinnamon
¼ teaspoon salt
3 cups regular or quick-cooking oats
Cooking spray
½ cup golden raisins

1. Preheat oven to 300°.

2. Combine first 5 ingredients in a small saucepan; stir well with a wire whisk. Bring to a boil; reduce heat, and simmer 1 minute.

3. Pour hot mixture over oats; stir well to coat oat mixture. Spread on a baking sheet coated with cooking spray. Bake at 300° for 15 minutes. Reduce heat to 250°; bake 15 minutes.

4. Add raisins, and stir well. Bake an additional 15 minutes. Turn oven off, and allow granola to cool in oven 20 to 30 minutes. **Yield:** 3⅔ cups (serving size: ⅓ cup).

Make Ahead
TRAIL BLAZIN' MIX

1 (18-ounce) box low-fat granola with raisins
   (such as Healthy Choice)
½ cup honey
1 (6-ounce) package dried chopped tropical
   fruit medley (such as Mariani)
1 cup tropical-flavored gourmet jelly beans
   (such as Jelly Belly)
¼ cup semisweet chocolate minichips

1. Preheat oven to 325°.

2. Spread granola in a jelly-roll pan; drizzle with honey, and toss well. Spread evenly in pan. Bake at 325° for 20 minutes, stirring every 7 minutes. Remove from oven, and stir in dried fruit; return to oven. Turn oven off, and let mixture stand in closed oven 30 minutes. Remove from oven, and let cool completely. Combine granola mixture, jelly beans, and minichips in a large bowl; toss well. Store mixture in an airtight container. **Yield:** 9 cups (serving size: ⅓ cup).

YIELD: 27 servings

EXCHANGES PER SERVING:
1 Starch
1 Fruit

PER SERVING:
Calories 143
(10% from fat)
Fat 1.6g
(saturated fat 0.8g)
Protein 1.7g
Carbohydrate 32.5g
Fiber 1.3g
Cholesterol 0mg
Sodium 52mg

Make Ahead
OLD-FASHIONED LEMONADE

YIELD: 6 servings

EXCHANGES PER SERVING:
2 Fruit

PER SERVING:
Calories 109
(0% from fat)
Fat 0g
(saturated fat 0g)
Protein 0.2g
Carbohydrate 29.4g
Fiber 0g
Cholesterol 0mg
Sodium 1mg

To make decorative lemon ice cubes, place a lemon twist inside each ice cube before freezing.

1¼ cups fresh lemon juice
¾ cup sugar
4¼ cups cold water
　 Lemon slices

1. Combine lemon juice and sugar in a large pitcher; stir until sugar dissolves. Add water and lemon slices; stir well, and chill. Serve lemonade over ice. **Yield:** 6 cups (serving size: 1 cup).

GINGER LEMONADE

YIELD: 8 servings

EXCHANGES PER SERVING:
2½ Fruit

PER SERVING:
Calories 133
(0% from fat)
Fat 0g
(saturated fat 0g)
Protein 0.2g
Carbohydrate 35.2g
Fiber 0g
Cholesterol 0mg
Sodium 1mg

This thirst quencher can be easily doubled.

6 cups water, divided
1¼ cups sugar
¼ cup grated peeled fresh ginger
1¼ cups fresh lemon juice (about 7 large lemons)
¼ cup fresh lime juice
　 Lemon slices (optional)
　 Lime slices (optional)

1. Combine 1 cup water, sugar, and ginger in a small saucepan; bring to a boil, and cook 1 minute or until sugar dissolves, stirring occasionally. Remove from heat; cool.

2. Strain ginger mixture through a sieve into a pitcher, and discard solids. Add 5 cups water and juices, and stir well. Serve over ice, and, if desired, garnish with lemon and lime slices. **Yield:** 8 cups (serving size: 1 cup).

Super Quick
KEY WEST MINTED LIMEADE

YIELD: 2 servings

¼ cup sugar
¼ cup fresh lime juice
4 fresh mint leaves
½ cup ice cubes
1 cup ginger ale, chilled
2 lime slices (optional)
    Mint sprigs (optional)

1. Combine first 3 ingredients in a blender; process until smooth. With blender on, add ice cubes, 1 at a time; process until smooth. Stir in ginger ale. Serve over ice; if desired, garnish with lime slices and mint. Serve immediately. **Yield:** 2 cups (serving size: 1 cup).

EXCHANGES PER SERVING:
2½ Fruit

PER SERVING:
Calories 144
(0% from fat)
Fat 0g
(saturated fat 0g)
Protein 0.1g
Carbohydrate 38.3g
Fiber 0g
Cholesterol 0mg
Sodium 7mg

Make Ahead
MOCK MARGARITAS

YIELD: 8 servings

3¼ cups crushed ice
½ cup sifted powdered sugar
1 (6-ounce) can frozen lemonade concentrate, thawed and undiluted
1 (6-ounce) can frozen limeade concentrate, thawed and undiluted
1½ cups club soda, chilled
    Lime slices (optional)

1. Combine first 4 ingredients in a large freezer container; cover and freeze several hours or until mixture is firm.

2. To serve, remove mixture from freezer, and let stand at room temperature 30 minutes. Spoon half of mixture into container of an electric blender; add half of club soda. Cover and process until smooth. Repeat blending process. Pour into glasses; garnish with lime slices, if desired. **Yield:** 6 cups (serving size: ¾ cup).

EXCHANGES PER SERVING:
2 Fruit

PER SERVING:
Calories 107
(1% from fat)
Fat 0.1g
(saturated fat 0g)
Protein 0.1g
Carbohydrate 28g
Fiber 0.1g
Cholesterol 0mg
Sodium 10mg

EXCHANGE PER SERVING:
1 Fruit

PER SERVING:
Calories 68
(0% from fat)
Fat 0g
(saturated fat 0g)
Protein 0.1g
Carbohydrate 17.4g
Fiber 0.1g
Cholesterol 0mg
Sodium 6mg

Make Ahead
CRANBERRY-APPLE ICED TEA

The fruity cranberry flavor in the tea will be stronger if you chill the beverage before pouring it over ice. Pouring hot tea over ice melts the ice and dilutes the tea's flavor.

  2 cups water
  2 cranberry-flavored tea bags
  1 cup cranberry-apple juice
  ½ cup apple juice
  2 teaspoons honey
     Ice cubes

1. Bring water to a boil in a medium saucepan. Add tea bags; remove from heat. Cover and steep (let stand) 10 minutes. Remove tea bags, squeezing gently.

2. Combine tea, juices, and honey, stirring well; cover and chill. Serve over ice. **Yield:** 4 cups (serving size: 1 cup).

Make Ahead
RASPBERRY-LEMON TEA

YIELD: 8 servings

6¼ cups boiling water
½ cup sugar
3 family-size tea bags
1 (10-ounce) package frozen raspberries in
   syrup, thawed and undrained
1 (6-ounce) can thawed lemonade
   concentrate, undiluted

**EXCHANGES PER
SERVING:**
2 Fruit

PER SERVING:
Calories 125
(0% from fat)
Fat 0.1g
(saturated fat 0g)
Protein 0.3g
Carbohydrate 32.3g
Fiber 1.6g
Cholesterol 0mg
Sodium 7mg

1. Combine first 3 ingredients; stir well. Cover and steep 5 minutes. Remove tea bags, squeezing gently.

2. Place raspberries in a blender. Process until smooth. Pour pureed berries through a fine sieve over a bowl, reserving liquid. Discard seeds.

3. Combine tea, raspberry liquid, and lemonade concentrate in a large pitcher. Chill. Serve over ice. **Yield:** 8 cups (serving size: 1 cup).

Make Ahead
MINT LIMEADE TEA

YIELD: 7 servings

2 cups boiling water
2 mint tea bags
1 (12-ounce) can frozen limeade concentrate,
   thawed

**EXCHANGES PER
SERVING:**
1½ Fruit

PER SERVING:
Calories 92
(0% from fat)
Fat 0g
(saturated fat 0g)
Protein 0.1g
Carbohydrate 24.3g
Fiber 0g
Cholesterol 0mg
Sodium 2mg

1. Combine water and tea bags in a 2–cup glass measure; cover and steep 7 minutes. Remove and discard tea bags. Cool to room temperature.

2. Combine limeade and 2 cans of water in a 2-quart pitcher; add tea, stirring well. Cover and chill. Serve over crushed ice, if desired. **Yield:** 7 cups (serving size: 1 cup).

BELLINI SPRITZERS

YIELD: 9 servings

EXCHANGE PER
SERVING:
1 Fruit

PER SERVING:
Calories 96
(1% from fat)
Fat 0.1g
(saturated fat 0g)
Protein 0.8g
Carbohydrate 9.4g
Fiber 1.2g
Cholesterol 0mg
Sodium 14mg

Substitute 4 cups frozen sliced peaches, thawed, for fresh peaches, if desired.

2 pounds medium to large fresh peaches, peeled and halved
1 (750-milliliter) bottle champagne, chilled
2 cups sparkling mineral water, chilled

1. Place peaches in container of an electric blender or food processor; cover and process until smooth, stopping once to scrape down sides.

2. Combine puree, champagne, and mineral water in a large pitcher; stir gently. Pour into chilled glasses. Serve immediately. **Yield:** 9 cups (serving size: 1 cup).

PASSION POTION

YIELD: 4 servings

EXCHANGES PER
SERVING:
2 Fruit

PER SERVING:
Calories 134
(3% from fat)
Fat 0.4g
(saturated fat 0.1g)
Protein 1.2g
Carbohydrate 33.7g
Fiber 1.9g
Cholesterol 0mg
Sodium 3mg

Substitute apricot or papaya nectar if you can't find passionfruit nectar.

2 cups cubed peeled ripe mango
1 cup cubed pineapple
1 1/2 cups orange juice, chilled
1/2 cup passionfruit nectar, chilled

1. Place mango cubes and pineapple cubes in separate shallow containers. Place into freezer, and freeze until firm (about 1 hour). Remove from freezer; let stand 10 minutes. Combine mango, juice, and nectar in a blender, and process until smooth. With blender on, add pineapple; process until smooth. Serve immediately. **Yield:** 4 cups (serving size: 1 cup).

TROPICAL WAVE

1½ cups sliced ripe banana
1 cup cubed fresh pineapple
1 cup cubed peeled ripe mango
1 cup papaya nectar, chilled
2 tablespoons fresh lime juice

1. Place banana, pineapple, and mango into freezer; freeze until firm (about 1 hour). Remove from freezer, and let stand 10 minutes. Combine fruit, nectar, and juice in a blender, and process until smooth. Serve immediately. **Yield:** 3 cups (serving size: 1 cup).

YIELD: 3 servings

EXCHANGES PER SERVING:
3 Fruit

PER SERVING:
Calories 184
(3% from fat)
Fat 0.7g
(saturated fat 0.2g)
Protein 1.3g
Carbohydrate 47g
Fiber 3.2g
Cholesterol 0mg
Sodium 2mg

FIVE-FRUIT CRUSH

¾ cup sliced ripe banana
½ cup chopped peeled ripe mango
2 cups whole strawberries
¾ cup pineapple juice, chilled
½ cup orange juice, chilled
½ cup ice cubes

1. Place banana and mango into freezer; freeze until firm (about 1 hour). Remove from freezer; let stand 10 minutes. Combine strawberries and juices in a blender; process until smooth. With blender on, add banana, mango, and ice cubes, 1 at a time; process until smooth. Serve immediately. **Yield:** 4 cups (serving size: 1 cup).

YIELD: 4 servings

EXCHANGES PER SERVING:
1½ Fruit

PER SERVING:
Calories 102
(4% from fat)
Fat 0.5g
(saturated fat 0.1g)
Protein 1.2g
Carbohydrate 25.2g
Fiber 2.8g
Cholesterol 0mg
Sodium 2mg

YIELD: 3 servings

EXCHANGES PER
SERVING:
2 Fruit

PER SERVING:
Calories 120
(5% from fat)
Fat 0.7g
(saturated fat 0.2g)
Protein 0.9g
Carbohydrate 29.7g
Fiber 0.6g
Cholesterol 0mg
Sodium 12mg

Super Quick
STRAWBERRY-CHERRY SLUSH

Don't thaw the cherries and strawberries before adding them to the blender; processing the frozen fruit is what makes the beverage slushy.

1⅓ cups frozen pitted sweet cherries
 1 cup frozen unsweetened whole strawberries
 1 cup cherry-flavored lemon-lime soda, chilled
 2 tablespoons sugar
 2 tablespoons thawed frozen reduced-calorie whipped topping
 1 tablespoon fresh lemon juice

1. Combine all ingredients in a blender; cover and process until smooth, stopping twice to scrape down sides. Pour into chilled glasses. **Yield:** 2¼ cups (serving size: ¾ cup).

YIELD: 4 servings

EXCHANGES PER
SERVING:
2 Fruit

PER SERVING:
Calories 121
(0% from fat)
Fat 0g
(saturated fat 0g)
Protein 0.9g
Carbohydrate 28.4g
Fiber 0g
Cholesterol 0mg
Sodium 23mg

Super Quick
SUNRISE SLUSH

½ (12-ounce) container frozen orange-strawberry-banana juice concentrate
 1 (6-ounce) can pineapple juice
 3 cups ice cubes

1. Combine all ingredients in a blender; cover and process until smooth, stopping once to scrape down sides. Serve immediately. **Yield:** 4 cups (serving size: 1 cup).

Make Ahead
PINEAPPLE-RUM SLUSH

Substitute orange juice for rum, if desired.

3 cups pineapple juice
1 cup fresh lemon juice (about 5 large lemons)
3/4 cup golden or dark rum
3/4 cup water
1/2 cup sugar

1. Combine all ingredients in a large plastic pitcher; cover and freeze at least 4 hours or until slushy. **Yield:** 6 cups (serving size: 1 cup).

YIELD: 6 servings

EXCHANGES PER SERVING:
2½ Fruit

PER SERVING:
Calories 228
(0% from fat)
Fat 0.1g
(saturated fat 0g)
Protein 0.6g
Carbohydrate 37.4g
Fiber 0.3g
Cholesterol 0mg
Sodium 2mg

Super Quick
BANANA-BERRY SMOOTHIE

Serve as a dessert beverage after a meal of spaghetti and a tossed green salad.

1 cup frozen unsweetened whole strawberries
1 small banana (about 5 ounces)
1/4 cup fat-free milk
1 cup vanilla fat-free ice cream
Banana slices (optional)

1. Combine first 3 ingredients in a blender; cover and process until smooth, stopping once to scrape down sides. Add ice cream; blend until smooth. Garnish with banana slices, if desired. **Yield:** 2 cups (serving size: 1 cup).

YIELD: 2 servings

EXCHANGES PER SERVING:
2 Starch
1 Fruit

PER SERVING:
Calories 202
(2% from fat)
Fat 0.4g
(saturated fat 0.2g)
Protein 5.1g
Carbohydrate 47.9g
Fiber 2.7g
Cholesterol 1mg
Sodium 63mg

Super Quick
STRAWBERRY SMOOTHIE

*If mango is not available, substitute half of a banana or
increase the strawberries to 2 cups.*

1½ cups halved fresh strawberries
1 (8-ounce) carton strawberry-banana low-fat
  yogurt
½ cup peeled, cubed mango
⅓ cup pineapple juice
2 tablespoons honey
  Ice cubes
4 whole strawberries

1. Combine first 5 ingredients in a blender. Cover
and process until smooth, stopping once to scrape
down sides.

2. Add enough ice cubes to bring mixture to 5–
cup level; process until smooth.

3. Pour into glasses to serve. Garnish with whole
strawberries. Serve immediately. **Yield:** 5 cups
(serving size: 1¼ cups).

♥ *Mangoes rate as the most-consumed fruit in the world,
and are certainly growing in popularity in the United
States. Besides their fabulous taste, mangoes are packed
with beta carotene, fiber, and vitamin C, all of which are
thought to be good for your heart.*

Super Quick
TROPICAL TOFU SMOOTHIE

²/₃ cup soft tofu, drained (about 3 ounces)
1 cup cubed pineapple, chilled
1 cup sliced strawberries, chilled
½ cup vanilla low-fat frozen yogurt
⅓ cup orange juice
1 teaspoon sugar
Dash of ground nutmeg (optional)

1. Place tofu in a blender; process until smooth. Add pineapple and next 4 ingredients; process until smooth. Serve immediately. Sprinkle with nutmeg, if desired. **Yield:** 2 cups (serving size: 1 cup).

YIELD: 2 servings

EXCHANGES PER SERVING:
1 Starch
1 Fruit
½ Fat

PER SERVING:
Calories 147
(15% from fat)
Fat 2.5g
(saturated fat 0.6g)
Protein 4.8g
Carbohydrate 28.9g
Fiber 2.8g
Cholesterol 4mg
Sodium 17mg

PEANUT BUTTER-CHOCOLATE-BANANA SHAKE

This healthy shake is yummy enough to serve as a dessert.

2 cups sliced banana
¾ cup 1% low-fat milk
½ cup vanilla low-fat ice cream
½ cup crushed ice
3 tablespoons chocolate-flavored syrup
2 tablespoons reduced-fat creamy peanut butter

1. Arrange banana slices in a single layer on a baking sheet; freeze 45 minutes or until firm.

2. Place frozen bananas and remaining ingredients in a blender; process until smooth. Serve immediately. **Yield:** 3 cups (serving size: 1 cup).

YIELD: 3 servings

EXCHANGES PER SERVING:
1½ Starch
1½ Fruit
½ Low-Fat Milk

PER SERVING:
Calories 260
(20% from fat)
Fat 5.7g
(saturated fat 1.6g)
Protein 7.3g
Carbohydrate 48g
Fiber 3.9g
Cholesterol 4mg
Sodium 110mg

Super Quick
FROSTY COFFEE SHAKE

Substitute fat-free chocolate ice cream for vanilla to make a mocha shake.

- 1/2 cup fat-free milk
- 1 to 2 teaspoons instant coffee granules
- 1 cup vanilla fat-free ice cream
- 1/2 teaspoon vanilla extract
- 1 cup crushed ice

1. Combine milk and coffee granules, stirring until coffee dissolves.

2. Place ice cream in a blender; add milk mixture and vanilla. Cover and process until smooth, stopping once to scrape down sides. Add enough ice to bring mixture to 2-cup level. Cover and process until smooth. Serve immediately. **Yield:** 2 cups (serving size: 1 cup).

Super Quick
ICED COFFEE FREEZE

Use a dark roast or specialty coffee for a stronger taste. We suggest amaretto, praline, and hazelnut varieties to boost the flavor.

- 1 cup vanilla fat-free frozen yogurt
- 1 cup fat-free milk
- 1/4 cup strongly brewed coffee, chilled
- 2 tablespoons powdered sugar
- 1 teaspoon vanilla extract
- 1/2 teaspoon ground cinnamon
- 1 1/4 cups large ice cubes

1. Combine all ingredients in container of an electric blender; cover and process until smooth, stopping once to scrape down sides. Serve immediately. **Yield:** 4 cups (serving size: 1 cup).

Super Quick
HOT CRANBERRY COCKTAIL

1 tablespoon whole cloves
2 teaspoons whole allspice
3 cups pineapple juice
1 (32-ounce) bottle cranberry juice drink
  Cinnamon sticks (optional)

1. Cut a 6-inch square of cheesecloth; place cloves and allspice in center, and tie with string.

2. Combine spice bag, pineapple juice, and cranberry juice in a large saucepan. Bring to a boil; cover, reduce heat, and simmer 5 minutes. Remove and discard spice bag. Serve warm with cinnamon-stick stirrers, if desired. **Yield:** 7 cups (serving size: 1 cup).

♥ *Don't forget that the cornerstone of a healthy lifestyle is exercise. Aerobic exercise, such as jogging and swimming, has long been promoted as the best exercise for your heart. But now the American Heart Association says that resistance exercise, such as weight lifting, improves your heart's health, too, by decreasing blood pressure, building muscle, and increasing the body's resting metabolic rate. Whatever the exercise, drink plenty of fluids, especially water, both during and after your workout.*

YIELD: 7 servings

EXCHANGES PER SERVING:
2 ½ Fruit

PER SERVING:
Calories 138
(1% from fat)
Fat 0.2g
(saturated fat 0g)
Protein 0.4g
Carbohydrate 34.9g
Fiber 0.1g
Cholesterol 0mg
Sodium 6mg

**EXCHANGES PER
SERVING:**
1 ½ Fruit

PER SERVING:
Calories 93
(2% from fat)
Fat 0.2g
(saturated fat 0g)
Protein 0.6g
Carbohydrate 22.8g
Fiber 0.3g
Cholesterol 0mg
Sodium 3mg

HOLIDAY HOT FRUIT PUNCH

*Plug in a large percolator to keep this beverage
warm during a party.*

1 (46-ounce) can apple juice
1 teaspoon ground nutmeg
1 (3-inch) stick cinnamon
2 teaspoons whole cloves
2 medium-size oranges, quartered
1 (46-ounce) can pineapple juice
1 (46-ounce) can orange juice
¼ cup sugar

1. Combine first 3 ingredients in a Dutch oven;
bring to a boil. Cover, reduce heat, and simmer 20
minutes, stirring occasionally.

2. Insert whole cloves into rinds of orange quarters; set aside.

3. Add pineapple juice, orange juice, and sugar to
apple juice mixture; stir well. Add orange quarters.
Cook 5 minutes or until mixture is thoroughly
heated (do not boil). Remove and discard orange
quarters and cinnamon stick. Serve warm. **Yield:**
17¼ cups (serving size: ¾ cup).

MOCHA PUNCH

Here's a punch so thick and rich it could double as dessert.

1 (2-ounce) jar instant coffee granules
1 cup boiling water
3/4 cup sugar
1 gallon fat-free milk
1/2 gallon chocolate fat-free frozen yogurt,
    softened
1/2 gallon vanilla fat-free frozen yogurt, softened
1 cup frozen reduced-calorie whipped
    topping, thawed

1. Combine coffee granules and boiling water, stirring until coffee granules dissolve. Add sugar, and stir until sugar dissolves. Cover and chill.

2. Combine coffee mixture and milk in a large punch bowl; gently stir in frozen yogurts. Spoon whipped topping on top. **Yield:** 34 cups (serving size: 1 cup).

YIELD: 34 servings

EXCHANGES PER SERVING:
1 1/2 Starch
1/2 Skim Milk

PER SERVING:
Calories 146
(3% from fat)
Fat 0.5g
(saturated fat 0.1g)
Protein 7.4g
Carbohydrate 29.1g
Fiber 0g
Cholesterol 2mg
Sodium 115mg

YIELD: 13 servings

EXCHANGES PER SERVING:
1½ Fruit

PER SERVING:
Calories 103
(1% from fat)
Fat 0.1g
(saturated fat 0g)
Protein 0.5g
Carbohydrate 25.9g
Fiber 0.2g
Cholesterol 0mg
Sodium 12mg

Make Ahead
CITRUS PUNCH

Freeze orange juice in ice cube trays for cubes that won't water down the punch.

4 cups water, divided
¼ cup sugar
3 cups pineapple juice
½ cup lemon juice
1 (6-ounce) can frozen orange juice concentrate, undiluted
3 (12-ounce) cans lemon-lime carbonated beverage, chilled
Lime slices (optional)

1. Combine 1 cup water and sugar in a small saucepan; cook over low heat until sugar dissolves, stirring occasionally. Cool. Combine sugar mixture, pineapple juice, 3 cups water, and next 2 ingredients in a bowl; cover and chill.

2. Just before serving, stir in carbonated beverage. Serve immediately over ice. Garnish with lime, if desired. **Yield:** 13 cups (serving size: 1 cup).

breads

PER SERVING:
Calories 58
(25% from fat)
Fat 1.6g
(saturated fat 0.1g)
Protein 1.7g
Carbohydrate 9.3g
Fiber 0.3g
Cholesterol 1mg
Sodium 90mg

LIGHT BISCUITS

The title of this recipe belies the rich, old-fashioned flavor of the biscuits. Use a reduced-calorie stick margarine that is 41% to 60% oil for this recipe.

2   cups all-purpose flour
1   tablespoon baking powder
1/4   teaspoon baking soda
1/2   teaspoon salt
1/4   cup reduced-calorie stick margarine
1   (8-ounce) carton plain low-fat yogurt
1   teaspoon honey
1   tablespoon all-purpose flour

1. Preheat oven to 425°.

2. Combine first 4 ingredients in a medium bowl; cut in margarine with a pastry blender until mixture is crumbly. Combine yogurt and honey; add to flour mixture, stirring with a fork just until dry ingredients are moistened.

3. Sprinkle 1 tablespoon flour over work surface. Turn dough out onto floured surface; knead lightly 4 or 5 times. Roll dough to 1/2-inch thickness; cut into rounds with a 2-inch biscuit cutter. Place biscuits on an ungreased baking sheet. Bake at 425° for 10 minutes or until golden. **Yield:** 22 servings (serving size: 1 biscuit).

BUTTERMILK BISCUITS

Handle dough with a light touch for fluffy biscuits. Biscuit dough should be slightly sticky and should be kneaded gently. Take care to keep the cutter straight as you cut the dough; the biscuits will rise evenly if you do.

2	cups all-purpose flour
2½	teaspoons baking powder
¼	teaspoon baking soda
¼	teaspoon salt
2	teaspoons sugar
3	tablespoons chilled reduced-calorie stick margarine, cut into small pieces
¾	cup low-fat or nonfat buttermilk
	Butter-flavored cooking spray (such as I Can't Believe It's Not Butter)
	Reduced-calorie jelly (optional)

1. Preheat oven to 425°.

2. Combine first 5 ingredients in a medium bowl; cut in margarine with a pastry blender until mixture resembles coarse meal. Add buttermilk, stirring just until dry ingredients are moistened.

3. Turn dough out onto a lightly floured surface, and knead 10 to 12 times. Roll dough to ½-inch thickness; cut into rounds with a 2-inch biscuit cutter.

4. Place rounds on an ungreased baking sheet. Bake at 425° for 10 to 12 minutes or until golden. Lightly spray biscuits with cooking spray. Serve with reduced-calorie jelly, if desired. **Yield:** 16 servings (serving size: 1 biscuit).

YIELD: 16 servings

EXCHANGE PER SERVING:
1 Starch

PER SERVING:
Calories 75
(19% from fat)
Fat 1.6g
(saturated fat 0.1g)
Protein 2g
Carbohydrate 13.2g
Fiber 0.4g
Cholesterol 0mg
Sodium 167mg

EXCHANGES PER
SERVING:
1½ Starch
1 Fat

PER SERVING:
Calories 146
(39% from fat)
Fat 6.3g
(saturated fat 1.2g)
Protein 2.8g
Carbohydrate 19.7g
Fiber 0.7g
Cholesterol 0mg
Sodium 150mg

HONEY ANGEL BISCUITS

*A drizzle of golden honey sweetens these
reach-for-the-sky biscuits.*

1   package active dry yeast
¼   cup warm water (105° to 115°)
3   cups all-purpose flour
1   teaspoon baking powder
1   teaspoon baking soda
½   teaspoon salt
1   cup low-fat or nonfat buttermilk
½   cup vegetable oil
3   tablespoons honey

1. Preheat oven to 400°.

2. Combine yeast and warm water in a 1-cup liquid measuring cup; let stand 5 minutes.

3. Combine flour and next 3 ingredients in a large
bowl. Combine yeast mixture, buttermilk, oil, and
honey, and add to dry ingredients, stirring just until
dry ingredients are moistened.

4. Turn dough out onto a lightly floured surface,
and knead 4 or 5 times. Pat dough to ½-inch
thickness. Cut with a 2-inch round cutter, and
place on an ungreased baking sheet. Bake at 400°
for 10 minutes or until golden. **Yield:** 1½ dozen
(serving size: 1 biscuit).

HERBED BISCUITS

YIELD: 18 servings

EXCHANGE PER SERVING:
1 Starch

PER SERVING:
Calories 83
(29% from fat)
Fat 2.7g
(saturated fat 0.6g)
Protein 2.3g
Carbohydrate 12.3g
Fiber 0.4g
Cholesterol 1mg
Sodium 122mg

2   cups all-purpose flour
1   tablespoon baking powder
½   teaspoon baking soda
¼   teaspoon salt
¼   teaspoon dried thyme, crushed
¼   teaspoon dried rosemary, crushed
¼   teaspoon dried basil, crushed
¼   cup stick margarine or butter
¾   cup plus 2 tablespoons low-fat or nonfat
      buttermilk
1   tablespoon all-purpose flour

1. Preheat oven to 400°.

2. Combine first 7 ingredients in a medium bowl; cut in margarine with a pastry blender until mixture is crumbly. Add buttermilk, stirring with a fork just until dry ingredients are moistened.

3. Sprinkle 1 tablespoon flour over work surface. Turn dough out onto floured surface; knead lightly 4 or 5 times. Roll dough to ½-inch thickness; cut into rounds with a 2-inch biscuit cutter. Place biscuits on an ungreased baking sheet. Bake at 400° for 10 minutes or until golden. **Yield:** 1½ dozen (serving size: 1 biscuit).

♥ *Fat helps tenderize, provides volume, and adds flavor to baked goods. For many of our breads and desserts, we recommend using a small amount of stick margarine or butter. Reduced-fat and liquid margarines are healthy choices for eating and to use in some recipes. But the first ingredient in these products is often water, which can cause sogginess in baked breads and desserts. See page 10 for more about margarine and butter in cooking.*

EXCHANGES PER
SERVING:
2 Starch
1 Fat

PER SERVING:
Calories 196
(24% from fat)
Fat 5.2g
(saturated fat 1.1g)
Protein 4.4g
Carbohydrate 33.7g
Fiber 1.3g
Cholesterol 37mg
Sodium 239mg

APRICOT SCONES

*Scones can be prepared a day ahead. Cool on a
wire rack, then wrap in aluminum foil.
Reheat at 350° for 25 minutes.*

2$^1/_2$ cups all-purpose flour
 $^1/_2$ cup sugar
 2 teaspoons baking powder
 $^1/_2$ teaspoon baking soda
 $^1/_4$ teaspoon salt
 $^1/_4$ cup chilled stick margarine or butter, cut
      into small pieces
 $^1/_2$ cup finely chopped dried apricots
 $^1/_2$ cup low-fat or nonfat buttermilk
 2 large eggs
    Cooking spray
 2 teaspoons sugar
 $^1/_2$ teaspoon ground cinnamon

1. Preheat oven to 400°.

2. Lightly spoon flour into dry measuring cups;
level with a knife. Combine flour and next 4 ingredients; cut in margarine with a pastry blender or
2 knives until the mixture resembles coarse meal.
Stir in apricots. Combine buttermilk and eggs, stirring with a whisk. Add to flour mixture, stirring
just until moist (dough will be sticky).

3. Turn dough out onto a lightly floured surface;
knead lightly 4 times. Pat dough into a 9-inch circle on a baking sheet coated with cooking spray.
Cut dough into 12 wedges, cutting into but not
through dough. Combine 2 teaspoons sugar and
cinnamon, and sprinkle over dough. Bake at 400°
for 20 minutes or until golden. Serve warm. **Yield:**
1 dozen (serving size: 1 scone).

BUTTERMILK-CHERRY SCONES

2 cups all-purpose flour
1 1/2 teaspoons baking powder
1/2 teaspoon baking soda
1/4 teaspoon salt
1/4 cup sugar
1/4 cup chilled stick margarine or butter, cut into small pieces
2/3 cup dried tart cherries
1 large egg, lightly beaten
1/2 cup low-fat or nonfat buttermilk
Cooking spray
1 large egg white, lightly beaten
1 tablespoon sugar

1. Preheat oven to 400°.

2. Combine first 5 ingredients in a bowl; cut in margarine with a pastry blender until mixture resembles coarse meal. Add cherries, and toss well. Combine egg and buttermilk; add to dry ingredients, stirring just until moistened (dough will be sticky).

3. Turn dough out onto a lightly floured surface; with floured hands, knead 4 or 5 times. Pat dough into an 8-inch circle on a baking sheet coated with cooking spray. Cut into 12 wedges, cutting to but not through bottom of dough. Brush with egg white, and sprinkle with 1 tablespoon sugar. Bake at 400° for 15 minutes or until golden. Serve hot.
Yield: 1 dozen (serving size: 1 scone).

YIELD: 12 servings

EXCHANGES PER SERVING:
2 Starch
1/2 Fat

PER SERVING:
Calories 173
(23% from fat)
Fat 4.5g
(saturated fat 1g)
Protein 4.1g
Carbohydrate 28.4g
Fiber 0.9g
Cholesterol 19mg
Sodium 239mg

EXCHANGES PER
SERVING:
1½ Starch

PER SERVING:
Calories 104
(10% from fat)
Fat 1.2g
(saturated fat 0.2g)
Protein 2.5g
Carbohydrate 20.9g
Fiber 0.8g
Cholesterol 0mg
Sodium 115mg

LEMON-BLUEBERRY MUFFINS

2   cups all-purpose flour
1   teaspoon baking powder
½   teaspoon baking soda
½   teaspoon salt
½   cup sugar
1   teaspoon grated lemon rind
¾   cup fresh blueberries
2   large egg whites, lightly beaten
1   (8-ounce) carton lemon fat-free yogurt
½   cup unsweetened applesauce
1   tablespoon vegetable oil
    Cooking spray

1. Preheat oven to 400°.

2. Combine first 6 ingredients in a large bowl; add blueberries, and toss to coat. Make a well in center of mixture. Combine egg whites and next 3 ingredients; add to dry ingredients, stirring just until dry ingredients are moistened.

3. Spoon batter into muffin pans coated with cooking spray, filling two-thirds full. Bake at 400° for 20 minutes. **Yield:** 16 servings (serving size: 1 muffin).

♥ *Many of the recipes in this book call for 2 egg whites in place of a whole egg to lower cholesterol and fat. Others specify egg substitute, which contains no cholesterol and little, if any, fat. Although some recipes work well with egg whites, others do not. So keep both egg whites and egg substitute on hand.*

Super Quick
APPLE BUTTER-BRAN MUFFINS

Apple butter has no fat, but is actually a thick preserve mixture of apples, sugar, spices, and cider. It adds moisture and a sweet apple flavor to these muffins.

1 (7.4-ounce) package honey bran muffin mix
1/2 cup apple butter
1/3 cup chopped dates
1 tablespoon fat-free milk
1 large egg, lightly beaten
  Cooking spray

1. Preheat oven to 450°.

2. Combine first 5 ingredients, stirring just until dry ingredients are moistened. Spoon batter into muffin pans coated with cooking spray, filling three-fourths full.

3. Bake at 450° for 10 to 12 minutes or until lightly browned. Remove from pans immediately. **Yield:** 8 servings (serving size: 1 muffin).

♥ *Health experts tell us that over half of the calories we eat should come from complex carbohydrates—good news for those who love bread—and that we should consume 25 to 30 grams of fiber daily. You can get extra fiber by eating whole grain breads or breads made with high-fiber cereal.*

YIELD: 8 servings

EXCHANGES PER SERVING:
2 Starch
1/2 Fat

PER SERVING:
Calories 174
(24% from fat)
Fat 4.7g
(saturated fat 1g)
Protein 2.5g
Carbohydrate 31.8g
Fiber 2.8g
Cholesterol 28mg
Sodium 212mg

YIELD: 12 servings

EXCHANGES PER SERVING:
1 1/2 Starch

PER SERVING:
Calories 124
(13% from fat)
Fat 1.8g
(saturated fat 0.3g)
Protein 3.1g
Carbohydrate 26.4g
Fiber 3.4g
Cholesterol 0mg
Sodium 128mg

MOLASSES-BRAN MUFFINS

Dark molasses gives these muffins a wonderful flavor similar to gingerbread.

1 1/4 cups unprocessed wheat bran
1 cup all-purpose flour
2 teaspoons baking powder
1/4 teaspoon baking soda
1/2 teaspoon ground cinnamon
3/4 cup unsweetened applesauce
1/2 cup fat-free milk
1/3 cup dark molasses
1/4 cup egg substitute
1 tablespoon vegetable oil
1/2 cup raisins
Cooking spray

1. Preheat oven to 400°.

2. Combine first 5 ingredients in a bowl; make a well in center of mixture. Combine applesauce and next 4 ingredients; add to dry ingredients, stirring just until moistened. Stir in raisins.

3. Spoon batter into muffin pans coated with cooking spray, filling two-thirds full. Bake at 400° for 18 to 20 minutes or until golden. Remove from pans immediately, and place on a wire rack. **Yield:** 1 dozen (serving size: 1 muffin).

GLAZED CITRUS MUFFINS

1³/₄ cups all-purpose flour
1 teaspoon baking powder
¹/₂ teaspoon baking soda
¹/₄ teaspoon salt
¹/₃ cup sugar
³/₄ cup low-fat or nonfat buttermilk
¹/₄ cup egg substitute
¹/₄ cup frozen orange juice concentrate,
    thawed
2 tablespoons vegetable oil
1 tablespoon grated orange rind
Cooking spray
¹/₄ cup orange marmalade spreadable fruit
1 tablespoon fresh lemon juice
1 tablespoon water

YIELD: 12 servings

EXCHANGES PER SERVING:
1¹/₂ Starch
¹/₂ Fat

PER SERVING:
Calories 138
(17% from fat)
Fat 2.6g
(saturated fat 0.5g)
Protein 3.1g
Carbohydrate 25.9g
Fiber 0.5g
Cholesterol 1mg
Sodium 126mg

1. Preheat oven to 400°.

2. Combine first 5 ingredients in a medium bowl; make a well in center of mixture. Combine buttermilk and next 4 ingredients, stirring well; add to dry ingredients, stirring just until dry ingredients are moistened.

3. Spoon batter into muffin pans coated with cooking spray, filling three-fourths full. Bake at 400° for 15 minutes. Do not remove muffins from pans.

4. Combine marmalade, lemon juice, and water in a small saucepan; place over low heat until melted, stirring often. Drizzle glaze evenly over warm muffins in pans. Remove from pans, and cool completely. **Yield:** 1 dozen (serving size: 1 muffin).

Glazed Citrus Mini-Muffins: Prepare batter as directed. Spoon into miniature muffin pans; bake at 400° for 14 minutes. Drizzle glaze over warm muffins in pans. Remove from pans, and cool completely. **Yield:** 3 dozen.

PER SERVING:
Calories 152
(21% from fat)
Fat 3.5g
(saturated fat 0.6g)
Protein 4.5g
Carbohydrate 25.9g
Fiber 1.5g
Cholesterol 1mg
Sodium 135mg

LEMON-POPPY SEED MUFFINS

*One large lemon should give you enough
rind and juice for this recipe.*

    1¼ cups unprocessed oat bran
     ¾ cup all-purpose flour
      1 teaspoon baking powder
     ½ teaspoon baking soda
     ½ cup sugar
      1 tablespoon grated lemon rind
      2 teaspoons poppy seeds
      1 (8-ounce) carton lemon fat-free yogurt
     ½ cup low-fat or nonfat buttermilk
     ¼ cup egg substitute
      2 tablespoons vegetable oil
     ½ teaspoon vanilla extract
     ¼ teaspoon lemon extract
        Cooking spray
     ⅓ cup sifted powdered sugar
      1 tablespoon fresh lemon juice

1. Preheat oven to 400°.

2. Combine first 7 ingredients in a bowl; make a
well in center of mixture. Combine yogurt and
next 5 ingredients; add yogurt mixture to dry
ingredients, stirring just until dry ingredients are
moistened.

3. Spoon batter into muffin pans coated with
cooking spray, filling three-fourths full. Bake at
400° for 20 to 22 minutes or until lightly browned.
Remove muffins from pans; place on a wire rack.

4. Combine powdered sugar and lemon juice, stirring mixture well; drizzle over warm muffins.
Yield: 1 dozen (serving size: 1 muffin).

PUMPKIN-RAISIN MUFFINS

1½ cups all-purpose flour
⅓ cup packed brown sugar
1 teaspoon baking powder
½ teaspoon baking soda
¼ teaspoon salt
1½ teaspoons pumpkin pie spice
⅓ cup raisins
1 large egg, lightly beaten
½ cup canned pumpkin
⅓ cup orange juice
1 tablespoon stick margarine or butter, melted
Cooking spray

1. Preheat oven to 400°.

2. Combine first 6 ingredients in a large bowl; stir in raisins. Make a well in center of mixture. Combine egg and next 3 ingredients in a small bowl. Add to dry ingredients, stirring just until dry ingredients are moistened (batter will be very thick).

3. Spoon batter into muffin pans coated with cooking spray, filling two-thirds full. Bake at 400° for 15 minutes. **Yield:** 1 dozen (serving size: 1 muffin).

♥ *Do you have a tough time getting out the door to exercise in the morning? It helps if you can keep in mind just how good exercise is for you. Scientific research has shown that exercise helps reduce your risk of heart disease, high blood pressure, stroke, adult-onset diabetes, osteoporosis, and cancer. So put on your jogging shoes— then enjoy a healthy muffin and juice when you return.*

YIELD: 12 servings

EXCHANGES PER SERVING:
1½ Starch

PER SERVING:
Calories 116
(14% from fat)
Fat 1.8g
(saturated fat 0.4g)
Protein 2.5g
Carbohydrate 22.9g
Fiber 1.1g
Cholesterol 18mg
Sodium 122mg

YIELD: 12 servings

EXCHANGES PER
SERVING:
1 Starch
1/2 Fat

PER SERVING:
Calories 111
(25% from fat)
Fat 3.1g
(saturated fat 0.6g)
Protein 3.8g
Carbohydrate 17.6g
Fiber 1.9g
Cholesterol 1mg
Sodium 120mg

CORN-OAT MUFFINS

These hearty muffins are proof positive that muffins aren't just for breakfast.

1 1/4 cups low-fat or nonfat buttermilk
1/2 cup yellow cornmeal
1/2 cup regular oats
1/4 cup egg substitute
3 tablespoons brown sugar
2 tablespoons vegetable oil
1 cup whole wheat flour
1 teaspoon baking powder
1/2 teaspoon baking soda
1/4 teaspoon salt
Cooking spray

1. Preheat oven to 400°.

2. Combine first 3 ingredients in a medium bowl; let stand 1 hour. Stir in egg substitute, brown sugar, and oil.

3. Combine flour and next 3 ingredients in a large bowl, and make a well in center of mixture. Add buttermilk mixture to flour mixture, stirring just until dry ingredients are moistened.

4. Spoon batter into muffin pans coated with cooking spray, filling two-thirds full. Bake at 400° for 20 minutes or until golden. Remove muffins from pans immediately. **Yield:** 1 dozen (serving size: 1 muffin).

CORN STICKS

A preheated cast-iron corn stick pan gives cornbread a crunchy, browned crust. The batter crisps quickly in the hot pan while the inside of the bread bakes slowly and stays moist.

  ³/₄ cup all-purpose flour
  ³/₄ cup yellow cornmeal
   2 teaspoons baking powder
  ¹/₄ teaspoon baking soda
  ¹/₄ teaspoon salt
1¹/₂ tablespoons sugar
  ¹/₈ teaspoon ground red pepper
   1 (6¹/₂-ounce) can whole-kernel corn, drained
   1 large egg, lightly beaten
   1 cup low-fat or nonfat buttermilk
     Cooking spray

1. Preheat oven to 425°.

2. Combine first 7 ingredients in a medium bowl. Add corn, stirring well; make a well in center of mixture. Combine egg and buttermilk; add to flour mixture, stirring just until moistened.

3. Place cast-iron corn stick pans in a 425° oven for 5 minutes or until hot. Remove pans from oven, and coat with cooking spray. Spoon batter evenly into pans. Bake at 425° for 10 minutes or until lightly browned. Remove corn sticks from pans immediately, and serve warm. **Yield:** 14 servings (serving size: 1 corn stick).

YIELD: 14 servings

EXCHANGE PER SERVING:
1 Starch

PER SERVING:
Calories 83
(10% from fat)
Fat 0.9g
(saturated fat 0.2g)
Protein 2.8g
Carbohydrate 16.3g
Fiber 0.7g
Cholesterol 16mg
Sodium 113mg

**EXCHANGES PER
SERVING:**
1 Starch
¹/₂ Fat

PER SERVING:
Calories 110
(39% from fat)
Fat 4.8g
(saturated fat 0.4g)
Protein 2.6g
Carbohydrate 13.8g
Fiber 0.8g
Cholesterol 26mg
Sodium 142mg

BAKED HUSH PUPPIES

*These hush puppies bake in miniature muffin pans for a
significant fat and calorie savings compared with
traditional deep-fried versions.*

1 cup yellow cornmeal
1 cup all-purpose flour
1 tablespoon baking powder
1 teaspoon sugar
1 teaspoon salt
¹/₈ teaspoon ground red pepper
2 large eggs, lightly beaten
³/₄ cup fat-free milk
¹/₄ cup vegetable oil
¹/₂ cup finely chopped onion
Cooking spray

1. Preheat oven to 425°.

2. Combine first 6 ingredients in a large bowl;
make a well in center of mixture. Set aside. Combine eggs and next 3 ingredients, stirring well; add
to dry mixture, stirring just until dry ingredients
are moistened.

3. Coat miniature (1³/₄-inch) muffin pans with
cooking spray. Spoon about 1 tablespoon batter
into each muffin cup (cups will be about three-
fourths full). Bake at 425° for 15 minutes or until
done. Remove from pans immediately. **Yield:** 3
dozen (serving size: 2 hush puppies).

EASY POPOVERS

Here's a quick fix for the breadtime dilemma: popovers. Crusty on the outside and almost hollow on the inside, these miniature "bread balloons" can be mixed up in about 10 minutes flat! Popovers can accompany everything from soup to hearty meats.

Cooking spray
³/₄ cup bread flour
³/₄ cup 1% low-fat milk
¹/₂ cup egg substitute
1 tablespoon sugar
1 tablespoon vegetable oil
¹/₄ teaspoon salt

1. Preheat oven to 450°.

2. Coat 6 popover cups heavily with cooking spray. Heat pans in oven 2 to 3 minutes or until hot.

3. Lightly spoon flour into a dry measuring cup; level with a knife. Place flour and next 5 ingredients in a food processor. Process until smooth, scraping sides of bowl once.

4. Divide batter evenly among hot cups; bake 15 minutes. Reduce oven temperature to 350° (do not remove popover cups from oven); bake an additional 15 minutes or until golden. Make a slit in top of each popover using a small sharp knife or scissors; bake 2 additional minutes. Serve immediately.
Yield: 6 servings (serving size: 1 popover).

YIELD: 6 servings

EXCHANGES PER SERVING:
1 Starch
¹/₂ Fat

PER SERVING:
Calories 105
(26% from fat)
Fat 3g
(saturated fat 0.6g)
Protein 4.7g
Carbohydrate 14.3g
Fiber 0.4g
Cholesterol 1mg
Sodium 143mg

Super Quick
HONEY PANCAKES

These light and fluffy flapjacks won high praise from our foods staff.

    3   cups all-purpose flour
1 1/2   tablespoons baking powder
  1/2   teaspoon salt
    2   cups fat-free milk
  1/2   cup egg substitute
  1/4   cup vegetable oil
  1/4   cup honey
        Cooking spray

1. Combine first 3 ingredients in a large bowl. Combine milk and next 3 ingredients; add to flour mixture, stirring just until batter is smooth.

2. Coat a nonstick griddle with cooking spray; preheat to 350°. For each pancake, pour 1/4 cup batter onto griddle. Turn pancakes when tops are covered with bubbles and edges look cooked. **Yield:** 16 servings (serving size: 1 pancake).

Note: To freeze, prepare pancakes as directed; cool. Place in a single layer on a wax paper-lined baking sheet; freeze. Place frozen pancakes in an airtight container, and freeze up to 1 month. To reheat, microwave 1 frozen pancake at HIGH 30 to 45 seconds, 2 pancakes at HIGH 1 minute to 1 minute and 10 seconds, and 3 pancakes at HIGH 1 1/2 minutes or until thoroughly heated.

BUCKWHEAT-HONEY PANCAKES

*Store any leftover buckwheat flour in your refrigerator
or freezer; whole-grain flours will spoil quickly
at room temperature.*

2/3 cup buckwheat flour
1/2 cup all-purpose flour
1 teaspoon baking powder
1/4 teaspoon baking soda
1/4 teaspoon salt
1/8 teaspoon ground nutmeg
3/4 cup plain fat-free yogurt
1/4 cup honey
1/4 cup fat-free milk
2 tablespoons vegetable oil
3/4 teaspoon vanilla extract
3 large eggs, lightly beaten

1. Lightly spoon flours into dry measuring cups,
and level with a knife. Combine flours and next 4
ingredients in a large bowl. Combine yogurt and remaining ingredients; add to flour mixture, stirring
until smooth.

2. For each pancake, spoon about 1/4 cup batter
onto a hot nonstick griddle or skillet. Turn pancakes
when tops are covered with bubbles and edges look
cooked. **Yield:** 12 servings (serving size: 1 pancake).

YIELD: 12 servings

**EXCHANGES PER
SERVING:**
1 Starch
1/2 Fat

PER SERVING:
Calories 117
(29% from fat)
Fat 3.8g
(saturated fat 0.9g)
Protein 4.3g
Carbohydrate 16.9g
Fiber 0.5g
Cholesterol 56mg
Sodium 148mg

PER SERVING:
Calories 105
(23% from fat)
Fat 2.7g
(saturated fat 0.5g)
Protein 3.8g
Carbohydrate 17.6g
Fiber 1.5g
Cholesterol 1mg
Sodium 86mg

WHOLE WHEAT-OAT PANCAKES

$^{2}/_{3}$ cup regular oats
$^{1}/_{2}$ cup whole wheat flour
$^{1}/_{2}$ cup all-purpose flour
  1 tablespoon baking powder
$^{1}/_{4}$ teaspoon salt
  1 cup fat-free milk
$^{1}/_{4}$ cup egg substitute
1$^{1}/_{2}$ tablespoons vegetable oil
  Cooking spray
  1 tablespoon powdered sugar
$^{3}/_{4}$ cup reduced-calorie maple-flavored syrup

1. Place oats in container of an electric blender;
cover and process until ground. Combine oats,
whole wheat flour, and next 3 ingredients in a
bowl. Combine milk, egg substitute, and oil; add to
oats mixture, stirring just until moistened.

2. For each pancake, pour ¼ cup batter onto a hot
griddle or skillet coated with cooking spray. Turn
pancakes when tops are covered with bubbles and
edges look cooked.

3. Sprinkle pancakes evenly with powdered sugar,
and serve with syrup. **Yield:** 10 servings (serving
size: 1 pancake with about 1 tablespoon syrup).

BLUEBERRY PANCAKES

Watch the surface of the pancake as it's cooking. When the top is full of bubbles, it's time to flip the pancake.

- 1 cup all-purpose flour
- 2 teaspoons baking powder
- ¼ teaspoon baking soda
- ¼ teaspoon salt
- 1 tablespoon sugar
- 1⅓ cups low-fat or nonfat buttermilk
- ¼ cup egg substitute
- 1 tablespoon vegetable oil
- ½ cup frozen blueberries
  Cooking spray

1. Combine first 5 ingredients in a large bowl. Combine buttermilk, egg substitute, and oil; add to dry ingredients, stirring just until dry ingredients are moistened. Stir in blueberries.

2. For each pancake, pour ¼ cup batter onto a hot griddle or skillet coated with cooking spray. Turn pancakes when tops are bubbly and edges look cooked. **Yield:** 12 servings (serving size: 1 pancake).

♥ *You can cut cholesterol and fat from your diet by using a commercial egg substitute instead of whole eggs. Egg whites are the main ingredient in most egg substitutes. Sodium, preservatives, and sometimes oil are added so that the product will taste and perform like whole eggs. When modifying your own recipes, use ¼ cup egg substitute for each whole egg.*

YIELD: 12 servings

EXCHANGE PER SERVING:
1 Starch

PER SERVING:
Calories 72
(19% from fat)
Fat 1.5g
(saturated fat 0.3g)
Protein 2.9g
Carbohydrate 11.8g
Fiber 0.5g
Cholesterol 1mg
Sodium 201mg

WAFFLES WITH TWO-BERRY SYRUP

EXCHANGES PER
SERVING:
2 Starch

PER SERVING:
Calories 166
(18% from fat)
Fat 3.3g
(saturated fat 0.4g)
Protein 5.4g
Carbohydrate 30.3g
Fiber 3.3g
Cholesterol 1mg
Sodium 200mg

2 tablespoons flaxseed
1 cup all-purpose flour
½ cup whole-wheat flour
¼ cup toasted wheat germ
2 tablespoons sugar
1½ teaspoons baking powder
½ teaspoon salt
1½ cups fat-free milk
¾ cup egg substitute
1½ tablespoons vegetable oil
1 teaspoon vanilla extract
 Cooking spray
1½ cups frozen blueberries
1½ cups frozen unsweetened raspberries
½ cup maple syrup
¼ teaspoon ground cinnamon

1. To prepare waffles, place flaxseed in a clean cof-fee grinder or blender; process until ground to measure ¼ cup flaxseed meal. Set the flaxseed meal aside. Lightly spoon flours into dry measuring cups; level with a knife. Combine the flaxseed meal, flours, wheat germ, sugar, baking powder, and salt in a large bowl; make a well in center of mixture. Combine milk, egg substitute, oil, and vanilla; add to flour mixture, stirring just until moist.

2. Coat a waffle iron with cooking spray; preheat. Spoon about ¼ cup of batter per 4-inch waffle onto the hot waffle iron, spreading batter to edges. Cook 5 to 6 minutes or until steaming stops; repeat procedure with remaining batter.

3. To prepare syrup, combine berries, maple syrup, and ground cinnamon in a saucepan. Cook over medium heat until thoroughly heated. Serve warm over waffles. **Yield:** 12 servings (serving size: 1 [4-inch] waffle and about 3 tablespoons syrup).

BANANA-OATMEAL BREAD

1 cup packed brown sugar
7 tablespoons vegetable oil
2 large egg whites
1 large egg
1⅓ cups mashed ripe banana (about 2 large)
1 cup regular oats
½ cup fat-free milk
2 cups all-purpose flour
1 tablespoon baking powder
½ teaspoon baking soda
½ teaspoon salt
½ teaspoon ground cinnamon
  Cooking spray

1. Preheat oven to 350°.

2. Combine first 4 ingredients in a large bowl; beat well at medium speed of a mixer. Combine banana, oats, and milk; add to sugar mixture, beating well. Lightly spoon flour into dry measuring cups; level with a knife. Combine flour, baking powder, baking soda, salt, and cinnamon; stir with a whisk. Add to sugar mixture; beat just until moist.

3. Spoon batter into a 9 x 5-inch loaf pan coated with cooking spray. Bake at 350° for 1 hour and 10 minutes or until a wooden pick inserted in center comes out clean. Cool 10 minutes in pan on a wire rack; remove from pan. Cool completely on wire rack. **Yield:** 18 servings (serving size: 1 [½-inch] slice).

YIELD: 18 servings

EXCHANGES PER SERVING:
2 Starch
½ Fat

PER SERVING:
Calories 185
(30% from fat)
Fat 6.1g
(saturated fat 1.2g)
Protein 3.3g
Carbohydrate 30.1g
Fiber 1.3g
Cholesterol 12mg
Sodium 200mg

EXCHANGES PER
SERVING:
1½ Starch
½ Fat

PER SERVING:
Calories 150
(24% from fat)
Fat 4g
(saturated fat 0.8g)
Protein 2.2g
Carbohydrate 27.3g
Fiber 1.5g
Cholesterol 0mg
Sodium 64mg

FRUITY BANANA BREAD

*We took a yummy banana bread recipe, stirred in some
chopped dried fruit, and came up with this quick bread
that's one of our favorites.*

⅓ cup stick margarine or butter, softened
¾ cup sugar
½ cup egg substitute
1¾ cups all-purpose flour
2¾ teaspoons baking powder
1 cup mashed ripe banana (about 2 medium)
¾ cup coarsely chopped mixed dried fruit
Cooking spray

1. Preheat oven to 350°.

2. Beat margarine at medium speed of an electric
mixer until creamy; gradually add sugar, beating
well. Add egg substitute; beat just until blended.

3. Combine flour and baking powder; add to margarine mixture, beating at low speed just until
blended. Stir in banana and dried fruit.

4. Spoon batter into an 8 x 4-inch loaf pan coated
with cooking spray. Bake at 350° for 1 hour or until a wooden pick inserted in center of loaf comes
out clean. Cool in pan on a wire rack 10 minutes;
remove from pan, and cool completely on wire
rack. **Yield:** 16 servings (serving size: 1 [½-inch]
slice).

POPPY SEED QUICK BREAD

YIELD: 16 servings

EXCHANGES PER SERVING:
1½ Starch
1 Fat

PER SERVING:
Calories 161
(29% from fat)
Fat 5.2g
(saturated fat 0.6g)
Protein 3.4g
Carbohydrate 26.1g
Fiber 0.8g
Cholesterol 0mg
Sodium 103mg

2¼ cups all-purpose flour
 1 teaspoon baking powder
½ teaspoon baking soda
¼ teaspoon salt
½ cup sugar
 2 tablespoons grated orange rind
 1 tablespoon poppy seeds
½ cup fat-free milk
½ cup orange juice
¼ cup egg substitute
 2 tablespoons stick margarine or butter, melted
½ cup chopped walnuts
  Cooking spray
½ cup sifted powdered sugar
 2 teaspoons orange juice

1. Preheat oven to 350°.

2. Combine first 7 ingredients in a large bowl; mix well. Combine milk and next 3 ingredients; add to dry ingredients, stirring just until dry ingredients are moistened. Stir in walnuts.

3. Spoon batter in an 8 x 4-inch loaf pan coated with cooking spray. Bake at 350° for 50 to 55 minutes or until a wooden pick inserted in center comes out clean.

4. Combine ½ cup powdered sugar and 2 teaspoons orange juice; stir well. Drizzle glaze over hot bread in pan. Cool in pan 10 minutes. Remove from pan, and let cool completely on a wire rack. **Yield:** 16 servings (serving size: 1 [½-inch] slice).

**EXCHANGES PER
SERVING:**
1 Starch
¹/₂ Fat

PER SERVING:
Calories 112
(30% from fat)
Fat 3.7g
(saturated fat 0.6g)
Protein 2.4g
Carbohydrate 17.6g
Fiber 1.1g
Cholesterol 18mg
Sodium 75mg

PUMPKIN-PECAN BREAD

*Make an extra batch of this aromatic nut bread
to share during the holidays.*

1³/₄ cups all-purpose flour
  1 teaspoon baking powder
 ¹/₂ teaspoon baking soda
 ¹/₄ teaspoon salt
 ¹/₂ cup sugar
 ³/₄ teaspoon ground cinnamon
 ¹/₂ teaspoon ground nutmeg
  1 cup canned pumpkin
 ¹/₂ cup egg substitute
2¹/₂ tablespoons vegetable oil
 ¹/₄ cup chopped pecans
    Cooking spray

1. Preheat oven to 350°.

2. Combine first 7 ingredients in a large bowl;
make a well in center of mixture. Combine pumpkin, egg substitute, and oil; add to flour mixture,
stirring just until dry ingredients are moistened.
Fold in pecans.

3. Spoon batter into an 8 x 4-inch loaf pan coated
with cooking spray. Bake at 350° for 45 minutes or
until a wooden pick inserted in center of loaf
comes out clean. Cool in pan on a wire rack 10
minutes; remove from pan, and cool completely on
wire rack. **Yield:** 16 servings (serving size: 1
[¹/₂-inch] slice).

STRAWBERRY BREAD

YIELD: 14 servings

1 ½ cups all-purpose flour
½ teaspoon baking soda
¼ teaspoon salt
½ cup sugar
½ teaspoon ground cinnamon
1 large egg white, lightly beaten
1 cup frozen unsweetened strawberries,
    thawed and coarsely chopped
2 tablespoons vegetable oil
⅓ cup chopped pecans
    Cooking spray

**EXCHANGES PER
SERVING:**
1 Starch
1 Fat

PER SERVING:
Calories 116
(30% from fat)
Fat 3.9g
(saturated fat 0.5g)
Protein 1.9g
Carbohydrate 18.8g
Fiber 0.6g
Cholesterol 0mg
Sodium 91mg

1. Preheat oven to 350°.

2. Combine first 5 ingredients in a large bowl; mix well. Combine egg white, strawberries, and oil, stirring well; add to flour mixture, stirring just until dry ingredients are moistened. Stir in pecans.

3. Spoon batter into a 7½ x 3-inch loaf pan coated with cooking spray. Bake at 350° for 1 hour or until a wooden pick inserted in center comes out clean. Cool in pan 10 minutes. Remove from pan, and let cool completely on a wire rack. **Yield:** 14 servings (serving size: 1 [½-inch] slice).

EXCHANGES PER
SERVING:
2½ Starch
1 Fat

PER SERVING:
Calories 248
(30% from fat)
Fat 8.4g
(saturated fat 1.8g)
Protein 3.4g
Carbohydrate 39.5g
Fiber 0.8g
Cholesterol 32mg
Sodium 206mg

CRANBERRY-ORANGE COFFEECAKE

Cooking spray
1 tablespoon all-purpose flour
½ cup stick margarine or butter, softened
1⅓ cups sugar
2 large eggs
2 teaspoons vanilla extract
1 cup 50%-less-fat sour cream (such as Daisy)
2 cups all-purpose flour
1 tablespoon baking powder
¼ teaspoon salt
½ cup dried cranberries
3 tablespoons chopped walnuts
2 tablespoons brown sugar
2 tablespoons grated orange rind
1 teaspoon ground cinnamon
⅔ cup sifted powdered sugar
2 teaspoons fresh orange juice

1. Preheat oven to 350°.

2. Coat a 12-cup Bundt pan with cooking spray; dust with 1 tablespoon flour, and set aside.

3. Beat margarine in a large bowl at medium speed of a mixer until creamy; gradually add sugar. Add eggs, one at a time, beating well after each addition. Add vanilla and sour cream, beating just until blended. Combine 2 cups flour, baking powder, and salt; gradually add to sour cream mixture, beating just until smooth.

4. Combine cranberries and next 4 ingredients. Spoon ⅓ of batter into prepared pan. Sprinkle cranberry mixture around center of batter. Spoon remaining batter over cranberry mixture, smoothing with a spatula. Bake at 350° for 45 minutes or until a wooden pick inserted in center comes out clean. Let cool in pan on a wire rack 10 minutes. Remove from pan, and let cool completely on a wire rack. Combine powdered sugar and orange juice, stirring well; drizzle over cake. **Yield:** 16 servings (serving size: 1 slice).

ORANGE COFFEECAKE WITH STREUSEL TOPPING

2 tablespoons nutlike cereal nuggets
2 tablespoons sugar
2 teaspoons stick margarine or butter, softened
2 large egg whites, lightly beaten
¼ cup unsweetened applesauce
3 tablespoons stick margarine or butter, melted
1 tablespoon frozen orange juice concentrate, thawed
1 (15-ounce) can mandarin oranges, drained
1 cup sifted cake flour
¼ cup sugar
1 teaspoon baking powder
⅛ teaspoon salt
¼ teaspoon ground cinnamon
Cooking spray

1. Preheat oven to 350°.

2. Combine first 3 ingredients in a small bowl until mixture resembles coarse meal. Set aside.

3. Combine egg whites and next 3 ingredients in a large bowl, stirring well with a wire whisk. Gently stir in oranges. Combine flour and next 4 ingredients. Add flour mixture to applesauce mixture, stirring just until dry ingredients are moistened.

4. Pour batter into an 8-inch round cake pan coated with cooking spray. Sprinkle with cereal mixture. Bake at 350° for 37 minutes. Let cool in pan on a wire rack 10 minutes. Cut into wedges. Serve warm or at room temperature. **Yield:** 9 servings (serving size: 1 wedge).

YIELD: 9 servings

EXCHANGES PER SERVING:
1½ Starch
½ Fat

PER SERVING:
Calories 152
(29% from fat)
Fat 4.9g
(saturated fat 0.9g)
Protein 2g
Carbohydrate 25.3g
Fiber 0.7g
Cholesterol 0mg
Sodium 110mg

PER SERVING:
Calories 101
(23% from fat)
Fat 2.6g
(saturated fat 0g)
Protein 3g
Carbohydrate 17.1g
Fiber 0.6g
Cholesterol 0g
Sodium 206mg

PARSLEY-GARLIC ROLLS

*Put your own spin on convenient frozen bread dough
with these little swirls. Pungent garlic and snippets of
fresh parsley dress them in savory fashion.*

2 tablespoons chopped fresh parsley
2 tablespoons reduced-calorie stick
  margarine, melted
2 garlic cloves, pressed
1 (16-ounce) loaf frozen bread dough, thawed
  Cooking spray

1. Combine first 3 ingredients; set aside.

2. Roll bread dough to a 12-inch square; spread
parsley mixture over dough, leaving a 1/2-inch border on top and bottom edges. Roll dough tightly,
jelly-roll fashion, from bottom edge. Press top edge
of dough into roll to seal edge. Cut roll of dough
into 1-inch slices. Place slices, cut sides down, in
muffin pans coated with cooking spray.

3. Cover and let rise in a warm place (85°), free
from drafts, 1 hour or until doubled in bulk.

4. Preheat oven to 400°.

5. Bake rolls at 400° for 9 to 11 minutes or until
golden. Remove from pans, and serve immediately.
Yield: 1 dozen (serving size: 1 roll).

MAKE-AHEAD YEAST ROLLS

Here's a convenient roll recipe you'll turn to again and again. We stripped a significant amount of fat from this recipe and still have a dough that would make Grandma jealous. It's so supple you can shape it any way you want.

2   packages dry yeast (about 4½ teaspoons)
¼   cup warm water (105° to 115°)
4½ cups bread flour, divided
1¾ cups low-fat or nonfat buttermilk
⅓   cup sugar
2   tablespoons stick margarine or butter, softened
1½ teaspoons salt
    Cooking spray

1. Combine yeast and warm water in a 1-cup liquid measuring cup; let stand 5 minutes. Combine yeast mixture, 2 cups flour, and next 4 ingredients in a large bowl; beat with a wooden spoon 2 minutes. Gradually stir in enough remaining flour to make a soft dough. Cover and let rise in a warm place (85°), free from drafts, 1 hour.

2. Punch dough down; cover and chill at least 8 hours.

3. Punch dough down; turn out onto a lightly floured surface, and knead 3 or 4 times. Divide dough in half; shape each portion into 16 (2-inch) balls. Place balls in two 9-inch square pans coated with cooking spray. Cover and let rise in a warm place (85°), free from drafts, 1½ hours or until dough is doubled in bulk.

4. Preheat oven to 375°.

5. Bake rolls at 375° for 12 minutes or until golden. **Yield:** 32 servings (serving size: 1 roll).

YIELD: 32 servings

EXCHANGE PER SERVING:
1 Starch

PER SERVING:
Calories 90
(11% from fat)
Fat 1.1g
(saturated fat 0.2g)
Protein 3g
Carbohydrate 16.9g
Fiber 0.1g
Cholesterol 0mg
Sodium 133mg

PER SERVING:
Calories 92
(8% from fat)
Fat 0.8g
(saturated fat 0.2g)
Protein 3g
Carbohydrate 17.7g
Fiber 0.7g
Cholesterol 0mg
Sodium 156mg

QUICK YEAST ROLLS

Enjoy these puffy pan rolls with dinner in about an hour.
We removed the egg from the original recipe, but kept its
rich egg flavor by using egg substitute.

      2 packages dry yeast (about 4$^{1}/_{2}$ teaspoons)
    $^{1}/_{2}$ cup warm water (105° to 115°)
      1 cup fat-free milk
    $^{1}/_{4}$ cup egg substitute
      2 tablespoons sugar
      1 tablespoon vegetable oil
  1$^{1}/_{2}$ teaspoons salt
      4 cups all-purpose flour, divided
         Butter-flavored cooking spray

1. Combine yeast and warm water in a 2-cup liquid measuring cup; let stand 5 minutes. Combine
yeast mixture, milk, and next 4 ingredients in a
large bowl. Gradually add 1 cup flour, stirring until
smooth. Gradually stir in enough remaining flour
to make a soft dough. Place in a bowl coated with
cooking spray, turning to coat top. Cover and let
stand in a warm place (85°), free from drafts, 15
minutes.

2. Punch dough down; cover and let stand in a
warm place (85°), free from drafts, 15 additional
minutes.

3. Turn dough out onto a lightly floured surface;
knead 3 or 4 times. Divide dough into 24 pieces;
shape into balls. Place in two 9-inch square pans or
round pans coated with cooking spray. Cover and
let stand in a warm place (85°), free from drafts, 15
minutes.

4. Preheat oven to 400°.

5. Bake rolls at 400° for 15 minutes or until
golden. **Yield:** 2 dozen (serving size: 1 roll).

Make Ahead
YOGURT CRESCENT ROLLS

*Yogurt adds so much richness to these soft twirls you'll
think you're eating buttery sour cream rolls.*

    2   packages dry yeast (about 4½ teaspoons)
    ½   cup warm water (105° to 115°)
    5¼ cups all-purpose flour, divided
    ½   cup sugar
    ⅓   cup vegetable oil
    1   teaspoon salt
    1   (8-ounce) carton plain low-fat yogurt
    1   large egg
    1   large egg white
        Butter-flavored cooking spray

1. Combine yeast and warm water; let stand 5 minutes. Combine yeast mixture, 2 cups flour, sugar, and
next 5 ingredients in a mixing bowl; beat at medium
speed of an electric mixer until smooth. Stir in 3
cups flour. Cover; chill 8 hours.

2. Sprinkle remaining ¼ cup flour over work surface. Punch dough down; divide into fourths. Roll
each fourth into a 10-inch circle on floured surface.
Coat circles with cooking spray; cut each circle into
12 wedges. Roll up wedges, beginning at wide
ends; place on baking sheets coated with cooking
spray, point sides down. Cover; let rise in a warm
place (85°), free from drafts, 45 minutes or until
doubled in bulk.

3. Preheat oven to 375°.

4. Bake rolls at 375° for 10 minutes or until golden.
Yield: 4 dozen (serving size: 1 roll).

YIELD: 48 servings

**EXCHANGE PER
SERVING:**
1 Starch

PER SERVING:
Calories 73
(22% from fat)
Fat 1.8g
(saturated fat 0.4g)
Protein 1.9g
Carbohydrate 12.1g
Fiber 0.4g
Cholesterol 5mg
Sodium 55mg

**EXCHANGE PER
SERVING:**
1 Starch

PER SERVING:
Calories 69
(18% from fat)
Fat 1.4g
(saturated fat 0.2g)
Protein 1.6g
Carbohydrate 12.3g
Fiber 0.5g
Cholesterol 0mg
Sodium 84mg

DINNER ROLLS

*Use a reduced-calorie stick margarine that is
41% to 60% oil for this recipe.*

```
  1  package dry yeast (about 2¼ teaspoons)
1½  cups warm water (105° to 115°)
4½  to 5 cups all-purpose flour, divided
  2  tablespoons sugar
  1  teaspoon salt
  6  tablespoons reduced-calorie stick
       margarine, softened
 ¼  cup all-purpose flour
     Cooking spray
```

1. Combine yeast and warm water; let stand 5
minutes. Combine yeast mixture, 1 cup flour, sugar,
salt, and margarine; beat at medium speed of an
electric mixer 2 minutes. Stir in 3½ to 4 cups flour
to make a soft dough.

2. Sprinkle ¼ cup flour over work surface. Turn
dough out onto surface; knead until smooth and
elastic (about 10 minutes). Place in a large bowl
coated with cooking spray; turn to coat top. Cover;
let rise in a warm place (85°), free from drafts, 1
hour or until doubled in bulk.

3. Punch dough down; divide into thirds. Divide
and shape each third into 12 balls. Arrange balls
evenly in three 8-inch square baking pans coated
with cooking spray. Cover and let rise in a warm
place, free from drafts, 40 minutes or until doubled
in bulk.

4. Preheat oven to 375°.

5. Bake rolls at 375° for 20 minutes or until
golden. **Yield:** 3 dozen (serving size: 1 roll).

WHOLE WHEAT ROLLS

YIELD: 36 servings

**EXCHANGE PER
SERVING:**
1 Starch

PER SERVING:
Calories 90
(24% from fat)
Fat 2.4g
(saturated fat 0.4g)
Protein 2.4g
Carbohydrate 15.2g
Fiber 1.3g
Cholesterol 6mg
Sodium 100mg

 2 packages dry yeast (about 4½ teaspoons)
 1¾ cups warm water (105° to 115°)
 ¼ cup vegetable oil
 1 large egg
 2¼ cups whole wheat flour
 ⅓ cup sugar
 1½ teaspoons salt
 2¾ to 3¼ cups all-purpose flour
 3 tablespoons all-purpose flour
 Butter-flavored cooking spray

1. Combine yeast and warm water in a 2-cup liquid measuring cup; let stand 5 minutes. Combine yeast mixture, oil, and next 4 ingredients in a large mixing bowl; beat at medium speed of an electric mixer 2 minutes. Gradually stir in enough of 2¾ to 3¼ cups all-purpose flour to make a soft dough.

2. Sprinkle 3 tablespoons flour evenly over work surface. Turn dough out onto floured surface, and knead until smooth and elastic (about 5 minutes). Place in a bowl coated with cooking spray, turning to coat top. Cover; let rise in a warm place (85°), free from drafts, 1 hour or until doubled in bulk.

3. Punch dough down; cover and let rise in a warm place, free from drafts, 20 minutes or until doubled in bulk.

4. Punch dough down; divide in half. Roll each half into a 14 x 9-inch rectangle. Cut each rectangle of dough in half crosswise; cut each half into 9 (1-inch-wide) strips. Roll each strip, jelly-roll fashion, into a spiral, and place in muffin pans coated with cooking spray. Coat rolls with cooking spray. Let rise, uncovered, in a warm place, free from drafts, 40 minutes or until doubled in bulk.

5. Preheat oven to 400°.

6. Bake rolls at 400° for 10 to 12 minutes or until golden. **Yield:** 3 dozen (serving size: 1 roll).

CORNMEAL YEAST MUFFINS

YIELD: 18 servings

EXCHANGES PER SERVING:
1½ Starch

PER SERVING:
Calories 130
(20% from fat)
Fat 2.9g
(saturated fat 0.4g)
Protein 3.4g
Carbohydrate 22.5g
Fiber 1.2g
Cholesterol 0mg
Sodium 90mg

¾ cup fat-free milk
3 tablespoons sugar
2 tablespoons reduced-calorie stick margarine
2 tablespoons vegetable oil
1 package dry yeast (about 2¼ teaspoons)
¼ cup warm water (105° to 115°)
3 cups all-purpose flour, divided
¾ cup plain yellow cornmeal
½ teaspoon salt
¼ cup egg substitute
¼ cup all-purpose flour
Butter-flavored cooking spray

1. Combine first 4 ingredients in a saucepan; heat until margarine melts. Cool to 105° to 115°. Combine yeast and warm water; let stand 5 minutes. Combine 1 cup flour, cornmeal, and salt in a mixing bowl; add milk mixture, yeast mixture, and egg substitute. Beat at medium speed of an electric mixer until smooth. Stir in enough of 2 cups flour to make a soft dough.

2. Sprinkle ¼ cup flour evenly over work surface. Turn dough out onto floured surface, and knead until smooth and elastic (about 8 minutes). Place in a bowl coated with cooking spray; turn to coat top. Cover; let rise in a warm place (85°), free from drafts, 1 hour or until doubled in bulk.

3. Punch dough down; divide into fourths. Divide and shape each fourth into 9 balls. Place 2 balls in each muffin cup coated with cooking spray. Cover and let rise in a warm place, free from drafts, 15 minutes or until doubled in bulk.

4. Preheat oven to 375°.

5. Bake muffins at 375° for 12 to 15 minutes or until golden. Spray muffin tops lightly with cooking spray; remove muffins from pans immediately. **Yield:** 1½ dozen (serving size: 1 muffin).

ENGLISH MUFFINS

1 cup 2% reduced-fat milk
3 tablespoons vegetable oil
2 tablespoons sugar
1 1/4 teaspoons salt
1 package dry yeast (about 2 1/4 teaspoons)
1/4 cup warm water (105° to 115°)
3 1/2 cups all-purpose flour, divided
1 large egg, lightly beaten
Cooking spray

1. Cook milk in a heavy saucepan over medium-high heat to 180° or until tiny bubbles form around edge (do not boil). Remove from heat. Pour milk into a large bowl. Stir in oil, sugar, and salt. Cool to about 90°.

2. Dissolve yeast in warm water in a small bowl; let stand 5 minutes. Add yeast mixture, 3 cups flour, and egg to milk mixture. Turn dough out onto a lightly floured surface. Knead until smooth and elastic (about 10 minutes); add enough of remaining flour, 1 tablespoon at a time, to prevent dough from sticking to hands (dough will feel tacky). Place dough in a large bowl coated with cooking spray, turning to coat top. Cover and let rise in a warm place (85°), free from drafts, 45 minutes or until doubled in size.

3. Punch dough down. Divide in half. Working with one portion at a time (cover remaining dough to keep from drying), roll each portion to 1/4-inch thickness. Let dough rest about 5 minutes. Cut with a 4-inch biscuit cutter into 8 muffins. Place muffins on a large baking sheet. Repeat procedure with remaining dough. Cover and let rise 30 minutes or until doubled in size.

4. Preheat oven to 350°.

5. Bake muffins at 350° for 7 minutes. Turn muffins over; bake an additional 7 minutes or until lightly browned. Cool. **Yield:** 16 servings (serving size: 1 muffin).

YIELD: 16 servings

EXCHANGES PER SERVING:
1 1/2 Starch
1/2 Fat

PER SERVING:
Calories 142
(22% from fat)
Fat 3.5g
(saturated fat 0.8g)
Protein 3.9g
Carbohydrate 23.4g
Fiber 0.9g
Cholesterol 15mg
Sodium 195mg

PER SERVING:
Calories 161
(22% from fat)
Fat 3.9g
(saturated fat 1.1g)
Protein 3.5g
Carbohydrate 27.5g
Fiber 0.6g
Cholesterol 22mg
Sodium 109mg

MARDI GRAS SWEET ROLLS

1 package dry yeast (about 2 1/4 teaspoons)
1/4 cup warm water (105° to 115°)
3 2/3 cups all-purpose flour
1/2 cup sugar
1/2 teaspoon salt
1 (8-ounce) carton 50%-less-fat sour cream
    (such as Daisy)
1/3 cup stick margarine or butter, melted
2 large eggs, lightly beaten
    Cooking spray
1 1/4 cups sifted powdered sugar
3 ounces fat-free cream cheese
1/2 teaspoon vanilla extract
1 tablespoon yellow sugar sprinkles
1 tablespoon green sugar sprinkles
1 tablespoon purple sugar sprinkles

1. Dissolve yeast in warm water in a small bowl; let stand 5 minutes. Combine flour, 1/2 cup sugar, and salt in a large mixing bowl. Combine sour cream, margarine, and eggs, stirring well. Add dissolved yeast and sour cream mixture to dry ingredients. Beat at medium speed of a mixer 2 minutes or until smooth. Cover tightly; chill 8 hours.

2. Divide dough in half; shape half of dough into 12 (2-inch) balls, smoothing out tops. Place 2 inches apart on a baking sheet coated with cooking spray. Repeat procedure with remaining dough. Cover and let rise 30 minutes or until doubled in bulk.

3. Preheat oven to 350°.

4. Bake rolls at 350° for 12 minutes or until very lightly browned. Let cool on wire racks. Combine powdered sugar, cream cheese, and vanilla in a bowl; beat at medium speed of a mixer until smooth. Combine sugar sprinkles in a small bowl. Spread 2 teaspoons frosting on each roll. Sprinkle each roll with 3/8 teaspoon of sugar sprinkles.
Yield: 2 dozen (serving size: 1 roll).

MONKEY BREAD

A pull-apart bread recipe like this one typically dips each piece of dough into a bowl of melted butter. But we simply brushed the dough with a little reduced-calorie margarine instead.

2 packages dry yeast (about 4½ teaspoons)
2 cups warm water (105° to 115°)
5½ cups all-purpose flour
⅓ cup sugar
1½ teaspoons salt
¼ cup reduced-calorie stick margarine, melted
   Cooking spray

1. Combine yeast and 1 cup warm water in a 2-cup liquid measuring cup; let stand 5 minutes. Add remaining 1 cup warm water, flour, sugar, and salt, stirring until blended. Cover and chill at least 8 hours.

2. Punch dough down; divide in half. Turn 1 portion out onto a heavily floured surface, and knead 3 or 4 times. Roll to ¼-inch thickness; cut into 4 x 1½-inch strips. Brush strips with half of melted margarine, and layer, overlapping, in a 12-cup Bundt or 10-inch tube pan coated with cooking spray. Repeat procedure with remaining dough and melted margarine in another coated Bundt or tube pan. Cover and let rise in a warm place (85°), free from drafts, 45 minutes or until doubled in bulk.

3. Preheat oven to 350°.

4. Bake bread at 350° for 30 to 35 minutes or until golden. **Yield:** 2 loaves, 10 servings per loaf.

YIELD: 20 servings

EXCHANGES PER SERVING:
2 Starch

PER SERVING:
Calories 152
(11% from fat)
Fat 1.9g
(saturated fat 0.3g)
Protein 3.8g
Carbohydrate 29.8g
Fiber 1.1g
Cholesterol 0mg
Sodium 198mg

EXCHANGES PER
SERVING:
1½ Starch

PER SERVING:
Calories 106
(8% from fat)
Fat 0.9g
(saturated fat 0.2g)
Protein 3.3g
Carbohydrate 20.6g
Fiber 0.8g
Cholesterol 0mg
Sodium 155mg

CLASSIC WHITE BREAD

  1 cup fat-free milk
  2 teaspoons vegetable oil
1½ teaspoons sugar
  1 teaspoon salt
3¼ cups all-purpose flour
  1 package dry yeast (about 2¼ teaspoons)
     Cooking spray

1. Combine milk, oil, sugar, and salt in a small saucepan; heat until very warm, stirring occasionally. Cool to 120° to 130°. Combine flour and yeast in a large mixing bowl; stir well. Gradually add milk mixture to flour mixture, beating well at low speed of a heavy-duty stand mixer. Beat 2 additional minutes at medium speed.

2. Turn dough out onto a lightly floured surface, and knead until smooth and elastic (about 6 to 8 minutes). Place in a large bowl coated with cooking spray, turning to coat top. Cover and let rise in a warm place (85°), free from drafts, 1 hour or until doubled in bulk.

3. Punch dough down; turn out onto a lightly floured surface and knead lightly 4 or 5 times. Roll dough into a 10 x 6-inch rectangle. Roll up dough, starting at short side, pressing firmly to eliminate air pockets; pinch ends to seal. Place dough, seam side down, in an 8 x 4-inch loaf pan coated with cooking spray. Cover and let rise in a warm place, free from drafts, 45 minutes or until doubled in bulk.

4. Preheat oven to 375°.

5. Bake bread at 375° for 25 minutes or until loaf sounds hollow when tapped. Remove bread from pan immediately; let cool on a wire rack. **Yield:** 16 servings (serving size: 1 slice).

CORNMEAL YEAST BREAD

3/4 cup evaporated fat-free milk
1/3 cup sugar
1/3 cup reduced-calorie stick margarine
1 teaspoon salt
2 packages dry yeast (about 4 1/2 teaspoons)
1/2 cup warm water (105° to 115°)
3 to 3 1/2 cups all-purpose flour, divided
3/4 cup yellow cornmeal
1 large egg
Cooking spray

1. Combine first 4 ingredients in a saucepan; heat until margarine melts. Cool to 105° to 115°. Combine yeast and warm water; let stand 5 minutes. Combine milk mixture, yeast mixture, 1 cup flour, cornmeal, and egg in a large mixing bowl; beat mixture at medium speed of an electric mixer until well blended. Gradually stir in enough of 2 to 2 1/2 cups flour to make a soft dough.

2. Turn dough out onto a lightly floured surface; knead until smooth and elastic (about 10 minutes). Place in a bowl coated with cooking spray; turn to coat top. Cover; let rise in a warm place (85°), free from drafts, 1 hour or until doubled in bulk.

3. Punch dough down; divide in half. Roll 1 portion into a 14 x 7-inch rectangle. Roll up, starting at short side, pressing firmly to eliminate air pockets; pinch ends to seal. Place, seam side down, in an 8 x 4-inch loaf pan coated with cooking spray. Repeat procedure with remaining dough. Cover and let rise in a warm place, free from drafts, 45 minutes or until doubled in bulk.

4. Preheat oven to 350°.

5. Bake bread at 350° for 30 to 35 minutes or until loaves sound hollow when tapped. Remove from pans immediately, and cool on wire racks. **Yield:** 32 servings (servng size: 1 [1/2-inch] slice).

YIELD: 32 servings

EXCHANGE PER SERVING:
1 Starch

PER SERVING:
Calories 77
(20% from fat)
Fat 1.7g
(saturated fat 0.3g)
Protein 2.2g
Carbohydrate 13.5g
Fiber 0.7g
Cholesterol 7mg
Sodium 102mg

PER SERVING:
Calories 77
(10% from fat)
Fat 0.9g
(saturated fat 0.1g)
Protein 2.5g
Carbohydrate 14.6g
Fiber 1g
Cholesterol 0mg
Sodium 154mg

ENGLISH MUFFIN BREAD

This bread resembles English muffins in texture and taste. Whole wheat flour, oat bran, and cornmeal team up to impart an earthy, whole grain goodness in every slice.

3½ to 3¾ cups all-purpose flour, divided
1 cup whole wheat flour
½ cup oat bran
2 teaspoons salt
1 package quick-rise yeast (about 2¼ teaspoons)
1 cup fat-free milk
1 cup water
3 tablespoons reduced-calorie stick margarine
Cooking spray
2 tablespoons cornmeal

1. Combine 1½ cups all-purpose flour, wheat flour, and next 3 ingredients in a large mixing bowl. Combine milk, water, and margarine in a 4-cup liquid measuring cup. Microwave at HIGH 2 minutes; pour over flour mixture. Beat at medium speed with an electric mixer 2 minutes. Gradually stir in 2 cups all-purpose flour. Turn dough out onto a lightly floured surface; if dough is sticky, knead in remaining ¼ cup flour. Cover dough with a large bowl; let stand 10 minutes.

2. Coat two 8 x 4-inch loaf pans with cooking spray; sprinkle evenly with cornmeal. Divide dough in half; shape each portion into a loaf, and place in pan. Cover and let dough rise in a warm place (85°), free from drafts, 1 hour or until dough is doubled in bulk.

3. Preheat oven to 400°.

4. Bake at 400° for 25 minutes. Remove loaves from pans, and cool on a wire rack. **Yield:** 2 loaves, 16 servings per loaf (serving size: 1 [½-inch] slice).

OATMEAL-MOLASSES BREAD

YIELD: 12 servings

¾ cup fat-free milk
¼ cup molasses
2 tablespoons stick margarine or butter
2½ to 2¾ cups all-purpose flour, divided
1 package quick-rise yeast (about 2¼ teaspoons)
½ teaspoon salt
¾ cup quick-cooking oats
Cooking spray
1 tablespoon quick-cooking oats

1. Combine milk, molasses, and margarine in a small saucepan; heat until margarine melts, stirring occasionally. Cool to 120° to 130°.

2. Combine 1 cup flour, yeast, and salt in a large mixing bowl. Gradually add milk mixture to flour mixture, beating well at low speed of a heavy–duty stand mixer. Beat 3 additional minutes at medium speed. Gradually stir in ¾ cup oats and enough remaining flour to make a soft dough. Turn dough out onto a lightly floured surface, and knead until smooth and elastic (about 5 minutes). Place in a large bowl coated with cooking spray, turning to coat top. Cover and let rise in a warm place (85°), free from drafts, 40 minutes or until doubled in bulk.

3. Punch dough down; let rest 10 minutes. Shape dough into a 6-inch diameter ball and flatten slightly; place on a baking sheet coated with cooking spray. Cover and let rise in a warm place, free from drafts, 30 minutes or until doubled in bulk.

4. Preheat oven to 375°.

5. Coat top of loaf with cooking spray; sprinkle with 1 tablespoon oats. Bake at 375° for 26 to 28 minutes or until loaf sounds hollow when tapped. Remove bread from baking sheet immediately; let cool on a wire rack. Cut into wedges. **Yield:** 12 servings (serving size: 1 wedge).

EXCHANGES PER SERVING:
2 Starch

PER SERVING:
Calories 158
(15% from fat)
Fat 2.6g
(saturated fat 0.5g)
Protein 4.3g
Carbohydrate 29.1g
Fiber 1.4g
Cholesterol 0mg
Sodium 131mg

YIELD: 54 servings

EXCHANGES PER
SERVING:
1½ Starch

PER SERVING:
Calories 104
(12% from fat)
Fat 1.4g
(saturated fat 0.2g)
Protein 3.3g
Carbohydrate 19.9g
Fiber 1.7g
Cholesterol 0mg
Sodium 94mg

ONION-HERB BREAD

  3 packages dry yeast (about 6¾ teaspoons)
  4 cups warm water (105° to 115°), divided
  4 cups whole wheat flour
  1 cup diced onion
  ½ cup instant nonfat dry milk powder
  ⅓ cup sugar
  ¼ cup vegetable oil
1½ tablespoons chopped fresh dill
  1 tablespoon chopped fresh rosemary
  2 teaspoons salt
6¼ to 6½ cups all-purpose flour
     Butter-flavored cooking spray

1. Combine yeast and 1 cup warm water; let stand
5 minutes. Combine yeast mixture, remaining 3
cups warm water, whole wheat flour, and next 7
ingredients in a large mixing bowl. Beat at medium
speed of an electric mixer until well blended.
Gradually stir in enough remaining all-purpose
flour to make a soft dough. Turn dough out onto a
lightly floured surface; knead until smooth and elastic (about 10 minutes). Place in a bowl coated with
cooking spray, turning to coat top. Cover; let rise in a
warm place (85°), free from drafts, 35 minutes or until doubled in bulk.

2. Punch dough down; divide into thirds. Roll 1
portion of dough into a 14 x 7-inch rectangle.
Roll up, starting at short side, pressing to eliminate
air pockets; pinch ends to seal. Place dough, seam
side down, in a 9 x 5-inch loaf pan coated with
cooking spray. Repeat with remaining 2 portions
of dough. Cover; let rise in a warm place, free from
drafts, 30 minutes or until doubled in bulk.

3. Preheat oven to 350°.

4. Bake at 350° for 40 to 45 minutes or until loaves
sound hollow when tapped. Coat tops of loaves
with cooking spray. Remove loaves from pans immediately; cool on wire racks. **Yield:** 3 loaves, 18
servings per loaf (serving size: 1 [½-inch] slice).

ROASTED RED BELL PEPPER BREAD

1 (7-ounce) jar roasted red bell peppers
1 package dry yeast (about 2 1/4 teaspoons)
1 teaspoon sugar
1 1/3 cups warm water (105° to 115°)
3 1/2 cups bread flour
1 cup grated fat-free Parmesan cheese
2 tablespoons chopped fresh rosemary
1 teaspoon salt
1 tablespoon cracked black pepper
  Cooking spray

1. Drain bell peppers on paper towels; chop and set aside.

2. Combine yeast, sugar, and warm water in a 2-cup liquid measuring cup; let stand 5 minutes. Combine flour, bell peppers, Parmesan cheese, and next 3 ingredients in a large bowl; gradually add yeast mixture, stirring until blended.

3. Turn dough out onto a well-floured surface; and knead until smooth and elastic (about 10 minutes). Place dough in a bowl coated with cooking spray, turning to coat top. Cover and let rise in a warm place (85°), free from drafts, 1 hour or until doubled in bulk.

4. Punch dough down; turn out onto a lightly floured surface, and knead 4 or 5 times. Divide dough in half. Shape each portion into a 12-inch loaf. Place loaves on a large baking sheet coated with cooking spray. Let rise in a warm place (85°), free from drafts, 45 minutes or until doubled in bulk.

5. Preheat oven to 450°.

6. Bake at 450° for 25 minutes or until loaves sound hollow when tapped, covering with aluminum foil after 15 minutes to prevent excessive browning. Remove from baking sheet immediately; cool on wire racks. **Yield:** 2 loaves, 12 servings per loaf (serving size: 1 [1-inch] slice).

YIELD: 24 servings

EXCHANGE PER SERVING:
1 Starch

PER SERVING:
Calories 93
(4% from fat)
Fat 0.4g
(saturated fat 0.1g)
Protein 2.5g
Carbohydrate 18.7g
Fiber 0.2g
Cholesterol 0mg
Sodium 191mg

FRENCH BREAD

EXCHANGE PER
SERVING:
½ Starch

PER SERVING:
Calories 48
(8% from fat)
Fat 0.4g
(saturated fat 0g)
Protein 1.4g
Carbohydrate 9.4g
Fiber 0.4g
Cholesterol 0mg
Sodium 74mg

1   cup water
¼   cup fat-free milk
1   tablespoon plus 1 teaspoon sugar
1   tablespoon reduced-calorie stick margarine
1   teaspoon salt
1   package dry yeast (about 2¼ teaspoons)
3¼ to 3½ cups all-purpose flour, divided
2   tablespoons all-purpose flour
    Cooking spray
1   large egg white, lightly beaten
1   tablespoon water

1. Combine first 5 ingredients in a saucepan; heat until margarine melts. Cool to 105° to 115°. Add yeast to warm milk mixture; let stand 5 minutes. Combine 1¼ cups flour and yeast mixture in a large mixing bowl; beat at medium speed of an electric mixer until blended. Stir in enough of 2 to 2¼ cups flour to make a soft dough; let stand 10 minutes. Stir dough gently for a few seconds; cover and let stand 40 minutes, stirring every 10 minutes.

2. Sprinkle 2 tablespoons flour evenly over work surface. Turn dough out onto floured surface, and divide in half. Flatten 1 portion of dough into an oval on floured surface. Fold dough over lengthwise; flatten with open hand. Fold again, and roll between palms of hands into a 17-inch rope. Pinch ends of rope to seal. Repeat procedure with remaining portion of dough. Place dough in two French bread pans coated with cooking spray. Using a sharp knife, cut ½-inch-deep slits across tops of loaves. Cover and let rise in a warm place (85°), free from drafts, 20 minutes or until doubled in bulk.

3. Preheat oven to 400°.

4. Combine egg white and 1 tablespoon water; brush mixture evenly over loaves. Bake at 400° for 15 minutes or until loaves sound hollow when tapped. **Yield:** 2 loaves, 17 servings per loaf (serving size: 1 [1-inch] slice).

ROSEMARY-HERB FRENCH BREAD

A bread machine mixes this dough and allows it to rise. You finish the shaping and baking.

2¼ cups bread flour
1 package dry yeast (about 2¼ teaspoons)
2 teaspoons sugar
1 teaspoon chopped fresh or dried rosemary
½ teaspoon dried basil
½ teaspoon dried thyme
½ teaspoon dried oregano
½ teaspoon salt
1 cup water
1 teaspoon olive oil
3 tablespoons preshredded fresh Parmesan cheese
1 teaspoon chopped fresh or dried rosemary
¼ teaspoon garlic powder

1. Following manufacturer's instructions, place first 9 ingredients into bread pan. Select dough cycle, and start bread machine. Remove dough from machine (do not bake).

2. Preheat oven to 350°.

3. Turn dough out onto a lightly floured surface; rub with oil. Shape into a 12-inch–long loaf. Place loaf on a baking sheet. Combine cheese, 1 teaspoon rosemary, and garlic powder; sprinkle cheese mixture over top of loaf.

4. Bake at 350° for 45 minutes or until loaf sounds hollow when tapped. Remove loaf from pan; cool on a wire rack. **Yield:** 12 servings (serving size: 1 [1-inch] slice).

YIELD: 12 servings

EXCHANGES PER SERVING:
1½ Starch

PER SERVING:
Calories 110
(13% from fat)
Fat 1.6g
(saturated fat 0.4g)
Protein 3.9g
Carbohydrate 19.8g
Fiber 0.2g
Cholesterol 1mg
Sodium 125mg

EXCHANGE PER
SERVING:
1 Starch

PER SERVING:
Calories 89
(17% from fat)
Fat 1.7g
(saturated fat 0.3g)
Protein 2.3g
Carbohydrate 15.8g
Fiber 0.6g
Cholesterol 0mg
Sodium 116mg

ROSEMARY FOCACCIA

1 package dry yeast (about 2¼ teaspoons)
1¼ cups warm water (105° to 115°), divided
3¾ cups all-purpose flour, divided
1 teaspoon salt, divided
3 tablespoons stick margarine or butter,
   melted
½ cup chopped fresh rosemary, divided
2 tablespoons all-purpose flour
   Olive oil-flavored cooking spray
4 garlic cloves, minced

1. Combine yeast and ¼ cup warm water; let stand 5 minutes. Combine yeast mixture, remaining 1 cup warm water, 2 cups flour, and ½ teaspoon salt in a large mixing bowl; beat at medium speed of an electric mixer until mixture is well blended. Cover and let rise in a warm place (85°), free from drafts, 1 hour or until doubled in bulk.

2. Preheat oven to 400°.

3. Punch dough down; stir in 1¾ cups flour, melted margarine, and ¼ cup rosemary. Sprinkle 2 tablespoons flour evenly over work surface. Turn dough out onto floured surface, and knead until smooth and elastic (about 10 minutes). Divide dough in half. For each focaccia, roll or press 1 portion of dough into an 11-inch circle on a baking sheet coated with cooking spray. Poke holes in dough at 1-inch intervals with handle of a wooden spoon.

4. Coat top of each round with cooking spray; sprinkle evenly with remaining ¼ cup rosemary, remaining ½ teaspoon salt, and garlic. Bake at 400° for 20 minutes. Cut each circle into 12 squares or wedges. **Yield:** 2 loaves, 12 servings per loaf (serving size: 1 wedge).

desserts

EXCHANGES PER
SERVING:
1 Starch
1 Fruit
½ Skim Milk

PER SERVING:
Calories 190
(2% from fat)
Fat 0.5g
(saturated fat 0g)
Protein 7.8g
Carbohydrate 37.5g
Fiber 3.3g
Cholesterol 5mg
Sodium 81mg

Super Quick
FRESH STRAWBERRIES WITH LIME CUSTARD

1 (8-ounce) container fat-free sour cream
½ cup fat-free sweetened condensed milk
½ teaspoon grated lime rind
1½ tablespoons fresh lime juice (about 1 medium lime)
3 cups sliced fresh strawberries

1. Combine first 4 ingredients, stirring well.

2. Spoon ¼ cup lime custard into each of 4 (6-ounce) custard cups or dessert dishes. Top each with ¾ cup strawberries. Top each serving with 2 tablespoons lime custard. **Yield:** 4 servings.

Fresh Strawberries with Orange Custard:
Substitute ½ teaspoon grated orange rind and 1½ tablespoons fresh orange juice for the lime rind and lime juice.

♥ *Fruit is naturally low in fat, high in fiber and complex carbohydrate, and a good source of vitamins and minerals. Health experts recommend 2 to 4 servings of fruit in each day's meal plan. Unsweetened canned fruit and frozen unsweetened fruit provide about the same nutrients as fresh but usually have less fiber than fresh, unpeeled fruit.*

Super Quick
CHOCOLATE-ALMOND FONDUE

*For a traditional fondue dessert, keep the sauce warm
in a fondue pot or chafing dish. Let guests dip
strawberries and cake into the warm sauce with
fondue sticks or wooden picks.*

1   (14-ounce) can fat-free sweetened
      condensed milk
½   cup reduced-fat semisweet chocolate
      baking chips
½   teaspoon almond extract
24 fresh strawberries
24 (1-inch) cubes angel food cake (about
      ¼ of 16-ounce cake)

1. Combine milk and chocolate in a medium
saucepan. Cook, stirring constantly, over low heat
about 3 minutes or until chocolate melts. Remove
from heat, and stir in almond extract. Serve warm
with strawberries and cake. **Yield:** 24 servings
(serving size: 1 tablespoon sauce, 1 strawberry, and 1
cake cube).

YIELD: 24 servings

**EXCHANGE PER
SERVING:**
1 Starch

PER SERVING:
Calories 81
(13% from fat)
Fat 1.2g
(saturated fat 1.2g)
Protein 0.5g
Carbohydrate 17.1g
Fiber 0.4g
Cholesterol 0mg
Sodium 38mg

**EXCHANGES PER
SERVING:**
2½ Fruit
2 Starch

PER SERVING:
Calories 290
(2% from fat)
Fat 0.8g
(saturated fat 0g)
Protein 1.4g
Carbohydrate 73.8g
Fiber 8.8g
Cholesterol 0mg
Sodium 5mg

Make Ahead
VERY BERRY SUMMER FRUIT COMPOTE

      1   vanilla bean
  1½   cups water
      1   cup sugar
      1   (3-inch) cinnamon stick
      2   cups fresh raspberries
      2   cups fresh blackberries
      2   cups fresh blueberries
           Pineapple-mint sprigs or spearmint sprigs
               (optional)

1. Split vanilla bean lengthwise, and scrape seeds from bean into a large saucepan. Add vanilla bean to pan. Add water, sugar, and cinnamon stick; stir well. Bring to a boil; reduce heat, and simmer 5 minutes, stirring occasionally. Add berries; cook 1 minute, stirring gently. Remove from heat; let stand 10 minutes.

2. Drain berry mixture, reserving sugar syrup. Place berries, vanilla bean, and cinnamon stick in a medium bowl; set aside. Return sugar syrup to pan; bring to a boil. Cook 10 minutes or until slightly thick. Pour syrup over berry mixture; cover and chill 2 hours. Discard vanilla bean and cinnamon stick before serving. Garnish with mint sprigs, if desired. **Yield:** 4 servings (serving size: 1 cup).

Super Quick
APRICOT-GLAZED PINEAPPLE SUNDAE

4 (1-inch-thick) peeled fresh pineapple slices
2 tablespoons apricot preserves, melted
1 teaspoon sugar
  Dash of ground cinnamon
1 cup vanilla low-fat frozen yogurt

1. Preheat broiler.

2. Place pineapple slices on a broiler pan. Brush pineapple with preserves; broil 6 minutes or until bubbly. Combine sugar and cinnamon, and sprinkle over pineapple. Serve warm with frozen yogurt. **Yield:** 2 servings (serving size: 2 pineapple slices and ½ cup frozen yogurt).

YIELD: 2 servings

EXCHANGES PER SERVING:
1½ Fruit
1 Starch

PER SERVING:
Calories 161
(9% from fat)
Fat 1.6g
(saturated fat 1g)
Protein 2.3g
Carbohydrate 35.8g
Fiber 0.2g
Cholesterol 7mg
Sodium 39mg

Super Quick
CARAMELIZED ORANGE BANANAS

2 large bananas
1½ teaspoons reduced-calorie stick margarine
¼ cup packed brown sugar
¼ cup orange juice
⅛ to ¼ teaspoon banana extract
2 cups vanilla fat-free ice cream

1. Peel bananas, and cut each in half. Cut banana halves lengthwise into quarters; set aside.

2. Add margarine to a medium skillet, and place over medium heat until margarine melts. Stir in brown sugar, and cook, stirring constantly, until sugar dissolves and mixture begins to bubble. Stir in orange juice, and add bananas to skillet. Increase heat to medium–high, and cook 2 minutes, stirring gently. Turn bananas, and sprinkle with banana extract.

3. Spoon ½ cup ice cream into each of 4 individual dessert bowls; spoon warm bananas evenly over ice cream. Serve immediately. **Yield:** 4 servings.

YIELD: 4 servings

EXCHANGES PER SERVING:
2 Fruit
1 Starch

PER SERVING:
Calories 199
(5% from fat)
Fat 1.2g
(saturated fat 0.1g)
Protein 2.7g
Carbohydrate 45.1g
Fiber 1.6g
Cholesterol 0mg
Sodium 58mg

YIELD: 4 servings

EXCHANGES PER SERVING:
2 Starch
1 1/2 Fruit

PER SERVING:
Calories 232
(16% from fat)
Fat 4g
(saturated fat 0.9g)
Protein 2.9g
Carbohydrate 49.7g
Fiber 3.3g
Cholesterol 3.3mg
Sodium 36mg

Make Ahead

PORT-GLAZED PEARS WITH TOASTED HAZELNUTS

2   large Anjou pears (about 1 pound)
1   cup port or other sweet red wine
1   cup cranberry juice cocktail
1/2 cup water
1/3 cup fresh mint leaves
3   tablespoons honey
1 1/3 cups vanilla low-fat ice cream
2   tablespoons chopped blanched hazelnuts, toasted

1. Peel and core pears; cut each pear in half lengthwise. Cut a 1/4-inch slice from rounded side of each pear half so pears sit flat. Combine wine and next 4 ingredients in a skillet; bring mixture to a boil. Cover, reduce heat, and simmer 5 minutes. Arrange pears, cut sides down, in skillet; cover and simmer 8 minutes (do not boil). Turn pear halves over; cover and simmer an additional 8 minutes or until tender. Remove pears from skillet with a slotted spoon; place pears in a shallow dish.

2. Bring poaching liquid to a boil; cook, uncovered, 10 minutes or until reduced to 1/2 cup. Pour poaching liquid through a sieve over pears in dish; discard mint leaves. Turn pears over to coat; cover and chill.

3. Arrange 1 pear half, cut side up, on each of 4 plates; top each with 1/3 cup ice cream. Drizzle 2 tablespoons poaching liquid over each serving, and sprinkle with 1 1/2 teaspoons hazelnuts. **Yield:** 4 servings.

BLACKBERRY COBBLER

*This recipe calls for reduced-calorie stick margarine—
use one with between 41% and 60% oil.*

6	cups fresh blackberries
1/2	cup sugar
2	tablespoons orange juice
1 1/2	tablespoons tapioca
1/4	teaspoon ground allspice
1	cup all-purpose flour
1 1/4	teaspoons baking powder
1/4	teaspoon baking soda
1/4	teaspoon salt
1/3	cup sugar
1/3	cup vanilla low-fat yogurt
1/3	cup fat-free milk
3	tablespoons reduced-calorie stick margarine, softened
1	tablespoon sugar

1. Preheat oven to 350°.

2. Combine first 5 ingredients; toss gently to coat. Spoon mixture into an 11 x 7–inch baking dish.

3. Combine flour and next 4 ingredients in a bowl; stir well. Add yogurt, milk, and margarine; beat at medium speed of an electric mixer until smooth. Pour over blackberry mixture.

4. Bake at 350° for 20 minutes. Sprinkle 1 tablespoon sugar evenly over cobbler. Bake an additional 25 minutes or until crust is golden. Serve warm. **Yield:** 10 servings (serving size: 1/2 cup).

YIELD: 10 servings

EXCHANGES PER SERVING:
2 Starch
1 Fruit

PER SERVING:
Calories 202
(12% from fat)
Fat 2.8g
(saturated fat 0.4g)
Protein 2.7g
Carbohydrate 43.7g
Fiber 5.8g
Cholesterol 0.7mg
Sodium 194mg

PER SERVING:
Calories 307
(18% from fat)
Fat 6.1g
(saturated fat 1g)
Protein 4.4g
Carbohydrate 60.7g
Fiber 2.9g
Cholesterol 18mg
Sodium 203mg

PLUM COBBLER

1¾ cups sugar, divided
2 tablespoons all-purpose flour
8 cups sliced ripe plums (about 3 pounds)
Cooking spray
2 cups all-purpose flour
2 teaspoons baking powder
½ teaspoon baking soda
½ teaspoon salt
¾ cup low-fat or nonfat buttermilk
¼ cup vegetable oil
1 teaspoon vanilla extract
1 large egg, lightly beaten
1 large egg white, lightly beaten
1½ teaspoons sugar

1. Preheat oven to 350°.

2. Combine 1 cup sugar and 2 tablespoons flour in a large bowl; stir well. Add plums, and toss well to coat. Spoon plum mixture into a 13 x 9–inch baking dish coated with cooking spray.

3. Combine 2 cups flour, baking powder, baking soda, and salt in a bowl; make a well in center of mixture. Combine ¾ cup sugar, buttermilk, and next 4 ingredients in a bowl; stir well. Add to flour mixture, stirring just until moist. Spoon batter over plum mixture, spreading gently to edges of dish. Sprinkle 1½ teaspoons sugar over batter.

4. Bake at 350° for 35 minutes or until golden. Cool on a wire rack. Serve cobbler warm or at room temperature. **Yield:** 12 servings.

CRANBERRY-ORANGE APPLE CRISP

¼ cup all-purpose flour
¼ cup cornmeal
¼ cup granulated sugar
¼ cup packed light brown sugar
¼ cup chilled stick margarine or butter, cut into small pieces
7 cups diced peeled Rome apple (about 3 pounds)
1 cup fresh or frozen cranberries
2 tablespoons granulated sugar
2 teaspoons grated orange rind
3 tablespoons orange juice

1. Preheat oven to 375°.

2. Lightly spoon flour into a dry measuring cup; level with a knife. Combine flour, cornmeal, ¼ cup granulated sugar, and brown sugar in a bowl; cut in margarine with a pastry blender or 2 knives until mixture is crumbly.

3. Combine apple and remaining ingredients in a large bowl; toss well. Spoon apple mixture into an 8-inch square baking dish or 1½-quart casserole. Sprinkle with crumb mixture. Bake at 375° for 45 minutes or until golden brown. **Yield:** 9 servings.

♥ *What would most desserts be without sugar or some other sweetener? Sugar contains no fat, but the calories it offers are "empty" calories, providing only simple carbohydrates but no vitamins, minerals, or fiber. Be cautious about the amount you use.*

YIELD: 9 servings

EXCHANGES PER SERVING:
1 Starch
1 Fruit
1 Fat

PER SERVING:
Calories 183
(27% from fat)
Fat 5.5g
(saturated fat 0.9g)
Protein 0.9g
Carbohydrate 34.6g
Fiber 2.1g
Cholesterol 0mg
Sodium 55mg

EXCHANGES PER
SERVING:
2 Starch
1½ Fruit
1 Fat

PER SERVING:
Calories 288
(26% from fat)
Fat 8.3g
(saturated fat 1.9g)
Protein 4.2g
Carbohydrate 52g
Fiber 3.8g
Cholesterol 5mg
Sodium 96mg

BLUEBERRY CRISP À LA MODE

*You can use almost any combination of fresh berries
in this dessert. Try cherries or blackberries instead
of blueberries, or a mixture of all three.*

    6   cups blueberries
    2   tablespoons brown sugar
    1   tablespoon all-purpose flour
    1   tablespoon fresh lemon juice
    ⅔   cup all-purpose flour
    ½   cup packed brown sugar
    ½   cup regular oats
    ¾   teaspoon ground cinnamon
 4½   tablespoons chilled stick margarine or
          butter, cut into small pieces
    2   cups vanilla low-fat frozen yogurt

1. Preheat oven to 375°.

2. Combine first 4 ingredients in a medium bowl;
spoon into an 11 x 7-inch baking dish. Lightly
spoon flour into a dry measuring cup, and level
with a knife. Combine ⅔ cup flour, ½ cup brown
sugar, oats, and cinnamon; cut in margarine with
a pastry blender or 2 knives until mixture resembles coarse meal. Sprinkle over blueberry mixture.
Bake at 375° for 30 minutes or until bubbly. Top
each serving with ¼ cup frozen yogurt. **Yield:** 8
servings.

Note: Topping may also be made in the food
processor. Place ⅔ cup flour, ½ cup brown sugar,
oats, and cinnamon in a food processor, and pulse 2
times or until combined. Add margarine; pulse 4
times or until mixture resembles coarse meal.

DOUBLE CHERRY CRISP

Make coarsely crumbled angel food cake by tearing the cake into small pieces or putting cubed cake into a food processor and pulsing several times.

2 (21-ounce) cans light cherry pie filling
³/₄ cup dried cherries, coarsely chopped
1 teaspoon grated lemon rind
2 cups coarsely crumbled angel food cake
2 tablespoons brown sugar
2 tablespoons chopped almonds

1. Preheat oven to 375°.

2. Combine cherry pie filling, dried cherries, and lemon rind in an 8-inch square baking dish.

3. Combine crumbled cake, brown sugar, and almonds in a small bowl; sprinkle evenly over cherry mixture. Bake at 375° for 25 to 30 minutes or until topping is golden and filling is bubbly. Serve warm. **Yield:** 8 servings (serving size: ½ cup).

♥ *It's easier said than done, but the truth is to lose weight you must burn more calories than you take in. One of the best ways to do this is to combine low-calorie, low-fat foods and exercise. Include some of your favorite foods, like dessert, occasionally, and plan on losing no more than 2 pounds a week in order to safely reach your weight-loss goal. This will make it easier for you to maintain your desired weight.*

YIELD: 8 servings

EXCHANGES PER SERVING:
1 Starch
1 Fruit

PER SERVING:
Calories 152
(6% from fat)
Fat 1g
(saturated fat 0.1g)
Protein 1.3g
Carbohydrate 33.4g
Fiber 2.7g
Cholesterol 0mg
Sodium 68mg

YIELD: 8 servings

**EXCHANGES PER
SERVING:**
1½ Fruit
1 Starch

PER SERVING:
Calories 175
(18% from fat)
Fat 3.5g
(saturated fat 0.5g)
Protein 2.6g
Carbohydrate 36g
Fiber 3.8g
Cholesterol 0mg
Sodium 48mg

STRAWBERRY-RHUBARB CRISP

*This recipe was tested with a reduced-calorie margarine
containing between 41% and 60% oil. Avoid
margarines labeled lower-fat or fat-free.*

  ¾ cup low-fat granola cereal without raisins
  ¼ cup all-purpose flour
1½ tablespoons dark brown sugar
   2 tablespoons reduced-calorie stick margarine
   1 cup sugar
   1 tablespoon cornstarch
   8 cups sliced fresh rhubarb
      Cooking spray
   2 cups strawberry halves

1. Preheat oven to 325°.

2. Combine first 4 ingredients, mixing until
crumbly; set aside.

3. Combine sugar and cornstarch; set aside 3 tablespoons mixture. Combine rhubarb and remaining
cornstarch mixture, tossing gently; spoon into a
13 x 9-inch baking dish coated with cooking spray.
Bake, uncovered, at 325° for 25 minutes or until
rhubarb is tender. Remove from oven; increase
oven temperature to 375°.

4. Combine strawberries and reserved cornstarch
mixture; spoon over cooked rhubarb. Sprinkle cereal mixture evenly over strawberries. Bake at 375°
for 15 minutes or until bubbly. **Yield:** 8 servings.

APPLE CRUMBLE

²/₃ cup quick-cooking oats
¼ cup packed brown sugar
¼ cup all-purpose flour
 3 tablespoons chilled stick margarine or butter,
    cut into small pieces
 3 (12-ounce) packages frozen escalloped
    apples (such as Stouffer's)
 4 teaspoons brown sugar

1. Preheat oven to 375°.

2. Combine oats, ¼ cup brown sugar, and flour; cut
in margarine with a pastry blender or 2 knives until
mixture resembles coarse meal.

3. Remove plastic film from apples. Place 3 packages apples in microwave oven; microwave at HIGH
11 minutes or until partially thawed. Spoon apples
into an 8-inch square baking dish. Add 4 teaspoons
brown sugar; stir well. Sprinkle oat mixture over apples. Bake at 375° for 40 minutes or until apple
mixture is bubbly and topping is golden. **Yield:** 8
servings.

YIELD: 8 servings

**EXCHANGES PER
SERVING:**
2½ Fruit
1 Starch
1 Fat

PER SERVING:
Calories 289
(21% from fat)
Fat 6.7g
(saturated fat 1.7g)
Protein 2.6g
Carbohydrate 54g
Fiber 4.1g
Cholesterol 0mg
Sodium 72mg

PER SERVING:
Calories 288
(23% from fat)
Fat 7.2g
(saturated fat 1.1g)
Protein 3.2g
Carbohydrate 56.2g
Fiber 3.8g
Cholesterol 0mg
Sodium 108mg

PEAR-ALMOND CRUMBLE

1/2 cup all-purpose flour
1/2 cup packed brown sugar
1/4 cup chilled stick margarine or butter, cut
         into small pieces
   2 tablespoons chopped almonds, toasted
   7 cups cubed peeled Anjou, Bartlett, or Bosc
         pear (about 3 pounds)
   1 tablespoon fresh lemon juice
   2 cups vanilla fat-free frozen yogurt
1/4 cup fat-free caramel sundae syrup

1. Preheat oven to 375°.

2. Lightly spoon flour into a dry measuring cup;
level with a knife. Combine flour and sugar in a
medium bowl; cut in margarine with a pastry
blender or 2 knives until mixture resembles coarse
meal. Stir in almonds.

3. Combine pear and lemon juice in a large bowl.
Spoon pear mixture into an 8-inch square baking
dish; sprinkle with crumb mixture. Bake at 375°
for 50 minutes or until golden brown. Spoon pear
mixture evenly into 8 bowls; top each serving with
1/4 cup frozen yogurt and 1 1/2 teaspoons syrup.
Yield: 8 servings.

CHERRY CLAFOUTI

Cooking spray
1 tablespoon all-purpose flour
1 (16-ounce) package pitted tart cherries, thawed and drained or 1 (16-ounce) can pitted dark sweet cherries in heavy syrup, drained
1 teaspoon cornstarch
2 teaspoons vanilla extract, divided
1/2 teaspoon almond extract
2 large eggs
2 large egg whites
1/2 cup sugar
1/3 cup all-purpose flour
3/4 cup plain fat-free yogurt
3/4 cup 1% low-fat milk
2 tablespoons sifted powdered sugar

1. Preheat oven to 325°.

2. Coat an 8-inch square baking dish with cooking spray; dust with 1 tablespoon flour, tapping out excess. Set aside.

3. Blot cherries dry on paper towels. Combine cherries, cornstarch, 1 teaspoon vanilla, and almond extract in a small bowl; toss gently. Place cherry mixture in baking dish.

4. Combine eggs, egg whites, and sugar in a medium bowl, stirring with a whisk. Add 1/3 cup flour, yogurt, milk, and remaining 1 teaspoon vanilla; stir with a wire whisk until smooth. Pour egg mixture slowly over cherries; do not stir. Bake at 325° for 50 minutes or until set and lightly browned. Sprinkle with sifted powdered sugar. Serve warm. **Yield:** 6 servings (serving size: 1 cup).

YIELD: 6 servings

EXCHANGES PER SERVING:
2 Starch
1/2 Fruit

PER SERVING:
Calories 191
(11% from fat)
Fat 2.3g
(saturated fat 0.8g)
Protein 7.4g
Carbohydrate 34.4g
Fiber 0.9g
Cholesterol 75mg
Sodium 85mg

EXCHANGES PER
SERVING:
2¹/₂ Starch
1 Fruit
1¹/₂ Fat

PER SERVING:
Calories 318
(27% from fat)
Fat 9.7g
(saturated fat 2.4g)
Protein 3.3g
Carbohydrate 57.3g
Fiber 2.5g
Cholesterol 0mg
Sodium 160mg

EASY CARAMEL-BANANA GALETTE

*The only trick to making this simple dessert is
leaving the caramel unstirred for 8 minutes;
stirring can cause it to harden.*

¹/₄ cup golden raisins
2 tablespoons dark rum
¹/₂ (15-ounce) package refrigerated pie dough
  (such as Pillsbury)
  Cooking spray
3 cups (¹/₄-inch-thick) diagonally sliced ripe
  banana (about 1¹/₂ pounds)
¹/₂ cup sugar
2 tablespoons water

1. Combine raisins and rum in a small bowl; set
aside.

2. Preheat oven to 425°.

3. Roll dough into a 10¹/₂-inch circle, and place
on a foil-lined baking sheet coated with cooking
spray. Arrange the banana slices in concentric circles on crust, leaving a 1-inch border (to prevent
discoloration of bananas, slice immediately before
placing on tart). Fold a 2-inch dough border over
banana slices, pressing gently to seal (dough will
partially cover slices). Bake at 425° for 30 minutes.

4. Combine sugar and water in a small saucepan;
cook over medium heat 8 minutes or until golden
(do not stir). Remove from heat; carefully stir in
raisin mixture until combined. Cool slightly. Pour
sauce over banana slices. Cut into 6 wedges. **Yield:**
6 servings (serving size: 1 wedge).

Note: Bottled fat-free caramel sauce may be
substituted for the sugar and water in step 4. Microwave the bottled sauce at HIGH 1 minute. Stir
in raisin mixture, and let stand 30 minutes. Pour
over banana slices.

CINNAMON-APPLE CAKE

1¾ cups sugar, divided
¾ cup (6 ounces) block-style fat-free cream
    cheese, softened
½ cup stick margarine or butter, softened
1 teaspoon vanilla extract
2 large eggs
1½ cups all-purpose flour
1½ teaspoons baking powder
¼ teaspoon salt
2 teaspoons ground cinnamon
3 cups chopped peeled Rome apple (about
    2 large)
    Cooking spray

1. Preheat oven to 350°.

2. Beat 1½ cups sugar, cream cheese, margarine, and vanilla at medium speed of a mixer until well-blended (about 4 minutes). Add eggs, 1 at a time, beating well after each addition; set aside.

3. Lightly spoon flour into dry measuring cups; level with a knife. Combine flour, baking powder, and salt. Add flour mixture to creamed mixture, and beat at low speed until blended. Combine ¼ cup sugar and cinnamon. Combine 2 tablespoons of the cinnamon mixture and apple in a bowl; stir apple mixture into batter. Pour batter into an 8-inch springform pan coated with cooking spray, and sprinkle with remaining cinnamon mixture.

4. Bake at 350° for 1 hour and 15 minutes or until cake pulls away from sides of pan. Cool cake completely on a wire rack, and cut using a serrated knife. **Yield:** 12 servings.

Note: Cake can be baked in a 9-inch square cake pan or a 9-inch springform pan; reduce baking time by 5 minutes.

YIELD: 12 servings

EXCHANGES PER SERVING:
3 Starch
1 Fat

PER SERVING:
Calories 281
(28% from fat)
Fat 8.7g
(saturated fat 1.8g)
Protein 4.8g
Carbohydrate 46.3g
Fiber 1.2g
Cholesterol 39mg
Sodium 234mg

PER SERVING:
Calories 192
(21% from fat)
Fat 4.5g
(saturated fat 1.3g)
Protein 5.2g
Carbohydrate 33g
Fiber 0.2g
Cholesterol 75mg
Sodium 78mg

LEMON PUDDING CAKE

3	large egg whites
¼	cup sugar
¼	cup all-purpose flour
7	tablespoons sugar
1½	cups 1% low-fat milk
2	large egg yolks
4	teaspoons grated lemon rind
¼	cup fresh lemon juice
1	tablespoon stick margarine or butter, melted and cooled slightly
1	teaspoon vanilla extract
	Cooking spray
2	tablespoons sifted powdered sugar

1. Preheat oven to 325°.

2. In a large bowl, beat egg whites at high speed of a mixer until foamy. Gradually add ¼ cup sugar, 1 tablespoon at a time, beating until stiff peaks form. Set aside.

3. Combine flour and 7 tablespoons sugar in a medium bowl; add milk, egg yolks, and lemon rind, stirring with a whisk until smooth. Stir in lemon juice, margarine, and vanilla (batter will be very thin). Add about one-fourth batter to beaten egg whites, stirring well. Stir remaining batter into egg white mixture.

4. Pour mixture into an 8-inch square baking dish coated with cooking spray. Place dish in a 13 x 9-inch baking pan; add hot water to pan to a depth of 1 inch. Bake at 325° for 45 minutes or until lightly browned and sides begin to pull away from the pan. Let stand in pan 5 minutes. Remove dish from pan; let cool 15 minutes. Sprinkle top with powdered sugar; serve warm. **Yield:** 6 servings.

CINNAMON-SWIRL ANGEL FOOD CAKE

A fragrant cinnamon swirl adds a delightful flavor to this classic cake.

1 cup sifted cake flour
1¼ cups plus 1 tablespoon sugar, divided
1 tablespoon ground cinnamon
12 large egg whites
1 teaspoon cream of tartar
¼ teaspoon salt
1 teaspoon vanilla extract
1 teaspoon lemon juice

1. Preheat oven to 350°.

2. Sift together cake flour and ½ cup sugar; set aside. Sift together 1 tablespoon sugar and cinnamon; set aside. Beat egg whites until foamy. Add cream of tartar and salt; beat until soft peaks form. Add ¾ cup sugar, 2 tablespoons at a time, beating until stiff peaks form. Sift flour mixture over egg white mixture, ¼ cup at a time, folding in flour mixture. Fold in vanilla and lemon juice.

3. Spoon one-third batter into an ungreased 10-inch tube pan. Run back of spoon around center of batter to indent. Sprinkle half of cinnamon mixture over batter. Repeat with remaining batter and cinnamon mixture, ending with batter.

4. Bake at 350° for 40 minutes or until cake springs back when lightly touched. Invert pan; cool 40 minutes. Loosen cake from sides of pan, using a narrow metal spatula; remove cake from pan. **Yield:** 10 servings.

YIELD: 10 servings

EXCHANGES PER SERVING:
2½ Starch

PER SERVING:
Calories 164
(1% from fat)
Fat 0.1g
(saturated fat 0g)
Protein 5g
Carbohydrate 36g
Fiber 0.4g
Cholesterol 0mg
Sodium 122mg

BROWN SUGAR POUND CAKE

*Brown sugar gives this pound cake a rich,
caramel-like flavor.*

　　Cooking spray
3　tablespoons dry breadcrumbs
3　cups all-purpose flour
1　teaspoon baking powder
1/4　teaspoon salt
3/4　cup stick margarine or butter, softened
2　cups packed light brown sugar
1　tablespoon vanilla extract
3　large eggs
1　cup fat-free milk
1　tablespoon powdered sugar

1. Preheat oven to 350°.

2. Coat a 10-inch tube pan with cooking spray,
and dust with breadcrumbs.

3. Lightly spoon flour into dry measuring cups,
and level with a knife. Combine flour, baking powder, and salt in a bowl; stir well with a whisk. Beat
margarine in a large bowl at medium speed of a
mixer until light and fluffy. Gradually add brown
sugar and vanilla, beating until well-blended. Add
eggs, 1 at a time, beating well after each addition.
Add flour mixture to sugar mixture alternately
with milk, beating at low speed, beginning and
ending with flour mixture.

4. Spoon batter into prepared pan. Bake at 350°
for 1 hour and 5 minutes or until a wooden pick
inserted in center comes out clean. Cool in pan 10
minutes on a wire rack, and remove from pan.
Cool completely on a wire rack. Sift powdered
sugar over top of cake. **Yield:** 18 servings (serving
size: 1 slice).

LEMON-BUTTERMILK POUND CAKE

Cooking spray
1 tablespoon all-purpose flour
¾ cup stick margarine or butter
2 cups sugar
4 large eggs
½ teaspoon baking soda
1 cup low-fat or nonfat buttermilk
3 cups all-purpose flour
⅛ teaspoon salt
1 tablespoon plus 1 teaspoon grated lemon rind, divided
¼ cup plus 2 tablespoons fresh lemon juice, divided
¾ cup sifted powdered sugar

1. Preheat oven to 350°.

2. Coat a 10-inch tube pan with cooking spray. Dust with 1 tablespoon flour.

3. Beat margarine at medium speed of a mixer until creamy. Gradually add sugar, beating well. Add eggs, 1 at a time, beating just until blended.

4. Combine baking soda and buttermilk. Combine 3 cups flour, salt, and 1 tablespoon lemon rind; add to margarine mixture alternately with buttermilk mixture, beginning and ending with flour mixture. Mix at low speed after each addition just until blended. Stir in ¼ cup lemon juice.

5. Pour batter into prepared pan. Bake at 350° for 1 hour or until a wooden pick inserted in center comes out clean. Let cool in pan 10 minutes; remove from pan, and place on a wire rack.

6. Poke holes in top of cake, using a wooden pick. Combine powdered sugar, 1 teaspoon lemon rind, and 2 tablespoons lemon juice. Beat at medium speed of a mixer until smooth. Drizzle glaze over warm cake. Let cool completely on a wire rack. **Yield:** 18 servings (serving size: 1 slice).

YIELD: 18 servings

EXCHANGES PER SERVING:
3 Starch
1 Fat

PER SERVING:
Calories 276
(30% from fat)
Fat 9.3g
(saturated fat 1.7g)
Protein 4.2g
Carbohydrate 44.7g
Fiber 0.6g
Cholesterol 49mg
Sodium 152mg

PER SERVING:
Calories 159
(23% from fat)
Fat 4.1g
(saturated fat 0.8g)
Protein 2.2g
Carbohydrate 29.5g
Fiber 1g
Cholesterol 0mg
Sodium 132mg

GINGERBREAD WITH CITRUS SAUCE

1 1/4 cups all-purpose flour
1/4 cup unprocessed wheat bran
1/2 teaspoon baking powder
1/2 teaspoon baking soda
1 teaspoon ground ginger
1 teaspoon ground cinnamon
1/4 cup packed brown sugar
1 teaspoon grated lemon rind
1/2 cup water
1/2 cup molasses
1/4 cup stick margarine or butter, melted
1/4 cup egg substitute
Cooking spray
Citrus Sauce

1. Preheat oven to 350°.

2. Combine first 8 ingredients in a large mixing bowl. Combine water and next 3 ingredients in a small bowl. Add to dry ingredients; stir just until moistened.

3. Pour batter into an 8-inch square pan coated with cooking spray. Bake at 350° for 30 to 40 minutes or until a wooden pick inserted in center comes out clean. Cool slightly on a wire rack. To serve, cut gingerbread into squares. Spoon Citrus Sauce over gingerbread. **Yield:** 12 servings (serving size: 1 square cake and 2 teaspoons sauce).

Citrus Sauce
3 tablespoons sugar
2 teaspoons cornstarch
1/2 cup orange juice
1 tablespoon lemon juice

1. Combine sugar and cornstarch in a small saucepan. Stir in orange juice and lemon juice. Cook over medium heat, stirring constantly, until mixture thickens. Boil 1 minute. **Yield:** 1/2 cup.

CARROT CAKE

YIELD: 24 servings

EXCHANGES PER SERVING:
2½ Starch

PER SERVING:
Calories 208
(19% from fat)
Fat 4.3g
(saturated fat 1.3g)
Protein 3.2g
Carbohydrate 39.9g
Fiber 1.1g
Cholesterol 4mg
Sodium 118mg

2   cups all-purpose flour
⅓   cup unprocessed wheat bran
1   teaspoon baking powder
1   teaspoon baking soda
2   teaspoons ground cinnamon
1½ cups sugar
3   cups shredded carrot
1   (8-ounce) carton lemon fat-free yogurt
1   cup egg substitute
⅓   cup vegetable oil
    Cooking spray
    Lemon-Cream Cheese Frosting

1. Preheat oven to 350°.

2. Combine first 6 ingredients in a large bowl; stir in carrot. Combine yogurt, egg substitute, and oil in a small bowl; add to dry ingredients, stirring just until moistened.

3. Pour batter into a 13 x 9-inch baking pan coated with cooking spray. Bake at 350° for 35 to 40 minutes or until a wooden pick inserted in center comes out clean. Cool completely in pan on a wire rack. Spread Lemon–Cream Cheese Frosting over cooled cake. **Yield:** 24 servings (serving size: 1 square).

Lemon-Cream Cheese Frosting

1   (8-ounce) block ⅓-less-fat cream cheese, softened
2   teaspoons vanilla extract
½   teaspoon grated lemon rind
3¼ cups sifted powdered sugar
2   to 3 teaspoons fat-free milk

1. Beat cream cheese, vanilla, and lemon rind at medium speed of an electric mixer until creamy; add powdered sugar, beating until smooth. Beat in milk, 1 teaspoon at a time, to reach desired consistency. **Yield:** 1½ cups.

EXCHANGES PER
SERVING:
1 Starch
1 Low-Fat Milk

PER SERVING:
Calories 206
(21% from fat)
Fat 4.9g
(saturated fat 2.4g)
Protein 8.8g
Carbohydrate 29.6g
Fiber 0.2g
Cholesterol 26mg
Sodium 289mg

Make Ahead
CHOCOLATE-ALMOND CHEESECAKE

Cooking spray
3/4 cup teddy bear-shaped chocolate graham
    cracker cookies, finely crushed and
    divided
1 (12-ounce) carton 1% low-fat cottage
    cheese
2/3 cup cocoa
1/3 cup all-purpose flour
1 (8-ounce) tub light cream cheese, softened
1 (8-ounce) block fat-free cream cheese,
    softened
1 1/2 cups sugar
1/4 cup amaretto
2 teaspoons vanilla extract
1 large egg
1 large egg white
1 cup frozen reduced-calorie whipped
    topping, thawed
2 tablespoons sliced almonds, lightly toasted

1. Preheat oven to 300°.

2. Coat bottom of a 9-inch springform pan with
cooking spray; sprinkle half of crushed cookies over
bottom of pan. Process cottage cheese in an electric
blender 2 to 3 minutes or until very smooth, scraping sides often. Sift cocoa and flour together.

3. Beat cream cheeses in a large bowl at medium
speed of a mixer 10 minutes. Gradually add sugar,
beating until well-blended. Add cottage cheese; beat
1 minute. Add cocoa mixture; beat 1 minute, scraping sides of bowl as needed. Add amaretto and next
3 ingredients; beat 1 minute. Pour into prepared
pan. Bake, uncovered, at 300° for 55 minutes or until set. Remove from oven; sprinkle with remaining
crushed cookies. Run a knife around edge of pan;
cool on a wire rack. Cover and chill at least 8 hours.

4. Remove sides of pan; place cheesecake on a plate.
Pipe whipped topping around edge; decorate with
almonds. **Yield:** 16 servings (serving size: 1 wedge).

Make Ahead
LEMON CHEESECAKE

YIELD: 12 servings

EXCHANGES PER SERVING:
1½ Starch
1 Skim Milk
1 Fat

PER SERVING:
Calories 255
(28% from fat)
Fat 8g
(saturated fat 3.1g)
Protein 9.3g
Carbohydrate 36.9g
Fiber 0.3g
Cholesterol 31mg
Sodium 365mg

1 cup low-fat gingersnap cookie crumbs
3 tablespoons reduced-calorie stick margarine, melted
Cooking spray
2 cups 1% low-fat cottage cheese
1 (8-ounce) block ⅓-less-fat cream cheese
1 cup sugar, divided
1 cup all-purpose flour, divided
1 large egg
2 large egg whites
1 tablespoon plus 1 teaspoon grated lemon rind, divided
2 tablespoons fresh lemon juice, divided
1 tablespoon reduced-calorie stick margarine, softened

1. Preheat oven to 325°.

2. Combine gingersnap crumbs and 3 tablespoons margarine. Press on bottom of an 8-inch springform pan coated with cooking spray.

3. Place cottage cheese and cream cheese in container of an electric blender or food processor bowl; cover and process 1½ minutes or until smooth, stopping once to scrape down sides. Add ¾ cup sugar, ¼ cup flour, egg, egg whites, 1 tablespoon lemon rind, and 1 tablespoon lemon juice; process until blended. Pour into prepared pan. Bake at 325° for 45 minutes (center will be soft).

4. Combine remaining ¼ cup sugar, ¾ cup flour, 1 teaspoon lemon rind, 1 tablespoon lemon juice, and 1 tablespoon margarine in a small bowl, stirring until mixture resembles coarse meal. Without moving cheesecake, sprinkle flour mixture carefully over cheesecake. Bake 15 additional minutes. Turn off oven; partially open oven door. Leave cheesecake in oven 1 hour. Remove from oven; let cool on a wire rack. Cover and chill 8 hours. **Yield:** 12 servings (serving size: 1 wedge).

BOILED CHRISTMAS CUSTARD

One taste of this smooth, old-fashioned custard will evoke memories of simpler times.

1   cup egg substitute
½   cup sugar
2   tablespoons all-purpose flour
2   teaspoons vanilla extract
1   quart fat-free milk

1. Combine first 4 ingredients in a small bowl, beating with a wire whisk until blended.

2. Cook milk in a medium–size heavy saucepan over medium heat 10 minutes or until hot.

3. Gradually stir 1 cup hot milk into egg mixture, and add to remaining hot milk, stirring constantly. Cook over medium heat, stirring constantly, 6 to 8 minutes or until mixture begins to thicken and thermometer registers 180° (do not boil). Pour into a bowl. Place heavy–duty plastic wrap directly on surface of custard, and chill. **Yield:** 5 cups (serving size: ½ cup).

♥ *Milk and other dairy products are the best food sources of calcium and are rich in protein, vitamins, and minerals. But whole milk and products made from it (such as ice cream) are high in fat, especially saturated fat. If a recipe calls for whole milk, you can often use fat-free milk instead.*

Make Ahead
CRÈME CARAMEL

YIELD: 4 servings

EXCHANGES PER SERVING:
1½ Starch
1 Skim Milk

PER SERVING:
Calories 182
(1% from fat)
Fat 0.2g
(saturated fat 0.1g)
Protein 9.4g
Carbohydrate 35.3g
Fiber 0g
Cholesterol 3mg
Sodium 143mg

½ cup sugar, divided
1 (12-ounce) can evaporated fat-free milk
½ cup egg substitute
½ teaspoon grated orange rind
1 teaspoon vanilla extract
¼ teaspoon almond extract

1. Preheat oven to 350°.

2. Place 6 tablespoons sugar in a cast-iron or heavy skillet. Cook over medium heat, stirring constantly, until sugar melts and turns light brown. Pour melted sugar into 4 (6-ounce) custard cups, tilting to coat bottoms; place in an 8- or 9-inch square pan. Set aside.

3. Heat milk in a small saucepan over medium heat until very hot (do not boil). Set aside. Combine remaining 2 tablespoons sugar, egg substitute, orange rind, and flavorings, stirring well. Gradually stir about one-fourth of hot milk into egg substitute mixture; add to remaining hot mixture, stirring constantly.

4. Pour milk mixture evenly into prepared custard cups; pour hot water into pan to depth of 1 inch. Bake at 350° for 30 minutes or until a knife inserted in center comes out clean. Remove custard cups from water, and let cool on a wire rack.

5. Cover and chill at least 2 hours. Loosen edges of custards with a knife; invert onto individual serving plates. **Yield:** 4 servings.

RUM AND COCONUT CRÈME BRÛLÉE

1 (12-ounce) package soft silken-style tofu (such as Mori-Nu), drained
$1/2$ cup coconut milk
$1/2$ cup maple syrup
2 tablespoons cornstarch
2 tablespoons rum
2 teaspoons coconut extract
$1/8$ teaspoon salt
1 tablespoon sugar
1 tablespoon brown sugar
4 teaspoons flaked sweetened coconut

1. Preheat oven to 325°.

2. Place first 7 ingredients in a food processor; process until smooth, scraping sides of processor bowl occasionally.

3. Spoon mixture evenly into 4 (4-ounce) ramekins or custard cups. Place ramekins in an 8-inch square baking dish; add hot water to baking dish to a depth of 1 inch. Cover and bake at 325° for 40 minutes or until a knife inserted near center comes out clean. Remove cups from baking dish; let cool on a wire rack. Cover and chill at least 2 hours.

4. Preheat broiler.

5. Combine sugars and coconut; sprinkle evenly over each serving. Place ramekins on a baking sheet; broil 2 minutes or until sugars melt and coconut is lightly browned. **Yield:** 4 servings.

Note: Regular coconut milk is high in saturated fat. If you use light coconut milk instead, you will cut the saturated fat to only 1.6 grams per serving.

Make Ahead
LOW-FAT FLAN

²/₃ cup sugar
1 (14-ounce) can fat-free sweetened
     condensed milk
1¼ cups 1% low-fat milk
1 cup egg substitute
1¼ teaspoons vanilla extract
⅛ teaspoon salt

1. Preheat oven to 325°.

2. Place sugar in a medium heavy skillet over medium–high heat; cook until sugar dissolves, stirring constantly. Cook 5 minutes or until golden, stirring constantly. Immediately pour into a 9-inch round cake pan, tipping quickly until caramelized sugar coats bottom of cake pan.

3. Combine sweetened condensed milk and remaining 4 ingredients, stirring until smooth. Pour milk mixture over syrup in cake pan.

4. Place cake pan in a large shallow baking pan; add hot water to a depth of 1 inch. Bake at 325° for 35 to 40 minutes or until almost set. Remove cake pan from water, and let cool completely on a wire rack. Cover and chill at least 3 hours. Loosen edges of flan with a knife. Place a plate, upside down, on top of pan; invert flan onto plate. Drizzle any remaining caramelized syrup over flan. **Yield:** 8 servings (serving size: 1 wedge).

YIELD: 8 servings

EXCHANGES PER SERVING:
2½ Starch
1 Skim Milk

PER SERVING:
Calories 237
(2% from fat)
Fat 0.4g
(saturated fat 0.2g)
Protein 8g
Carbohydrate 49.6g
Fiber 0g
Cholesterol 8mg
Sodium 150mg

YIELD: 16 servings

EXCHANGES PER SERVING:
3 Starch

PER SERVING:
Calories 231
(7% from fat)
Fat 1.7g
(saturated fat 0.5g)
Protein 10.5g
Carbohydrate 43.3g
Fiber 0.5g
Cholesterol 4mg
Sodium 140mg

Make Ahead
SWEET POTATO FLAN

 ½ cup sugar
 1 cup mashed cooked sweet potato, divided
 2 (14-ounce) cans fat-free sweetened condensed milk
 2 cups fat-free milk
 2½ cups egg substitute
 1 teaspoon ground cinnamon
 ½ teaspoon ground allspice
 ¼ teaspoon ground cloves
 1 teaspoon vanilla extract
 1 tablespoon flaked coconut, toasted

1. Sprinkle sugar in a 10-inch round cakepan; place over medium heat, and cook, shaking pan constantly, until sugar melts and turns light golden brown. Remove from heat; set aside to cool (caramelized sugar may crack slightly as it cools).

2. Preheat oven to 325°.

3. Combine ½ cup sweet potato, 1 can sweetened condensed milk, and half of next 6 ingredients in container of an electric blender; process until smooth, stopping once to scrape down sides. Pour mixture into a large bowl. Repeat procedure; add mixture to bowl, stirring well with a wire whisk.

4. Pour mixture over caramelized sugar in cakepan; cover with aluminum foil, and place in a larger shallow pan. Add hot water to larger pan to depth of ½ inch.

5. Bake at 325° for 1 hour and 15 minutes or until a knife inserted in center comes out clean. Remove pan from water, and uncover; cool in pan on a wire rack 30 minutes. Cover and chill at least 8 hours.

6. Run a knife around edge of flan to loosen; invert flan onto a serving plate, and sprinkle with toasted coconut. **Yield:** 16 servings (serving size: 1 wedge).

OLD-FASHIONED BANANA PUDDING

Simply mention the words "homemade banana pudding," and you'll see eyes sparkle and faces light up. This recipe lives up to those expectations.

½	cup sugar
3	tablespoons cornstarch
⅓	cup water
⅓	cup egg substitute
1	(12-ounce) can evaporated fat-free milk
½	cup fat-free sour cream
1	teaspoon vanilla extract
29	vanilla wafers
3	medium bananas, sliced
2	large egg whites
¼	teaspoon cream of tartar
1	tablespoon sugar

1. Preheat oven to 325°.

2. Combine ½ cup sugar and cornstarch in a medium-size heavy saucepan; gradually stir in water, egg substitute, and milk. Bring to a boil over medium heat, stirring constantly. Boil, stirring constantly, 1 minute. Remove from heat; fold in sour cream and vanilla.

3. Place a layer of vanilla wafers in bottom of a 1½-quart casserole, and spoon one-third of pudding over wafers. Top pudding with half of banana slices. Repeat layers. Spread remaining pudding over top. Arrange remaining vanilla wafers in pudding around edge of dish. Set aside.

4. Beat egg whites and cream of tartar at high speed of an electric mixer until foamy. Add 1 tablespoon sugar; beat until stiff peaks form and sugar dissolves (about 2 minutes). Spread meringue over pudding, sealing to wafers. Bake at 325° for 25 minutes. Let pudding stand 10 minutes before serving. **Yield:** 8 servings.

YIELD: 8 servings

EXCHANGES PER SERVING:
1½ Starch
1 Fruit
½ Skim Milk

PER SERVING:
Calories 212
(12% from fat)
Fat 2.8g
(saturated fat 0.6g)
Protein 7g
Carbohydrate 39.8g
Fiber 1.2g
Cholesterol 2mg
Sodium 135mg

Make Ahead
MOCHA FUDGE PUDDING

*Strong brewed coffee can be substituted in equal measure
for the Kahlúa in this rich, creamy pudding.*

   ½ cup sugar
   3 tablespoons cornstarch
   3 tablespoons unsweetened cocoa
   ⅛ teaspoon salt
2¼ cups fat-free milk
   ½ cup egg substitute
   2 tablespoons Kahlúa
   2 teaspoons vanilla extract
   1 tablespoon reduced-calorie stick margarine

1. Combine first 4 ingredients in a medium
saucepan; gradually add milk and egg substitute,
stirring until smooth.

2. Bring mixture to a boil over medium heat, stirring constantly; boil 1 minute, stirring constantly.
Add Kahlúa and vanilla; cook over low heat 1
minute.

3. Remove from heat; stir in margarine. Spoon
pudding into 6 individual dessert dishes. Cover and
chill thoroughly. **Yield:** 6 servings (serving size:
½ cup).

TURKISH RICE PUDDING

1¼ cups water
3 tablespoons light butter
1 (3-inch) cinnamon stick
1 cup uncooked long-grain rice
3 cups fat-free milk, divided
⅔ cup sugar
¼ cup nonfat dry milk
1 teaspoon vanilla extract
4 teaspoons cinnamon-sugar
8 teaspoons chopped almonds
8 whole almonds (optional)
  Cinnamon sticks (optional)

1. Bring first 3 ingredients to a boil in a medium saucepan. Stir in rice; cover, reduce heat to medium–low, and simmer 10 minutes or until liquid is absorbed.

2. Stir in 1 cup milk and sugar; cook, uncovered, 10 minutes or until liquid is nearly absorbed, stirring frequently. Add 1 cup milk and ¼ cup dry milk; cook, uncovered, 10 minutes or until liquid is nearly absorbed, stirring frequently. Add ½ cup milk; cook, uncovered, 15 minutes or until liquid is nearly absorbed, stirring constantly. Add remaining milk; cook until rice is tender and mixture is thick and creamy. Remove from heat; stir in vanilla.

3. Serve pudding warm or chilled topped with cinnamon–sugar and chopped almonds. If desired, garnish with whole almonds and cinnamon sticks. **Yield:** 8 servings (serving size: ½ cup pudding, ½ teaspoon cinnamon–sugar, and 1 teaspoon chopped almonds).

YIELD: 8 servings

EXCHANGES PER SERVING:
2½ Starch
½ Low-Fat Milk

PER SERVING:
Calories 239
(21% from fat)
Fat 5.5g
(saturated fat 1.8g)
Protein 6.9g
Carbohydrate 44.3g
Fiber 0.6g
Cholesterol 10mg
Sodium 96mg

EXCHANGES PER SERVING:
3 Starch
1 Fat

PER SERVING:
Calories 282
(27% from fat)
Fat 8.4g
(saturated fat 3.3g)
Protein 4.3g
Carbohydrate 44.3g
Fiber 0g
Cholesterol 6.3mg
Sodium 249mg

Make Ahead
CHOCOLATE CREAM PIE

Pressing plastic wrap directly onto the surface of the filling prevents a thick skin from forming as the filling cools.

$^1/_2$ (15-ounce) package refrigerated piecrusts
$^1/_2$ cup sugar
$^1/_4$ cup cornstarch
$^1/_4$ cup unsweetened cocoa
$^1/_4$ teaspoon salt
 2 cups fat-free milk
$^1/_4$ cup egg substitute
 1 tablespoon reduced-calorie stick margarine
 1 teaspoon vanilla extract
 1 (8-ounce) container frozen fat-free whipped topping, thawed
   Grated chocolate (optional)

1. Fit piecrust into a 9-inch pie plate, and bake according to package directions. Set aside.

2. Combine sugar, cornstarch, cocoa, and salt in a heavy saucepan; gradually stir in milk. Bring mixture to a boil over medium heat, stirring constantly. Boil 1 minute, stirring constantly.

3. Gradually stir about one-fourth of hot mixture into egg substitute; add to remaining hot mixture, stirring constantly. Cook, stirring constantly, 1 minute. Remove from heat; stir in margarine and vanilla. Pour mixture into baked pastry shell; cover surface with plastic wrap, and chill at least 3 hours.

4. Spoon whipped topping evenly over filling, and garnish with grated chocolate, if desired. **Yield:** 8 servings (serving size: 1 wedge).

Make Ahead
KEY LIME PIE

YIELD: 8 servings

2 large eggs
2 large egg whites
1/2 cup Key lime juice (such as Nellie and Joe's
   Famous Key West Lime Juice)
1 teaspoon grated lime rind
1 (14-ounce) can fat-free sweetened
   condensed milk
1 (6-ounce) reduced-fat graham cracker
   crust
1 1/2 cups frozen reduced-calorie whipped
   topping, thawed

EXCHANGES PER SERVING:
3 1/2 Starch
1/2 Fat

PER SERVING:
Calories 288
(18% from fat)
Fat 5.9g
(saturated fat 3g)
Protein 7.6g
Carbohydrate 49.2g
Fiber 0.8g
Cholesterol 56mg
Sodium 198mg

1. Preheat oven to 350°.

2. Beat eggs and egg whites at medium speed of a mixer until well-blended. Gradually add lime juice, rind, and milk to egg mixture, beating until well-blended. Spoon mixture into crust, and bake at 350° for 20 minutes or until almost set (the center will not be firm but will set up as it chills). Cool pie on a wire rack. Cover loosely, and chill 4 hours. Spread whipped topping evenly over filling. **Yield:** 8 servings (serving size: 1 wedge).

YIELD: 8 servings

EXCHANGES PER SERVING:
2½ Starch
1 Fat

PER SERVING:
Calories 239
(32% from fat)
Fat 8.6g
(saturated fat 3.5g)
Protein 4.9g
Carbohydrate 35.5g
Fiber 2.3g
Cholesterol 61mg
Sodium 147mg

*The blend of spices gives this pumpkin pie
a wonderful flavor.*

½ (15-ounce) package refrigerated piecrusts
1 (15-ounce) can unsweetened pumpkin
½ cup sugar
2 tablespoons all-purpose flour
1½ teaspoons ground cinnamon
½ teaspoon ground ginger
⅛ teaspoon ground allspice
¾ cup fat-free evaporated milk
2 large eggs, lightly beaten
½ cup frozen fat-free whipped topping,
   thawed

1. Fit piecrust into a 9–inch pie plate and bake according to package directions. Set aside.

2. Reduce oven to 350°.

3. Combine pumpkin and next 5 ingredients in a large bowl; stir in milk. Add beaten eggs; stir well. Pour into baked pastry shell. Bake at 350° for 45 minutes or until a knife inserted in center comes out clean. Cool on a wire rack. Cover and store in refrigerator. Serve each wedge with 1 tablespoon whipped topping. **Yield:** 8 servings (serving size: 1 wedge and 1 tablespoon whipped topping).

Make Ahead
FROZEN CHOCOLATE BROWNIE PIE

1/4 cup stick margarine or butter
2/3 cup packed brown sugar
1/2 cup egg substitute
1/4 cup low-fat or nonfat buttermilk
1/3 cup cocoa
1/4 cup all-purpose flour
1/4 teaspoon salt
1 teaspoon vanilla extract
   Cooking spray
1/2 gallon vanilla fat-free frozen yogurt, softened
   and divided
1 quart chocolate fat-free frozen yogurt,
   softened
3/4 cup fat-free chocolate sundae syrup
   Fresh strawberry halves (optional)

YIELD: 12 servings

EXCHANGES PER SERVING:
4 Starch

PER SERVING:
Calories 295
(13% from fat)
Fat 4.2g
(saturated fat 1g)
Protein 9.1g
Carbohydrate 63.4g
Fiber 0.1g
Cholesterol 0mg
Sodium 257mg

1. Preheat oven to 350°.

2. Melt margarine in a large saucepan over medium heat; add brown sugar, stirring until dissolved. Remove from heat; cool slightly.

3. Add egg substitute and buttermilk to margarine mixture; stir well. Combine cocoa, flour, and salt; add to buttermilk mixture, stirring until blended. Stir in vanilla. Pour batter into a 9–inch springform pan lightly coated with cooking spray. Bake at 350° for 15 minutes. Cool in pan on a wire rack.

4. Spread half of vanilla frozen yogurt over cooled brownie layer; freeze at least 30 minutes or until firm. Spread chocolate frozen yogurt over vanilla frozen yogurt, and freeze at least 30 minutes or until firm.

5. Spread remaining vanilla frozen yogurt over chocolate frozen yogurt. Cover and freeze at least 8 hours. Cut pie into 12 wedges; drizzle each serving with 1 tablespoon chocolate syrup. Garnish with strawberry halves, if desired. **Yield:** 12 servings (serving size: 1 wedge and 1 tablespoon chocolate syrup).

VANILLA ICE CREAM

Crème de cacao is a dark, chocolate-flavored liqueur with a hint of vanilla. It gives this ice cream a wonderful flavor, but may be omitted, if desired.

YIELD: 8 servings

EXCHANGES PER
SERVING:
1½ Starch
1 Skim Milk

PER SERVING:
Calories 203
(10% from fat)
Fat 2.3g
(saturated fat 1g)
Protein 7.9g
Carbohydrate 35g
Fiber 0g
Cholesterol 59mg
Sodium 135mg

2 tablespoons vanilla extract
1 tablespoon crème de cacao (optional)
1½ teaspoons unflavored gelatin
1 (14-ounce) can fat-free sweetened
   condensed milk
2 large egg yolks, lightly beaten
⅛ teaspoon salt
3 cups 1% low-fat milk, divided

1. Combine vanilla and crème de cacao, if desired, in a small bowl; sprinkle gelatin over vanilla mixture, and set aside to soften. Combine condensed milk, egg yolks, and salt in a small bowl; stir well with a whisk. Set aside.

2. Heat 1½ cups milk in a heavy saucepan over medium heat until very hot (do not boil). Slowly add condensed milk mixture to milk in saucepan, stirring constantly. Cook, stirring constantly, 3 to 5 minutes or until mixture coats back of spoon (do not boil).

3. Add gelatin mixture to milk mixture; stir with a whisk until gelatin dissolves. Stir in remaining 1½ cups milk. Pour into a medium bowl; cover and chill at least 2 hours.

4. Pour mixture into freezer can of an electric ice cream freezer. Freeze according to manufacturer's instructions.

5. Pack freezer with additional ice and rock salt, and let stand 1 hour before serving. **Yield:** 8 servings (serving size: ½ cup).

Make Ahead
MANGO FREEZE

Let Mango Freeze soften a little before serving.

4 cups peeled ripe mango, cut into 1-inch
    pieces (about 4 large)
3/4 cup powdered sugar
1/2 cup mashed ripe banana
1 tablespoon fresh lime juice
1 (8-ounce) carton vanilla low-fat yogurt

1. Place mango pieces on a baking sheet lined with plastic wrap; freeze at least 4 hours. Remove from freezer; let stand 10 minutes.

2. Place mango pieces in a food processor or blender; process until smooth, scraping sides of bowl occasionally. Add sugar, banana, and lime juice. With food processor on, slowly spoon yogurt through food chute; process until smooth, scraping sides of bowl once. Spoon mixture into a freezer-safe container; cover and freeze 3 hours or until firm. **Yield:** 10 servings (serving size: 1/2 cup).

♥ *Remember that portion sizes are important in healthy cooking. Measuring cups and food scales can assist you in determining proper portion sizes as well as correct ingredient amounts.*

YIELD: 10 servings

EXCHANGES PER SERVING:
2 Fruit

PER SERVING:
Calories 108
(4% from fat)
Fat 0.5g
(saturated fat 0.2g)
Protein 1.6g
Carbohydrate 26.1g
Fiber 1.3g
Cholesterol 1mg
Sodium 17mg

EXCHANGES PER SERVING:
2 Fruit

PER SERVING:
Calories 123
(4% from fat)
Fat 0.5g
(saturated fat 0.3g)
Protein 2.5g
Carbohydrate 29.1g
Fiber 0.9g
Cholesterol 2mg
Sodium 26mg

Make Ahead
PEACH SHERBET

Keep this cool, refreshing dessert on hand in the freezer to satisfy a craving for a sweet treat anytime.

  2 cups peeled, sliced ripe peaches or 2 cups
        frozen sliced peaches, partially thawed
 ½ cup orange juice
 ⅓ cup honey
  1 (8-ounce) carton vanilla low-fat yogurt
      Fresh mint sprigs (optional)

1. Place first 4 ingredients in food processor. Process until peaches are finely chopped. Pour into an 8-inch square pan; cover. Freeze until almost firm.

2. Break frozen mixture into large pieces, and place in food processor; process until fluffy, but not thawed. Return mixture to pan; cover and freeze until firm.

3. Remove mixture from freezer; let stand at room temperature 10 to 15 minutes. Scoop mixture evenly into 6 individual dessert dishes; garnish with mint sprigs, if desired. **Yield:** 6 servings (serving size: ½ cup).

Make Ahead
PASSIONFRUIT SORBET

  2 cups water
 ¾ cup sugar
1½ cups passionfruit nectar
  3 tablespoons fresh lemon juice

1. Combine water and sugar in a small saucepan; bring to a boil, and cook 5 minutes. Pour into an 8-inch square baking dish; freeze 20 minutes. Stir in nectar and lemon juice, and freeze 30 minutes. Stir well with a fork; freeze 1½ hours or until solid (do not stir).

2. Let frozen mixture stand at room temperature until slightly softened. Break frozen mixture into chunks. Place frozen chunks in a food processor; pulse 5 times or until smooth. Serve immediately. **Yield:** 6 servings (serving size: ½ cup).

♥ *When buying fruit juice, choose refrigerated, bottled, or canned juices that are 100 percent juice. Although fruit drinks and fruit-flavored sodas have little or no fat, they usually have a high sugar content and are not good sources of vitamins and minerals.*

YIELD: 6 servings

EXCHANGES PER SERVING:
2 Fruit

PER SERVING:
Calories 124
(0% from fat)
Fat 0g
(saturated fat 0g)
Protein 0.1g
Carbohydrate 32g
Fiber 1g
Cholesterol 0mg
Sodium 4.8mg

Make Ahead
PINEAPPLE-BROWN SUGAR FROZEN YOGURT

1 1/2 cups packed light brown sugar
   2 (15 1/4-ounce) cans crushed pineapple in
        juice, undrained
   4 cups vanilla low-fat yogurt
   2 teaspoons vanilla extract

1. Combine sugar and pineapple in a medium saucepan over medium heat, and cook until sugar dissolves, stirring occasionally. Remove from heat, and cool slightly. Chill.

2. Combine pineapple mixture, yogurt, and vanilla in a large bowl. Pour mixture into the freezer can of an ice-cream freezer, and freeze according to manufacturer's instructions. Spoon yogurt into a freezer-safe container; cover and freeze 1 hour or until firm. **Yield:** 18 servings (serving size: 1/2 cup).

Make Ahead
RASPBERRY-ORANGE YOGURT

   2 (10-ounce) packages frozen raspberries in
        light syrup, thawed
 1/2 teaspoon grated orange rind
 1/2 cup orange juice
   1 (8-ounce) carton raspberry fat-free yogurt

1. Place raspberries in food processor; process until smooth. Pour puree into a wire-mesh strainer; press with back of a spoon against the sides of strainer to squeeze out juice. Discard seeds remaining in strainer. Combine strained puree, orange rind, orange juice, and yogurt, stirring well with a wire whisk. Pour mixture into an 8-inch square pan. Cover and freeze 8 hours or until firm.

2. Place frozen raspberry mixture in food processor; process until smooth, but not thawed. To serve, scoop into 8 individual dessert dishes. Serve immediately. **Yield:** 8 servings (serving size: 1/2 cup).

BUTTERSCOTCH BARS

YIELD: 16 servings

½ cup granulated sugar
½ cup packed brown sugar
¼ cup stick margarine or butter, softened
2 large egg whites
1 teaspoon vanilla extract
1¼ cups all-purpose flour
½ teaspoon baking powder
¼ teaspoon salt
   Cooking spray
½ cup butterscotch morsels

EXCHANGES PER SERVING:
1½ Starch
½ Fat

PER SERVING:
Calories 142
(27% from fat)
Fat 4.3g
(saturated fat 1.3g)
Protein 1.6g
Carbohydrate 24g
Fiber 0.3g
Cholesterol 0mg
Sodium 95mg

1. Preheat oven to 350°.

2. Beat sugars and margarine at medium speed of a mixer until well–blended (about 4 minutes). Add egg whites and vanilla; beat well. Lightly spoon flour into dry measuring cups, and level with a knife. Combine flour, baking powder, and salt; stir well with a whisk. Add flour mixture to sugar mixture; beat at low speed just until blended.

3. Spread batter evenly into an 8-inch square baking pan coated with cooking spray; sprinkle evenly with morsels. Bake at 350° for 28 minutes or until a wooden pick inserted in center comes out clean. Cool in pan on a wire rack. **Yield:** 16 servings (serving size: 1 bar).

♥ *Unless the recipe calls for reduced-calorie stick margarine, use regular margarine or butter (see page 10 for more details).*

YIELD: 16 servings

EXCHANGES PER
SERVING:
1½ Starch

PER SERVING:
Calories 118
(24% from fat)
Fat 3.2g
(saturated fat 0.7g)
Protein 2.2g
Carbohydrate 20.5g
Fiber 0.3g
Cholesterol 41mg
Sodium 68mg

EASY LEMON SQUARES

¼ cup granulated sugar
3 tablespoons stick margarine or butter, softened
1 cup all-purpose flour
3 large eggs
¾ cup granulated sugar
2 teaspoons grated lemon rind
⅓ cup fresh lemon juice
3 tablespoons all-purpose flour
½ teaspoon baking powder
⅛ teaspoon salt
2 teaspoons powdered sugar

1. Preheat oven to 350°.

2. To prepare crust, beat ¼ cup granulated sugar and margarine at medium speed of a mixer until creamy. Lightly spoon 1 cup flour into a dry measuring cup; level with a knife. Gradually add 1 cup flour to sugar mixture, beating at low speed until mixture resembles fine crumbs. Gently press mixture into bottom of an 8-inch square baking pan. Bake at 350° for 15 minutes; cool on a wire rack.

3. To prepare topping, beat eggs at medium speed until foamy. Add ¾ cup granulated sugar and next 5 ingredients, and beat until well-blended. Pour mixture over partially baked crust. Bake at 350° for 20 to 25 minutes or until set. Cool on wire rack. Sift powdered sugar evenly over top. **Yield:** 16 servings (serving size: 1 square).

Make Ahead
BUTTER PECAN-TOFFEE BROWNIES

Cooking spray
1 cup packed brown sugar
3 tablespoons stick margarine or butter,
 melted
1 teaspoon vanilla extract
1 large egg
3/4 cup all-purpose flour
2 tablespoons chopped pecans
1/2 teaspoon baking powder
1/8 teaspoon salt
2/3 cup powdered sugar
2 tablespoons semisweet chocolate minichips,
 melted
1 tablespoon hot water
2 tablespoons almond brickle chips (such as
 Heath)

1. Preheat oven to 350°.

2. To prepare brownies, coat bottom of an 8-inch square baking pan with cooking spray (do not coat sides of pan).

3. Combine brown sugar and next 3 ingredients in a large bowl; stir well with a whisk. Lightly spoon flour into dry measuring cups, and level with a knife. Combine flour, pecans, baking powder, and salt; add to brown sugar mixture. Spread batter in bottom of prepared pan. Bake at 350° for 22 minutes or until a wooden pick inserted in center comes out almost clean. Cool on a wire rack.

4. To prepare the topping, combine powdered sugar, minichips, and hot water in a small bowl; stir until smooth. Spread topping over brownies, and sprinkle with brickle chips. Chill 30 minutes or until topping is set. **Yield:** 16 servings (serving size: 1 brownie).

YIELD: 16 servings

EXCHANGES PER SERVING:
1 1/2 Starch
1/2 Fat

PER SERVING:
Calories 141
(27% from fat)
Fat 4.3g
(saturated fat 1g)
Protein 1.2g
Carbohydrate 25g
Fiber 0.2g
Cholesterol 14mg
Sodium 75mg

**EXCHANGES PER
SERVING:**
1 Starch
1/2 Fat

PER SERVING:
Calories 90
(29% from fat)
Fat 2.9g
(saturated fat 0.6g)
Protein 2.1g
Carbohydrate 14.1g
Fiber 0.2g
Cholesterol 0mg
Sodium 86mg

FUDGY BROWNIES

1/2 cup unsweetened cocoa
1/2 cup sugar
1/3 cup all-purpose flour
1/2 teaspoon baking powder
1/2 teaspoon salt
1/2 cup apple butter
1/2 cup egg substitute
2 tablespoons vegetable oil
1 teaspoon vanilla extract
Cooking spray
2 tablespoons chopped walnuts

1. Preheat oven to 350°.

2. Combine first 5 ingredients in a medium bowl, stirring well. Combine apple butter and next 3 ingredients in a large bowl. Gradually add cocoa mixture to apple butter mixture, stirring with a wire whisk.

3. Pour batter into an 8-inch square pan coated with cooking spray; sprinkle evenly with chopped walnuts. Bake at 350° for 25 minutes or until a wooden pick inserted in center comes out clean. Cool completely on a wire rack. Cut into 16 squares. **Yield:** 16 servings (serving size: 1 brownie).

♥ *Chocolate, a favorite dessert ingredient, comes in many forms. Powdered unsweetened cocoa is much lower in fat than unsweetened, semisweet, and milk chocolate. You can cut the fat in your own recipes by substituting cocoa for unsweetened chocolate. The general guideline is to use 3 tablespoons cocoa plus 1 tablespoon oil or melted margarine for each ounce of unsweetened chocolate. You may omit the oil to reduce the fat even more.*

FUDGY-MINT BROWNIE BITES

1 (20.5-ounce) package low-fat fudge
    brownie mix
¹/₂ cup water
¹/₃ cup reduced-fat semisweet chocolate
    morsels
¹/₂ teaspoon peppermint extract
    Cooking spray

1. Preheat oven to 350°.

2. Combine brownie mix and water in a large bowl, stirring well. Stir in chocolate morsels and peppermint extract.

3. Spoon 1 tablespoon batter into each of 30 miniature muffin cups heavily coated with cooking spray. Bake at 350° for 16 minutes. Cool completely in pans. **Yield:** 2½ dozen (serving size: 1 brownie).

Fudgy-Mint Pan Brownies: Prepare batter as directed above; spoon into a 13 x 9–inch pan heavily coated with cooking spray. Bake at 350° for 25 to 27 minutes. Place on wire rack, and cool completely. **Yield:** 2½ dozen (serving size: 1 brownie).

YIELD: 30 servings

EXCHANGE PER SERVING:
1 Starch

PER SERVING:
Calories 89
(21% from fat)
Fat 2.1g
(saturated fat 0.9g)
Protein 1.2g
Carbohydrate 16.4g
Fiber 0.6g
Cholesterol 0mg
Sodium 72mg

CRANBERRY-CHOCOLATE CHIP BISCOTTI

YIELD: 30 servings

EXCHANGE PER SERVING:
1 Starch

PER SERVING:
Calories 98
(17% from fat)
Fat 1.8g
(saturated fat 0.7g)
Protein 2g
Carbohydrate 18.6g
Fiber 0.4g
Cholesterol 22mg
Sodium 50mg

2¾ cups all-purpose flour
1 cup sugar
½ cup dried cranberries
⅓ cup semisweet chocolate chips
2 teaspoons baking powder
⅛ teaspoon salt
1 tablespoon vegetable oil
1 teaspoon almond extract
1 teaspoon vanilla extract
3 large eggs
  Cooking spray

1. Preheat oven to 350°.

2. Lightly spoon flour into dry measuring cups, and level with a knife. Combine flour and next 5 ingredients in a large bowl. Combine oil, extracts, and eggs; add to flour mixture, stirring until well-blended (dough will be dry and crumbly).

3. Turn dough out onto a lightly floured surface; knead lightly 7 to 8 times. Divide the dough in half. Shape each portion into an 8-inch-long roll. Place rolls 6 inches apart on a baking sheet coated with cooking spray; flatten each roll to 1-inch thickness.

4. Bake at 350° for 35 minutes. Remove rolls from baking sheet; cool 10 minutes on a wire rack. Cut each roll diagonally into 15 (½-inch) slices. Place slices, cut sides down, on baking sheet.

5. Reduce oven temperature to 325°, and bake 10 minutes. Turn cookies over, and bake an additional 10 minutes (cookies will be slightly soft in center but will harden as they cool). Remove from baking sheet, and cool completely on wire rack. **Yield:** 2½ dozen (serving size: 1 biscotto).

Make Ahead
SNICKERDOODLE BISCOTTI

2³/₄ cups all-purpose flour
1 cup sugar
2 teaspoons baking powder
¹/₄ teaspoon salt
1 tablespoon vegetable oil
1 teaspoon vanilla extract
3 large eggs
Cooking spray
2 tablespoons sugar
1 teaspoon ground cinnamon
1 large egg white

1. Preheat oven to 350°.

2. Lightly spoon flour into dry measuring cups, and level with a knife. Combine flour, 1 cup sugar, baking powder, and salt in a large bowl. Combine oil, vanilla, and eggs; add to flour mixture, stirring until well-blended (dough will be dry and crumbly).

3. Turn dough out onto a lightly floured surface, and knead lightly 7 to 8 times. Divide the dough in half. Shape each portion into an 8-inch-long roll. Place rolls 6 inches apart on a baking sheet coated with cooking spray, and flatten each roll to 1-inch thickness. Combine 2 tablespoons sugar and cinnamon. Gently brush tops of rolls with egg white, and sprinkle with the cinnamon mixture.

4. Bake at 350° for 30 minutes. Remove rolls from baking sheet; cool 10 minutes on a wire rack. Cut each roll diagonally into 15 (½-inch) slices. Place slices, cut sides down, on baking sheet.

5. Reduce oven temperature to 325°; bake 10 minutes. Turn cookies over, and bake an additional 10 minutes (the cookies will be slightly soft in center but will harden as they cool). Remove from baking sheet; cool completely on wire rack. **Yield:** 2½ dozen (serving size: 1 biscotto).

YIELD: 30 servings

EXCHANGE PER SERVING:
1 Starch

PER SERVING:
Calories 84
(13% from fat)
Fat 1.2g
(saturated fat 0.3g)
Protein 1.9g
Carbohydrate 16.5g
Fiber 0.3g
Cholesterol 22mg
Sodium 61mg

YIELD: 30 servings

EXCHANGES PER SERVING:
1 Starch
1/2 Fat

PER SERVING:
Calories 87
(24% from fat)
Fat 2.3g
(saturated fat 0.7g)
Protein 1.1g
Carbohydrate 16.4g
Fiber 0.1g
Cholesterol 7.4mg
Sodium 113mg

Make Ahead
CARAMEL APPLE CHEWS

1 (18.25-ounce) package caramel cake mix (such as Duncan Hines)
1/2 (8-ounce) container frozen reduced-calorie whipped topping, thawed (about 1 1/2 cups)
1 1/2 cups peeled diced Golden Delicious apple (about 8 ounces)
1 large egg, lightly beaten
   Cooking spray

1. Combine first 4 ingredients in a large bowl; beat at medium speed of a heavy–duty stand mixer just until moistened. Chill batter 30 minutes.

2. Preheat oven to 350°.

3. Drop by level tablespoonfuls onto cookie sheets coated with cooking spray. Bake at 350° for 16 minutes or just until tops of cookies spring back when touched (do not overbake). Remove cookies from pan; let cool on wire racks. **Yield:** 2½ dozen (serving size: 1 cookie).

Crispy Caramel Apple Chews: Shape dough, 1 tablespoon at a time, into small balls. Roll balls in ⅓ cup low-fat cinnamon graham cracker crumbs (about 1½ cracker sheets). Bake at 350° for 16 minutes. Remove from pan, and let cool on wire racks. **Yield:** 2½ dozen (serving size: 1 cookie).

RAISIN-BRAN COOKIES

YIELD: 24 servings

EXCHANGE PER SERVING:
1 Starch

PER SERVING:
Calories 86
(23% from fat)
Fat 2.2g
(saturated fat 0.4g)
Protein 2.2g
Carbohydrate 15.1g
Fiber 0.9g
Cholesterol 0mg
Sodium 90mg

¼ cup stick margarine or butter, softened
⅓ cup sugar
2 tablespoons honey
¼ cup egg substitute
1 teaspoon vanilla extract
1 cup regular oats
¾ cup all-purpose flour
½ teaspoon baking powder
¼ teaspoon baking soda
¼ teaspoon salt
⅓ cup instant nonfat dry milk
¾ cup raisins
1¼ cups wheat bran flakes cereal
Cooking spray

1. Preheat oven to 350°.

2. Beat margarine, sugar, and honey in a large mixing bowl at medium-high speed of a mixer until creamy. Add egg substitute and vanilla, beating well.

3. Combine oats and next 5 ingredients; gradually add to creamed mixture, beating well. Stir in raisins and bran flakes.

4. Drop dough by rounded tablespoonfuls onto a baking sheet coated with cooking spray. Bake at 350° for 10 minutes or until golden. Transfer to a wire rack, and let cool completely. **Yield:** 2 dozen (serving size: 1 cookie).

**EXCHANGE PER
SERVING:**
½ Starch

PER SERVING:
Calories 47
(23% from fat)
Fat 1.2g
(saturated fat 0.2g)
Protein 0.6g
Carbohydrate 8.8g
Fiber 0.4g
Cholesterol 3mg
Sodium 31mg

Make Ahead
DATE SWIRL COOKIES

1 (8-ounce) package chopped dates
⅓ cup water
⅓ cup stick margarine or butter
¾ cup packed brown sugar
¼ cup apricot-flavored baby food
1 large egg
2 cups all-purpose flour
1 teaspoon baking powder
¾ teaspoon pumpkin pie spice
¼ teaspoon salt
   Cooking spray

1. Combine dates and water in a medium sauce-pan. Cook over medium heat, stirring constantly, 5 minutes or until thickened. Remove from heat, and cool.

2. Beat margarine at medium speed of a mixer until light and fluffy; add sugar, and beat well. Add baby food and egg; beat well.

3. Combine flour and next 3 ingredients; gradually add to margarine mixture. Shape dough into a ball. Place dough on a lightly floured surface, and roll into an 18 x 8-inch rectangle. Spread date mixture over dough, leaving a ½-inch margin on each side. Beginning at 1 long edge, roll up dough tightly, jelly-roll fashion; pinch seam to seal. Cut roll in half, and wrap rolls in wax paper; freeze 3 hours or chill 8 hours.

4. Preheat oven to 350°.

5. Unwrap rolls; cut each roll into 30 (⅜-inch) slices. Place slices on baking sheets coated with cooking spray. Bake at 350° for 13 minutes or just until lightly browned. **Yield:** 5 dozen (serving size: 1 cookie).

BRANDIED FRUITCAKE COOKIES

4 ounces red candied cherries, chopped
4 ounces green candied cherries, chopped
4 ounces candied pineapple, chopped
½ cup raisins
1½ cups all-purpose flour, divided
¼ teaspoon baking soda
1½ teaspoons apple pie spice
½ cup stick margarine or butter, softened
½ cup packed brown sugar
1 large egg
2 teaspoons vanilla extract
⅓ cup brandy
Cooking spray

1. Preheat oven to 325°.

2. Combine first 4 ingredients in a bowl; toss with ½ cup flour.

3. Combine remaining 1 cup flour, baking soda, and apple pie spice.

4. Beat margarine at medium speed of a mixer until creamy; gradually add sugar, beating well. Add egg, mixing well. Stir in vanilla and brandy. Add flour mixture to margarine mixture, mixing just until blended; stir in fruit mixture.

5. Drop dough by level tablespoonfuls onto baking sheets coated with cooking spray. Flatten cookies slightly with back of a spoon. Bake at 325° for 12 to 14 minutes or until golden. Remove from oven; let stand 2 to 3 minutes or until firm. Remove cookies from pan; let cool on wire racks. **Yield:** 3 dozen (serving size: 1 cookie).

YIELD: 36 servings

EXCHANGES PER SERVING:
1 Starch
½ Fat

PER SERVING:
Calories 95
(27% from fat)
Fat 2.8g
(saturated fat 0.5g)
Protein 1g
Carbohydrate 16.8g
Fiber 0.3g
Cholesterol 6mg
Sodium 49mg

YIELD: 24 servings

**EXCHANGE PER
SERVING:**
½ Starch

PER SERVING:
Calories 44
(12% from fat)
Fat 0.6g
(saturated fat 0.4g)
Protein 0.6g
Carbohydrate 9.4g
Fiber 0g
Cholesterol 0mg
Sodium 32mg

CHOCOLATE-CHIP MERINGUE COOKIES

3 large egg whites
¼ teaspoon cream of tartar
¼ teaspoon salt
1 cup sugar
3 tablespoons unsweetened cocoa
3 tablespoons semisweet chocolate minichips

1. Preheat oven to 300°.

2. Beat egg whites, cream of tartar, and salt at high speed of a mixer until soft peaks form. Add sugar, 1 tablespoon at a time, beating until stiff peaks form. Sift cocoa over egg white mixture; fold in. Fold in minichips.

3. Cover a baking sheet with parchment paper; secure to baking sheet with masking tape. Drop batter by level tablespoonfuls onto prepared baking sheet. Bake at 300° for 40 minutes or until crisp. Cool on pan on a wire rack. Repeat procedure with remaining batter, reusing parchment paper. Store in an airtight container. **Yield:** 4 dozen (serving size: 2 cookies).

OATMEAL-RAISIN COOKIES

If you bake cookies often, invest in sturdy, shiny aluminum baking sheets, large wire cooling racks, and a good metal spatula.

3/4 cup sugar
1/4 cup packed brown sugar
1/3 cup stick margarine or butter, softened
1/4 cup apple butter
1/4 cup egg substitute
1/2 teaspoon vanilla extract
1/2 teaspoon ground cinnamon
1/2 teaspoon baking soda
1 1/2 cups quick-cooking oats
1 cup all-purpose flour
1/2 cup raisins
   Cooking spray

1. Preheat oven to 375°.

2. Beat first 3 ingredients in a large bowl at medium speed of an electric mixer until blended. Add apple butter and next 4 ingredients; beating well. Stir in oats, flour, and raisins.

3. Drop dough by rounded tablespoonfuls onto baking sheets coated with cooking spray. Bake at 375° for 9 minutes or until lightly browned. Cool 1 minute on baking sheets. Remove cookies from baking sheets, and let cool completely on wire racks. **Yield:** 34 servings (serving size: 1 cookie).

YIELD: 34 servings

EXCHANGE PER SERVING:
1 Starch

PER SERVING:
Calories 78
(24% from fat)
Fat 2.1g
(saturated fat 0.4g)
Protein 1.2g
Carbohydrate 14.1g
Fiber 0.6g
Cholesterol 0mg
Sodium 43mg

**EXCHANGES PER
SERVING:**
1 Starch
¹/₂ Fat

PER SERVING:
Calories 105
(27% from fat)
Fat 3.1g
(saturated fat 0.4g)
Protein 1.6g
Carbohydrate 18g
Fiber 0.4g
Cholesterol 9mg
Sodium 82mg

Make Ahead
PEANUT BUTTER-AND-JELLY COOKIES

*Natural peanut butter (made from ground peanuts with
no added sugar) is the best choice for these
thumbprint-style cookies.*

¹/₂ cup packed brown sugar
¹/₄ cup natural creamy peanut butter (such as
  Smucker's)
¹/₄ cup dark corn syrup
 3 tablespoons stick margarine or butter,
  softened
 1 large egg
 2 teaspoons vanilla extract
1¹/₃ cups all-purpose flour
 2 tablespoons cornstarch
¹/₂ teaspoon baking powder
¹/₄ teaspoon baking soda
¹/₄ teaspoon salt
¹/₄ cup granulated sugar
  Cooking spray
¹/₄ cup grape or other flavored jelly or jam

1. Beat first 4 ingredients at medium speed of a
mixer until well-blended. Add egg; beat well. Beat
in vanilla. Lightly spoon flour into dry measuring
cups; level with a knife. Combine flour and next 4
ingredients, stirring well with a whisk. Add flour
mixture to sugar mixture; beat well. Cover; freeze
30 minutes or until firm.

2. Preheat oven to 375°.

3. Shape dough into 24 balls; roll in granulated
sugar. Place 1 inch apart on baking sheets coated
with cooking spray. Press thumb into center of
each cookie, leaving an indentation. Spoon about
¹/₂ teaspoon jelly into center of each cookie. Bake
at 375° for 12 minutes or until lightly browned.
Cool 2 minutes on pans. Remove from pans, and
cool completely on wire racks. **Yield:** 2 dozen
(serving size: 1 cookie).

fish & shellfish

**EXCHANGES PER
SERVING:**
3 Very Lean Meat
1 Vegetable

PER SERVING:
Calories 142
(20% from fat)
Fat 3.2g
(saturated fat 0.8g)
Protein 24.6g
Carbohydrate 3.4g
Fiber 0.9g
Cholesterol 49mg
Sodium 95mg

SEASONED FISH AND TOMATOES

6 (4-ounce) amberjack fillets
1 teaspoon dried oregano
1/2 teaspoon cracked pepper
6 plum tomatoes, cut into 1/4-inch-thick slices
  Cooking spray
3/4 cup dry white wine
2 tablespoons sliced ripe olives
  Fresh oregano sprigs (optional)
  Whole peppercorns (optional)

1. Preheat oven to 350°.

2. Sprinkle fillets with oregano and cracked pepper. Place fillets and tomato in a 13 x 9-inch baking dish coated with cooking spray. Add wine. Bake, uncovered, at 350° for 15 minutes or until fish flakes easily when tested with a fork.

3. To serve, place tomato slices evenly on individual serving plates, using a slotted spoon. Top each serving with a fillet and 1 teaspoon olives. If desired, garnish each serving with a fresh oregano sprig and whole peppercorns. **Yield:** 6 servings.

♥ *Fish is a vitamin-rich source of low-fat protein, making it a perfect choice for heart-healthy eating. When you buy fish, choose what's freshest and cook it that day or the next. The fish's flesh should appear firm and unblemished. And it should not have a "fishy" smell.*

Super Quick
BLACKENED AMBERJACK

1 (1-pound) amberjack fillet
1 tablespoon paprika
2 teaspoons onion powder
2 teaspoons garlic powder
1 teaspoon dried thyme
1 teaspoon dried oregano
1 teaspoon black pepper
1/2 teaspoon ground red pepper
   Cooking spray

1. Cut fillet into 4 equal pieces. Combine paprika and next 6 ingredients in a small bowl; stir well. Dredge fish in spice mixture; let stand 5 minutes.

2. Coat a large cast-iron skillet with cooking spray; place over high heat until very hot. Add fish, and cook 3 minutes. Turn fish, and cook 3 to 4 additional minutes or until fish flakes easily when tested with a fork. Fish should look charred. (You may prefer to do this procedure outside due to the small amount of smoke that is created.) **Yield:** 4 servings.

YIELD: 4 servings

EXCHANGES PER SERVING:
4 Very Lean Meat
1 Fat

PER SERVING:
Calories 182
(30% from fat)
Fat 6g
(saturated fat 1.5g)
Protein 27.2g
Carbohydrate 3.8g
Fiber 1.2g
Cholesterol 43mg
Sodium 46mg

LIME-MARINATED GRILLED SEA BASS

If you can't find sea bass, substitute grouper since they're from the same family. Grouper fillets are not as thick, though, so you'll need to cut the grilling time.

$^1/_4$ cup dry vermouth or dry white wine
2 tablespoons fresh lime juice
2 tablespoons minced fresh cilantro
1 tablespoon low-sodium soy sauce
2 teaspoons olive oil
4 (4-ounce) sea bass fillets (1 inch thick)
Cooking spray

1. Combine first 5 ingredients in a heavy-duty zip-top plastic bag; add fish fillets. Seal bag securely, and shake gently to coat fillets. Marinate in refrigerator 30 minutes.

2. Prepare grill.

3. Coat grill rack with cooking spray; place on grill over hot coals (400° to 500°). Remove fish from marinade, reserving marinade. Place fish fillets on rack; grill, covered, 4 to 5 minutes on each side or until fish flakes easily when tested with a fork.

4. Place reserved marinade in a small saucepan, and bring to a boil; remove from heat. To serve, spoon hot marinade over fish. **Yield:** 4 servings.

KOREAN-STYLE STRIPED BASS

*Striped bass is a mild, firm fish from the Atlantic coast.
It is also sold in fish markets as striper, greenhead, or
squidhound. It cooks best under the broiler because
fillets are usually cut thin and fall apart easily.*

1/4 cup low-sodium soy sauce
1 tablespoon brown sugar
1 tablespoon dry sherry
1 tablespoon rice vinegar
2 teaspoons grated peeled fresh ginger
1 teaspoon sesame seeds, toasted
1 teaspoon dark sesame oil
1/2 teaspoon chile paste with garlic
1 garlic clove, minced
4 (6-ounce) striped bass fillets
  Cooking spray

1. Combine all ingredients except cooking spray in
a large zip-top plastic bag. Seal bag, and marinate in
refrigerator 20 minutes. Remove fish from bag; discard marinade.

2. Preheat broiler.

3. Place fillets on a broiler pan coated with cooking
spray. Broil 4 minutes or until fish flakes easily when
tested with a fork. **Yield:** 4 servings.

YIELD: 4 servings

**EXCHANGES PER
SERVING:**
5 Very Lean Meat
1/2 Fat

PER SERVING:
Calories 213
(30% from fat)
Fat 7.2g
(saturated fat 1.4g)
Protein 32.6g
Carbohydrate 2.2g
Fiber 0g
Cholesterol 116mg
Sodium 366mg

OVEN-FRIED CATFISH

*The crispy oven-fried crust comes from baking the
crumb-coated fillets at a high temperature. Creole
seasoning gives the crunchy crust its great flavor.*

    1 cup plus 2 tablespoons crushed corn flakes
       cereal
 1 ¹/₂ teaspoons salt-free Creole seasoning
    ¹/₈ teaspoon salt
    ¹/₄ cup fat-free mayonnaise
    1 tablespoon lemon juice
    ¹/₂ teaspoon hot sauce
    8 (4-ounce) farm-raised catfish fillets
       Cooking spray
    8 lemon wedges

1. Preheat oven to 450°.

2. Combine first 3 ingredients in a small bowl,
stirring well; set aside. Combine mayonnaise,
lemon juice, and hot sauce, stirring well.

3. Brush mayonnaise mixture evenly over both
sides of fillets; dredge in cereal mixture. Place fillets
on rack of a broiler pan coated with cooking spray.
Bake at 450° for 18 minutes or until fish flakes easily when tested with a fork. Serve with lemon
wedges. **Yield:** 8 servings.

CRISPY PAN-FRIED CATFISH

A fish's texture determines how it should be prepared. Dense, sturdy fish, such as amberjack, can be cooked almost any way, while softer-textured fish, such as catfish and red snapper, should be baked or sautéed—they tend to fall apart when grilled or steamed.

1 large egg white, lightly beaten
1 tablespoon water
1/4 cup yellow cornmeal
2 tablespoons grated Parmesan cheese
1 tablespoon chopped fresh thyme
1/4 teaspoon pepper
4 (4-ounce) farm-raised catfish fillets
3 tablespoons all-purpose flour
  Cooking spray
  Lemon wedges (optional)

1. Combine egg white and water; stir well, and set aside. Combine cornmeal and next 3 ingredients. Dredge fillets in flour; dip in egg white mixture, and dredge in cornmeal mixture.

2. Coat a large nonstick skillet with cooking spray, and place over medium-high heat until hot. Add fillets, and cook 3 minutes on each side or until fish flakes easily when tested with a fork. Transfer to a serving platter; garnish with lemon wedges, if desired. **Yield:** 4 servings.

YIELD: 4 servings

EXCHANGES PER SERVING:
3 Very Lean Meat
1 Starch
1/2 Fat

PER SERVING:
Calories 202
(27% from fat)
Fat 6g
(saturated fat 1.6g)
Protein 23.9g
Carbohydrate 11.5g
Fiber 0g
Cholesterol 68mg
Sodium 132mg

EXCHANGES PER
SERVING:
3 Lean Meat

PER SERVING:
Calories 151
(36% from fat)
Fat 6.1g
(saturated fat 1.3g)
Protein 21.1g
Carbohydrate 1.9g
Fiber 0.4g
Cholesterol 66mg
Sodium 223mg

BAKED CATFISH IN FOIL PACKETS

*You can substitute flounder, orange roughy, sole, perch, or
grouper for catfish in this recipe.*

1 tablespoon reduced-sodium soy sauce
1 teaspoon ground ginger
1 teaspoon sesame oil
4 (4-ounce) catfish fillets
1/4 cup sliced green onions (about 2 large)
1/2 cup chopped red bell pepper (about
    1/2 medium)
1/2 cup peeled, finely chopped cucumber
    (about 1/2 small)

1. Preheat oven to 450°.

2. Combine soy sauce, ginger, and sesame oil, stir-ring well.

3. Cut 4 (12-inch) squares of aluminum foil; place a fish fillet in center of each square. Spoon green onions, bell pepper, and cucumber evenly over each fillet. Spoon soy sauce mixture evenly over vegetables. Fold foil over fillets to make packets, and seal edges tightly.

4. Place fish packets on a baking sheet; bake at 450° for 12 minutes. **Yield:** 4 servings.

CATFISH NUGGETS WITH TARTAR SAUCE

1 large egg white
2 teaspoons water
$1/2$ cup fine, dry breadcrumbs
$1/4$ teaspoon ground red pepper
12 ounces farm-raised catfish, cut into 2-inch
  pieces
  Butter-flavored cooking spray
2 teaspoons margarine or butter, melted
$1/4$ cup fat-free mayonnaise
2 teaspoons sweet pickle relish
2 teaspoons fresh lemon juice
1 teaspoon Dijon mustard
  Lemon wedges (optional)

1. Preheat oven to 450°.

2. Combine egg white and water in a small bowl; beat well with a wire whisk. Combine breadcrumbs and pepper in a shallow dish. Dip fish pieces into egg white mixture, letting excess drip off. Roll fish pieces in breadcrumb mixture to coat.

3. Place fish on a baking sheet coated with cooking spray. Coat fish with cooking spray. Drizzle evenly with margarine. Bake at 450° for 12 to 14 minutes or until fish flakes easily when tested with a fork.

4. Combine mayonnaise and next 3 ingredients; stir mixture well. Serve fish with tartar sauce and, if desired, lemon wedges. **Yield:** 4 servings.

YIELD: 4 servings

EXCHANGES PER SERVING:
2 Lean Meat
$1/2$ Starch

PER SERVING:
Calories 166
(34% from fat)
Fat 6.2g
(saturated fat 1.3g)
Protein 17.2g
Carbohydrate 9.3g
Fiber 0.3g
Cholesterol 49mg
Sodium 395mg

FLOUNDER IN ORANGE SAUCE

YIELD: 4 servings

EXCHANGES PER SERVING:
3 Very Lean Meat

PER SERVING:
Calories 117
(12% from fat)
Fat 1.5g
(saturated fat 0.3g)
Protein 21.8g
Carbohydrate 2.9g
Fiber 0.3g
Cholesterol 54mg
Sodium 98mg

Keep this recipe quick by slicing the green onions with kitchen scissors. Just hold a bunch of onions together and snip them over a measuring cup to save cleanup.

⅓ cup low-sugar orange marmalade
2 tablespoons orange juice
¼ teaspoon ground ginger
⅓ cup sliced green onions (about 3 medium)
4 (4-ounce) flounder fillets (or orange roughy, cod, or perch)
Cooking spray

1. Preheat oven to 400°.

2. Combine first 3 ingredients in a small saucepan. Cook over medium heat until marmalade melts, stirring often. Remove from heat, and stir in green onions.

3. Place fillets in a 13 x 9-inch baking dish coated with cooking spray. Spoon orange marmalade mixture evenly over fillets. Bake at 400° for 10 minutes or until fish flakes easily when tested with a fork. **Yield:** 4 servings.

Super Quick
FLOUNDER WITH PIMIENTO

Serve with angel hair pasta, steamed snow peas, and dinner rolls.

1 small lemon
1 (2-ounce) jar diced pimiento, drained
4 (4-ounce) flounder fillets (or orange roughy, cod, or perch)
   Butter-flavored cooking spray
1 teaspoon extra-spicy salt-free herb-and-spice blend (such as Mrs. Dash)
   Fresh oregano sprigs (optional)

1. Preheat oven to 425°.

2. Cut lemon in half. Squeeze juice from half of lemon (about 1 tablespoon) into a small bowl; set remaining lemon half aside. Add pimiento to lemon juice, mixing well; set aside.

3. Place flounder in an 11 x 7-inch baking dish coated with cooking spray. Coat fish with cooking spray; sprinkle with herb-and-spice blend.

4. Spoon pimiento mixture evenly over fish. Bake, uncovered, at 425° for 12 minutes or until fish flakes easily when tested with a fork. While fish bakes, cut remaining lemon half into slices to serve with fish. Garnish with oregano sprigs, if desired.
Yield: 4 servings.

YIELD: 4 servings

EXCHANGES PER SERVING:
3 Very Lean Meat

PER SERVING:
Calories 108
(13% from fat)
Fat 1.5g
(saturated fat 0.3g)
Protein 21.5g
Carbohydrate 1.6g
Fiber 0g
Cholesterol 54mg
Sodium 93mg

EXCHANGES PER SERVING:
3 Very Lean Meat
1 Vegetable

PER SERVING:
Calories 134
(18% from fat)
Fat 2.7g
(saturated fat 0.3g)
Protein 21.9g
Carbohydrate 3.3g
Fiber 0.7g
Cholesterol 54mg
Sodium 113mg

FLOUNDER WITH PEPPERS AND GREEN ONIONS

2 teaspoons reduced-calorie margarine
1/3 cup sliced green onions
1 teaspoon bottled minced garlic
1 small red bell pepper, cut into thin strips
1 pound flounder fillets, cut into 4 pieces
3 tablespoons dry white wine
1/2 teaspoon grated lime rind
2 tablespoons fresh lime juice

1. Melt margarine in a large nonstick skillet over medium–high heat. Add green onions, garlic, and pepper strips; cook 2 minutes, stirring often.

2. Add fish, and cook 2 minutes on each side. Sprinkle wine, lime rind, and lime juice over fish. Cover, reduce heat, and simmer 3 minutes or until fish flakes easily when tested with a fork. Carefully remove fish to a serving platter; top with pepper mixture. **Yield:** 4 servings.

FLOUNDER IN FOIL POUCHES

4 green onions, cut into 1-inch pieces
2 medium carrots, scraped and cut into thin strips
1 tablespoon fresh lemon juice
1 teaspoon olive oil
¼ teaspoon paprika
Cooking spray
4 (4-ounce) flounder fillets
¼ teaspoon salt
4 thin slices lemon

1. Preheat oven to 400°.

2. Place green onions and carrot strips in a 2-cup glass measuring cup; cover with heavy-duty plastic wrap, and microwave at HIGH 3 minutes. Drain and set aside.

3. Combine lemon juice, olive oil, and paprika in a small bowl; stir well.

4. Cut 4 (15-inch) squares of aluminum foil. Place foil on a large baking sheet. Lightly coat squares with cooking spray. Place a fillet in center of each square; top fillets evenly with green onion mixture. Spoon lemon juice mixture evenly over fillets and green onion mixture; sprinkle with salt. Top each serving with a lemon slice. Fold foil over fillets and vegetables, and crimp edges to seal. Bake at 400° for 8 minutes. Transfer pouches to individual serving plates; cut an X in top of each pouch, and fold cut edges back. **Yield:** 4 servings.

YIELD: 4 servings

EXCHANGES PER SERVING:
3 Very Lean Meat
1 Vegetable

PER SERVING:
Calories 138
(18% from fat)
Fat 2.7g
(saturated fat 0.5g)
Protein 22.2g
Carbohydrate 5.6g
Fiber 1.7g
Cholesterol 54mg
Sodium 254mg

**EXCHANGES PER
SERVING:**
3 Very Lean Meat
1 Fruit

PER SERVING:
Calories 161
(8% from fat)
Fat 1.4g
(saturated fat 0.3g)
Protein 22.4g
Carbohydrate 14.1g
Fiber 0.2g
Cholesterol 42mg
Sodium 50mg

Super Quick
GROUPER WITH HONEY CITRUS GLAZE

3 tablespoons orange juice concentrate,
   thawed
2 tablespoons honey
1 teaspoon dried basil
¼ teaspoon garlic powder
6 dashes of hot sauce
4 (4-ounce) grouper fillets (or red snapper or
   halibut)
   Cooking spray
   Orange rind strips (optional)

1. Prepare grill.

2. Combine first 5 ingredients, stirring well.

3. Arrange fillets in a single layer in a grill basket coated with cooking spray. Grill, covered, over medium–hot coals (350° to 400°) for 5 minutes on each side or until fish flakes easily when tested with a fork, basting occasionally with orange juice mixture. Transfer fillets to a serving platter. Garnish with orange rind, if desired. **Yield:** 4 servings.

Note: To broil instead of grill, place fish on a broiler pan coated with cooking spray. Broil 5½ inches from heat 5 minutes on each side. Baste fish occasionally with orange juice mixture.

Make Ahead
GRILLED GROUPER WITH
PINEAPPLE SALSA

*Serve with steamed Sugar Snap peas and
warm whole wheat rolls.*

1 (15-ounce) can pineapple tidbits in juice,
    drained
1 small red bell pepper, finely chopped
    (about ½ cup)
2 tablespoons chopped fresh mint or parsley
1 tablespoon lime juice
2 teaspoons finely chopped fresh jalapeño
    pepper
1 teaspoon grated peeled fresh ginger or
    ¼ teaspoon ground ginger
½ teaspoon salt, divided
¼ teaspoon black pepper
4 (4-ounce) grouper fillets
    Cooking spray

1. Combine first 6 ingredients in a small bowl; stir
in ¼ teaspoon salt. Cover and set aside; chill
overnight, if desired.

2. Prepare grill.

3. Sprinkle remaining ¼ teaspoon salt and ¼
teaspoon black pepper over fish; coat lightly with
cooking spray.

4. Coat grill rack with cooking spray; place on grill
over medium–hot coals (350° to 400°). Arrange fish
on rack or in a grill basket coated with cooking
spray; grill, uncovered, 5 minutes on each side or
until fish flakes easily when tested with a fork. Remove fish from grill; top with pineapple mixture.
Yield: 4 servings.

YIELD: 4 servings

**EXCHANGES PER
SERVING:**
3 Very Lean Meat
1 Fruit

PER SERVING:
Calories 155
(8% from fat)
Fat 1.4g
(saturated fat 0.3g)
Protein 22.2g
Carbohydrate 12.1g
Fiber 1.4g
Cholesterol 42mg
Sodium 341mg

EXCHANGES PER SERVING:
3 Very Lean Meat
1 Fruit

PER SERVING:
Calories 159
(9% from fat)
Fat 1.6g
(saturated fat 0.3g)
Protein 22.7g
Carbohydrate 13.5g
Fiber 1.6g
Cholesterol 42mg
Sodium 343mg

GROUPER À LA MANGO

Mango, red bell pepper, onion, cilantro, and lime juice make a colorful, tropical-tasting salsa that's good with fish or grilled chicken. Serve the salsa at room temperature or chilled.

1½ cups finely chopped fresh mango (about 2 mangoes)
½ cup finely chopped red bell pepper
⅓ cup finely chopped red onion
¼ cup chopped fresh cilantro
2 tablespoons fresh lime juice
½ teaspoon salt, divided
4 (4-ounce) grouper fillets
¼ teaspoon ground red pepper
Cooking spray
Fresh cilantro sprigs (optional)

1. Combine mango, bell pepper, onion, chopped cilantro, lime juice, and ¼ teaspoon salt in a small bowl; toss well to combine. Set aside or chill, if desired.

2. Preheat oven to 425°.

3. Sprinkle fillets evenly with remaining ¼ teaspoon salt and ground red pepper; arrange in an 11 x 7-inch baking dish coated with cooking spray. Bake at 425° for 20 minutes or until fish flakes easily when tested with a fork. Serve with mango salsa. Garnish with cilantro sprigs, if desired. **Yield:** 4 servings (serving size: 1 fillet and ½ cup salsa).

GROUPER WITH CHARMOULA

*Charmoula is a Moroccan herb paste used
primarily as a marinade for fish.*

1/2 cup chopped fresh cilantro
1/2 cup chopped fresh parsley
3 garlic cloves, peeled
1/4 cup fresh lemon juice
1 tablespoon olive oil
3/4 teaspoon ground cumin
1/4 teaspoon salt
1/4 teaspoon ground red pepper
1/4 teaspoon paprika
1/8 teaspoon ground cinnamon
4 (6-ounce) grouper or other white fish fillets
   (1 inch thick)
   Cooking spray
4 cups hot cooked couscous (cooked without
   salt or fat)

1. Combine first 3 ingredients in a food processor;
process until chopped. Add juice and next 6 ingredients; process until smooth. Arrange fish in a single
layer in a shallow dish; spread cilantro mixture
evenly over both sides of fish. Cover and marinate
in refrigerator 30 minutes. Remove fish from dish;
discard marinade.

2. Preheat broiler.

3. Place fish on a broiler pan coated with cooking
spray; broil 7 minutes or until fish flakes easily when
tested with a fork. Serve with couscous. **Yield:** 4
servings (serving size: 1 fillet and 1 cup couscous).

YIELD: 4 servings

**EXCHANGES PER
SERVING:**
4 Very Lean Meat
3 Starch

PER SERVING:
Calories 371
(10% from fat)
Fat 4.3g
(saturated fat 0.7g)
Protein 40.3g
Carbohydrate 41.7g
Fiber 2.4g
Cholesterol 63mg
Sodium 171mg

EXCHANGES PER SERVING:
3 Very Lean Meat
1 Vegetable

PER SERVING:
Calories 145
(23% from fat)
Fat 3.7g
(saturated fat 0.5g)
Protein 24.2g
Carbohydrate 3g
Fiber 0.9g
Cholesterol 36mg
Sodium 251mg

HALIBUT PROVENÇALE

You can pit kalamata olives quickly by pressing the olives with the side of a chef's knife.

 1 cup chopped plum tomato (about 4 plum tomatoes)
 2 tablespoons pitted, coarsely chopped kalamata olives or sliced ripe olives
 2 tablespoons chopped fresh basil or parsley
 1 garlic clove, minced
 1/4 teaspoon seasoned salt
 1/4 teaspoon pepper
 4 (4-ounce) halibut steaks
    Olive oil-flavored cooking spray

1. Prepare grill.

2. Combine first 4 ingredients; set aside.

3. Sprinkle salt and pepper over both sides of fish; coat with cooking spray. Arrange fish in a grill basket coated with cooking spray.

4. Place on grill over medium–hot coals (350° to 400°); grill, covered, 5 to 6 minutes on each side or until fish flakes easily when tested with a fork. Top fish with tomato mixture. **Yield:** 4 servings.

GRILLED MAHIMAHI WITH TOMATO VINAIGRETTE

This tangy-sweet tomato vinaigrette tastes just as good served with other firm white fish fillets. You can use red wine vinegar instead of balsamic, but balsamic vinegar has a distinctive mellow flavor that makes it worth keeping on your pantry shelf.

6   medium tomatoes, sliced
    Olive oil-flavored cooking spray
2   tablespoons balsamic vinegar
1   tablespoon olive oil
½   teaspoon sugar
¼   teaspoon black pepper
1   tablespoon capers, drained
6   (4-ounce) mahimahi fillets (½ inch thick)

1. Preheat broiler.

2. Arrange tomato slices on a large baking sheet. Coat slices with cooking spray, and broil 3 inches from heat 6 to 8 minutes or until browned.

3. Position knife blade in food processor bowl; add tomato, vinegar, and next 3 ingredients. Process until smooth, stopping once to scrape down sides. Add capers, and set aside.

4. Prepare grill.

5. Coat grill rack with cooking spray. Place on grill over medium-hot coals (350° to 400°). Place fillets on rack; grill, covered, 4 to 5 minutes on each side or until fish flakes easily when tested with a fork. Transfer fillets to a serving platter; top evenly with vinaigrette. **Yield:** 6 servings (serving size: 1 fillet and ¼ cup vinaigrette).

YIELD: 6 servings

EXCHANGES PER SERVING:
3 Very Lean Meat
1 Vegetable

PER SERVING:
Calories 139
(23% from fat)
Fat 3.5g
(saturated fat 0.6g)
Protein 21.8g
Carbohydrate 4.7g
Fiber 1.2g
Cholesterol 83mg
Sodium 220mg

EXCHANGES PER SERVING:
3 Very Lean Meat

PER SERVING:
Calories 102
(10% from fat)
Fat 1.1g
(saturated fat 0g)
Protein 17.2g
Carbohydrate 3.3g
Fiber 0.2g
Cholesterol 23mg
Sodium 223mg

Super Quick
WINE-BAKED ORANGE ROUGHY

To determine if fish is done, prick the thickest part with a fork. The fish will fall apart in flakes and the juices will be milky white if the fish is done.

4 (4-ounce) orange roughy fillets (or flounder or sole)
Cooking spray
¼ teaspoon salt
¼ teaspoon black pepper
⅛ teaspoon garlic powder
¼ cup sliced green onions (about 2 large)
1 (2-ounce) jar diced pimiento, drained
¼ cup lemon juice
¼ cup dry white wine

1. Preheat oven to 400°.

2. Place fillets in an 11 x 7-inch baking dish coated with cooking spray; sprinkle fillets evenly with salt, pepper, garlic powder, green onions, and pimiento. Pour lemon juice and wine over fish.

3. Cover and bake at 400° for 10 minutes or until fish flakes easily when tested with a fork. Serve with a slotted spatula. **Yield:** 4 servings.

NEWPORT ORANGE ROUGHY

6 (4-ounce) orange roughy fillets
   Cooking spray
2 tablespoons lemon juice
1 tablespoon reduced-calorie margarine,
   melted
2 teaspoons salt-free garlic and herb
   seasoning (such as Mrs. Dash)
1 (2-ounce) jar diced pimiento, drained
2 tablespoons sliced almonds

1. Preheat broiler.

2. Arrange fish in a single layer on rack of a broiler pan coated with cooking spray. Combine lemon juice and next 3 ingredients in a small bowl. Drizzle evenly over fish.

3. Broil fish 5½ inches from heat 12 minutes or until fish flakes easily when tested with a fork. Sprinkle fish with almonds the last minute of broiling. **Yield:** 6 servings.

YIELD: 6 servings

EXCHANGES PER SERVING:
3 Very Lean Meat

PER SERVING:
Calories 107
(29% from fat)
Fat 3.4g
(saturated fat 0.1g)
Protein 17.3g
Carbohydrate 2.6g
Fiber 0.3g
Cholesterol 23mg
Sodium 91mg

**EXCHANGES PER
SERVING:**
5 Very Lean Meat

PER SERVING:
Calories 180
(19% from fat)
Fat 3.7g
(saturated fat 0.5g)
Protein 33.2g
Carbohydrate 1.4g
Fiber 0.1g
Cholesterol 121mg
Sodium 292mg

LEMON-DILL POLLOCK

*Pollock (POL-uhk) is a delicately flavored, firm white
fish that is a cousin to the cod. It's often used to make the
imitation shellfish look-alike called surimi.*

¹/₃	cup minced fresh dill
¹/₄	cup fresh lemon juice
1	tablespoon olive oil
4	teaspoons Dijon mustard
¹/₄	teaspoon salt
¹/₄	teaspoon sugar
¹/₄	teaspoon black pepper
1	garlic clove, minced
4	(6-ounce) pollock or other firm white fish fillets
	Cooking spray

1. Combine all ingredients except cooking spray
in a large zip-top plastic bag; seal and marinate in
refrigerator 20 minutes. Remove fish from bag; discard marinade.

2. Prepare grill or broiler.

3. Place fish on a grill rack or broiler pan coated
with cooking spray. Cook for 4 minutes on each
side or until fish flakes easily when tested with a
fork. **Yield:** 4 servings.

WINE-POACHED SALMON

1 cup fat-free, less-sodium chicken broth
¼ cup dry white wine
1 cup slivered onion (about 1 small)
2 teaspoons dried dill or 2 tablespoons
    chopped fresh dill
4 (4-ounce) skinless salmon fillets
½ cup fat-free sour cream
¼ cup chopped cucumber (about ½ small)
1 teaspoon dried dill or 1 tablespoon chopped
    fresh dill

1. Bring first 4 ingredients to a boil in a large skillet. Reduce heat to medium-low, and add fish; cover and simmer 7 minutes or until fish is firm when touched in center. Remove from heat; cover and let stand 3 minutes.

2. While fish cooks, combine sour cream, cucumber, and 1 teaspoon dried dill in a small bowl. Remove salmon and onion from poaching liquid, using a slotted spoon; top with sour cream mixture.
Yield: 4 servings.

YIELD: 4 servings

EXCHANGES PER SERVING:
3½ Lean Meat

PER SERVING:
Calories 204
(43% from fat)
Fat 9.7g
(saturated fat 1.7g)
Protein 25.3g
Carbohydrate 1.4g
Fiber 0.1g
Cholesterol 77mg
Sodium 69mg

**EXCHANGES PER
SERVING:**
5 Lean Meat
¹/₂ Starch

PER SERVING:
Calories 316
(41% from fat)
Fat 14.4g
(saturated fat 2.5g)
Protein 35g
Carbohydrate 9.3g
Fiber 0.1g
Cholesterol 111mg
Sodium 184mg

MAPLE-GLAZED SALMON

*Hoisin sauce and five-spice powder can be found in the
Asian-food sections of large supermarkets.*

2	tablespoons maple syrup
1¹/₂	tablespoons apple juice
1¹/₂	tablespoons fresh lemon juice
2	teaspoons hoisin sauce
1¹/₂	teaspoons grated peeled fresh ginger
1¹/₂	teaspoons country-style Dijon mustard
¹/₄	teaspoon five-spice powder
4	(6-ounce) salmon fillets (about 1 inch thick)
	Cooking spray

1. Preheat broiler.

2. Combine first 7 ingredients in a large zip-top
plastic bag. Add salmon to bag; seal. Marinate in
refrigerator 15 minutes.

3. Remove salmon from bag, reserving marinade.
Place salmon fillets, skin sides down, on a broiler
rack coated with cooking spray. Broil 12 minutes
or until fish flakes easily when tested with a fork,
and baste salmon occasionally with reserved marinade. **Yield:** 4 servings.

BROILED SALMON WITH HONEY AND VERMOUTH

Leave the skin on the salmon while it cooks, then remove it to serve.

2 tablespoons honey
2 tablespoons dry vermouth or white wine
1½ teaspoons grated peeled fresh ginger
1½ teaspoons country-style Dijon mustard
⅛ teaspoon salt
⅛ teaspoon black pepper
2 (6-ounce) salmon fillets (about 1 inch thick)
   Cooking spray

1. Preheat broiler.

2. Combine first 6 ingredients in a small bowl; stir with a whisk. Place salmon on a broiler pan coated with cooking spray; brush with half of honey mixture. Broil 8 minutes or until fish flakes easily when tested with a fork, basting frequently with remaining honey mixture. **Yield:** 2 servings.

♥ *One reason that salmon tastes so good is that it is relatively high in fat. Fortunately, the types of fat in salmon are monounsaturated and polyunsaturated—those don't raise unhealthy blood cholesterol levels. Keep your total fat percentage low by serving salmon with low-fat side dishes such as rice or potatoes.*

YIELD: 2 servings

EXCHANGES PER SERVING:
5 Lean Meat
1 Starch

PER SERVING:
Calories 366
(36% from fat)
Fat 14.6g
(saturated fat 2.5g)
Protein 35g
Carbohydrate 18.8g
Fiber 0.1g
Cholesterol 111mg
Sodium 346mg

YIELD: 5 servings

EXCHANGES PER
SERVING:
5 Lean Meat
1/2 Starch

PER SERVING:
Calories 348
(44% from fat)
Fat 16.9g
(saturated fat 3.2g)
Protein 40.2g
Carbohydrate 6.7g
Fiber 0.7g
Cholesterol 121mg
Sodium 179mg

BAKED SALMON WITH A GREEN ONION GARNISH

 1 (8-ounce) carton plain low-fat yogurt
1/2 cup diced seeded peeled cucumber
 1 tablespoon chopped fresh dill
 2 teaspoons prepared horseradish
 2 teaspoons stone-ground mustard
 1 teaspoon honey
 1 (2-pound) salmon fillet (about 2 inches
      thick)
    Cooking spray
 1 teaspoon dark sesame oil
1/2 teaspoon low-sodium soy sauce
 8 green onion tops, split lengthwise

1. Spoon yogurt onto several layers of heavy-duty paper towels; spread to 1/2-inch thickness. Cover with additional paper towels, and let stand 5 minutes. Scrape into a bowl using a rubber spatula. Combine yogurt, cucumber, and next 4 ingredients; cover and refrigerate.

2. Preheat oven to 425°.

3. Place fillet on a baking sheet coated with cooking spray. Brush fillet with oil and soy sauce. Bring water to a boil in a medium saucepan; add onion strips. Cook 10 seconds or until limp. Drain. Arrange onion strips over fillet. Bake at 425° for 20 minutes or until fillet flakes easily when tested with a fork. Serve with yogurt sauce. **Yield:** 5 servings (serving size: about 5 ounces salmon and about 2 tablespoons yogurt sauce).

Super Quick

TERIYAKI-GLAZED SALMON WITH PEACH SALSA

Serve with steamed asparagus. For extra flavor, drizzle lemon juice over the asparagus.

- 3 tablespoons low-sodium teriyaki sauce
- 2 tablespoons lime juice
- 1½ tablespoons honey
- 4 (4-ounce) skinless salmon fillets
- 1½ cups frozen peach slices, thawed and chopped, or 1½ cups drained and chopped canned peaches
- ¼ cup minced fresh cilantro or mint
- 2 teaspoons honey
- 1 teaspoon lime juice
  Cooking spray

1. Prepare grill.

2. Combine first 3 ingredients in a shallow dish; stir well. Add fish, and let stand 5 minutes.

3. While fish marinates, combine peach slices and next 3 ingredients in a small bowl; stir well. Set aside.

4. Coat grill rack with cooking spray; place on grill over medium–hot coals (350° to 400°). Remove fish from marinade, discarding marinade. Place fish on rack or in a grill basket coated with cooking spray; grill fish, uncovered, 3 to 5 minutes on each side or until fish flakes easily when tested with a fork. Remove fish from grill, and top with peach mixture. **Yield:** 4 servings.

YIELD: 4 servings

EXCHANGES PER SERVING:
3 Lean Meat
1 Fruit

PER SERVING:
Calories 233
(39% from fat)
Fat 10.2g
(saturated fat 1.7g)
Protein 24.5g
Carbohydrate 10.4g
Fiber 0.8g
Cholesterol 77mg
Sodium 140mg

YIELD: 4 servings

EXCHANGES PER SERVING:
3 Lean Meat
1 Fruit
1 Vegetable

PER SERVING:
Calories 255
(35% from fat)
Fat 10g
(saturated fat 1.7g)
Protein 24.7g
Carbohydrate 15.2g
Fiber 0.5g
Cholesterol 77mg
Sodium 181mg

Super Quick
SALMON WITH PINEAPPLE SALSA

Use rubber or plastic gloves to protect your skin when handling jalapeño or other hot peppers. If you want to reduce the heat in the salsa, remove the seeds and inner white skins of membranes from the pepper.

4 (4-ounce) salmon fillets (1/2 inch thick)
  Cooking spray
1 tablespoon low-sodium soy sauce
1 (20-ounce) can pineapple tidbits in juice, drained
1/2 cup finely chopped green bell pepper (about 1/2 medium)
1/4 cup finely chopped red onion (about 1/2 small)
1 medium jalapeño pepper, seeded and minced
1 tablespoon fresh lime juice

1. Preheat broiler.

2. Arrange fillets on rack of a broiler pan coated with cooking spray; brush fillets with soy sauce. Broil 5½ inches from heat 4 minutes on each side.

3. While salmon broils, combine pineapple and remaining 4 ingredients in a small bowl.

4. Transfer salmon fillets to a serving platter; top evenly with salsa. **Yield:** 4 servings.

Super Quick
SPICY LEMON RED SNAPPER

4 (4-ounce) red snapper fillets
¼ cup fresh lemon juice
1 teaspoon black and red pepper blend (such as McCormick's)
1 teaspoon dry mustard
1 teaspoon onion powder
1 teaspoon dried thyme
Cooking spray
Lemon wedges (optional)

1. Preheat grill.

2. Place fish in a large shallow dish; pour lemon juice over fish. Let stand 5 minutes.

3. While fish marinates, combine pepper blend and next 3 ingredients. Remove fish from lemon juice, discarding juice. Rub pepper mixture over both sides of fillets.

4. Coat grill rack with cooking spray; place on grill over medium-hot coals (350° to 400°). Place fish on rack or in a grill basket coated with cooking spray; grill, covered, 3 minutes on each side or until fish flakes easily when tested with a fork. Serve with lemon wedges, if desired. **Yield:** 4 servings.

YIELD: 4 servings

EXCHANGES PER SERVING:
3 Very Lean Meat

PER SERVING:
Calories 121
(14% from fat)
Fat 1.9g
(saturated fat 0.3g)
Protein 23.5g
Carbohydrate 1.1g
Fiber 0.1g
Cholesterol 42mg
Sodium 51mg

EXCHANGES PER
SERVING:
5 Very Lean Meat
1 Starch

PER SERVING:
Calories 257
(19% from fat)
Fat 5.3g
(saturated fat 0.3g)
Protein 36.1g
Carbohydrate 14.4g
Fiber 0.5g
Cholesterol 55mg
Sodium 313mg

Super Quick
CURRY-CHUTNEY SNAPPER

2 tablespoons all-purpose flour
2 teaspoons curry powder
1/8 teaspoon salt
4 (6-ounce) red snapper or mahimahi fillets
1 tablespoon margarine or butter
1/2 cup fat-free, less-sodium chicken broth
1/4 cup mango chutney
1/4 teaspoon hot sauce
2 tablespoons minced fresh cilantro

1. Combine first 3 ingredients in a shallow dish. Dredge fish in flour mixture. Melt margarine in a large nonstick skillet over medium–high heat. Add fish; cook 3 minutes on each side or until fish flakes easily when tested with a fork. Remove from skillet; keep warm.

2. Add broth, chutney, and hot sauce to skillet; bring to a boil. Cook 1 minute, stirring constantly. Spoon sauce over fish; sprinkle with cilantro. **Yield:** 4 servings (serving size: 1 fillet and 2 tablespoons sauce).

GRILLED LEMON-BASIL SNAPPER WITH ROASTED PEPPERS

3 large red bell peppers
2 tablespoons minced fresh basil
3 tablespoons water
2 tablespoons balsamic vinegar
1 tablespoon extra-virgin olive oil
2 teaspoons grated lemon rind
¼ teaspoon salt
¼ teaspoon freshly ground black pepper
4 (6-ounce) red snapper fillets or other firm
    white fish fillets
    Cooking spray
    Fresh chives (optional)

1. Preheat broiler.

2. Cut bell peppers in half lengthwise; discard seeds and membranes. Place pepper halves, skin sides up, on a foil-lined baking sheet; flatten with hand. Broil 12 minutes or until blackened. Place in a zip-top plastic bag; seal. Let stand 15 minutes. Peel and cut into ½-inch-wide strips.

3. Combine basil and next 6 ingredients in a medium bowl; stir well with a whisk. Add pepper strips; toss well. Let stand 1 hour. Drain peppers, reserving marinade.

4. Prepare grill.

5. Brush both sides of fillets with reserved marinade. Place fish on a grill rack coated with cooking spray. Grill 5 minutes on each side or until fish flakes easily when tested with a fork, basting frequently with remaining marinade.

6. Divide pepper mixture evenly among 4 plates. Top each serving with a fillet. Garnish with fresh chives, if desired. **Yield:** 4 servings.

YIELD: 4 servings

EXCHANGES PER SERVING:
5 Very Lean Meat
1 Vegetable
½ Fat

PER SERVING:
Calories 241
(24% from fat)
Fat 6.5g
(saturated fat 1.1g)
Protein 38.3g
Carbohydrate 6.5g
Fiber 1.8g
Cholesterol 67mg
Sodium 231mg

3 Very Lean Meat
1 Vegetable
$^1/_2$ Fat

PER SERVING:
Calories 147
(23% from fat)
Fat 3.7g
(saturated fat 0.7g)
Protein 23.9g
Carbohydrate 3.4g
Fiber 0.8g
Cholesterol 42mg
Sodium 224mg

RED SNAPPER VERACRUZ

     Cooking spray
$^1/_2$ cup chopped green bell pepper
$^1/_4$ cup chopped onion
  2 garlic cloves, minced
$1^1/_2$ cups peeled, chopped tomato (about 2
       medium)
  2 tablespoons drained chopped green chiles
  1 tablespoon chopped fresh cilantro
$^1/_4$ teaspoon salt
$^1/_4$ teaspoon hot sauce
     Dash of ground white pepper
  4 (4-ounce) red snapper fillets
  2 teaspoons margarine or butter, melted

1. Prepare grill.

2. Coat a large nonstick skillet with cooking spray;
place over medium-high heat until hot. Add bell
pepper, onion, and garlic; cook, stirring constantly,
until tender. Stir in tomato and next 5 ingredients;
cook until mixture is thoroughly heated, stirring
often. Set aside, and keep warm.

3. Brush fillets with margarine, and arrange in a
grill basket coated with cooking spray. Grill, covered, over medium–hot coals (350° to 400°) for 5
minutes on each side or until fish flakes easily
when tested with a fork. Serve fillets with tomato
mixture. **Yield:** 4 servings.

CHEESE-STUFFED SWORDFISH

If you're cooking for guests, stuff the fish before your company arrives and keep the prepared fish in the refrigerator. Then coat the fish with the crumb mixture, and grill it for 10 minutes before dinnertime.

3 tablespoons grated Parmesan cheese
2 tablespoons fine, dry breadcrumbs
1 tablespoon drained capers, minced
1 tablespoon minced fresh parsley
½ teaspoon black pepper
1 garlic clove, minced
1 (1-pound) swordfish fillet (about 2 inches thick)
2 ounces part-skim mozzarella cheese, cut into 4 equal slices
Olive oil-flavored cooking spray

1. Combine first 6 ingredients; mix well. Set aside.

2. Prepare grill.

3. Cut swordfish fillet into 4 equal pieces; cut a pocket in each piece, cutting to, but not through, remaining 3 sides. Place cheese slices in fish pockets; secure openings with wooden picks. Coat fillets with cooking spray; dredge in crumb mixture.

4. Coat grill rack with cooking spray; place on grill over medium–hot coals (350° to 400°). Place fish on rack; grill, covered, 5 minutes on each side or until fish flakes easily when tested with a fork. Serve immediately. **Yield:** 4 servings.

YIELD: 4 servings

EXCHANGES PER SERVING:
4 Very Lean Meat
1 Fat

PER SERVING:
Calories 205
(36% from fat)
Fat 8.1g
(saturated fat 3.3g)
Protein 27.8g
Carbohydrate 3.4g
Fiber 0.3g
Cholesterol 55mg
Sodium 424mg

EXCHANGES PER
SERVING:
3 Very Lean Meat
1 Fat

PER SERVING:
Calories 165
(37% from fat)
Fat 6.8g
(saturated fat 1.5g)
Protein 21.8g
Carbohydrate 2.5g
Fiber 0.2g
Cholesterol 43mg
Sodium 277mg

Make Ahead
HERB-GRILLED SWORDFISH

¼ cup orange juice
3 tablespoons minced onion
1 tablespoon chopped fresh thyme
1 tablespoon chopped fresh basil
2 tablespoons low-sodium soy sauce
1½ tablespoons fresh lemon juice
1 tablespoon olive oil
½ teaspoon sugar
⅛ teaspoon salt
⅛ teaspoon pepper
1 garlic clove, minced
6 (4-ounce) swordfish steaks (½ inch thick)
Cooking spray
Fresh basil sprigs (optional)

1. Combine first 11 ingredients in a large zip-top plastic bag. Add swordfish steaks; seal bag, and shake until steaks are well coated. Marinate in refrigerator 2 hours, turning bag occasionally.

2. Prepare grill.

3. Remove steaks from marinade, reserving marinade. Place marinade in a small saucepan. Bring to a boil; boil 1 minute.

4. Coat grill rack with cooking spray. Place on grill over medium-hot coals (350° to 400°). Place swordfish steaks on rack; grill, covered, 3 to 4 minutes on each side or until fish flakes easily when tested with a fork, basting occasionally with marinade. Garnish swordfish steaks with fresh basil sprigs, if desired. **Yield:** 6 servings.

GRILLED ROSEMARY SWORDFISH

4 (4-ounce) swordfish steaks (about 1 inch thick)
1 teaspoon minced fresh rosemary
1 teaspoon grated lemon rind
1 garlic clove, minced
  Cooking spray
1 tablespoon fresh lemon juice
¼ teaspoon pepper
  Lemon wedges (optional)
  Fresh rosemary sprigs (optional)

1. Arrange steaks in a large baking dish. Combine minced rosemary, lemon rind, and garlic; press evenly onto one side of each steak. Cover and marinate in refrigerator 1 hour.

2. Prepare grill.

3. Coat grill rack with cooking spray; place rack on grill over medium–hot coals (350° to 400°). Place steaks on rack. Combine lemon juice and pepper, and brush over steaks. Grill, uncovered, 6 minutes on each side or until done, basting frequently with lemon juice mixture. Garnish with lemon wedges and rosemary sprigs, if desired. **Yield:** 4 servings.

♥ *We're told by health experts to eat fish often—it's good for our hearts. But some types of predatory fish, such as swordfish and shark, should be eaten only once a week since these fish absorb and store mercury and other contaminants from the water in which they live.*

YIELD: 4 servings

EXCHANGES PER SERVING:
3 Very Lean Meat
½ Fat

PER SERVING:
Calories 136
(30% from fat)
Fat 4.6g
(saturated fat 1.2g)
Protein 21.7g
Carbohydrate 0.8g
Fiber 0.1g
Cholesterol 43mg
Sodium 98mg

EXCHANGES PER
SERVING:
3 Very Lean Meat
1 Fat

PER SERVING:
Calories 155
(34% from fat)
Fat 5.8g
(saturated fat 1g)
Protein 23.5g
Carbohydrate 1.3g
Fiber 0.1g
Cholesterol 65mg
Sodium 177mg

HERB-BAKED TROUT

*Substitute ¼ cup of your favorite fresh herb for basil in
this dish. To mince the leafy herbs quickly, pack the herbs
in a measuring cup, and use kitchen shears.*

¼ cup minced fresh basil
¼ cup fresh lemon juice
2 teaspoons olive oil
4 (4-ounce) rainbow trout fillets
   Cooking spray
½ teaspoon black pepper
¼ teaspoon salt
1 small lemon, thinly sliced

1. Preheat oven to 350°.

2. Combine first 3 ingredients in a liquid measuring cup; set aside.

3. Place trout in a 13 x 9-inch baking dish coated
with cooking spray. Sprinkle fillets with pepper and
salt; top with lemon slices. Pour half of basil mixture over trout. Bake at 350° for 13 to 15 minutes
or until fish flakes easily when tested with a fork.
Spoon remaining basil mixture over fish, and serve
immediately. **Yield:** 4 servings.

Super Quick
BALSAMIC-GLAZED TUNA

Cooking spray
1 1/4 teaspoons coarsely ground black pepper
1/4 teaspoon salt
4 (6-ounce) tuna steaks (about 3/4 inch thick)
1/4 cup fat-free, less-sodium chicken broth
1 tablespoon balsamic vinegar
4 teaspoons dark brown sugar
1 tablespoon low-sodium soy sauce
1/2 teaspoon cornstarch
1/4 cup diagonally sliced green onions

1. Place a grill pan coated with cooking spray over medium-high heat until hot. Sprinkle pepper and salt over fish. Place fish in grill pan; cook 3 minutes on each side until medium-rare or desired degree of doneness. Remove from heat.

2. Combine broth, vinegar, sugar, soy sauce, and cornstarch in a small saucepan. Bring to a boil; cook 1 minute, stirring constantly. Spoon glaze over fish; top with green onions. **Yield:** 4 servings (serving size: 1 steak and 1 tablespoon glaze).

♥ *Some fish with a dark, moist flesh contain high amounts of omega-3 fatty acid—a type of polyunsaturated fat that may help reduce the risk of heart attacks. Fish with the highest amounts of omega-3 fatty acids include herring, mackerel, pompano, salmon, sardines, lake trout, and tuna.*

YIELD: 4 servings

EXCHANGES PER SERVING:
5 1/2 Very Lean Meat
1/2 Starch
1/2 Fat

PER SERVING:
Calories 266
(29% from fat)
Fat 8.5g
(saturated fat 2.2g)
Protein 40.3g
Carbohydrate 4.6g
Fiber 0.3g
Cholesterol 65mg
Sodium 366mg

PER SERVING:
Calories 285
(26% from fat)
Fat 8.1g
(saturated fat 2.1g)
Protein 39.5g
Carbohydrate 11.7g
Fiber 0.4g
Cholesterol 63mg
Sodium 323mg

CITRUS-TERIYAKI TUNA

    1 cup orange juice
    ¼ cup peeled minced fresh ginger
    ¼ cup chopped green onions
    ¼ cup low-sodium teriyaki sauce
    3 tablespoons fresh lemon juice
    2 garlic cloves, minced
    3 drops of hot sauce
    4 (6-ounce) tuna steaks (about ¾ inch thick)
       Cooking spray
       Sliced green onions (optional)

1. Combine first 7 ingredients in a shallow dish. Add tuna, turning to coat. Cover. Marinate in refrigerator 30 minutes, turning tuna occasionally. Remove tuna from dish; reserve marinade.

2. Strain marinade through a sieve into a saucepan, discarding solids. Bring marinade to a boil over high heat; cook 6 minutes or slightly thick. Set sauce aside; keep warm.

3. Prepare grill.

4. Place tuna steaks on grill rack coated with cooking spray, and grill 4 minutes on each side until tuna is medium-rare or until desired degree of doneness. Serve tuna with prepared sauce, and sprinkle with sliced green onions, if desired. **Yield:** 4 servings.

Note: To prepare indoors, place a grill pan over medium-high heat until hot; coat with cooking spray. Add tuna, and cook 3 minutes on each side until tuna is medium-rare or desired degree of doneness.

GRILLED TUNA WITH PAPAYA CHUTNEY

6 (6-ounce) tuna steaks (about ¾ inch thick)
2 tablespoons low-sodium soy sauce
3 cups diced peeled papaya or mango
½ cup golden raisins
⅓ cup cider or balsamic vinegar
¼ cup water
2 tablespoons brown sugar
½ teaspoon ground ginger
   Dash of salt
   Cooking spray

1. Place tuna steaks in a shallow dish. Drizzle soy sauce over both sides of fish; cover and marinate in refrigerator 30 minutes.

2. Combine diced papaya and next 6 ingredients in a small saucepan, and bring mixture to a boil. Cover, reduce heat, and simmer papaya mixture 20 minutes or until papaya is tender. Remove chutney from heat, and keep warm.

3. Prepare grill.

4. Place tuna on a grill rack coated with cooking spray, and grill for 4 minutes on each side or until tuna is medium-rare or desired degree of doneness. Serve tuna steaks with papaya chutney. **Yield:** 6 servings (serving size: 1 tuna steak and about ⅓ cup chutney).

YIELD: 6 servings

EXCHANGES PER SERVING:
5½ Very Lean Meat
1½ Fruit
1 Fat

PER SERVING:
Calories 336
(24% from fat)
Fat 9.1g
(saturated fat 2.3g)
Protein 40.9g
Carbohydrate 22.1g
Fiber 1.8g
Cholesterol 65mg
Sodium 201mg

EXCHANGES PER
SERVING:
3 Lean Meat
1 Vegetable
1 Fruit

PER SERVING:
Calories 254
(26% from fat)
Fat 7.3g
(saturated fat 1.6g)
Protein 27.1g
Carbohydrate 18.5g
Fiber 2.4g
Cholesterol 43mg
Sodium 340mg

Super Quick
GRILLED TUNA SKEWERS

8 ounces tuna steaks, trimmed and cut into
   1-inch pieces
1 medium-size green bell pepper, cut into
   1-inch pieces (about 1 cup)
1 cup pineapple chunks
¼ cup lemon juice
¼ cup dry white wine
2 teaspoons minced garlic
1 teaspoon dried oregano
1 teaspoon olive oil
½ teaspoon salt
   Cooking spray

1. Prepare grill.

2. Thread first 3 ingredients alternately onto 4
(12-inch) metal skewers. Combine lemon juice and
next 5 ingredients, stirring well; brush over kabobs.

3. Coat grill rack with cooking spray; place on
grill over medium–hot coals (350° to 400°). Place
kabobs on rack; grill, covered, 8 to 12 minutes or
until tuna flakes easily when tested with a fork,
turning and basting with lemon juice mixture.
Yield: 2 servings (serving size: 2 kabobs).

ANGEL HAIR PASTA WITH FRESH CLAMS

YIELD: 2 servings

EXCHANGES PER SERVING:
1 Very Lean Meat
2½ Starch
2 Vegetable

PER SERVING:
Calories 282
(7% from fat)
Fat 2.2g
(saturated fat 0.3g)
Protein 12.9g
Carbohydrate 53.4g
Fiber 3.1g
Cholesterol 9mg
Sodium 106mg

- 12 littleneck clams
- 2 teaspoons cornmeal
- Olive oil-flavored cooking spray
- 1½ teaspoons minced garlic
- 2 cups peeled, seeded, and chopped tomato
- ¼ cup clam juice
- ¼ cup dry white wine
- ⅛ teaspoon dried crushed red pepper
- 4 ounces uncooked capellini (angel hair pasta)
- 1½ teaspoons chopped fresh flat-leaf parsley

1. Scrub clams thoroughly with a brush, discarding any that are cracked or open. Place remaining clams in a large bowl; cover with cold water, and sprinkle with cornmeal. Let stand 30 minutes. Drain and rinse clams, discarding cornmeal. Set clams aside.

2. Coat a medium nonstick skillet with cooking spray. Place over medium–high heat until hot. Add garlic, and sauté 30 seconds. Add tomato and next 3 ingredients. Bring to a boil; reduce heat, and simmer, uncovered, 15 minutes, stirring occasionally.

3. Place clams on top of tomato mixture. Cover and cook 8 minutes or until clams open. Remove and discard any unopened clams.

4. Cook pasta according to package directions, omitting salt and fat. Drain. Remove clams from tomato mixture; set aside. Toss pasta with tomato mixture, and transfer to serving plates. Arrange clams evenly over pasta. Sprinkle with parsley. **Yield:** 2 servings.

CURRIED CORN-CRAB CAKES

³/₄ cup fresh corn kernels (about 2 ears)
¹/₄ cup finely chopped onion
¹/₄ cup diced red bell pepper
¹/₂ teaspoon curry powder
 1 garlic clove, minced
 1 pound lump crabmeat, shells removed
¹/₃ cup low-fat mayonnaise
 3 tablespoons minced fresh cilantro
 2 tablespoons chopped fresh mint
 2 tablespoons fresh lime juice
 1 tablespoon low-sodium soy sauce
 2 large egg whites
10 tablespoons dry breadcrumbs, divided
 4 teaspoons vegetable oil
   Lime wedges

1. Heat a large nonstick skillet over medium–high heat. Add first 5 ingredients; sauté 4 minutes or until vegetables are soft. Place mixture in a large bowl; cool completely. Stir in crabmeat; set aside.

2. Combine mayonnaise and next 5 ingredients in a small bowl. Gently fold mayonnaise mixture into crab mixture. Stir in 7 tablespoons breadcrumbs. Divide mixture into 8 (¾-inch-thick) patties. Dredge patties in 3 tablespoons breadcrumbs.

3. Heat oil in pan over medium–high heat. Place patties in pan; cook 4 minutes. Turn patties, and cover pan; cook 4 minutes or until done. Serve with lime wedges. **Yield:** 8 servings.

Super Quick
STEAMED MUSSELS WITH GARLIC AND SHALLOTS

  1 teaspoon olive oil
 ⅓ cup minced shallots
  2 garlic cloves, minced
  1 cup Riesling or other slightly sweet white
     wine
 12 mussels (about 8 ounces), scrubbed and
     debearded
  2 teaspoons chopped fresh thyme

1. Heat oil in a large nonstick skillet over medium heat. Add shallots and garlic; sauté 3 minutes, stirring occasionally. Add wine, and bring to a simmer. Add mussels; cover and cook 6 minutes or until shells open. Discard any unopened shells. Divide evenly between 2 shallow dishes, and sprinkle with thyme. **Yield:** 2 servings (serving size: 6 mussels and ⅓ cup sauce).

YIELD: 2 servings

EXCHANGES PER SERVING:
2 Very Lean Meat
½ Starch
½ Fat

PER SERVING:
Calories 132
(30% from fat)
Fat 4.4g
(saturated fat 0.7g)
Protein 12.5g
Carbohydrate 10.7g
Fiber 0.3g
Cholesterol 27mg
Sodium 189mg

LEMON-DILL SCALLOPS AND SNOW PEAS

When fresh snow peas aren't available, use frozen Sugar Snap peas instead.

Cooking spray
1 teaspoon reduced-calorie margarine
8 ounces bay scallops
6 ounces fresh snow pea pods, trimmed at stem end
⅛ teaspoon salt
¼ teaspoon dried dill or ¾ teaspoon chopped fresh dill
1½ teaspoons fresh lemon juice

1. Lightly coat a nonstick skillet with cooking spray; add margarine, and place over high heat until margarine melts. Add scallops, and cook 2 minutes, stirring often. Add snow peas and remaining ingredients; cook 2 minutes, stirring often. Serve immediately. **Yield:** 2 servings.

CITRUS SCALLOPS WITH PEAS IN PARCHMENT

1 pound sea scallops
1/4 cup sliced green onions
2 tablespoons frozen orange juice
   concentrate, thawed
1 teaspoon grated peeled fresh ginger
3/4 teaspoon curry powder
1/4 teaspoon pepper
1/8 teaspoon salt
1/2 pound fresh Sugar Snap peas, trimmed

1. Preheat oven to 400°.

2. Combine first 7 ingredients in a medium bowl. Toss well, and set aside. Cut 4 (15 x 14-inch) pieces of parchment paper; fold each in half crosswise, creasing firmly, and trim into a heart shape. Unfold hearts, and place on baking sheets.

3. Place ½ cup scallop mixture on each parchment heart, near the crease; arrange Sugar Snap peas around scallop mixture. Fold over remaining half of each parchment heart. Starting with rounded edge, pleat and crimp edges of parchment together to make a seal; twist ends tightly to seal. Bake at 400° for 10 minutes or until puffed and lightly browned. Place on individual serving plates, and cut open; serve immediately. **Yield:** 4 servings.

YIELD: 4 servings

EXCHANGES PER SERVING:
3 Very Lean Meat
1 Vegetable

PER SERVING:
Calories 140
(7% from fat)
Fat 1.1g
(saturated fat 0.1g)
Protein 20.9g
Carbohydrate 10.9g
Fiber 2g
Cholesterol 37mg
Sodium 257mg

EXCHANGES PER
SERVING:
3 Very Lean Meat
2 Starch
1/2 Fruit

PER SERVING:
Calories 295
(7% from fat)
Fat 2.4g
(saturated fat 0.1g)
Protein 26.7g
Carbohydrate 39.1g
Fiber 2.2g
Cholesterol 38mg
Sodium 326mg

SEA SCALLOPS ON FETTUCCINE

2 teaspoons grated lime rind, divided
1/2 cup fresh lime juice
1/2 cup fresh orange juice
1/2 teaspoon ground white pepper
1 pound sea scallops, halved lengthwise
1 (9-ounce) package refrigerated spinach
    fettuccine, uncooked
    Cooking spray
3/4 cup sliced green onions (about 3 large)

1. Combine 1 teaspoon lime rind and next 3 ingredients in a shallow dish; add scallops, and let stand 5 minutes, turning once.

2. While scallops marinate, cook pasta according to package directions, omitting salt and fat. Drain well. Set aside; keep warm.

3. Remove scallops from marinade, reserving marinade. Coat a large nonstick skillet with cooking spray; place over medium-high heat until hot. Add scallops; cook 1 minute on each side or until lightly browned. Remove scallops from skillet; set aside, and keep warm. Add marinade mixture to skillet, and cook 1 minute, stirring to scrape particles that cling to bottom of skillet.

4. Combine pasta and green onions in a large bowl. Add scallops and marinade mixture to pasta mixture; toss lightly. Sprinkle with remaining 1 teaspoon lime rind. **Yield:** 4 servings.

Super Quick
SPICY BAKED SHRIMP

Rinse a measuring spoon or cup with cold water or spray with cooking spray before measuring honey; the honey will slide out easily.

Olive oil-flavored cooking spray
2 tablespoons lemon juice
1 tablespoon honey
2 teaspoons dried parsley flakes
2 teaspoons salt-free Creole seasoning
1 teaspoon olive oil
2 teaspoons reduced-sodium soy sauce
12 ounces peeled, deveined large fresh shrimp
   (1 pound unpeeled)

1. Preheat oven to 450°.

2. Coat an 11 x 7–inch baking dish with cooking spray. Add lemon juice and next 5 ingredients to dish, stirring well. Add shrimp; toss well to coat. Bake at 450° for 8 minutes or until shrimp turn pink, stirring occasionally. **Yield:** 4 servings.

♥*Although shrimp contain higher levels of cholesterol than most seafood, they are low in both total fat and satu-rated fat. A 4-ounce serving of steamed shrimp contains only 1.2 grams of fat and 221 milligrams of cholesterol, which is below the recommended limit of 300 milligrams cholesterol per day. (Compare that to a 4-ounce lean T-bone, which contains over 11 grams of fat!)*

YIELD: 4 servings

EXCHANGES PER SERVING:
2 Very Lean Meat
1/2 Starch

PER SERVING:
Calories 121
(21% from fat)
Fat 2.8g
(saturated fat 0.4g)
Protein 17.5g
Carbohydrate 6.1g
Fiber 0g
Cholesterol 129mg
Sodium 208mg

EXCHANGES PER SERVING:
3 Very Lean Meat
½ Starch

PER SERVING:
Calories 151
(12% from fat)
Fat 2g
(saturated fat 0.3g)
Protein 24.3g
Carbohydrate 6.9g
Fiber 0.3g
Cholesterol 221mg
Sodium 263mg

BARBECUED SHRIMP

This recipe received our highest rating. We love its distinctive tangy-sweet flavor and how quick and easy it is to prepare.

24	unpeeled jumbo fresh shrimp
	Cooking spray
¼	cup diced onion
½	cup reduced-calorie ketchup
2	tablespoons chopped fresh rosemary
1	tablespoon dry mustard
1	tablespoon brown sugar
1	tablespoon white vinegar
¼	teaspoon garlic powder
	Dash of hot sauce
1	lemon, cut into 4 wedges

1. Peel shrimp, leaving tails intact. Devein shrimp, if desired. Place shrimp in a large heavy-duty zip-top plastic bag. Set aside.

2. Coat a large nonstick skillet with cooking spray; place over medium-high heat until hot. Add onion; cook, stirring constantly, until tender. Stir in ketchup and next 6 ingredients; pour over shrimp. Seal bag; shake until shrimp is coated. Marinate in refrigerator 1 hour, turning bag occasionally.

3. Soak 4 (8-inch) wooden skewers in water at least 30 minutes.

4. Prepare grill.

5. Thread 6 shrimp onto each skewer, running skewer through neck and tail. Coat grill rack with cooking spray; place on grill over medium-hot coals (350° to 400°). Place skewers on rack; grill, covered, 3 to 4 minutes on each side or until shrimp turn pink. Squeeze 1 lemon wedge over each skewer, and serve immediately. **Yield:** 4 servings (serving size: 1 kabob).

GLAZED SHRIMP KABOBS

*Substitute one 20-ounce can pineapple chunks in juice,
drained, for fresh pineapple, if desired.*

1½ pounds unpeeled large fresh shrimp
2 cups fresh pineapple chunks
⅓ cup no-sugar-added all-fruit apricot spread
1 tablespoon rice vinegar
1 tablespoon low-sodium soy sauce
1 teaspoon bottled minced ginger
1 teaspoon dark sesame oil
Cooking spray

1. Peel and devein shrimp, leaving tails intact, if desired. Thread shrimp and pineapple alternately onto 8 (12-inch) skewers; set aside.

2. Preheat broiler.

3. Spoon apricot spread into a medium bowl; chop any large chunks of apricot, if desired. Add rice vinegar and next 3 ingredients, and stir well. Divide apricot mixture in half; reserve half of mixture.

4. Place kabobs on a broiler pan coated with cooking spray. Brush kabobs with apricot mixture; broil 3 minutes. Turn kabobs over, and brush with apricot mixture. Broil an additional 3 minutes or until done. Brush with reserved apricot mixture before serving. **Yield:** 4 servings (serving size: 2 kabobs).

YIELD: 4 servings

EXCHANGES PER SERVING:
3 Very Lean Meat
1½ Fruit

PER SERVING:
Calories 201
(11% from fat)
Fat 2.4g
(saturated fat 0.5g)
Protein 20.5g
Carbohydrate 23.6g
Fiber 0.6g
Cholesterol 187mg
Sodium 313mg

YIELD: 8 servings

EXCHANGES PER SERVING:
2 Very Lean Meat
2½ Starch
1 Vegetable

PER SERVING:
Calories 312
(10% from fat)
Fat 3.4g
(saturated fat 0.5g)
Protein 22.4g
Carbohydrate 47.2g
Fiber 3.9g
Cholesterol 101mg
Sodium 220mg

SHRIMP AND MUSSELS MEDLEY

1½ pounds unpeeled medium-size fresh shrimp
1 pound fresh mussels
    Cooking spray
1 teaspoon olive oil
¾ cup chopped onion
⅔ cup chopped green bell pepper
⅔ cup chopped red bell pepper
⅔ cup chopped yellow bell pepper
5 garlic cloves, minced
2 cups peeled, seeded, and chopped tomato
1½ cups dry white wine
⅓ cup chopped fresh cilantro
¼ teaspoon salt
8 cups hot cooked linguine (cooked without
    salt or fat)

1. Peel and devein shrimp, leaving tails intact. Set aside. Remove beards on mussels, and scrub shells with a brush. Discard opened, cracked, or heavy mussels (they're filled with sand). Set aside.

2. Coat a Dutch oven with cooking spray; add oil. Place over medium–high heat until hot. Add onion and next 4 ingredients; sauté 3 minutes or until vegetables are tender. Add tomato, wine, cilantro, and salt; bring to a boil. Add shrimp and mussels. Cover and cook 8 minutes or until mussels are open and shrimp turn pink.

3. Place 1 cup cooked linguine in each individual serving bowl; spoon shrimp mixture evenly over linguine. **Yield:** 8 servings.

grains & pasta

**EXCHANGES PER
SERVING:**
1½ Starch

PER SERVING:
Calories 109
(4% from fat)
Fat 0.5g
(saturated fat 0.1g)
Protein 3.4g
Carbohydrate 23g
Fiber 4.7g
Cholesterol 0mg
Sodium 93mg

MUSHROOM BARLEY

*Look for barley on the same aisle in the
supermarket as rice and other grains.*

1 (14¼-ounce) can low-salt beef broth
1 tablespoon low-sodium Worcestershire
    sauce
¼ teaspoon salt
¼ teaspoon black pepper
1 cup uncooked quick-cooking barley
    Cooking spray
1 (8-ounce) package sliced fresh mushrooms
¾ cup frozen chopped onion, thawed
½ cup finely chopped celery

1. Combine first 4 ingredients in a medium
saucepan; bring to a boil. Add barley; cover, reduce
heat, and simmer 10 minutes. Remove from heat,
and let stand 5 minutes.

2. While barley stands, coat a large nonstick skillet
with cooking spray, and place over medium–high
heat until hot. Add mushrooms, onion, and celery;
cook 3 minutes or until tender, stirring often. Stir
into cooked barley. **Yield:** 8 servings (serving size:
½ cup).

BULGUR PILAF

Many recipes call for pouring boiling water over bulgur and letting it stand for 30 minutes. This recipe takes the quick route by simmering for 10 minutes. This not only tenderizes the bulgur, but it also plumps the currants and allows the flavors of the vegetables to be absorbed.

Cooking spray
1 cup chopped onion
1 cup shredded carrot
1 1/2 cups plus 2 tablespoons uncooked bulgur or cracked wheat
1/2 cup currants
1/2 teaspoon salt
2 cups water
2 tablespoons pine nuts, toasted

1. Place a medium saucepan coated with cooking spray over medium heat until hot. Add onion and carrot; sauté 5 minutes or until tender. Stir in bulgur, currants, and salt. Add water; bring to a boil. Cover, reduce heat, and simmer 10 minutes or until bulgur is tender and liquid is absorbed. Spoon bulgur mixture into a bowl; sprinkle with pine nuts. **Yield:** 12 servings (serving size: 1/2 cup).

♥ *Complex carbohydrates are so important that heart experts recommend you eat at least six servings of starchy foods (including pasta, rice, grains, breads, and cereals) a day. These foods are generally low in fat and provide vitamins, minerals, and fiber.*

YIELD: 12 servings

EXCHANGES PER SERVING:
1 1/2 Starch

PER SERVING:
Calories 105
(17% from fat)
Fat 2g
(saturated fat 0.4g)
Protein 3.1g
Carbohydrate 21.2g
Fiber 4.2g
Cholesterol 0mg
Sodium 109mg

EXCHANGES PER
SERVING:
2 Starch

PER SERVING:
Calories 144
(3% from fat)
Fat 0.5g
(saturated fat 0g)
Protein 5.3g
Carbohydrate 30.9g
Fiber 2.1g
Cholesterol 0mg
Sodium 125mg

Super Quick
CALICO COUSCOUS

To seed the tomato, slice it in half horizontally, and use a spoon to remove the seeds from the seed pockets.

1½ cups water
½ cup frozen whole-kernel corn
1½ tablespoons lime juice
1 teaspoon minced garlic (about 2 cloves)
¼ teaspoon salt
¼ teaspoon black pepper
1 cup uncooked couscous
¾ cup seeded, chopped tomato (1 medium)
2 tablespoons chopped fresh cilantro or
     parsley

1. Combine first 6 ingredients in a medium saucepan; place over medium–high heat, and bring to a boil. Stir in couscous, and cover; remove from heat, and let stand 5 minutes.

2. Fluff couscous mixture with a fork. Add tomato and cilantro, tossing well. **Yield:** 5 servings (serving size: ½ cup).

COUSCOUS WITH MIXED FRUIT

Couscous (KOOS-koos) is perfect to keep on hand for a quick, healthy side dish. Just add it to boiling water, and it practically cooks itself.

1 cup fat-free, less-sodium chicken broth
½ cup chopped mixed dried fruit
½ cup chopped Rome apple
½ cup apple juice
¼ teaspoon salt
1 cup uncooked couscous

1. Combine first 4 ingredients in a nonaluminum saucepan; let stand 15 minutes.

2. Add salt to fruit mixture; bring to a boil over medium heat. Stir in couscous; cover and remove from heat. Let stand 5 to 7 minutes or until liquid is absorbed. Fluff with a fork before serving. **Yield:** 8 servings (serving size: ½ cup).

YIELD: 8 servings

EXCHANGES PER SERVING:
1 Starch
1 Fruit

PER SERVING:
Calories 138
(7% from fat)
Fat 1g
(saturated fat 0g)
Protein 4.4g
Carbohydrate 27.7g
Fiber 1.1g
Cholesterol 0mg
Sodium 123mg

YIELD: 6 servings

EXCHANGES PER
SERVING:
2½ Starch

PER SERVING:
Calories 205
(12% from fat)
Fat 2.8g
(saturated fat 0.3g)
Protein 7.2g
Carbohydrate 39g
Fiber 2.1g
Cholesterol 0mg
Sodium 18mg

Super Quick
ORANGE-SCENTED COUSCOUS TIMBALES

If you don't have custard cups for shaping the couscous into timbales, just fluff it with a fork and serve it as you would rice.

1 cup orange juice
1 cup low-sodium chicken broth
1 (10-ounce) package uncooked couscous
2 teaspoons grated orange rind
   Cooking spray
2 tablespoons sliced almonds, toasted
   Orange rind strips (optional)

1. Combine orange juice and chicken broth in a medium saucepan; bring to a boil. Stir in couscous and orange rind; cover and remove from heat. Let stand 5 minutes.

2. Spoon mixture evenly into 6 (6-ounce) custard cups coated with cooking spray. Invert onto a serving platter; sprinkle with almonds. Garnish with orange rind strips, if desired. **Yield:** 6 servings (serving size: ¾ cup).

CURRIED BASMATI RICE

If you're tired of plain white rice, here's a recipe to try soon. The basmati rice has a nutty flavor that blends well with curry powder.

2 tablespoons reduced-calorie margarine
1/2 cup finely chopped onion
2 garlic cloves, minced
1 1/2 cups uncooked basmati rice
1 teaspoon curry powder
1/2 teaspoon salt
2 (10 1/2-ounce) cans low-sodium chicken broth
1/2 cup water
1/4 cup chopped fresh parsley
1/4 teaspoon grated lemon rind
1 tablespoon fresh lemon juice

1. Melt margarine in a saucepan over medium heat. Add onion and garlic; sauté 5 minutes. Add rice and curry powder; cook, stirring constantly, 1 minute. Add salt, broth, and water; bring to a boil. Cover, reduce heat, and simmer 20 minutes or until liquid is absorbed. Remove from heat; stir in parsley, lemon rind, and lemon juice. Cover and let stand 10 minutes; fluff with a fork. **Yield:** 12 servings (serving size: 1/2 cup).

YIELD: 12 servings

EXCHANGES PER SERVING:
1 1/2 Starch

PER SERVING:
Calories 104
(13% from fat)
Fat 1.5g
(saturated fat 0.3g)
Protein 2.4g
Carbohydrate 20.1g
Fiber 0.4g
Cholesterol 0mg
Sodium 140mg

PER SERVING:
Calories 117
(20% from fat)
Fat 2.6g
(saturated fat 0.3g)
Protein 2.8g
Carbohydrate 20.2g
Fiber 1.6g
Cholesterol 0mg
Sodium 159mg

BROWN RICE PILAF

Brown rice's characteristic color comes from the natural bran layer left on the rice grain during processing. The bran also gives cooked brown rice its chewy texture, nutty flavor, and healthy dose of fiber.

```
2   cups fat-free, less-sodium chicken broth
1   cup uncooked brown rice
½   cup shredded carrot
½   cup finely chopped celery
¼   cup finely sliced green onions
½   teaspoon salt
¼   teaspoon ground red pepper
1   garlic clove, minced
3   tablespoons slivered almonds, toasted
```

1. Bring broth to a boil in a heavy saucepan; stir in rice and next 6 ingredients. Cover, reduce heat, and simmer 50 to 55 minutes or until rice is tender and liquid is absorbed. Stir in almonds. Serve immediately. **Yield:** 8 servings (serving size: ½ cup).

Super Quick
FRUITED BROWN RICE

1 cup uncooked instant brown rice
²/₃ cup halved seedless red or green grapes
¹/₄ cup coarsely chopped pecans, toasted
2 tablespoons sherry vinegar or rice wine
   vinegar
1 teaspoon extra-virgin olive oil
¹/₄ teaspoon salt
¹/₂ teaspoon black pepper

1. Cook rice according to package directions, omitting salt and fat.

2. Combine rice, grapes, and pecans in a medium bowl. Stir in vinegar and remaining ingredients. Serve immediately, or cover and chill up to 24 hours, if desired. **Yield:** 5 servings (serving size: ½ cup).

♥ *Take a hike! For fitness, that is. A few times around the block can help you lose weight, burn fat, and decrease your risk of heart disease. Walking can be done almost anywhere or anytime and it requires no equipment except a sturdy pair of shoes.*

YIELD: 5 servings

EXCHANGES PER SERVING:
1 Starch
½ Fruit
1 Fat

PER SERVING:
Calories 157
(33% from fat)
Fat 5.8g
(saturated fat 0.6g)
Protein 2.7g
Carbohydrate 24.2g
Fiber 2.2g
Cholesterol 0mg
Sodium 181mg

STIR-FRIED BROWN RICE

EXCHANGES PER
SERVING:
1½ Starch
1 Vegetable

PER SERVING:
Calories 138
(14% from fat)
Fat 2.2g
(saturated fat 0.4g)
Protein 5g
Carbohydrate 26g
Fiber 4.2g
Cholesterol 0mg
Sodium 110mg

Be sure to use instant brown rice in this recipe; it cooks in less than half the time of regular rice.

Cooking spray
1 teaspoon olive oil
1 cup chopped celery
1 cup thinly sliced carrot
1 cup chopped onion
2 teaspoons ground cumin
2 teaspoons minced peeled fresh ginger
2½ cups low-sodium chicken broth
2 cups uncooked instant brown rice
⅓ cup dried tomato sprinkles
2 cups frozen English peas, thawed

1. Coat a large nonstick skillet with cooking spray; add oil, and place over medium–high heat until hot. Add celery, carrot, and onion; cook 4 minutes or until vegetables are tender, stirring often. Stir in cumin and ginger; cook, stirring constantly, 1 minute. Add broth, rice, and tomato sprinkles; bring to a boil. Cover, reduce heat, and simmer 15 minutes or until liquid is absorbed and rice is tender. Stir in peas. **Yield:** 7 servings (serving size: 1 cup).

GREEK RICE

1   regular-size package boil-in-bag rice
1   cup chopped tomato
1 1/2 tablespoons chopped ripe olives
1   tablespoon lemon juice
1/2   teaspoon salt-free Greek seasoning

1. Cook rice according to package directions, omitting salt and fat. Drain. Place in a serving bowl; add tomato, ripe olives, lemon juice, and seasoning. Toss. **Yield:** 3 servings (serving size: 3/4 cup).

YIELD: 3 servings

EXCHANGES PER SERVING:
1 1/2 Starch
1 Vegetable

PER SERVING:
Calories 136
(4% from fat)
Fat 0.6g
(saturated fat 0.1g)
Protein 2.7g
Carbohydrate 29.8g
Fiber 1.3g
Cholesterol 0mg
Sodium 48mg

Super Quick
QUICK SPANISH RICE

Frozen seasoning blend is a mix of chopped onions, celery, red bell peppers, green bell peppers, and parsley. It's handy to use for soups, stews, and sauces, too.

1   cup water
1   (8-ounce) can no-salt-added tomato sauce
3/4   cup frozen seasoning blend (such as McKenzie's)
1/2   cup thick and chunky salsa
1/2   teaspoon chili powder
1/4   teaspoon salt
2   cups uncooked instant rice

1. Combine first 6 ingredients in a medium saucepan; bring to a boil. Stir in rice. Cover, remove from heat, and let stand 5 minutes or until liquid is absorbed and rice is tender. **Yield:** 8 servings (serving size: 1/2 cup).

YIELD: 8 servings

EXCHANGES PER SERVING:
1 1/2 Starch

PER SERVING:
Calories 108
(1% from fat)
Fat 0.1g
(saturated fat 0g)
Protein 2.5g
Carbohydrate 23.8g
Fiber 0.7g
Cholesterol 0mg
Sodium 128mg

EXCHANGES PER
SERVING:
2½ Starch

PER SERVING:
Calories 185
(2% from fat)
Fat 0.5g
(saturated fat 0.1g)
Protein 3.6g
Carbohydrate 38.7g
Fiber 0.6g
Cholesterol 0mg
Sodium 152mg

YELLOW RICE

*Onion, turmeric, and a bay leaf punch up the flavor
of plain rice.*

     Cooking spray
¼ cup diced onion
2 cups fat-free, less-sodium chicken broth
1 cup uncooked long-grain rice
¼ teaspoon salt
⅛ teaspoon ground turmeric
1 bay leaf

1. Coat a large nonstick skillet with cooking spray;
place over medium-high heat until hot. Add onion;
cook, stirring constantly, until tender.

2. Stir in chicken broth and remaining ingredients;
bring to a boil. Cover, reduce heat, and simmer 25
minutes or until rice is tender and liquid is absorbed. Remove and discard bay leaf. **Yield:** 4
servings (serving size: ¾ cup).

ORANGE RICE PILAF

1 teaspoon olive oil
¼ cup chopped onion
1 cup uncooked long-grain rice
1 cup fat-free, less-sodium chicken broth
1 cup fresh orange juice
½ cup golden raisins
1 tablespoon grated orange rind
¼ teaspoon salt
¼ teaspoon freshly ground black pepper

1. Heat oil in a medium nonstick skillet. Add onion; sauté until tender. Add rice; stir well. Cook, stirring constantly, 2 minutes. Add broth, juice, and raisins. Bring to a boil; cover, reduce heat, and simmer 20 to 25 minutes or until rice is tender and liquid is absorbed. Add orange rind, salt, and pepper; toss lightly. **Yield:** 5 servings (serving size: ¾ cup).

♥ *When you add butter, margarine, cheese, or heavy cream to rice or pasta, you're also adding calories, fat, and cholesterol to an otherwise low-fat dish. To avoid this, use creative recipes that call for herbs, fruit, and other seasonings to boost flavor while keeping cholesterol low.*

YIELD: 5 servings

EXCHANGES PER SERVING:
2 Starch
1 Fruit

PER SERVING:
Calories 223
(5% from fat)
Fat 1.3g
(saturated fat 0.2g)
Protein 3.8g
Carbohydrate 49.8g
Fiber 1.5g
Cholesterol 0mg
Sodium 123mg

VEGETABLE-RICE TOSS

YIELD: 8 servings

EXCHANGES PER SERVING:
1½ Starch

PER SERVING:
Calories 139
(8% from fat)
Fat 1.3g
(saturated fat 0.2g)
Protein 3.6g
Carbohydrate 27.7g
Fiber 1.3g
Cholesterol 0mg
Sodium 113mg

Cooking spray
1 teaspoon sesame oil
¾ cup diced onion
½ cup diced carrot
2 garlic cloves, minced
2 (10½-ounce) cans low-sodium chicken broth
¼ teaspoon salt
¼ teaspoon pepper
¼ teaspoon Chinese five-spice powder
1¼ cups uncooked long-grain rice
½ cup frozen English peas, thawed
½ cup sliced green onions
Sliced green onion tops (optional)

1. Coat a large nonstick skillet with cooking spray; add oil. Place over medium–high heat until hot. Add onion, carrot, and garlic; cook until tender.

2. Stir broth and next 3 ingredients into vegetable mixture; bring to a boil. Stir in rice; return to a boil. Cover, reduce heat, and cook 20 minutes or until rice is tender and liquid is absorbed. Remove from heat. Add peas and ½ cup green onions; toss gently. Garnish with green onion tops, if desired. **Yield:** 8 servings (serving size: ⅔ cup).

MUSHROOM RISOTTO

Risotto is an Italian rice specialty that is worth the time required to stir the rice until it is delectably creamy.

    3   cups fat-free, less-sodium chicken broth
    2   teaspoons reduced-calorie margarine
    ½   teaspoon olive oil
    1   small onion, finely chopped
    ½   (8-ounce) package sliced fresh mushrooms
    ¼   cup chopped green bell pepper
 1 ¼   cups uncooked Arborio rice
    ½   cup dry white wine
    2   tablespoons grated fresh Parmesan cheese
    ⅛   teaspoon freshly ground black pepper
        Shaved fresh Parmesan cheese (optional)

1. Heat broth in a medium saucepan over low heat; keep warm.

2. Heat margarine and olive oil in a large saucepan over medium heat. Add onion, mushrooms, and bell pepper. Cook, stirring constantly, 3 minutes or until vegetables are tender.

3. Add rice, stirring well. Add wine, and cook over medium–low heat, stirring constantly, until wine has been absorbed. Add enough hot broth to cover rice. Cook over medium heat, stirring constantly, until broth is absorbed. Continue adding broth 1 ladle at a time until broth is absorbed and rice is done, stirring constantly. (Add water as needed if rice is not done after all broth has been used.)

4. Stir in 2 tablespoons Parmesan cheese and black pepper. Serve immediately. Garnish with shaved fresh Parmesan cheese, if desired. **Yield:** 8 servings (serving size: ½ cup).

YIELD: 8 servings

EXCHANGES PER SERVING:
2 Starch

PER SERVING:
Calories 140
(10% from fat)
Fat 1.5g
(saturated fat 0.3g)
Protein 3.1g
Carbohydrate 27.1g
Fiber 0.8g
Cholesterol 1mg
Sodium 242mg

PER SERVING:
Calories 199
(19% from fat)
Fat 4.3g
(saturated fat 0.8g)
Protein 4.1g
Carbohydrate 35.3g
Fiber 0.8g
Cholesterol 0mg
Sodium 139mg

RICE-AND-NOODLE PILAF

To make this unusual pilaf, first sauté dry rice and noodles in butter, then boil them. The result is a texture that is partially soft and partially crunchy. In countries such as Spain, this type of pilaf is typically made with fideos (fih-DAY-ohs), skinny egg noodles found in Latin and Middle Eastern markets. We've substituted easier-to-find spaghetti noodles.

2 tablespoons margarine or butter
3 ounces uncooked thin spaghetti, broken into
    1-inch pieces, or fideo egg noodles
1 cup uncooked long-grain rice
2 cups boiling water
1/4 teaspoon salt
1/4 teaspoon black pepper

1. Melt margarine in a large saucepan over medium heat, and add spaghetti. Sauté spaghetti for 5 minutes or until lightly browned. Add rice, stirring to coat. Stir in water, salt, and pepper, and bring to a boil. Cover; reduce heat, and simmer for 20 minutes or until liquid is absorbed. Remove pilaf from heat; let stand for 10 minutes. Fluff with a fork. **Yield:** 6 servings (serving size: 2/3 cup).

Super Quick
HERBED CHERRY TOMATOES OVER PASTA

Replacing most of the olive oil with chicken broth and balsamic vinegar makes this pasta moist and flavorful.

12   ounces uncooked bow tie pasta
¼   cup chopped fresh basil
⅓   cup balsamic vinegar
¼   cup fat-free, less-sodium chicken broth
2   tablespoons olive oil
4   cups cherry tomatoes, cut in half

1. Cook pasta according to package directions, omitting salt and fat; drain.

2. Combine basil and next 3 ingredients; pour over pasta. Add cherry tomatoes, and toss gently. **Yield:** 6 servings (serving size: 1½ cups).

YIELD: 6 servings

EXCHANGES PER SERVING:
1 Starch
1 Vegetable
1 Fat

PER SERVING:
Calories 144
(33% from fat)
Fat 5.3g
(saturated fat 0.7g)
Protein 4g
Carbohydrate 21.6g
Fiber 2.4g
Cholesterol 0mg
Sodium 51mg

Super Quick
GARLIC AND LEMON LINGUINE

Recipes don't get much easier or tastier than this. If you have the time, grate fresh Parmesan cheese and use freshly squeezed lemon juice for maximum flavor.

1½   tablespoons reduced-calorie margarine
¼   cup grated Parmesan cheese
2   tablespoons lemon juice
½   teaspoon pepper
2   garlic cloves, crushed
2½   cups hot cooked linguine (cooked without salt or fat)

1. Melt margarine in a small saucepan over medium heat; stir in Parmesan cheese and next 3 ingredients. Pour over pasta; toss gently. Serve immediately. **Yield:** 3 servings (serving size: ¾ cup).

YIELD: 3 servings

EXCHANGES PER SERVING:
1 Starch
1 Fat

PER SERVING:
Calories 133
(41% from fat)
Fat 6g
(saturated fat 1.8g)
Protein 5.1g
Carbohydrate 15.3g
Fiber 0.8g
Cholesterol 5mg
Sodium 180mg

LINGUINE WITH RED PEPPER SAUCE

EXCHANGES PER
SERVING:
2½ Starch
1 Vegetable

PER SERVING:
Calories 240
(10% from fat)
Fat 2.7g
(saturated fat 0.4g)
Protein 7.9g
Carbohydrate 45.8g
Fiber 2.2g
Cholesterol 0mg
Sodium 104mg

*The natural sweetness of red bell peppers, balsamic
vinegar, and fresh basil adds flair to the thick,
rich sauce that tops this pasta. We liked this recipe
so much that as soon as we tasted it, we jotted it
down to slip into our own files.*

　　Cooking spray
　2　teaspoons olive oil
　3　cups chopped red bell pepper
　2　small garlic cloves, crushed
　⅓　cup chopped fresh basil
　¼　cup balsamic vinegar
　¼　teaspoon salt
　⅛　teaspoon pepper
　6　cups hot cooked linguine (cooked without
　　　salt or fat)
　　Fresh basil sprigs (optional)

1. Coat a nonstick skillet with cooking spray; add
oil. Place over medium heat until hot. Add red bell
pepper and garlic; cook, uncovered, 30 minutes,
stirring occasionally. Set aside, and cool slightly.

2. Place pepper mixture in container of an electric
blender or food processor; add chopped basil and
next 3 ingredients. Cover and process until
smooth, stopping once to scrape down sides. For
each serving, top 1 cup pasta with ¼ cup pepper
sauce. Garnish, if desired. Serve immediately.
Yield: 6 servings (serving size: 1¼ cups).

LINGUINE VERDE

Buy bags of prewashed spinach leaves for the fastest preparation time. (One 10-ounce bag yields 2½ cups torn spinach.)

8 ounces uncooked linguine
3 cups loosely packed spinach leaves
2 cups trimmed watercress
2 large plum tomatoes, each cut into 8 wedges
¾ cup loosely packed sliced fresh basil leaves
2 teaspoons extra-virgin olive oil
¼ teaspoon salt
½ cup grated Parmesan cheese
½ teaspoon black pepper

1. Cook linguine according to package directions, omitting salt and fat. Set aside, and keep warm.

2. Combine spinach and next 5 ingredients in a large bowl; toss well. Add linguine to spinach mixture; sprinkle with Parmesan cheese and pepper, tossing well. Serve immediately. **Yield:** 8 servings (serving size: 1 cup).

♥ *Many healthy pasta sauces are available at the grocery store for quick pasta fix-ups. Check the nutrient labels to determine which are lower in fat and sodium. If you choose one that is higher in sodium, watch out for additional sources of sodium (such as salt you might add to the pasta's cooking water).*

YIELD: 8 servings

EXCHANGES PER SERVING:
2 Vegetable
1 Starch
½ Fat

PER SERVING:
Calories 156
(22% from fat)
Fat 3.8g
(saturated fat 1.6g)
Protein 7.3g
Carbohydrate 23.2g
Fiber 1.6g
Cholesterol 6mg
Sodium 220mg

EXCHANGES PER SERVING:
1½ Starch
½ Fat

PER SERVING:
Calories 146
(19% from fat)
Fat 3.1g
(saturated fat 1.1g)
Protein 6.5g
Carbohydrate 21.8g
Fiber 2.1g
Cholesterol 4mg
Sodium 168mg

PARMESAN ORZO AND PEAS

Try sun-dried tomatoes for intense tomato flavor. You can store an unopened package in the pantry up to one year; it will keep for three months once opened.

 ⅓ cup dried tomato bits (packed without oil)
 ¾ cup hot water
 1 tablespoon margarine or butter
 1 cup chopped onion
 1 teaspoon minced garlic
 1 cup uncooked orzo
 1 (14½-ounce) can fat-free, less-sodium chicken broth
1¼ cups frozen English peas
 ½ cup grated Parmesan cheese
 ½ cup evaporated fat-free milk

1. Combine tomato bits and hot water in a small bowl; let stand 10 minutes. Drain and set aside.

2. Melt margarine in a saucepan over medium-high heat. Add onion and garlic; sauté 5 minutes or until tender. Add orzo, and sauté 3 minutes or until orzo is lightly browned. Add broth, and bring to a boil. Cover, reduce heat, and simmer 12 to 15 minutes or until broth is absorbed and orzo is tender.

3. Stir in peas, cheese, and milk; cook over medium heat until cheese melts. Stir in tomato; serve immediately. **Yield:** 10 servings (serving size: ½ cup).

Super Quick
LEMON PASTA

There will be excess liquid in the skillet when you first add the mushroom mixture, but the pasta absorbs a good bit of it, leaving the pasta well coated.

  6 ounces uncooked penne (1½ cups tubular
       pasta)
  1 teaspoon garlic-flavored olive oil
1½ cups sliced fresh mushrooms
  ⅓ cup sliced green onions (about 3 medium)
  ½ cup dry white wine
  ½ to 1 teaspoon grated lemon rind
  ¼ teaspoon salt
  ½ teaspoon lemon-pepper seasoning

1. Cook pasta according to package directions, omitting salt and fat; drain well.

2. While pasta cooks, add olive oil to a large non-stick skillet; place over medium–high heat until hot. Add mushrooms and green onions, and cook 3 minutes, stirring often. Add wine; cook 5 minutes or until wine is reduced by half. Pour mushroom mixture over pasta; add lemon rind, salt, and lemon-pepper seasoning. Toss well. Serve immediately. **Yield:** 6 servings (serving size: ¾ cup).

YIELD: 6 servings

EXCHANGES PER SERVING:
1½ Starch

PER SERVING:
Calories 118
(10% from fat)
Fat 1.3g
(saturated fat 0.2g)
Protein 4.1g
Carbohydrate 22.5g
Fiber 1g
Cholesterol 0mg
Sodium 137mg

SPAGHETTI AGLIO E OLIO

In Italian, aglio e olio (AH-lyoh ay OH-lyoh) means "garlic and oil." Typically, the garlic is fried in olive oil on the stovetop, but we've cooked it with olive oil in the microwave, which is easier and omits the risk of burning the garlic. You can add some crushed red pepper flakes for a spicier version.

  2 tablespoons extra-virgin olive oil
1/4 teaspoon dried oregano
  4 large garlic cloves, minced
  4 quarts water
  8 ounces uncooked spaghetti
1/2 cup fat-free, less-sodium chicken broth
  2 tablespoons minced fresh parsley

1. Combine olive oil, oregano, and minced garlic in a small microwave–safe bowl. Cover with wax paper, and microwave at HIGH 1 minute.

2. Bring water to a boil in a large stockpot. Add spaghetti; return to a boil. Cook, uncovered, 10 minutes or until "al dente," stirring occasionally. Drain. Return to pot. Stir in garlic mixture and broth. Cook over medium heat 4 minutes or until broth is absorbed, stirring constantly. Stir in parsley. **Yield:** 4 servings (serving size: 1 cup).

VERMICELLI WITH TOMATO-BASIL SAUCE

A trip to the garden or farmers' market for ripe red tomatoes and fresh basil will yield a pasta sauce that boasts a bounty of summertime flavors.

8   ounces uncooked vermicelli
    Cooking spray
2   garlic cloves, minced
1   medium onion, thinly sliced
5   cups peeled, chopped tomato (about
      5 medium tomatoes)
¼   cup minced fresh basil
¼   teaspoon salt
⅛   teaspoon pepper
1   (8-ounce) can no-salt-added tomato sauce
¼   cup (1 ounce) grated fresh Parmesan cheese

1. Cook pasta according to package directions, omitting salt and fat. Drain.

2. Coat a Dutch oven with cooking spray; place over medium heat until hot. Add garlic and onion; cook, stirring constantly, 5 minutes or until onion is tender. Stir in tomato and next 4 ingredients; bring to a boil. Reduce heat, and simmer, uncovered, 15 minutes, stirring occasionally.

3. Add cooked pasta to tomato mixture; cook, uncovered, until mixture is thoroughly heated, stirring occasionally. Sprinkle with cheese. Serve immediately. **Yield:** 8 servings (serving size: 1 cup).

YIELD: 8 servings

EXCHANGES PER SERVING:
1½ Starch
1 Vegetable

PER SERVING:
Calories 163
(10% from fat)
Fat 1.9g
(saturated fat 0.6g)
Protein 6.3g
Carbohydrate 29.9g
Fiber 2.9g
Cholesterol 2mg
Sodium 147mg

YIELD: 4 servings

EXCHANGES PER
SERVING:
2 Very Lean Meat
3 Starch
2 Vegetable

PER SERVING:
Calories 371
(10% from fat)
Fat 4.1g
(saturated fat 1.5g)
Protein 25.6g
Carbohydrate 57.1g
Fiber 2.2g
Cholesterol 41mg
Sodium 216mg

LINGUINE WITH RED CLAM SAUCE

8 ounces uncooked linguine
   Cooking spray
3 garlic cloves, minced
2 (14½-ounce) cans no-salt-added stewed
   tomatoes, undrained
¼ teaspoon dried crushed red pepper
3 (6½-ounce) cans clams, drained
⅓ cup grated Parmesan or Romano cheese

1. Cook pasta according to package directions, omitting salt and fat.

2. Coat a large deep skillet with cooking spray, and place over medium heat. Add garlic; cook, stirring constantly, 2 minutes. Add tomatoes and crushed red pepper to skillet. Bring mixture to a boil; reduce heat, and simmer, uncovered, 7 to 8 minutes.

3. Stir in clams; cook until thoroughly heated.

4. Drain pasta; arrange on four serving plates. Top evenly with clam sauce, and sprinkle with cheese. **Yield:** 4 servings (serving size: 1 cup pasta and about 1 cup sauce).

DILLED SHRIMP WITH ANGEL HAIR PASTA

6 ounces uncooked angel hair pasta
2 tablespoons reduced-calorie margarine
3/4 cup sliced green onions (about 3 large)
3 tablespoons fresh lemon juice (1 large)
2 large garlic cloves, minced
1 pound peeled, deveined large fresh shrimp
1/2 cup fat-free half-and-half or fat-free
    evaporated milk
1/4 cup tub-style light cream cheese
2 tablespoons chopped fresh dill or 1 1/2
    teaspoons dried dill

1. Cook pasta according to package directions, omitting salt and fat. Drain.

2. While pasta cooks, melt margarine in a large nonstick skillet over medium-high heat. Add green onions, lemon juice, and garlic; cook 2 minutes, stirring often. Add shrimp, and cook 5 minutes or until shrimp turn pink. Remove shrimp from skillet; set aside.

3. Add half-and-half, cream cheese, and dill to skillet, stirring until smooth. Cook 1 to 2 minutes or until mixture is bubbly. Return shrimp to skillet, and cook until thoroughly heated. Combine shrimp mixture and pasta, tossing well. Serve immediately.
Yield: 4 servings (serving size: 1 1/2 cups).

YIELD: 4 servings

EXCHANGES PER SERVING:
3 Very Lean Meat
2 1/2 Starch
1 Fat

PER SERVING:
Calories 368
(23% from fat)
Fat 9.5g
(saturated fat 1.8g)
Protein 31g
Carbohydrate 37.4g
Fiber 0.3g
Cholesterol 180mg
Sodium 366mg

EXCHANGES PER
SERVING:
2 Very Lean Meat
2½ Starch
1 Vegetable
1 Fat

PER SERVING:
Calories 351
(24% from fat)
Fat 9.2g
(saturated fat 2.1g)
Protein 24.1g
Carbohydrate 43.7g
Fiber 3.6g
Cholesterol 107mg
Sodium 317mg

SHRIMP-AND-SQUASH PENNE

*Start with about 8 ounces uncooked pasta to yield
4 cups cooked pasta. Ziti, rigatoni, and mostaccioli
are good substitutes for the penne.*

2 tablespoons olive oil
4 cups thinly sliced yellow squash (about
   4 small)
3 cups thinly sliced zucchini (about 2)
1 pound medium shrimp, peeled and
   deveined
¼ cup fresh lemon juice
1 teaspoon dried basil
1 teaspoon dried oregano
¼ teaspoon salt
¼ teaspoon black pepper
3 garlic cloves, minced
4 cups hot cooked penne (cooked without salt
   or fat)
½ cup thinly sliced fresh chives or green
   onions
¼ cup (1 ounce) grated fresh Parmesan cheese

1. Heat oil in a large nonstick skillet over
medium–high heat. Add squash and zucchini, and
sauté 10 minutes. Add shrimp; sauté 3 minutes. Add
lemon juice and next 5 ingredients; cook 2 minutes or until shrimp are done. Combine shrimp
mixture, pasta, chives, and cheese in a large bowl;
toss gently. **Yield:** 5 servings (serving size: 2 cups).

LAZY LASAGNA

Precooked noodles and prepackaged convenience products make this recipe easy to prepare.

1 pound ground round
1 (26-ounce) bottle low-fat pasta sauce
½ cup water
2 cups fat-free cottage cheese
2 tablespoons grated Parmesan cheese
  Cooking spray
1 (8-ounce) package precooked lasagna
  noodles
1 cup (4 ounces) preshredded reduced-fat
  mild Cheddar cheese
  Chopped fresh parsley (optional)

1. Preheat oven to 350°.

2. Cook beef in a large nonstick skillet over medium-high heat until browned, stirring to crumble. Drain; wipe drippings from pan with paper towels. Return beef to pan. Stir in pasta sauce and water; bring to a boil. Reduce heat, and simmer 5 minutes. Combine cottage and Parmesan cheeses in a bowl.

3. Spread ½ cup beef mixture in bottom of a 13 x 9-inch baking dish coated with cooking spray. Arrange 4 noodles over beef mixture; top with half of cottage cheese mixture, 1 cup beef mixture, and ⅓ cup Cheddar cheese. Repeat layers once, ending with noodles. Spread remaining beef mixture over noodles. Cover and bake at 350° for 30 minutes. Uncover; sprinkle with ⅓ cup Cheddar cheese, and bake 5 additional minutes or until cheese melts. Let stand 10 minutes before serving. Garnish with parsley, if desired. **Yield:** 9 servings.

YIELD: 9 servings

EXCHANGES PER SERVING:
3 Very Lean Meat
1½ Starch
1 Fat

PER SERVING:
Calories 273
(25% from fat)
Fat 7.5g
(saturated fat 2.8g)
Protein 25.7g
Carbohydrate 24.5g
Fiber 2.5g
Cholesterol 42mg
Sodium 536mg

SPAGHETTI WITH BEEF, TOMATOES, AND ZUCCHINI

YIELD: 4 servings

EXCHANGES PER SERVING:
2 Lean Meat
2 Starch
2 Vegetable

PER SERVING:
Calories 332
(21% from fat)
Fat 7.9g
(saturated fat 2.9g)
Protein 19.3g
Carbohydrate 46.4g
Fiber 2.2g
Cholesterol 35mg
Sodium 336mg

1   (7-ounce) package thin spaghetti
½   pound lean ground round
¼   cup chopped onion
2   (8-ounce) cans no-salt-added tomato sauce
1   teaspoon dried Italian seasoning
½   teaspoon salt
¼   teaspoon garlic powder
¼   teaspoon dried crushed red pepper
1½ cups coarsely chopped zucchini (about 1 medium)
1½ cups coarsely chopped tomato (about 1 medium)

1. Cook spaghetti according to package directions, omitting salt and fat.

2. While spaghetti cooks, cook ground round and onion in a large nonstick skillet over high heat 4 to 5 minutes or until beef is browned, stirring until beef crumbles. Drain beef mixture, if necessary; wipe skillet with paper towels.

3. Return beef mixture to skillet. Stir in tomato sauce and next 4 ingredients. Cook over medium heat 2 to 4 minutes or until hot and bubbly, stirring occasionally.

4. Stir in cooked spaghetti and zucchini. Cook 2 minutes, stirring occasionally. Stir in tomato. **Yield:** 4 servings (serving size: 1½ cups).

CASSEROLE SPAGHETTI

YIELD: 8 servings

EXCHANGES PER SERVING:
3 Lean Meat
2 Starch

PER SERVING:
Calories 331
(27% from fat)
Fat 9.8g
(saturated fat 3.9g)
Protein 27.5g
Carbohydrate 32.5g
Fiber 2.8g
Cholesterol 65mg
Sodium 400mg

1½ pounds ground round
1½ cups chopped onion
1 cup chopped green bell pepper
½ cup chopped celery
2 garlic cloves, crushed
1 (10¾-ounce) can reduced-fat, reduced-sodium cream of mushroom soup, undiluted
¾ cup water
1 (14.5-ounce) can no-salt-added whole tomatoes, undrained and chopped
2 tablespoons chili powder
⅛ teaspoon salt
¼ teaspoon pepper
1 (8-ounce) package spaghetti
2 ounces reduced-fat sharp Cheddar cheese, cut into ½-inch cubes
2 tablespoons chopped pimiento-stuffed olives
Cooking spray
½ cup (2 ounces) shredded reduced-fat sharp Cheddar cheese

1. Cook first 5 ingredients in a Dutch oven, stirring until meat crumbles; drain well, and return to Dutch oven. Stir in soup and next 5 ingredients. Bring to a boil over medium heat. Cover, reduce heat, and simmer 1 hour, stirring occasionally.

2. Preheat oven to 325°.

3. Cook spaghetti according to package directions, omitting salt and fat; drain.

4. Stir spaghetti, cheese cubes, and olives into meat sauce. Spoon mixture into a 13 x 9-inch baking dish coated with cooking spray. Cover and bake at 325° for 20 minutes or until thoroughly heated. Sprinkle with ½ cup shredded cheese, and bake, uncovered, 10 additional minutes. **Yield:** 8 servings.

CREOLE CHICKEN PASTA

EXCHANGES PER
SERVING:
3 Very Lean Meat
1½ Starch
1 Vegetable

PER SERVING:
Calories 269
(12% from fat)
Fat 3.7g
(saturated fat 0.5g)
Protein 23.4g
Carbohydrate 32.2g
Fiber 2g
Cholesterol 44mg
Sodium 172mg

Serve with a spinach salad and crusty French bread.

3   tablespoons all-purpose flour
2   teaspoons no-salt-added Creole seasoning,
      divided
4   (4-ounce) skinned, boned chicken breast
      halves, cut into strips
    Cooking spray
2   teaspoons hot pepper oil
1   medium onion, cut into vertical strips (about
      1 cup)
1   medium-size green bell pepper, cut into
      julienne strips
1   teaspoon minced garlic
1   (9-ounce) package refrigerated fettuccine,
      uncooked
1   cup fat-free half-and-half or fat-free
      evaporated milk

1. Combine flour and 1½ teaspoons Creole seasoning in a large heavy-duty zip-top plastic bag; add chicken, and shake to coat.

2. Coat a large nonstick skillet with cooking spray; add oil. Place over medium-high heat until hot. Add chicken, onion, bell pepper, and garlic; cook 8 to 10 minutes or until chicken is done and vegetables are tender, stirring occasionally.

3. While chicken mixture cooks, cook fettuccine according to package directions, omitting salt and fat; drain well.

4. Combine remaining ½ teaspoon Creole seasoning and half-and-half; add to chicken mixture in skillet, scraping bottom of skillet to deglaze. Cook 1 minute or until sauce is slightly thickened. Toss with cooked fettuccine; serve immediately. **Yield:** 6 servings (serving size: 1 cup).

Super Quick
DIJON CHICKEN FETTUCCINE

1   (9-ounce) package refrigerated fettuccine,
     uncooked
½   (16-ounce) package fresh broccoli flowerets
     (4 cups)
⅓   cup commercial fat-free honey Dijon
     dressing (such as Hellman's)
¼   cup red wine vinegar
1   tablespoon Dijon mustard
1   teaspoon olive oil
1   teaspoon bottled minced garlic
1   (10.11-ounce) package cooked chicken
     breast (such as Tyson's roasted chicken),
     skinned and shredded
¼   teaspoon freshly ground black pepper

1. Cut pasta in half before cooking. Cook pasta according to package directions, omitting salt and fat.
Add broccoli to pasta during last 3 minutes of
cooking time. Drain well; place in a large bowl.

2. While pasta cooks, combine dressing and next 4
ingredients; stir well. Pour dressing mixture over
pasta mixture. Add chicken, and toss gently. Sprinkle
with pepper. **Yield:** 8 servings (serving size: 1 cup).

YIELD: 8 servings

**EXCHANGES PER
SERVING:**
1 Very Lean Meat
1 Starch
1 Vegetable

PER SERVING:
Calories 162
(13% from fat)
Fat 2.4g
(saturated fat 0.6g)
Protein 12.5g
Carbohydrate 22.9g
Fiber 1.1g
Cholesterol 54mg
Sodium 296mg

**EXCHANGES PER
SERVING:**
2¹/₂ Very Lean Meat
3 Starch

PER SERVING:
Calories 315
(11% from fat)
Fat 3.7g
(saturated fat 1.3g)
Protein 26.5g
Carbohydrate 41.3g
Fiber 1.7g
Cholesterol 48mg
Sodium 305mg

CHICKEN TETRAZZINI

Cooking spray
8 ounces uncooked spaghetti
1 (14¹/₂-ounce) can fat-free, less-sodium
    chicken broth
¹/₂ (8-ounce) package sliced fresh mushrooms
¹/₂ cup chopped green bell pepper
¹/₃ cup chopped onion
1 cup fat-free evaporated milk
¹/₃ cup all-purpose flour
¹/₄ teaspoon pepper
¹/₈ teaspoon ground nutmeg
2 cups chopped, cooked chicken breast
2 tablespoons dry sherry or fat-free evaporated
    milk
¹/₄ cup (1 ounce) grated fresh Parmesan cheese

1. Coat an 8-inch square baking dish with cooking spray; set aside. Cook spaghetti according to
package directions, omitting salt and fat. Drain and
set aside.

2. Preheat oven to 400°.

3. Combine broth and next 3 ingredients in a
large saucepan. Bring to a boil; cover, reduce heat,
and simmer 5 minutes or until vegetables are tender. Combine 1 cup evaporated milk and next 3
ingredients in a small bowl, stirring well with a
whisk. Add to vegetable mixture. Cook over
medium heat until mixture is thickened and bubbly, stirring constantly. Add chicken and sherry.

4. Toss cooked spaghetti with chicken mixture.
Spoon into prepared baking dish. Sprinkle with
Parmesan cheese. Bake, uncovered, at 400° for 10
minutes or until golden. **Yield:** 6 servings (serving
size: 1 cup).

meatless main dishes

PER SERVING:
Calories 354
(15% from fat)
Fat 5.8g
(saturated fat 1.9g)
Protein 15.3g
Carbohydrate 58.7g
Fiber 5.7g
Cholesterol 8mg
Sodium 399mg

RICE AND BEAN SOFT TACOS

*Leftover rice works well in this recipe. Or use quick-
cooking rice that cooks in just 10 minutes.*

  4 (10-inch) flour tortillas
    Cooking spray
1/2 cup thinly sliced green bell pepper (about
    1/2 small)
1/2 cup thinly sliced onion (about 1/2 medium)
  1 cup cooked long-grain rice (cooked without
    salt or fat)
  1 (15-ounce) can no-salt-added black beans,
    drained
1/3 cup mild salsa
1/2 teaspoon chili powder
1/8 teaspoon salt
1/2 cup fat-free sour cream
1/4 cup (1 ounce) shredded Monterey Jack
    cheese with peppers

1. Preheat oven to 350°.

2. Wrap tortillas in aluminum foil. Bake at 350° for
10 minutes or until tortillas are warm.

3. While tortillas bake, coat a nonstick skillet with
cooking spray. Place over medium–high heat until
hot. Add bell pepper and onion; cook 4 minutes or
until tender, stirring often.

4. Combine rice and next 4 ingredients. Divide
mixture evenly among warm tortillas; roll up, and
place tortillas, seam side down, on a serving platter.
Top with sour cream and cheese. **Yield:** 4 servings
(serving size: 1 taco with 2 tablespoons sour cream
and 1 tablespoon cheese).

SPICY CARIBBEAN BLACK BEANS AND RICE

You may decrease the sodium content of canned beans by rinsing the beans with water.

    1   teaspoon olive oil
 1 ¼   cups diced onion
   ¾   cup finely chopped carrot
    1   tablespoon bottled minced garlic
    2   cups cooked rice (cooked without salt or fat)
    2   tablespoons dry sherry
    1   tablespoon balsamic vinegar
    1   teaspoon dried thyme
   ½   teaspoon black pepper
   ⅛   teaspoon salt
    2   (15-ounce) cans black beans, rinsed and
         drained
    2   bay leaves

1. Heat oil in a large saucepan over medium heat. Add onion, carrot, and garlic; sauté 10 minutes. Add rice and remaining ingredients; cover, reduce heat, and simmer 5 minutes or until thoroughly heated. Discard bay leaves. **Yield:** 4 servings (serving size: 1¾ cups).

♥ *It's easy to meet your protein needs without meat if you include a variety of high-protein foods such as beans, tofu, grains, and low-fat dairy products. In fact, 1 cup of cooked kidney beans contains more protein than 2 ounces of lean ground beef.*

YIELD: 4 servings

EXCHANGES PER SERVING:
4 Starch

PER SERVING:
Calories 325
(6% from fat)
Fat 2.3g
(saturated fat 0.4g)
Protein 13.9g
Carbohydrate 62.2g
Fiber 7.5g
Cholesterol 0mg
Sodium 411mg

YIELD: 4 servings

EXCHANGES PER SERVING:
1 Very Lean Meat
3 Starch
1 Fat

PER SERVING:
Calories 307
(22% from fat)
Fat 7.5g
(saturated fat 1g)
Protein 14.4g
Carbohydrate 49g
Fiber 7g
Cholesterol 0mg
Sodium 456mg

GARLICKY STEWED WHITE BEANS WITH MIXED PEPPERS

To complement this stew, try French bread slices that have been sprinkled with Parmesan cheese, then broiled.

1 tablespoon olive oil
1 cup chopped green bell pepper
1 cup chopped yellow or red bell pepper
1 tablespoon bottled minced garlic (about 4 cloves)
1/8 teaspoon dried crushed red pepper
1/2 cup water
1/4 teaspoon dried rubbed sage
2 (15-ounce) cans cannellini beans or other white beans, rinsed and drained
1 (14.5-ounce) can diced tomatoes, undrained
1/4 teaspoon coarsely ground black pepper

1. Heat olive oil in a large skillet over medium-high heat. Add bell peppers, and cook 5 minutes or until tender, stirring frequently. Add garlic and crushed red pepper; cook 1 minute, stirring constantly. Stir in water, sage, beans, and tomatoes; bring to a boil. Reduce heat, and simmer 10 minutes or until thick, stirring occasionally. Sprinkle with black pepper. **Yield:** 4 servings (serving size: 1 cup).

CREAMY INDIAN LENTILS AND RICE

We've added salt to season the otherwise bland rice and lentils. If you're on a sodium-restricted diet, you can cut the salt to ¼ teaspoon—one serving will provide only 118 milligrams of sodium. Omit the salt, and the sodium will be under 30 milligrams per serving.

1 tablespoon vegetable oil
2 cups thinly sliced onion
1 cup uncooked long-grain brown rice
1 tablespoon curry powder
2 teaspoons mustard seeds
1 teaspoon salt
½ teaspoon black pepper
4 cups water
1 cup dried lentils
1 cup chopped fresh cilantro
½ cup low-fat sour cream

1. Heat oil in a large Dutch oven over medium-high heat. Add onion; sauté 8 minutes or until golden brown, stirring occasionally. Add rice and next 4 ingredients; sauté 1 minute. Add water and lentils; bring to a boil. Cover, reduce heat, and simmer 1 hour. Remove from heat; stir in cilantro and sour cream. **Yield:** 6 servings (serving size: 1 cup).

♥ *If you're concerned about your heart's health, eat plenty of lentils and other legumes such as dried beans and split peas. They are rich in fiber, protein, and complex carbohydrates, yet low in fat and sodium. Unlike most legumes, lentils do not need to be presoaked, but will cook in less than 40 minutes.*

YIELD: 6 servings

EXCHANGES PER SERVING:
1 Very Lean Meat
3 Starch
½ Fat

PER SERVING:
Calories 297
(20% from fat)
Fat 6.5g
(saturated fat 2.1g)
Protein 13.2g
Carbohydrate 48g
Fiber 6.3g
Cholesterol 8mg
Sodium 411mg

EXCHANGES PER
SERVING:
1 Very Lean Meat
2½ Starch
1 Vegetable
1 Fat

PER SERVING:
Calories 310
(30% from fat)
Fat 10.2g
(saturated fat 1.6g)
Protein 11.5g
Carbohydrate 44.1g
Fiber 5.2g
Cholesterol 0mg
Sodium 423mg

SESAME VEGETABLE TOFU STIR-FRY

1 (10½-ounce) package extra firm tofu
¼ cup low-sodium soy sauce
1 tablespoon grated peeled fresh ginger
2 teaspoons sugar
2 teaspoons dark sesame oil
2 garlic cloves, minced
2 teaspoons vegetable oil
2 cups fresh broccoli flowerets
1 cup thinly sliced red bell pepper
2 cups thinly sliced napa cabbage
1 cup fresh bean sprouts
2 teaspoons sesame seeds, toasted
3 cups hot cooked brown rice (cooked
   without salt or fat)

1. Place tofu between 2 flat plates or cutting boards. Weight the top with a heavy can (sides of tofu should be bulging slightly, but not cracking). Let stand 40 to 45 minutes; pour off liquid, and discard. Cut tofu into ½-inch cubes, and set aside.

2. Combine soy sauce and next 4 ingredients in a medium bowl, stirring well. Add tofu, and toss to coat. Let stand 10 minutes. Remove tofu from marinade, reserving marinade.

3. Drizzle vegetable oil around top of wok, coating sides. Heat at medium-high (375°) until hot. Add tofu, and stir-fry 4 minutes. Add broccoli and red bell pepper; stir-fry 2 minutes. Add cabbage and bean sprouts, and stir-fry 2 additional minutes or until vegetables are crisp-tender. Add reserved marinade; toss gently, and cook 30 seconds or until thoroughly heated. Stir in sesame seeds.

4. Spoon ¾ cup rice onto each individual serving plate. Top evenly with vegetable mixture. **Yield:** 4 servings.

FRIED RICE WITH PINEAPPLE AND TOFU

The brown rice in this dish is nuttier tasting and better for you than white. Long-grain brown rice tends to be a little milder than short-grain, but whichever you use, be sure to start this recipe using cold cooked rice.

- 1 (14-ounce) package firm tofu, drained and cut into ¹/₂-inch cubes
- 2 tablespoons roasted peanut oil or regular peanut oil, divided
- ¹/₄ teaspoon salt
- 1 cup (¹/₂-inch) pieces red bell pepper
- ³/₄ cup thinly sliced green onions
- 1 cup shelled green peas
- ¹/₄ pound snow peas, trimmed and cut lengthwise into thin strips
- 4 cups cooked long-grain brown rice (cooked without salt or fat), chilled
- ¹/₄ cup chopped fresh cilantro, divided
- 1 (15¹/₄-ounce) can pineapple chunks in juice, drained
- ¹/₄ cup low-sodium soy sauce
- 1 tablespoon chopped unsalted, dry-roasted peanuts

1. Place tofu between paper towels until barely moist. Heat 1 tablespoon oil in a large nonstick skillet or stir-fry pan over medium-high heat. Add tofu, and cook 8 minutes or until golden. Sprinkle with salt. Remove tofu from pan.

2. Heat 1 tablespoon oil in pan over medium-high heat. Add bell pepper and onions, and sauté 2 minutes. Add peas, and sauté 30 seconds. Stir in rice, and cook 2 minutes. Add tofu, 2 tablespoons cilantro, and pineapple; cook 1 minute, stirring gently. Remove from heat. Stir in soy sauce and peanuts. Sprinkle with 2 tablespoons cilantro. **Yield:** 7 servings (serving size: 1 cup).

YIELD: 7 servings

EXCHANGES PER SERVING:
1 Medium-Fat Meat
1 Starch
1 Fruit
1 Vegetable

PER SERVING:
Calories 256
(30% from fat)
Fat 8.5g
(saturated fat 1.4g)
Protein 10.3g
Carbohydrate 36.5g
Fiber 4.5g
Cholesterol 0mg
Sodium 375mg

YIELD: 6 servings

EXCHANGES PER
SERVING:
2½ Starch
1 Vegetable
1 Fat

PER SERVING:
Calories 254
(25% from fat)
Fat 7g
(saturated fat 0.8g)
Protein 12g
Carbohydrate 42g
Fiber 3.5g
Cholesterol 0mg
Sodium 453mg

MEDITERRANEAN BULGUR PILAF

1   teaspoon olive oil
1   cup sliced green onions
½   cup sliced celery
2   garlic cloves, minced
1¼ cups water
1¼ cups canned vegetable broth
1½ teaspoons curry powder
1   teaspoon ground cumin
¼   teaspoon salt
¼   teaspoon ground red pepper
1⅓ cups uncooked bulgur wheat with soy grits
       (such as Hodgson Mill) or bulgur
¼   cup dried currants
¼   cup pine nuts, toasted
1   tablespoon chopped fresh parsley
1   (15-ounce) can chickpeas (garbanzo beans),
       drained

1. Heat oil in a large saucepan over medium–high heat until hot. Add green onions, celery, and garlic; cook, stirring constantly, 3 minutes. Add water and next 5 ingredients; bring to a boil. Stir in bulgur; remove from heat. Cover and let stand 30 minutes or until liquid is absorbed.

2. Add currants and remaining ingredients to bulgur mixture; toss well. Serve at room temperature. **Yield:** 6 servings (serving size: 1 cup).

Super Quick
CURRIED VEGETABLE COUSCOUS

Couscous, made from wheat, fluffs up like rice when cooked. The best part is that it takes only 5 minutes to prepare. Find couscous in the rice section of your supermarket.

1 (14½-ounce) can vegetable broth, divided
⅓ cup raisins
1 cup couscous, uncooked
½ (16-ounce) package fresh stir-fry vegetables
¼ cup water
2 teaspoons curry powder
¼ teaspoon ground red pepper
1 (15.8-ounce) can black-eyed peas, rinsed and drained

1. Combine 1¼ cups broth and raisins in a small saucepan. Bring to a boil, and stir in couscous. Cover, remove from heat, and let stand 5 minutes.

2. Meanwhile, combine remaining broth, stir-fry vegetables, and remaining 4 ingredients in a saucepan; stir well. Cover and simmer 7 minutes or until vegetables are crisp-tender. Serve over couscous mixture. **Yield:** 4 servings.

YIELD: 4 servings

EXCHANGES PER SERVING:
2 Starch
2 Vegetable
1 Fruit

PER SERVING:
Calories 293
(5% from fat)
Fat 1.6g
(saturated fat 0.2g)
Protein 13.2g
Carbohydrate 58.6g
Fiber 5.2g
Cholesterol 0mg
Sodium 364mg

EXCHANGES PER
SERVING:
4 Starch

PER SERVING:
Calories 295
(4% from fat)
Fat 1.4g
(saturated fat 0.1g)
Protein 11.2g
Carbohydrate 61.6g
Fiber 5.9g
Cholesterol 0mg
Sodium 503mg

COUSCOUS WITH ITALIAN VEGETABLE RAGOÛT

*One (10-ounce) package of couscous makes about
5 cups of cooked couscous, so be sure to buy
two packages for this recipe.*

4   cups thinly sliced zucchini (about 4 small)
2   cups coarsely chopped onion (about 1
      medium)
2   (14¹⁄₂-ounce) cans Italian-style stewed
      tomatoes, undrained
1   (15-ounce) can no-salt-added chickpeas
      (garbanzo beans), drained
1   teaspoon dried Italian seasoning
¹⁄₄   teaspoon salt
¹⁄₄   teaspoon ground pepper
7   cups cooked couscous (cooked without salt
      or fat)

1. Combine first 7 ingredients in a large skillet.
Bring to a boil; cover, reduce heat, and simmer 10
minutes, stirring occasionally. Uncover and simmer
an additional 5 minutes or until most of liquid
evaporates.

2. Arrange 1 cup couscous on each of 7 individual
serving plates; top with vegetable mixture. **Yield:** 7
servings.

CREAMY POLENTA WITH ROASTED VEGETABLES

1/2 pound fresh asparagus spears
2 medium zucchini, cut into 1/4-inch slices
     (about 2 1/2 cups)
1 small red onion, cut into 3/4-inch pieces
     (about 1 1/2 cups)
   Cooking spray
1 teaspoon olive oil
1 teaspoon minced garlic
1/8 teaspoon salt
1 3/4 cups fat-free milk
1/2 cup yellow cornmeal
1/4 teaspoon salt
1 1/2 tablespoons red wine vinegar
1/2 teaspoon sugar
2 tablespoons grated fresh Parmesan cheese
   Freshly ground black pepper (optional)

YIELD: 3 servings

EXCHANGES PER SERVING:
2 Starch
1 Vegetable
1 Fat

PER SERVING:
Calories 221
(20% from fat)
Fat 5g
(saturated fat 1.8g)
Protein 12.3g
Carbohydrate 34.1g
Fiber 4.3g
Cholesterol 8mg
Sodium 505mg

1. Preheat oven to 475°.

2. Snap off and discard tough ends of asparagus; cut asparagus into 1-inch pieces. Combine asparagus, zucchini, and onion in a 15 x 10-inch jelly-roll pan coated with cooking spray. Drizzle with oil; sprinkle with garlic and 1/8 teaspoon salt. Stir gently until vegetables are coated. Bake at 475° for 18 minutes or until vegetables are crisp-tender and begin to brown, stirring once.

3. Meanwhile, pour milk into a medium saucepan; place over medium heat. Gradually stir in cornmeal and 1/4 teaspoon salt. Cook over medium heat, stirring constantly, 5 minutes or until very thick.

4. Immediately spoon cornmeal mixture onto 3 individual serving plates. Combine vinegar and sugar; sprinkle over vegetables. Toss well; spoon vegetables evenly over cornmeal mixture. Sprinkle evenly with cheese; sprinkle with pepper, if desired. **Yield:** 3 servings.

EXCHANGES PER
SERVING:
1 Lean Meat
4 Starch

PER SERVING:
Calories 361
(10% from fat)
Fat 4g
(saturated fat 1.6g)
Protein 17.7g
Carbohydrate 62.2g
Fiber 3.1g
Cholesterol 9mg
Sodium 363mg

HERBED ALFREDO SAUCE OVER PASTA

*For extra flavor, we used roasted garlic and red pepper
angel hair pasta (by Skinner) to test this recipe. You can
use 10 ounces of any pasta you have on hand.*

10	ounces roasted garlic- and red pepper-flavored angel hair pasta, uncooked
	Cooking spray
1/4	cup sliced green onions (about 2)
1	teaspoon minced garlic
2	tablespoons all-purpose flour
1	(12-ounce) can evaporated fat-free milk, divided
1/2	cup grated Parmesan cheese
1/4	cup chopped fresh parsley or 1 tablespoon dried parsley
1	tablespoon chopped fresh basil or 1 teaspoon dried basil
1/4	teaspoon salt
1/4	teaspoon pepper

1. Cook pasta according to package directions,
omitting salt and fat. Drain and set aside.

2. While pasta cooks, coat a medium saucepan
with cooking spray; place over medium heat until
hot. Add green onions and garlic; cook, stirring
constantly, 2 minutes.

3. Combine flour and 1/3 cup milk, stirring until
smooth. Add remaining milk, stirring well. Add to
saucepan; cook over medium heat, stirring constantly, until thickened. Add cheese and remaining
4 ingredients; cook until thoroughly heated. Toss
with pasta; serve immediately. **Yield:** 5 servings
(serving size: 1 cup).

VEGETABLE LASAGNA

YIELD: 10 servings

1 1/2 cups chopped onion
1 cup chopped green bell pepper
3/4 cup chopped celery
3 garlic cloves, minced
Cooking spray
2 1/2 cups coarsely chopped zucchini
2 cups peeled, chopped tomato
2 cups sliced fresh mushrooms
3/4 cup shredded carrot
2 tablespoons red wine vinegar
1 tablespoon dried Italian seasoning
1/2 teaspoon salt
1/2 teaspoon pepper
2 (8-ounce) cans no-salt-added tomato sauce
1 (6-ounce) can no-salt-added tomato paste
2 cups part-skim ricotta cheese
1 1/4 cups (5 ounces) shredded part-skim mozzarella cheese, divided
6 cooked lasagna noodles (cooked without salt or fat)
2 tablespoons grated Parmesan cheese

EXCHANGES PER SERVING:
1 Very Lean Meat
2 Starch
1 Fat

PER SERVING:
Calories 238
(28% from fat)
Fat 7.3g
(saturated fat 4.2g)
Protein 14.5g
Carbohydrate 30.4g
Fiber 3.5g
Cholesterol 24mg
Sodium 300mg

1. Sauté first 4 ingredients in a Dutch oven coated with cooking spray over medium–high heat until tender. Stir in zucchini and next 9 ingredients; bring to a boil. Cover, reduce heat, and simmer 30 minutes, stirring occasionally. Remove from heat.

2. Preheat oven to 350°.

3. Combine ricotta cheese and 3/4 cup mozzarella cheese. Spoon 2 cups vegetable mixture into a 13 x 9-inch baking dish coated with cooking spray. Place 3 noodles lengthwise in a single layer over vegetable mixture; top with half of ricotta cheese mixture. Repeat layers, ending with vegetable mixture. Cover and bake at 350° for 25 minutes. Uncover and sprinkle with remaining 1/2 cup mozzarella cheese and Parmesan cheese. Bake, uncovered, 8 to 10 additional minutes or until cheeses melt. Let stand 10 minutes before serving. **Yield:** 10 servings.

EXCHANGES PER SERVING:
1 Lean Meat
1 Low-Fat Milk
½ Starch

PER SERVING:
Calories 204
(37% from fat)
Fat 8.4g
(saturated fat 3.7g)
Protein 13.9g
Carbohydrate 18g
Fiber 0.7g
Cholesterol 21mg
Sodium 491mg

MACARONI AND CHEESE

Mention "macaroni and cheese," and visions of creamy, cheesy, down-home goodness pop into most minds. Our lightened version of this revered comfort food will meet your highest expectations.

　1　(8-ounce) package elbow macaroni
　2　tablespoons reduced-calorie margarine
　2　tablespoons all-purpose flour
　2　cups fat-free milk
1½　cups (6 ounces) shredded reduced-fat sharp Cheddar cheese
　½　teaspoon salt
　3　tablespoons egg substitute
　　　Cooking spray
　¼　teaspoon paprika

1. Cook pasta according to package directions, omitting salt and fat. Drain and set aside.

2. Preheat oven to 350°.

3. Melt margarine in a heavy saucepan over low heat; add flour, stirring until smooth. Cook, stirring constantly, 1 minute. Gradually add milk; cook over medium heat, stirring constantly, until thickened and bubbly. Add cheese and salt, stirring until cheese melts. Gradually stir about one-fourth of hot cheese mixture into egg substitute. Add to remaining hot mixture, stirring constantly.

4. Combine cheese sauce and pasta; pour into a 2-quart baking dish coated with cooking spray. Sprinkle with paprika. Bake at 350° for 25 to 30 minutes or until thoroughly heated. **Yield:** 6 servings (serving size: 1 cup).

EASY CHEESY MANICOTTI

Take the easy way when it comes to stuffing manicotti shells. First, fill a heavy-duty zip-top plastic bag with the cheese mixture. Then seal the bag, and snip a large hole in 1 corner of the bag. Finally, just squeeze the bag to pipe the cheese mixture into the shells.

½ cup (2 ounces) grated fresh Parmesan cheese, divided
2 cups 1% low-fat cottage cheese
½ cup part-skim ricotta cheese
2 tablespoons chopped fresh parsley
½ teaspoon dried Italian seasoning
¼ teaspoon garlic powder
1 large egg, lightly beaten
12 cooked manicotti shells (cooked without salt or fat)
1 (15½-ounce) jar no-salt-added spaghetti sauce

1. Preheat oven to 375°.

2. Combine ⅓ cup Parmesan cheese, cottage cheese, and next 5 ingredients; stuff each shell with about ¼ cup cheese mixture. Arrange shells in a 13 x 9-inch baking dish. Pour spaghetti sauce over shells. Cover and bake at 375° for 25 minutes or until heated. Sprinkle with remaining Parmesan cheese before serving. **Yield:** 6 servings (serving size: 2 stuffed shells).

YIELD: 6 servings

EXCHANGES PER SERVING:
1 Lean Meat
1 Skim Milk
3 Starch

PER SERVING:
Calories 408
(17% from fat)
Fat 7.5g
(saturated fat 3.3g)
Protein 25.7g
Carbohydrate 57.4g
Fiber 1.4g
Cholesterol 53mg
Sodium 518mg

PASTA CAPONATA

Penne pasta looks like straightened tubes of large macaroni. It will take about 11 ounces of dried pasta to equal 6 cups of cooked penne.

Olive oil-flavored cooking spray
2 cups cubed eggplant
1½ cups cubed yellow squash
¾ cup chopped celery
½ cup coarsely chopped onion
2 garlic cloves, minced
2 cups sliced fresh mushrooms
2 (14½-ounce) cans no-salt-added whole tomatoes, undrained and chopped
¼ cup chopped pimiento-stuffed olives
1 tablespoon balsamic vinegar
1 tablespoon no-salt-added tomato paste
1 teaspoon dried oregano
½ teaspoon ground pepper
¼ teaspoon salt
6 cups hot cooked penne (cooked without salt or fat)
2 tablespoons grated Parmesan cheese

1. Preheat broiler.

2. Coat a 15 x 10-inch jelly-roll pan with cooking spray. Arrange eggplant and squash in pan in a single layer; coat with cooking spray. Broil 5½ inches from heat 7 to 8 minutes or until tender, stirring occasionally. Set aside.

3. Coat a Dutch oven with cooking spray; place over medium-high heat until hot. Add celery, onion, and garlic; cook, stirring constantly, 4 to 5 minutes or until tender. Add mushrooms; cook 4 minutes. Stir in tomato and next 6 ingredients; bring to a boil. Reduce heat, and simmer, uncovered, 20 minutes or until slightly thickened. Stir in eggplant and squash. Serve over pasta, and sprinkle with cheese. **Yield:** 6 servings.

CREAMY PENNE PRIMAVERA

YIELD: 5 servings

10 ounces penne (short tubular pasta),
     uncooked
 1 (16-ounce) package frozen Sugar Snap
     stir-fry vegetable blend
 ½ (8-ounce) tub light cream cheese (about
     ½ cup)
 ½ cup fat-free sour cream
 3 tablespoons fat-free milk
1 ½ teaspoons salt-free herb-and-spice blend
     (such as Mrs. Dash)
 ½ teaspoon salt
 ¼ cup (1 ounce) shredded fresh Parmesan
     cheese

EXCHANGES PER SERVING:
1 Medium-Fat Meat
3 Starch
1 Vegetable

PER SERVING:
Calories 337
(17% from fat)
Fat 6.3g
(saturated fat 3.2g)
Protein 14.2g
Carbohydrate 50.5g
Fiber 1.8g
Cholesterol 17mg
Sodium 497mg

1. Cook pasta according to package directions, omitting salt and fat. Add vegetables to pasta the last 2 minutes of cooking. Drain; set aside.

2. Using the same saucepan (pan will still be warm), melt cream cheese over low heat; add sour cream, stirring until smooth. Add milk, stirring until smooth. Add spice blend and salt; stir well. Add pasta mixture, and toss well. Sprinkle with Parmesan cheese. Serve immediately. **Yield:** 5 servings (serving size: 1½ cups).

**EXCHANGES PER
SERVING:**
1 High-Fat Meat
3 Starch
1 Vegetable

PER SERVING:
Calories 362
(28% from fat)
Fat 11.2g
(saturated fat 5.3g)
Protein 16.3g
Carbohydrate 50.8g
Fiber 6.3g
Cholesterol 70mg
Sodium 356mg

Super Quick
CHEESE RAVIOLI WITH TOMATOES AND PEPPERS

*For an easy meal, serve with warm Italian bread
sprinkled with garlic powder and a green salad.*

1 (9-ounce) package refrigerated cheese-filled
  ravioli, uncooked
1 teaspoon olive oil
1 medium-size green bell pepper, cut into thin
  strips
1 medium onion, cut into thin strips
2 teaspoons minced garlic
3 cups chopped fresh tomato (2 medium)
¾ teaspoon freshly ground black pepper
1 cup loosely packed basil leaves, slivered

1. Cook pasta according to package directions,
omitting salt and fat.

2. While pasta cooks, heat oil in a large nonstick
skillet over medium–high heat. Add green bell
pepper, onion, and garlic; cook 3 minutes or until
vegetables begin to wilt. Stir in tomato, and cook 2
additional minutes or until tomatoes are soft. Stir
in ground pepper and basil; remove from heat.

3. Drain pasta, and place in a large serving bowl;
pour sauce over pasta. Serve immediately. **Yield:**
3 servings (serving size: 1½ cups).

RATATOUILLE RIGATONI

Eight ounces of uncooked rigatoni equals about 2½ cups of dried noodles. Penne pasta is a good substitute for rigatoni; they're similar in size and shape.

8 ounces rigatoni (tube-shaped pasta), uncooked
Cooking spray
1 teaspoon olive oil
3 medium zucchini, sliced
1 medium-size green bell pepper, sliced
1 (8-ounce) package sliced fresh mushrooms
1 (14½-ounce) can no-salt-added stewed tomatoes, undrained
1 (8-ounce) can no-salt-added tomato sauce
1 teaspoon dried oregano
½ teaspoon black pepper
¼ teaspoon salt
1 garlic clove, minced
1 bay leaf
2 tablespoons plus 2 teaspoons grated fresh Parmesan cheese

1. Cook pasta according to package directions, omitting salt and fat. Drain and set aside.

2. Coat a large nonstick skillet with cooking spray; add oil. Place over medium–high heat until hot. Add zucchini, green bell pepper, and mushrooms; cook 8 minutes or until crisp–tender, stirring often. Add tomato and next 6 ingredients. Cover, reduce heat, and simmer 10 minutes. Uncover and simmer 5 minutes or until slightly thickened. Remove and discard bay leaf.

3. Combine pasta and tomato mixture in a large bowl; toss well. To serve, spoon into individual serving bowls. Sprinkle 2 teaspoons Parmesan cheese over each serving. **Yield:** 4 servings.

YIELD: 4 servings

EXCHANGES PER SERVING:
3½ Starch
2 Vegetable

PER SERVING:
Calories 352
(14% from fat)
Fat 5.3g
(saturated fat 2g)
Protein 15.4g
Carbohydrate 62.6g
Fiber 4.9g
Cholesterol 7mg
Sodium 347mg

Super Quick
VEGETARIAN PEANUT PASTA

EXCHANGES PER SERVING:
1 Medium-Fat Meat
3 Starch
1 Vegetable

PER SERVING:
Calories 339
(22% from fat)
Fat 8.1g
(saturated fat 0.1g)
Protein 12.3g
Carbohydrate 54.2g
Fiber 4.3g
Cholesterol 0mg
Sodium 398mg

*You can substitute 1¹/₂ cups broccoli flowerets for snow
peas in this recipe. For a bit of crunch, sprinkle each
serving with 2 teaspoons chopped dry-roasted peanuts.*

¹/₄ cup plus 2 tablespoons reduced-fat peanut
      butter
¹/₄ cup plus 1¹/₂ teaspoons water
  3 tablespoons brown sugar
  3 tablespoons low-sodium soy sauce
  3 tablespoons rice vinegar
¹/₄ to ¹/₂ teaspoon dried crushed red pepper
  8 ounces spaghetti, uncooked
10 ounces fresh snow pea pods, trimmed
  1 large carrot, shredded

1. Combine first 6 ingredients in a small saucepan.
Cook over medium heat until mixture begins to
boil, stirring often; remove from heat, and set sauce
aside.

2. While sauce cooks, cook pasta according to
package directions, omitting salt and fat; add snow
peas to pasta the last 3 minutes of cooking time.
Drain and place in a large serving bowl. Add carrot
and sauce, tossing to coat. **Yield:** 5 servings.

HEARTY SPAGHETTI

*Serve with a romaine salad tossed with fresh apple slices
and creamy reduced-fat Ranch-style dressing. Lightly spray
slices of Italian bread with butter-flavored cooking spray
and toast them until golden.*

12 ounces spaghetti, uncooked
    Cooking spray
 1 teaspoon bottled minced garlic
 1 (10-ounce) package frozen chopped onion
 1 (8-ounce) package sliced fresh mushrooms
 1 (14½-ounce) can no-salt-added stewed
    tomatoes, undrained
 1 (6-ounce) can tomato paste
 1 cup water
 1 (12-ounce) package all-vegetable burger
    crumbles
¼ teaspoon salt
 1 tablespoon dried Italian seasoning

1. Cook pasta according to package directions,
omitting salt and fat; drain and keep warm.

2. While pasta cooks, coat a Dutch oven with
cooking spray; place over medium–high heat until
hot. Add garlic, onion, and mushrooms; cook mixture 5 minutes or until liquid is absorbed, stirring
occasionally.

3. Reduce heat to medium; add tomatoes, tomato
paste, and water. Cook 1 minute, stirring well. Add
vegetable crumbles, salt, and Italian seasoning.
Cover, reduce heat to medium-low, and simmer 10
minutes, stirring once. Serve sauce over pasta.
Yield: 6 servings.

YIELD: 6 servings

**EXCHANGES PER
SERVING:**
1 Very Lean Meat
3½ Starch
2 Vegetable

PER SERVING:
Calories 349
(4% from fat)
Fat 1.6g
(saturated fat 0.2g)
Protein 20.7g
Carbohydrate 63.6g
Fiber 6.3g
Cholesterol 0mg
Sodium 396mg

YIELD: 4 servings

EXCHANGES PER
SERVING:
1 Medium-Fat Meat
4 Starch
1 Vegetable

PER SERVING:
Calories 415
(17% from fat)
Fat 7.9g
(saturated fat 3.7g)
Protein 19.9g
Carbohydrate 68.1g
Fiber 6.1g
Cholesterol 21mg
Sodium 479mg

BROCCOLI-CHEDDAR POTATOES

*Add the reduced-fat cheese at the end of cooking
to maintain a creamy texture.*

 4 (10-ounce) baking potatoes
 2 teaspoons margarine or butter
 1/2 cup chopped onion
 1 1/2 cups broccoli flowerets
 1 medium-size yellow squash, sliced
 1 tablespoon all-purpose flour
 1 cup evaporated fat-free milk
 1/2 teaspoon dried thyme
 1/4 teaspoon salt
 1/4 teaspoon pepper
 1 cup (4 ounces) shredded reduced-fat
      Cheddar cheese, divided

1. Place potatoes on a paper towel in microwave oven. Microwave at HIGH 8 minutes. Rotate potatoes a half-turn; microwave about 7 minutes or until tender. Let stand 5 minutes.

2. Meanwhile, melt margarine in a large nonstick skillet over medium heat. Add onion; cook 3 minutes, stirring often. Add broccoli and squash; cook 3 minutes, stirring often. Sprinkle flour over vegetables; stir well, and cook 30 seconds. Add milk and next 3 ingredients; stir well. Bring to a boil; reduce heat, and simmer 3 minutes or until sauce is thickened. Remove from heat; stir in 1/2 cup cheese.

3. Cut a lengthwise slit in top of each potato. Press ends of each potato toward center, pushing pulp up. Top evenly with vegetable mixture; sprinkle with remaining 1/2 cup cheese. **Yield:** 4 servings.

VEGETABLE PIZZA

Cooking spray
1 tablespoon cornmeal
1 (10-ounce) can refrigerated pizza dough
1 medium-size red onion, thinly sliced
2 garlic cloves, very thinly sliced
1 teaspoon olive oil
¼ pound fresh green beans
1 cup (4 ounces) shredded part-skim
   mozzarella cheese
½ cup fat-free ricotta cheese
¼ cup minced fresh basil
½ teaspoon pepper
3 tablespoons sliced ripe olives
4 plum tomatoes, thinly sliced
¼ cup (1 ounce) grated fresh Parmesan cheese

1. Preheat oven to 450°.

2. Coat a 15 x 10-inch jelly-roll pan with cooking spray; sprinkle with cornmeal. Unroll pizza dough; press into pan.

3. Coat a large nonstick skillet with cooking spray; place over medium–high heat until hot. Add onion, and cook 6 minutes or until tender, stirring often. Add garlic, and cook 2 minutes, stirring often. Remove from skillet, and set aside. Add olive oil to skillet; place over medium–high heat until hot. Add green beans, and cook 2 minutes, stirring often. Set aside.

4. Combine mozzarella cheese and next 3 ingredients; stir well. Spread mixture evenly over pizza crust, leaving a ½-inch border. Arrange onion, garlic, and beans over cheese mixture; top with olives and tomato. Sprinkle with Parmesan cheese. Bake at 450° for 12 minutes or until crust is browned. Let pizza stand 5 minutes. To serve, cut into squares.
Yield: 6 servings (serving size: 1 square).

YIELD: 6 servings

EXCHANGES PER SERVING:
1 Medium-Fat Meat
2 Starch
1 Vegetable

PER SERVING:
Calories 252
(26% from fat)
Fat 7.4g
(saturated fat 3g)
Protein 14.3g
Carbohydrate 33.8g
Fiber 3g
Cholesterol 15mg
Sodium 470mg

THREE-CHEESE VEGETABLE PIZZA

EXCHANGES PER
SERVING:
1 Medium-Fat Meat
1½ Starch
1 Vegetable

PER SERVING:
Calories 217
(26% from fat)
Fat 6.3g
(saturated fat 2.9g)
Protein 10.9g
Carbohydrate 30.2g
Fiber 2.3g
Cholesterol 10mg
Sodium 413mg

*This hearty pizza is a veggie-lover's delight.
Serve it with a tossed green salad and
for dessert, fruit sorbet or Italian ice.*

Olive oil-flavored cooking spray
½ (8-ounce) package sliced fresh mushrooms
1 (10-ounce) thin crust Italian bread shell
  (such as Boboli)
3 plum tomatoes, thinly sliced
1 small onion, thinly sliced and separated
  into rings
1 medium-size green or red bell pepper,
  thinly sliced
2 tablespoons chopped fresh basil
3 tablespoons sliced ripe olives
1 cup (4 ounces) shredded part-skim
  mozzarella cheese
1 tablespoon grated Parmesan cheese
1 tablespoon grated Romano cheese

1. Preheat oven to 475°.

2. Coat a medium skillet with cooking spray. Place over medium–high heat until hot. Add mushrooms and cook, stirring constantly, 5 minutes or until golden. Set aside.

3. Place bread shell on an ungreased baking sheet or pizza pan. Top bread shell with mushrooms, tomato, onion, bell pepper, basil, and olives; sprinkle with mozzarella, Parmesan, and Romano cheeses. Bake at 475° for 6 to 9 minutes or until cheeses melt. Cut into 8 wedges. **Yield:** 8 servings (serving size: 1 wedge).

ALL-PURPOSE PIZZA DOUGH

1 package dry yeast (about 2¼ teaspoons)
1¼ cups warm water (105° to 115°)
3¼ cups all-purpose flour, divided
½ teaspoon salt
   Cooking spray

1. Dissolve yeast in warm water in a large bowl, and let stand 5 minutes. Lightly spoon flour into dry measuring cups, and level with a knife. Add 1 cup flour and salt to yeast mixture, and stir well. Stir in 2 cups flour, 1 cup at a time, stirring well after each addition. Turn dough out onto a floured surface. Knead until smooth and elastic (about 10 minutes), and add enough of remaining flour, 1 tablespoon at a time, to prevent the dough from sticking to hands (dough will feel tacky).

2. Place dough in a large bowl coated with cooking spray, turning to coat top. Cover and let rise in a warm place (85°), free from drafts, 1 hour or until doubled in size. (Press two fingers into dough. If an indentation remains, the dough has risen enough.) Punch dough down; cover and let rest 5 minutes. Shape dough according to recipe directions. **Yield:** 1 (15-inch) pizza crust, 8 servings (serving size: 1 wedge).

Note: To freeze, let the dough rise once, punch down, and shape into a ball. Place in a heavy-duty zip-top plastic bag coated with cooking spray; squeeze out all air, and seal. Store in freezer up to 1 month. To thaw, place dough in refrigerator 12 hours or overnight. With scissors, cut away the plastic bag. Place dough on a floured surface, and shape according to recipe directions. Alternatively, for pizza, you can make the dough, roll out, wrap in foil, and freeze. To bake, remove from freezer; top and bake according to recipe instructions (no need to thaw).

YIELD: 8 servings

EXCHANGES PER SERVING:
2½ Starch

PER SERVING:
Calories 188
(3% from fat)
Fat 0.6g
(saturated fat 0.1g)
Protein 5.6g
Carbohydrate 39.1g
Fiber 1.6g
Cholesterol 0mg
Sodium 148mg

PER SERVING:
Calories 274
(21% from fat)
Fat 6.5g
(saturated fat 3g)
Protein 10.9g
Carbohydrate 42.3g
Fiber 2g
Cholesterol 15mg
Sodium 334mg

TOMATO-AND-BASIL PIZZA

*We love this pizza's flavor with Gruyère cheese, but you
can use mozzarella if you prefer.*

   All-Purpose Pizza Dough (recipe on
     page 267)
2 teaspoons yellow cornmeal
2 teaspoons olive oil
2 garlic cloves, minced
1 (14.5-ounce) can diced tomatoes, undrained
   Cooking spray
3/4 cup (3 ounces) shredded Gruyère or Swiss
     cheese
1/4 cup thinly sliced fresh basil
1/4 cup (1 ounce) grated fresh Parmesan cheese

1. Roll prepared dough into a 15-inch circle on a
floured surface. Place dough on a 15-inch round
pizza pan sprinkled with cornmeal. Cover dough,
and let rise in a warm place 20 minutes or until
puffy.

2. Preheat oven to 450°.

3. Heat oil in a large nonstick skillet over
medium-high heat. Add garlic; sauté 30 seconds.
Add tomatoes; cook 5 minutes or until liquid almost evaporates.

4. Lightly coat dough with cooking spray. Spread
tomato mixture over dough, leaving a 1-inch border, and top with Gruyère, basil, and Parmesan.
Bake at 450° for 15 minutes or until golden.
Yield: 8 servings (serving size: 1 wedge).

Note: In a hurry? Try this pizza with refrigerated
pizza dough or a commercial Italian bread shell
(such as Boboli) instead.

THREE-CHEESE PIZZA BIANCA

Bianca, which means white in Italian, refers to a dish without tomato sauce.

All-Purpose Pizza Dough (recipe on page 267)
2 teaspoons yellow cornmeal
2 teaspoons olive oil
3 garlic cloves, minced
Cooking spray
3/4 cup fat-free ricotta cheese
3/4 cup (3 ounces) finely shredded Gruyère cheese
2 tablespoons (1/2 ounce) grated fresh Parmesan cheese

1. Roll prepared dough into a 15-inch circle on a floured surface. Place dough on a 15-inch round pizza pan sprinkled with cornmeal. Cover dough; let rise in a warm place 20 minutes or until puffy.

2. Preheat oven to 450°.

3. Combine oil and garlic in a small bowl. Cover and microwave at MEDIUM-HIGH (70% power) for 1 minute or until bubbly. Cool 10 minutes.

4. Lightly coat dough with cooking spray. Combine garlic mixture and ricotta. Spread ricotta mixture over dough, leaving a 1-inch border. Sprinkle with Gruyère and Parmesan cheeses. Bake pizza at 450° for 15 minutes or until golden. **Yield:** 8 servings (serving size: 1 wedge).

YIELD: 8 servings

EXCHANGES PER SERVING:
2 1/2 Starch
1/2 Low-Fat Milk

PER SERVING:
Calories 271
(19% from fat)
Fat 5.8g
(saturated fat 2.6g)
Protein 12.8g
Carbohydrate 41.8g
Fiber 1.7g
Cholesterol 16mg
Sodium 225mg

YIELD: 4 servings

EXCHANGES PER
SERVING:
1 Medium-Fat Meat
2½ Starch
1 Vegetable

PER SERVING:
Calories 293
(22% from fat)
Fat 7g
(saturated fat 1.8g)
Protein 17.7g
Carbohydrate 40.8g
Fiber 5.1g
Cholesterol 221mg
Sodium 417mg

MEXICAN-STYLE POACHED EGGS

1 (16-ounce) can red beans, rinsed and
  drained
1 (14½-ounce) can Mexican-style stewed
  tomatoes, undrained
2 tablespoons sliced green onions
4 large eggs
4 (6-inch) corn tortillas
  Cooking spray
¼ teaspoon garlic powder
¼ teaspoon ground cumin
¼ cup no-salt-added salsa
¼ cup fat-free sour cream
  Chopped fresh cilantro (optional)

1. Preheat oven to 475°.

2. Combine first 3 ingredients in a saucepan; cook, uncovered, over medium heat 10 minutes, stirring occasionally.

3. Pour water to depth of 2 inches into a large skillet. Bring water to a boil; reduce heat, and simmer. Break 1 egg into a saucer, and slip egg into simmering water, holding saucer as close as possible to water. Repeat with remaining 3 eggs. Simmer eggs 5 minutes or until done; remove from water with a slotted spoon. Drain.

4. Coat tortillas on both sides with cooking spray. Combine garlic powder and cumin; sprinkle on 1 side of tortillas. Stack tortillas, and cut stack into quarters. Place tortilla wedges in a single layer on a baking sheet; bake at 475° for 5 minutes or until crisp and golden, turning once.

5. Arrange tortilla wedges around edges of 4 individual serving plates, and top evenly with bean mixture. Top each serving with a poached egg. Spoon 1 tablespoon salsa and 1 tablespoon sour cream over each serving. Sprinkle with cilantro, if desired. **Yield:** 4 servings.

VEGETABLE FRITTATA

1 cup egg substitute
1 tablespoon fat-free milk
¼ teaspoon dried oregano
⅛ teaspoon garlic powder
⅛ teaspoon salt
⅛ teaspoon pepper
  Cooking spray
¼ cup chopped red bell pepper
¼ cup chopped broccoli flowerets
2 tablespoons sliced fresh mushrooms
¼ cup alfalfa sprouts
½ cup (2 ounces) shredded reduced-fat Swiss
  cheese

1. Combine first 6 ingredients; set aside.

2. Coat a small nonstick skillet with cooking spray; place over medium-high heat until hot. Add bell pepper, broccoli, and mushrooms; cook, stirring constantly, until tender. Remove vegetable mixture from skillet, and set aside.

3. Add egg substitute mixture to skillet; cover and cook over medium-low heat 8 to 10 minutes or until mixture is set. Remove skillet from heat; top egg substitute mixture with alfalfa sprouts and vegetable mixture, and sprinkle evenly with cheese. Cover and let stand 3 to 5 minutes or until cheese melts. Cut into 4 wedges. Serve immediately. **Yield:** 2 servings (serving size: 2 wedges).

♥ *The American Heart Association says it's okay to eat up to 4 egg yolks a week and as many egg whites as you wish. (Egg whites contain no fat or cholesterol.)*

YIELD: 2 servings

EXCHANGES PER SERVING:
3 Very Lean Meat
1 Vegetable
½ Fat

PER SERVING:
Calories 162
(31% from fat)
Fat 5.5g
(saturated fat 2.8g)
Protein 22.6g
Carbohydrate 5g
Fiber 0.8g
Cholesterol 18mg
Sodium 372mg

CHEESE AND VEGETABLE OMELET

YIELD: 2 servings

EXCHANGES PER SERVING:
3 Very Lean Meat
1 Vegetable
1 Fat

PER SERVING:
Calories 168
(32% from fat)
Fat 5.9g
(saturated fat 3.2g)
Protein 21.9g
Carbohydrate 6.9g
Fiber 1g
Cholesterol 18mg
Sodium 469mg

Serve with toasted English muffins and sliced tomatoes.

Butter-flavored cooking spray
1¾ cups finely chopped zucchini (about 1 small)
¼ teaspoon dried dill
1 (8-ounce) carton egg substitute
⅓ cup thinly sliced green onions
¼ teaspoon freshly ground black pepper
Dash of salt
½ cup (2 ounces) reduced-fat shredded Cheddar cheese

1. Coat a 10-inch nonstick skillet with cooking spray; place over medium-high heat until hot. Add zucchini, and cook 4 minutes or until crisp-tender, stirring occasionally. Stir in dill; remove mixture from skillet, and set aside. Wipe skillet with paper towels.

2. Coat skillet with cooking spray; place over medium-high heat until hot. Combine egg substitute and next 3 ingredients, stirring well. Add egg substitute mixture to skillet, and cook 2 minutes. Carefully lift edges of omelet using a spatula; allow uncooked portion to flow underneath cooked portion. Cook 2 additional minutes or until center is almost set.

3. Spoon cheese and zucchini mixture down center of omelet. Fold omelet in half. Reduce heat to low; cook 1 additional minute or until cheese melts and omelet is set. **Yield:** 2 servings.

meats

PICADILLO-STUFFED PEPPERS

4 large green bell peppers
6 ounces ground round
1 cup chopped onion
2 garlic cloves, minced
2 cups cooked brown rice (cooked without salt or fat)
1 (8-ounce) can no-salt-added tomato sauce
¼ cup currants or raisins
¼ cup sliced pimiento-stuffed green olives
2 teaspoons chili powder
1 teaspoon ground cumin
¼ teaspoon ground cinnamon

1. Cut tops off peppers, and remove seeds. Cook tops and bottoms of peppers in boiling water 5 minutes. Drain peppers; set aside.

2. Preheat oven to 350°.

3. Cook ground round, onion, and garlic in a large nonstick skillet over medium heat until meat is browned, stirring until it crumbles; drain. Wipe drippings from skillet with a paper towel. Return meat mixture to skillet, and add rice and remaining 6 ingredients. Cook 3 minutes or until thoroughly heated, stirring occasionally.

4. Spoon meat mixture evenly into pepper shells, and replace tops; place stuffed shells in an 8-inch square baking dish. Add hot water to dish to a depth of 1 inch. Bake, uncovered, at 350° for 20 minutes. **Yield:** 4 servings.

FAVORITE MEAT LOAF

Use leftovers to make satisfying meat loaf sandwiches for lunch or dinner.

Cooking spray
½ cup chopped onion
¼ cup finely chopped celery
2 garlic cloves, minced
1½ pounds ground round
1 (14½-ounce) can diced tomatoes with Italian herbs, drained (such as Contadina)
3 (1-ounce) slices reduced-calorie whole wheat bread, torn into small pieces
1 tablespoon reduced-sodium Worcestershire sauce
¼ teaspoon pepper
1 large egg, lightly beaten
1 large egg white, lightly beaten
2 tablespoons chili sauce
1 tablespoon water

1. Preheat oven to 350°.

2. Coat a nonstick skillet with cooking spray; place over medium-high heat until hot. Add onion, celery, and garlic; cook 3 minutes or until vegetables are tender, stirring constantly.

3. Combine onion mixture, ground round, and next 6 ingredients in a bowl; stir well. Shape meat mixture into a 9 x 5-inch loaf; place on a rack in a broiler pan coated with cooking spray. Combine chili sauce and water; brush over loaf. Bake loaf, uncovered, at 350° for 1 hour or until a meat thermometer inserted in center of loaf registers 160°. Let stand 10 minutes before slicing. **Yield:** 10 servings.

YIELD: 10 servings

EXCHANGES PER SERVING:
2 Lean Meat
½ Starch

PER SERVING:
Calories 137
(27% from fat)
Fat 4.1g
(saturated fat 1.4g)
Protein 17.2g
Carbohydrate 7.7g
Fiber 1.2g
Cholesterol 62mg
Sodium 213mg

**EXCHANGES PER
SERVING:**
3 Lean Meat
1 Starch
1 Vegetable

PER SERVING:
Calories 267
(32% from fat)
Fat 9.4g
(saturated fat 2.8g)
Protein 26.6g
Carbohydrate 18.6g
Fiber 2.9g
Cholesterol 68mg
Sodium 374mg

SWISS STEAK

4	(4-ounce) boned chuck steaks
2	garlic cloves, chopped
¼	cup all-purpose flour
½	teaspoon salt
½	teaspoon black pepper
1	tablespoon vegetable oil
5	cups sliced onion
1¼	cups water

1. Trim fat from steaks. Place each steak between 2 sheets of heavy-duty plastic wrap; flatten each piece to ¼-inch thickness using a meat mallet or rolling pin. Rub steaks with garlic. Lightly spoon flour into a dry measuring cup, and level with a knife. Combine flour, salt, and pepper. Sprinkle steaks with flour mixture.

2. Heat oil in a large cast-iron skillet over medium-high heat. Add steaks, and cook 4 minutes or until brown. Turn steaks over. Add onion, and cook 4 minutes. Add water. Cover, reduce heat, and simmer for 1½ hours or until meat is tender.
Yield: 4 servings (serving size: 1 steak and about ½ cup onions).

Make Ahead
MARINATED FLANK STEAKS

Just a small amount of this aromatic marinade adds flavor and tenderness to these flank steaks.

2 (1-pound) flank steaks
1½ tablespoons prepared mustard
3 tablespoons dry red wine
3 tablespoons low-sodium soy sauce
3 tablespoons lemon juice
3 tablespoons low-sodium Worcestershire
  sauce
  Cooking spray

1. Make shallow cuts in steaks diagonally across grain at 1-inch intervals. Brush both sides of steaks with mustard. Place steaks in a large shallow dish. Combine wine and next 3 ingredients; pour over steaks. Cover and marinate in refrigerator 8 to 12 hours, turning steaks occasionally.

2. Preheat broiler.

3. Remove steaks from marinade, reserving marinade. Place reserved marinade in a small saucepan; bring to a boil. Remove from heat, and set aside.

4. Place steaks on a rack in a broiler pan coated with cooking spray. Broil 5½ inches from heat 5 to 7 minutes on each side or to desired degree of doneness, basting with reserved marinade. Cut steaks diagonally across grain into thin slices. **Yield:** 8 servings.

YIELD: 8 servings

EXCHANGES PER SERVING:
3 Medium-Fat Meat

PER SERVING:
Calories 226
(53% from fat)
Fat 13.2g
(saturated fat 5.6g)
Protein 22.3g
Carbohydrate 1.8g
Fiber 0g
Cholesterol 61mg
Sodium 277mg

**EXCHANGES PER
SERVING:**
2 Medium-Fat Meat
2 Starch
1½ Fruit

PER SERVING:
Calories 388
(25% from fat)
Fat 10.6g
(saturated fat 3.9g)
Protein 20.9g
Carbohydrate 53g
Fiber 3.4g
Cholesterol 43mg
Sodium 267mg

BEEF, PINEAPPLE, AND RED ONION STIR-FRY WITH GINGER SAUCE

¾ pound lean beef flank steak
1 tablespoon dry sherry
¼ teaspoon pepper
1 (20-ounce) can unsweetened pineapple
    chunks, undrained
2 tablespoons low-sodium soy sauce
1 tablespoon rice vinegar
2 teaspoons peanut oil or vegetable oil
1 medium-size red onion, cut into thin
    wedges
2 tablespoons minced peeled fresh ginger or
    bottled chopped fresh ginger
2 garlic cloves, minced
1 cup finely chopped green onions
4 cups hot cooked rice (cooked without salt
    or fat)
¼ cup diagonally sliced green onions

1. Cut steak in half lengthwise (with the grain).
Cut steak across grain into ⅛-inch-thick slices.
Combine steak, sherry, and pepper in a bowl;
toss well.

2. Drain pineapple chunks, reserving pineapple
and ½ cup juice. Combine juice, soy sauce, and
vinegar.

3. Heat oil in a large nonstick skillet or wok over
high heat. Add steak; stir-fry 3 minutes or until
browned. Remove steak from skillet; drain well.

4. Add onion, ginger, garlic, and 1 cup green
onions to skillet; stir-fry 3 minutes or until lightly
browned. Add pineapple; stir-fry 1 minute or until
lightly browned. Return steak to skillet; add juice
mixture. Stir-fry 2 minutes or until thoroughly
heated. Serve over rice. Top with sliced green
onions. **Yield:** 4 servings (serving size: 1 cup stir-
fry and 1 cup rice).

SKILLET BEEF STROGANOFF

The thinner you cut the steak into slices, the more tender the cooked meat will be.

1 (12-ounce) lean boneless round steak
  Cooking spray
1 large onion, sliced
2 cups sliced fresh mushrooms
3/4 cup water
1 tablespoon all-purpose flour
1 tablespoon sweet Hungarian paprika
1/2 teaspoon beef-flavored bouillon granules
1/2 cup low-fat sour cream
1/4 teaspoon salt
1/2 teaspoon pepper
3 cups hot cooked wide egg noodles (cooked without salt or fat)
  Minced fresh parsley (optional)

1. Partially freeze steak; trim fat. Slice steak diagonally across grain into very thin strips; cut strips into 2-inch pieces.

2. Coat a large nonstick skillet with cooking spray; place over medium-high heat until hot. Add steak, and cook 5 minutes or until browned on all sides. Remove steak from skillet; drain. Wipe drippings from skillet with a paper towel. Coat skillet with cooking spray. Add onion; cook, stirring constantly, 5 minutes. Add mushrooms; cook, stirring constantly, 3 minutes. Combine water, flour, paprika, and bouillon granules, stirring until smooth; add to skillet. Stir in steak. Reduce heat to medium-low; cook, stirring constantly, until mixture reaches a simmer. Cook, uncovered, an additional 10 minutes, stirring occasionally.

3. Remove skillet from heat; stir in sour cream, salt, and pepper. To serve, spoon 3/4 cup noodles onto each serving plate; spoon beef mixture evenly over noodles. Sprinkle with minced parsley, if desired. **Yield:** 4 servings.

YIELD: 4 servings

EXCHANGES PER SERVING:
3 Lean Meat
2 Starch
2 Vegetable

PER SERVING:
Calories 368
(25% from fat)
Fat 10.1g
(saturated fat 4.1g)
Protein 28.7g
Carbohydrate 40.3g
Fiber 4.6g
Cholesterol 105mg
Sodium 334mg

EXCHANGES PER
SERVING:
3 Lean Meat

PER SERVING:
Calories 170
(31% from fat)
Fat 5.8g
(saturated fat 2.1g)
Protein 24.3g
Carbohydrate 1.1g
Fiber 0.3g
Cholesterol 69mg
Sodium 215mg

STEAK AU POIVRE

1 pound lean boneless top sirloin steak
2 teaspoons cracked black pepper
$^1/_2$ teaspoon garlic powder
$^1/_4$ teaspoon salt
   Cooking spray
$^1/_4$ cup no-salt-added beef broth
$^1/_4$ cup dry red wine
   Fresh rosemary sprigs (optional)

1. Trim fat from steak. Combine pepper, garlic powder, and salt; rub over both sides of steak.

2. Coat a large nonstick skillet with cooking spray; place skillet over medium heat until hot. Add steak, and cook 7 minutes on each side or to desired degree of doneness. Transfer to a serving platter; set aside, and keep warm.

3. Add broth and wine to skillet; cook over medium heat 4 minutes or until reduced by half, stirring occasionally. Cut steak diagonally across grain into thin slices; drizzle with broth mixture. Garnish with fresh rosemary, if desired. **Yield:** 4 servings.

♥ You can enjoy steak, even on a low-fat diet, by eating small portions of lean cuts like sirloin and round steak. Just remember that 3 ounces of meat—about the size of a deck of cards—is the American Heart Association's recommendation for one serving. And the nutrition experts say that you can eat up to 6 ounces of lean meat a day.

SIRLOIN STEAK WITH GARLIC SAUCE

Serve with mashed potatoes and steamed broccoli.

  Cooking spray
1 pound well-trimmed boneless top sirloin
    steak (1 inch thick)
1 teaspoon dried thyme
¼ teaspoon salt
¼ teaspoon pepper
8 large garlic cloves, unpeeled
⅓ cup no-salt-added beef broth

1. Preheat broiler.

2. Coat rack of a broiler pan with cooking spray. Sprinkle both sides of steak with thyme, salt, and pepper. Place steaks on rack; arrange garlic cloves around steak. Broil steak and garlic 5½ inches from heat 5 to 6 minutes on each side or to desired degree of doneness. Transfer steak to cutting board; cover loosely with aluminum foil to keep warm.

3. Position knife blade in food processor bowl. Cut off bottom of each garlic clove, and squeeze out soft garlic into processor bowl; process until smooth. Add broth; process until combined. Transfer garlic sauce to a microwave-safe dish. Microwave at HIGH 40 seconds.

4. Slice steak diagonally across grain into thin slices; spoon garlic sauce over steak. **Yield:** 4 servings.

YIELD: 4 servings

EXCHANGES PER SERVING:
4 Lean Meat

PER SERVING:
Calories 188
(32% from fat)
Fat 6.6g
(saturated fat 2.5g)
Protein 27.7g
Carbohydrate 2.5g
Fiber 0.2g
Cholesterol 80mg
Sodium 208mg

**EXCHANGES PER
SERVING:**
4 Lean Meat

PER SERVING:
Calories 191
(32% from fat)
Fat 6.7g
(saturated fat 2.6g)
Protein 27.9g
Carbohydrate 3.6g
Fiber 1.2g
Cholesterol 80mg
Sodium 111mg

Make Ahead
PORT MARINATED STEAKS

Steak marinated in port, a sweet red wine with a bit of brandy added to it, takes on a unique flavor. The steak will taste fine if you substitute another sweet red wine, but use port for special occasions.

1½ pounds lean boneless top sirloin steak
½ cup port or sweet red wine
2 tablespoons Worcestershire sauce
2 tablespoons balsamic vinegar
2 garlic cloves, crushed
3 tablespoons minced fresh thyme
Cooking spray

1. Trim fat from steak. Combine wine and next 4 ingredients in a heavy-duty zip-top plastic bag. Add steak; seal bag, and turn bag to coat steak. Marinate steak in refrigerator 8 hours, turning bag occasionally.

2. Remove steak from marinade; pour marinade into a small saucepan. Bring marinade to a boil; cook until reduced to ¼ cup. Set aside.

3. Prepare grill.

4. Coat grill rack with cooking spray; place on grill over medium-hot coals (350° to 400°). Place steak on rack; grill, covered, 5 minutes on each side or to desired degree of doneness. Let steak stand 5 minutes. Cut diagonally across grain into thin slices; drizzle with hot marinade. **Yield:** 6 servings.

Super Quick
CHILI-RUBBED SIRLOIN WITH CORN-BEAN SALSA

1 tablespoon chili powder
1 teaspoon ground cumin
1/2 teaspoon ground red pepper
1 (1-pound) lean boneless top sirloin steak
  (1 inch thick)
  Cooking spray
  Corn-Bean Salsa

1. Combine first 3 ingredients in a small bowl; rub evenly over steak, pressing into steak.

2. Prepare grill.

3. Coat grill rack with cooking spray; place on grill over hot coals (400° to 500°). Place steak on rack; grill, covered, 6 minutes on each side or to desired degree of doneness. Slice steak diagonally across grain into 1/4-inch-thick slices. Top with Corn-Bean Salsa. **Yield:** 4 servings (serving size: 3 ounces steak and 2/3 cup salsa).

Corn-Bean Salsa
1/2 cup thick and chunky cilantro-flavored salsa
1 cup frozen whole-kernel corn, thawed
1 cup drained canned no-salt-added pinto
  beans
1/2 cup sliced green onions

1. Combine all ingredients; serve at room temperature or chill. **Yield:** 2/3 cups.

YIELD: 4 servings

EXCHANGES PER SERVING:
3 Lean Meat
1 1/2 Starch

PER SERVING:
Calories 283
(24% from fat)
Fat 7.5g
(saturated fat 2.6g)
Protein 32.4g
Carbohydrate 22.6g
Fiber 4g
Cholesterol 80mg
Sodium 240mg

EXCHANGES PER
SERVING:
3 Lean Meat
1 Vegetable
1/2 Starch

PER SERVING:
Calories 249
(31% from fat)
Fat 8.7g
(saturated fat 2.5g)
Protein 28.8g
Carbohydrate 12.1g
Fiber 3.7g
Cholesterol 69mg
Sodium 316mg

Super Quick
GINGERED BEEF STIR-FRY

*You can substitute snow peas or zucchini strips
for Sugar Snap peas.*

1/2 cup no-salt-added beef broth
1 tablespoon reduced-sodium soy sauce
1 teaspoon cornstarch
1 teaspoon ground ginger
1/4 to 1/2 teaspoon dried crushed red pepper
Cooking spray
1 teaspoon dark sesame oil
1/2 pound lean boneless sirloin steak, cut
crosswise into 1/4-inch-thick slices
1 (9-ounce) package frozen Sugar Snap peas

1. Combine first 5 ingredients; stir well.

2. Coat a wok or large nonstick skillet with cooking spray; drizzle oil around top of wok, coating
sides. Heat at medium–high (375°) until hot. Add
steak, and stir-fry 2 minutes or until lightly
browned.

3. Add peas and broth mixture to wok; stir-fry 3
minutes or until thickened. **Yield:** 2 servings.

BEEF FILETS WITH VEGETABLES

Cooking spray
1 teaspoon olive oil
2 medium-size red bell peppers, seeded and
    cut into thin strips
2 medium zucchini, thinly sliced
1 small onion, thinly sliced
1 cup no-salt-added beef broth, divided
2 teaspoons minced fresh thyme or ½
    teaspoon dried thyme
2 teaspoons all-purpose flour
4 (4-ounce) beef tenderloin steaks (about
    1 inch thick)
2 large garlic cloves, halved
½ teaspoon freshly ground black pepper

1. Coat a large nonstick skillet with cooking spray; add oil. Place over medium–high heat until hot. Add pepper strips, zucchini, and onion; cook 5 minutes, stirring often. Add ½ cup broth and thyme. Cover, reduce heat, and simmer 5 minutes.

2. Combine remaining ½ cup broth and flour, stirring well. Add to vegetable mixture, stirring well. Cook, stirring constantly, until slightly thickened and bubbly.

3. Prepare grill.

4. Rub steaks with garlic halves, and sprinkle with ½ teaspoon black pepper. Coat grill rack with cooking spray; place on grill over medium–hot coals (350° to 400°). Place steak on rack, and grill, covered, 4 minutes on each side or to desired degree of doneness. Spoon vegetables evenly onto individual serving plates; arrange steaks over vegetables. **Yield:** 4 servings.

YIELD: 4 servings

EXCHANGES PER SERVING:
3 Lean Meat
2 Vegetable

PER SERVING:
Calories 238
(37% from fat)
Fat 9.8g
(saturated fat 3.3g)
Protein 26.2g
Carbohydrate 10.4g
Fiber 2.2g
Cholesterol 71mg
Sodium 61mg

**EXCHANGES PER
SERVING:**
3 Lean Meat
4 Starch

PER SERVING:
Calories 496
(20% from fat)
Fat 10.9g
(saturated fat 3.4g)
Protein 30.2g
Carbohydrate 65.9g
Fiber 2.9g
Cholesterol 71mg
Sodium 298mg

Make Ahead
HOISIN BEEF WITH SHIITAKE MUSHROOM SAUCE

1½ tablespoons hoisin sauce
  1 tablespoon dry white wine
  1 teaspoon minced peeled fresh ginger
  2 garlic cloves, minced and divided
  2 (4-ounce) beef tenderloin steaks (about
       1 inch thick)
1½ cups water
  1 (0.5-ounce) package dried shiitake
       mushrooms (about ½ cup)
     Cooking spray
  1 teaspoon dark sesame oil
 ⅔ cup sliced green onions
  2 cups hot cooked long-grain rice (cooked
       without salt or fat)

1. Combine hoisin sauce, wine, ginger, and 1 garlic clove in a shallow dish. Add steaks; cover and marinate in refrigerator 2 hours, turning occasionally.

2. Combine water and mushrooms in a saucepan; bring to a boil. Remove from heat; cover and let stand 30 minutes. Remove mushrooms from pan, reserving liquid. Discard mushroom stems; cut caps into quarters; set aside. Bring liquid to a boil; cook until reduced to ⅓ cup (about 5 minutes). Remove from heat. Remove steaks from marinade; add marinade to reduced mushroom liquid; set aside.

3. Prepare grill.

4. Place steaks on grill rack coated with cooking spray; cook 6 minutes on each side or until done. Heat sesame oil in a nonstick skillet over medium-high heat. Add mushrooms, green onions, and 1 garlic clove; sauté 2 minutes. Add marinade mixture, and cook 2 minutes. Cut steaks diagonally across grain into thin slices. Arrange steak on each of 2 plates; top with mushroom sauce. Serve with rice. **Yield:** 2 servings (serving size: 3 ounces steak, 1 cup rice, and ¼ cup sauce).

SAVORY STEAKS WITH MUSHROOM SAUCE

Make a nonalcoholic version of this recipe by substituting no-salt-added beef broth or water for the red wine.

4 (4-ounce) beef tenderloin steaks (about 1 inch thick)
1/2 teaspoon freshly ground black pepper
     Cooking spray
1 tablespoon Dijon mustard
1 tablespoon Worcestershire sauce
1/2 cup minced onion
1 (8-ounce) package sliced fresh mushrooms
1 teaspoon dried thyme
1 teaspoon minced garlic
1/4 cup dry red wine

1. Sprinkle steaks with black pepper. Coat a large nonstick skillet with cooking spray; place over medium-high heat until hot. Add steaks; cook 2 minutes on each side. Reduce heat to medium; cook 3 additional minutes, turning once.

2. Remove steaks from skillet; spread mustard over steaks, and top with Worcestershire sauce. Set aside, and keep warm.

3. Coat skillet with cooking spray; add onion, and cook, stirring constantly, 2 minutes. Add mushrooms and remaining 3 ingredients; cook, stirring constantly, 5 minutes.

4. Return steaks to skillet. Cook 4 to 5 minutes or to desired degree of doneness. Transfer steaks to 4 individual serving plates; spoon mushroom mixture over steaks. **Yield:** 4 servings.

YIELD: 4 servings

EXCHANGES PER SERVING:
3 Lean Meat
1 Vegetable

PER SERVING:
Calories 211
(35% from fat)
Fat 8.1g
(saturated fat 3g)
Protein 25.2g
Carbohydrate 6g
Fiber 1.3g
Cholesterol 70mg
Sodium 214mg

BEEF TENDERLOIN WITH HORSERADISH CREAM SAUCE

YIELD: 4 servings

EXCHANGES PER SERVING:
3 Lean Meat

PER SERVING:
Calories 193
(39% from fat)
Fat 8.3g
(saturated fat 3.2g)
Protein 25.7g
Carbohydrate 1.9g
Fiber 0.1g
Cholesterol 73mg
Sodium 155mg

¼ cup red wine vinegar
1 teaspoon chopped fresh thyme or
  ½ teaspoon dried thyme
¼ teaspoon pepper
4 (4-ounce) beef tenderloin steaks (about
  1 inch thick)
  Cooking spray
  Horseradish Cream Sauce
  Fresh thyme sprigs (optional)

1. Combine vinegar, chopped thyme, and ¼ teaspoon pepper in a large heavy-duty zip-top plastic bag. Add steaks; seal bag, and shake until meat is well coated. Marinate steaks in refrigerator 8 hours or overnight, turning bag occasionally.

2. Preheat broiler.

3. Remove steaks from marinade, discarding marinade. Place steaks on rack of a broiler pan coated with cooking spray. Broil 3 inches from heat for 3 to 4 minutes on each side or to desired degree of doneness.

4. Place steaks on 4 individual serving plates; serve each steak with 2½ tablespoons Horseradish Cream Sauce. Garnish with thyme sprigs, if desired. **Yield:** 4 servings.

Horseradish Cream Sauce
  ½ cup fat-free sour cream
  2 tablespoons prepared horseradish
  ¾ teaspoon white wine Worcestershire sauce
  ⅛ teaspoon salt
  ⅛ teaspoon pepper

1. Combine all ingredients. Cover and chill 8 hours or overnight. **Yield:** ⅔ cup.

SLOW-COOKED BEEF POT ROAST

Long, slow cooking tenderizes lean cuts of meat. Other lean roasts you can substitute include round and tip.

      Cooking spray
  1 (3-pound) eye-of-round roast, trimmed
 ½ teaspoon pepper
1¼ cups water, divided
  1 (0.8-ounce) package brown gravy mix with
      onions
  1 teaspoon cornstarch

1. Coat a large nonstick skillet with cooking spray; place over medium-high heat. Sprinkle roast on all sides with pepper. Add roast to skillet, and cook until browned on all sides; place in a 3½- to 4-quart electric slow cooker coated with cooking spray.

2. Combine 1 cup water and gravy mix; pour gravy over roast. Cover and cook on low-heat setting for 8 to 10 hours or on high-heat setting for 4 to 5 hours. Remove roast from sauce; cover roast, and keep warm.

3. Combine remaining ¼ cup water and cornstarch, stirring until smooth. Slowly stir cornstarch mixture into gravy in slow cooker. Pour mixture into a 1-quart microwave-safe glass measure, stirring until blended. Microwave at HIGH 2 minutes or until thickened, stirring after 1 minute. Serve roast with gravy. **Yield:** 12 servings.

YIELD: 12 servings

EXCHANGES PER SERVING:
4 Very Lean Meat

PER SERVING:
Calories 162
(27% from fat)
Fat 4.8g
(saturated fat 1.7g)
Protein 26g
Carbohydrate 1.9g
Fiber 0g
Cholesterol 65mg
Sodium 192mg

SUNDAY POT ROAST

YIELD: 6 servings

EXCHANGES PER
SERVING:
4 Very Lean Meat
1½ Starch
1 Vegetable

PER SERVING:
Calories 311
(16% from fat)
Fat 5.6g
(saturated fat 2g)
Protein 36.3g
Carbohydrate 27.9g
Fiber 3.6g
Cholesterol 74mg
Sodium 469mg

Substitute no-salt-added beef broth if you're concerned about the sodium in this recipe.

1 (2-pound) lean boneless bottom round roast
3 garlic cloves, sliced
½ teaspoon freshly ground black pepper
    Cooking spray
1 (14.5-ounce) can beef broth
½ cup dry red wine
1 large onion, sliced
18 small round red potatoes, halved (about
      1½ pounds)
18 baby carrots (about ½ pound)

1. Trim fat from roast. Make slits in top of roast. Insert a garlic slice into each slit. Rub roast with pepper. Brown roast on all sides over medium–high heat in an ovenproof Dutch oven coated with cooking spray.

2. Preheat oven to 325°.

3. Add beef broth, wine, and onion to Dutch oven. Cover and bake at 325° for 2 hours. Add potato and carrot. Cover and bake 1 to 1½ hours or until roast and vegetables are tender. **Yield:** 6 servings (serving size: 3 ounces roast, 3 potatoes, 3 carrots, and ¼ cup gravy).

Super Quick
GRILLED VEAL CHOPS WITH GREENS

2 tablespoons lemon juice, divided
1 teaspoon olive oil
½ teaspoon pepper, divided
8 cups packaged European-style Italian salad
     greens (romaine, radicchio, and endive)
¼ teaspoon garlic powder
½ teaspoon dried rosemary
4 (6-ounce) lean center-cut loin veal chops
     (about ½ inch thick)
   Cooking spray

1. Combine 1 tablespoon lemon juice, oil, and
¼ teaspoon pepper in a large bowl, stirring well.
Add salad greens, and toss to coat.

2. Combine remaining 1 tablespoon lemon juice,
remaining ¼ teaspoon pepper, garlic powder, and
rosemary in a bowl; rub mixture over veal.

3. Prepare grill.

4. Coat grill rack with cooking spray; place on grill
over hot coals (400° to 500°). Place veal on rack;
grill, covered, 3 to 4 minutes on each side or until
done. Serve veal on top of greens mixture. **Yield:** 4
servings.

YIELD: 4 servings

**EXCHANGES PER
SERVING:**
4 Very Lean Meat
1 Vegetable
1 Fat

PER SERVING:
Calories 205
(32% from fat)
Fat 7.2g
(saturated fat 1.8g)
Protein 29.1g
Carbohydrate 5.1g
Fiber 1.3g
Cholesterol 101mg
Sodium 97mg

VEAL PICCATA

EXCHANGES PER SERVING:
3 Very Lean Meat

PER SERVING:
Calories 143
(23% from fat)
Fat 3.6g
(saturated fat 1g)
Protein 23.1g
Carbohydrate 3.2g
Fiber 0.1g
Cholesterol 94mg
Sodium 243mg

You can substitute pork medaillons or boneless chicken breasts for the veal cutlets, though you may have to cook them a little longer. Be sure to flatten or pound both pork and chicken to about ¼ inch thickness.

⅓ cup dry vermouth
2 tablespoons fresh lemon juice (about 1 small)
¼ teaspoon garlic powder
⅛ teaspoon salt
  Butter-flavored cooking spray
½ pound (¼-inch-thick) veal cutlets
2 tablespoons chopped fresh parsley

1. Combine first 4 ingredients, stirring well.

2. Coat a medium nonstick skillet with cooking spray; place over medium–high heat until hot. Add half of veal cutlets to skillet; cook 1 minute on each side. Transfer veal to a serving platter, and keep warm. Recoat skillet with cooking spray, and repeat procedure with remaining veal cutlets.

3. Add vermouth mixture to skillet. Cook over high heat 1 minute, stirring constantly, scraping particles that cling to bottom. Pour sauce over veal; sprinkle with parsley, and serve immediately. **Yield:** 2 servings.

VEAL MARSALA

Cooking spray
1 (8-ounce) package sliced fresh mushrooms
¼ cup all-purpose flour
¼ teaspoon salt
⅛ teaspoon cracked black pepper
½ pound veal scaloppine or very thin veal cutlets
1½ teaspoons margarine or butter
½ cup Marsala wine

1. Coat a large nonstick skillet with cooking spray; place skillet over medium-high heat until hot. Add mushrooms, and cook 5 minutes or until tender. Set aside; keep warm.

2. While mushrooms cook, place flour, salt, and pepper in a large heavy-duty zip-top plastic bag. Seal bag; shake to mix. Add veal; seal bag, and shake to coat veal. Remove veal from flour mixture, and reserve 1 tablespoon flour mixture; discard remaining flour mixture.

3. Melt margarine in skillet over medium-high heat. Add veal, and cook 3 minutes on each side or until browned. Transfer veal to a serving platter, and keep warm.

4. Combine wine and reserved 1 tablespoon flour mixture, stirring well with a wire whisk; add to skillet. Bring to a boil, scraping browned particles that cling to bottom of skillet. Spoon mushroom mixture and wine mixture over veal. **Yield:** 2 servings.

YIELD: 2 servings

EXCHANGES PER SERVING:
3 Lean Meat
1 Starch
1 Vegetable

PER SERVING:
Calories 253
(25% from fat)
Fat 7g
(saturated fat 1.6g)
Protein 27g
Carbohydrate 19.7g
Fiber 1.9g
Cholesterol 94mg
Sodium 434mg

MOROCCAN LAMB MEAT LOAF

EXCHANGES PER
SERVING:
4 Lean Meat
1 Starch
1/2 Fruit

PER SERVING:
Calories 318
(30% from fat)
Fat 10.7g
(saturated fat 3.6g)
Protein 32.2g
Carbohydrate 23.7g
Fiber 3.5g
Cholesterol 91mg
Sodium 369mg

1　cup finely chopped onion
1/3　cup golden raisins
1/4　cup uncooked bulgur or cracked wheat
1/4　cup chopped fresh mint
1/4　cup coarsely chopped pimiento-stuffed
　　　olives
2　tablespoons lemon juice
1　teaspoon ground cumin
1/4　teasoon salt
1/2　teaspoon ground coriander
1/4　teasoon ground red pepper
2　large egg whites, lightly beaten
1　pound lean ground lamb
　　Cooking spray

1. Preheat oven to 375°.

2. Combine first 11 ingredients in a bowl; stir
well. Crumble lamb over onion mixture; stir just
until blended. Shape mixture into an 8 x 4-inch
loaf. Place loaf in an 11 x 7-inch baking dish
coated with cooking spray.

3. Bake at 375° for 45 minutes or until an instant-
read thermometer registers 160°. Let meat loaf
stand 5 minutes before slicing. **Yield:** 4 servings.

Super Quick
ROSEMARY GRILLED LAMB CHOPS

If you have time, marinate the chops 1 to 2 hours in the refrigerator and they will be even more flavorful.

- ¼ cup balsamic vinegar
- 1 tablespoon lemon juice
- 1 tablespoon dried rosemary, crushed
- ¼ teaspoon garlic powder
- ¼ teaspoon pepper
- 4 (4-ounce) lean lamb loin chops (about 1 inch thick)
  Cooking spray
  Additional balsamic vinegar (optional)

1. Combine first 5 ingredients; stir well.

2. Prepare grill.

3. Trim fat from chops. Coat grill rack with cooking spray; place on grill over medium-hot coals (350° to 400°). Place chops on rack; grill, covered, 6 minutes on each side or until desired degree of doneness, basting occasionally with vinegar mixture. Serve with balsamic vinegar, if desired. **Yield:** 2 servings (serving size: 2 chops).

YIELD: 2 servings

EXCHANGES PER SERVING:
4 Lean Meat

PER SERVING:
Calories 241
(40% from fat)
Fat 10.7g
(saturated fat 3.6g)
Protein 31.5g
Carbohydrate 3.6g
Fiber 0.4g
Cholesterol 99mg
Sodium 89mg

**EXCHANGES PER
SERVING:**
3 Lean Meat

PER SERVING:
Calories 173
(41% from fat)
Fat 7.9g
(saturated fat 2.9g)
Protein 23g
Carbohydrate 1.2g
Fiber 0.1g
Cholesterol 74mg
Sodium 66mg

Super Quick
MINT-GRILLED LAMB CHOPS

⅓ cup fresh mint leaves, chopped
2 tablespoons plain low-fat yogurt
2 garlic cloves, crushed
4 (5-ounce) lean lamb loin chops (about
    1 inch thick)
1 small lemon, cut in half
    Cooking spray
    Fresh mint sprigs (optional)

1. Combine first 3 ingredients in a small bowl.

2. Prepare grill.

3. Trim fat from lamb. Rub lemon halves on both
sides of lamb. Coat grill rack with cooking spray,
and place on grill over medium–hot coals (350° to
400°). Place lamb on rack; grill, covered, 5 minutes.
Turn lamb; spread mint mixture evenly over lamb.
Cook 5 additional minutes or to desired degree of
doneness. Garnish with mint sprigs, if desired.
Yield: 4 servings.

♥ *In a heart-healthy diet, no more than 30 percent of
your calories should come from fat. But not every food
you eat has to fall under the 30 percent limit. For instance, when you serve lamb chops (which are naturally
higher in fat), be sure to serve a low-fat side dish such as
pasta or rice to keep your total fat percentage down at a
healthy level.*

MUSTARD-GARLIC LAMB CHOPS

We assigned our highest flavor rating to this easy recipe. All you do is spread on a paste of spices, Dijon mustard, and lemon juice, then broil the chops.

2 garlic cloves, minced
½ teaspoon pepper
¼ teaspoon dried thyme
⅛ teaspoon salt
2 teaspoons fresh lemon juice
2 teaspoons Dijon mustard
1 teaspoon olive oil
4 (5-ounce) lean lamb loin chops
Cooking spray

1. Combine garlic, pepper, thyme, and salt in a small bowl; mash with back of a spoon until mixture forms a paste. Stir in lemon juice, mustard, and olive oil.

2. Preheat broiler.

3. Trim fat from chops. Spread garlic mixture over both sides of chops. Place chops on rack of a broiler pan coated with cooking spray. Broil 5½ inches from heat 6 to 7 minutes on each side or to desired degree of doneness. **Yield:** 4 servings.

YIELD: 4 servings

EXCHANGES PER SERVING:
3 Lean Meat

PER SERVING:
Calories 192
(44% from fat)
Fat 9.3g
(saturated fat 3g)
Protein 24.3g
Carbohydrate 1.1g
Fiber 0.1g
Cholesterol 77mg
Sodium 216mg

YIELD: 4 servings

EXCHANGES PER
SERVING:
3 Lean Meat

PER SERVING:
Calories 190
(37% from fat)
Fat 7.9g
(saturated fat 2.8g)
Protein 24g
Carbohydrate 4.2g
Fiber 0.2g
Cholesterol 76mg
Sodium 215mg

Make Ahead
HERBED LAMB CHOPS

The longer you allow the lamb and herbs to marinate, the stronger the herb flavor will be when the meat is cooked.

$1/2$ teaspoon dried rosemary, crushed
$1/2$ teaspoon pepper
$1/4$ teaspoon salt
$1/4$ teaspoon dried oregano
$1/4$ teaspoon rubbed sage
1 garlic clove, minced
4 (5-ounce) lean lamb loin chops (about 1 inch thick)
$1/4$ cup balsamic vinegar
$1/4$ cup no-salt-added beef broth
1 tablespoon sugar
1 teaspoon dried rosemary, crushed
Cooking spray

1. Combine first 6 ingredients in a small bowl; stir well. Press mixture evenly onto all sides of lamb chops; place chops on a plate. Cover and marinate in refrigerator 1 to 2 hours.

2. Combine vinegar and next 3 ingredients in a small saucepan; bring to a boil over low heat. Cook 1 minute; remove from heat, and let cool. Strain through a wire mesh strainer, reserving liquid.

3. Preheat broiler.

4. Arrange chops on rack of a broiler pan coated with cooking spray. Broil $5\frac{1}{2}$ inches from heat 7 to 8 minutes on each side or to desired degree of doneness. To serve, spoon vinegar mixture over lamb chops. **Yield:** 4 servings.

LAMB CHOPS WITH HONEY-BALSAMIC GLAZE

4 (5-ounce) lean lamb loin chops
  Cooking spray
¾ cup no-salt-added beef broth
¼ cup dry red wine
2 tablespoons balsamic vinegar
1 tablespoon honey
2 teaspoons cornstarch
1 tablespoon minced fresh mint

1. Coat both sides of lamb chops with cooking spray. Place a large nonstick skillet over medium-high heat until hot; add lamb, and cook 5 minutes on each side.

2. Combine broth and next 4 ingredients, stirring until smooth; add to lamb in skillet, stirring well. Cook lamb in glaze 3 minutes on each side or to desired degree of doneness, stirring glaze often. Transfer lamb to a serving platter. Stir mint into glaze. Pour over lamb, and serve immediately.
Yield: 4 servings.

YIELD: 4 servings

EXCHANGES PER SERVING:
4 Lean Meat
½ Starch

PER SERVING:
Calories 270
(37% from fat)
Fat 11.1g
(saturated fat 3.9g)
Protein 33.7g
Carbohydrate 6.2g
Fiber 0g
Cholesterol 106mg
Sodium 97mg

EXCHANGES PER SERVING:
3 Lean Meat
1 Vegetable

PER SERVING:
Calories 187
(34% from fat)
Fat 7.1g
(saturated fat 2.5g)
Protein 24.2g
Carbohydrate 5.3g
Fiber 1.3g
Cholesterol 74mg
Sodium 316mg

SIMMERED LAMB AND PEPPERS

2 small red bell peppers, cut into thin strips
   (about 2 cups)
1 small onion, vertically sliced (about 1 cup)
   Cooking spray
4 (5-ounce) lean lamb loin chops
½ cup dry red wine
1 teaspoon instant beef-flavored bouillon
   granules
¼ teaspoon garlic powder
⅛ teaspoon pepper

1. Coat bell pepper and onion with cooking spray. Place a large nonstick skillet over medium-high heat until hot. Add bell pepper and onion; stir-fry 2 minutes. Remove from skillet, and set aside. Coat both sides of lamb with cooking spray; add lamb to skillet, and cook 3 minutes on each side.

2. Combine wine and remaining 3 ingredients, stirring well. Pour over lamb; bring to a boil over medium-high heat. Cook 6 minutes or to desired degree of doneness, turning lamb once and stirring occasionally.

3. Transfer lamb to a serving platter. Stir vegetables into wine mixture; cook until thoroughly heated, stirring occasionally. Spoon vegetables over lamb. **Yield:** 4 servings.

Make Ahead
CURRIED LAMB KABOBS

1 pound lean boneless leg of lamb
½ cup plain fat-free yogurt
1 tablespoon low-sodium soy sauce
1 teaspoon curry powder
2 small onions
1 large green bell pepper, seeded and cut into
   16 pieces
16 medium-size fresh mushrooms
   Cooking spray

1. Trim fat from lamb; cut lamb into 1¼-inch cubes. Place lamb in a shallow dish. Combine yogurt, soy sauce, and curry powder; add to lamb, and stir to coat. Cover and marinate in refrigerator at least 2 hours.

2. Cook onions in boiling water to cover in a medium saucepan 10 minutes. Drain and cut each onion into 4 wedges.

3. Prepare grill.

4. Remove lamb from marinade; reserve marinade. Thread lamb, onion, bell pepper, and mushrooms alternately onto 8 (10-inch) skewers; brush with reserved marinade.

5. Coat a grill rack with cooking spray; place on grill over medium-hot coals (350° to 400°). Place kabobs on rack; grill, covered, 10 minutes or to desired degree of doneness, turning kabobs once. Serve immediately. **Yield:** 4 servings.

YIELD: 4 servings

EXCHANGES PER SERVING:
3 Lean Meat
2 Vegetable
½ Starch

PER SERVING:
Calories 257
(32% from fat)
Fat 9g
(saturated fat 3.1g)
Protein 29.5g
Carbohydrate 14.1g
Fiber 2.2g
Cholesterol 81mg
Sodium 201mg

**EXCHANGES PER
SERVING:**
4 Lean Meat
½ Starch

PER SERVING:
Calories 258
(37% from fat)
Fat 10.6g
(saturated fat 3.7g)
Protein 31.9g
Carbohydrate 6.7g
Fiber 0g
Cholesterol 101mg
Sodium 118mg

TANGY RASPBERRY LAMB KABOBS

*For a quick meal, serve with rice and
grilled onions or mushrooms.*

¼ cup seedless raspberry jam
¼ cup balsamic vinegar
 1 teaspoon Dijon mustard
½ teaspoon crumbled dried rosemary
1¼ pounds lean boneless leg of lamb, cut into
     1-inch pieces
    Cooking spray

1. Combine first 4 ingredients in a bowl. Add
lamb, tossing to coat. Thread lamb onto 4 (6-inch)
skewers, leaving space between pieces. Brush
kabobs with jam mixture.

2. Prepare grill.

3. Coat grill rack with cooking spray; place on
grill over medium–hot coals (350° to 400°). Place
kabobs on rack; grill, covered, 3 to 4 minutes. Turn
kabobs, and brush with jam mixture. Grill, covered,
3 to 4 additional minutes or to desired degree of
doneness. **Yield:** 4 servings.

BRAISED LAMB WITH LEMON AND ROSEMARY BEANS

YIELD: 7 servings

EXCHANGES PER SERVING:
2 Lean Meat
3 Starch

PER SERVING:
Calories 340
(19% from fat)
Fat 7.2g
(saturated fat 2.5g)
Protein 26.9g
Carbohydrate 42.8g
Fiber 7.3g
Cholesterol 44mg
Sodium 390mg

     2   cups dried cannellini beans
  2½   pounds lamb shanks
          Cooking spray
     1   medium onion, chopped (about 1 cup)
     1   medium carrot, chopped (about ¾ cup)
    ½   cup dry white wine
     6   cups water
     3   sprigs fresh thyme
     1   sprig fresh rosemary
     1   tablespoon chopped fresh rosemary
     1   teaspoon salt
    ½   teaspoon pepper
     3   garlic cloves, minced
     3   tablespoons fresh lemon juice

1. Sort and wash beans; drain well, and set aside.

2. Place a 6-quart ovenproof Dutch oven over medium heat until hot. Coat lamb shanks with cooking spray; add to pan, and cook 12 minutes or until brown on all sides, turning often. Remove shanks from pan; set aside, and keep warm.

3. Preheat oven to 350°.

4. Add onion and carrot to pan; cook 5 minutes, stirring constantly. Add wine, and bring to a boil, stirring constantly. Reduce heat, and simmer, uncovered, 2 minutes. Add beans, lamb shanks, water, thyme, and rosemary sprig. Bring to a boil. Transfer to oven, and bake, covered, at 350° for 2 hours or until beans are done and meat is tender. Stir in chopped rosemary and next 3 ingredients. Cover and bake 30 additional minutes.

5. Remove meat from bones, and return to pan; stir in lemon juice. Cook over medium–high heat until slightly thickened. Serve immediately. **Yield:** 7 servings (serving size: 1 cup).

Super Quick
MEDITERRANEAN PORK CHOPS

**EXCHANGES PER
SERVING:**
4 Lean Meat
½ Starch

PER SERVING:
Calories 247
(34% from fat)
Fat 9.2g
(saturated fat 3.1g)
Protein 29.7g
Carbohydrate 9.7g
Fiber 0.5g
Cholesterol 82mg
Sodium 205mg

2   teaspoons chopped fresh mint
2   teaspoons sugar
1   (8-ounce) carton plain fat-free yogurt
1½ tablespoons hoisin sauce
2   teaspoons curry powder
4   (4-ounce) boneless center-cut pork loin
        chops (½ inch thick), trimmed
    Cooking spray

1. Combine mint and sugar in a small bowl, press-ing mint into sugar with back of a spoon until blended. Stir in yogurt. Set aside.

2. Combine hoisin sauce and curry powder, stir-ring well; spread evenly on both sides of pork.

3. Prepare grill.

4. Coat grill rack with cooking spray; place on grill over medium–hot coals (350° to 400°). Place pork on rack; grill, covered, 5 minutes or until done, turning once. Serve pork with yogurt mix-ture. **Yield:** 4 servings.

CURRANT GLAZED PORK CHOPS

Serve with roasted new potatoes and green beans.

2 tablespoons red currant jelly
1½ tablespoons ketchup
1½ teaspoons white vinegar
   Dash of ground cinnamon
   Dash of ground cloves
4 (4-ounce) boneless center-cut pork loin
   chops (½ inch thick)
¼ teaspoon pepper
⅛ teaspoon salt
   Cooking spray

1. Combine first 5 ingredients in a small saucepan. Cook over medium heat until jelly melts, stirring constantly.

2. Preheat grill.

3. Sprinkle both sides of pork with pepper and salt. Coat grill rack with cooking spray; place on grill over medium–hot coals (350° to 400°). Place pork on rack; brush with jelly mixture. Grill, covered, 5 minutes on each side or until done, basting frequently with jelly mixture. **Yield:** 4 servings.

YIELD: 4 servings

EXCHANGES PER SERVING:
3 Lean Meat
½ Starch

PER SERVING:
Calories 214
(35% from fat)
Fat 8.3g
(saturated fat 2.8g)
Protein 25.1g
Carbohydrate 8.4g
Fiber 0.2g
Cholesterol 71mg
Sodium 218mg

YIELD: 4 servings

EXCHANGES PER SERVING:
3 Lean Meat
½ Starch

PER SERVING:
Calories 221
(38% from fat)
Fat 9.4g
(saturated fat 3g)
Protein 25.1g
Carbohydrate 7.1g
Fiber 0g
Cholesterol 71mg
Sodium 245mg

Super Quick
MARMALADE PORK CHOPS

If you're watching sodium, look for salt-free lemon-herb seasoning. The flavor is similar to lemon-pepper seasoning, but without the salt.

    Cooking spray
1 teaspoon olive oil
4 (4-ounce) lean boneless pork loin chops, trimmed
2 teaspoons lemon-pepper seasoning
2 tablespoons cider vinegar
¼ cup low-sugar orange marmalade

1. Coat a large nonstick skillet with cooking spray; add oil, and place over medium-high heat until hot. Sprinkle chops on both sides with 2 teaspoons lemon-pepper seasoning; add chops to skillet, and cook 5 minutes on each side or until done. Remove from pan, and keep warm.

2. Add vinegar to skillet; stir in marmalade. Return chops to skillet, turning once to coat; cook 1 minute or until thoroughly heated. Serve immediately. **Yield:** 4 servings.

PEPPERED PORK WITH CORN RELISH

When chopping green onions and bell pepper, chop extra, and store in the freezer in zip-top freezer bags.

Cooking spray
4 (4-ounce) lean boneless pork loin chops (about ½ inch thick)
2 tablespoons jalapeño pepper jelly, divided
1½ cups frozen whole-kernel corn, thawed
½ cup diced red bell pepper
⅓ cup chopped green onions (about 3 green onions)

1. Coat a large nonstick skillet with cooking spray, and place over medium heat until hot. Add pork; top evenly with 1 tablespoon jelly. Cook pork 3 minutes on each side. Remove pork from skillet, and keep warm.

2. Add remaining 1 tablespoon jelly to skillet; cook over low heat, stirring constantly, until melted. Add corn, red bell pepper, and green onions; cook over medium–high heat, stirring constantly, 2 minutes. Add pork; cook 3 minutes or until pork is done. **Yield:** 4 servings.

♥*Think pork is fatty? Actually, roasted pork tenderloin has about the same amount of fat as the same size portion of skinless roasted chicken breast. To make sure you buy the leanest cuts of pork, look for "loin" or "leg" on the package label (pork tenderloin, top loin roast, top leg roast, loin chops, and pork sirloin roast).*

YIELD: 4 servings

EXCHANGES PER SERVING:
3 Lean Meat
1 Starch
1 Vegetable

PER SERVING:
Calories 268
(30% from fat)
Fat 8.8g
(saturated fat 2.9g)
Protein 27.1g
Carbohydrate 20.8g
Fiber 2g
Cholesterol 71mg
Sodium 82mg

YIELD: 4 servings

**EXCHANGES PER
SERVING:**
3 Lean Meat
1½ Fruit

PER SERVING:
Calories 279
(31% from fat)
Fat 9.5g
(saturated fat 3g)
Protein 25.4g
Carbohydrate 23.1g
Fiber 2.7g
Cholesterol 71mg
Sodium 234mg

PORK MEDAILLONS WITH
PEAR SAUCE

  4 (4-ounce) boneless center-cut pork loin
       chops (½ inch thick)
 ½ teaspoon pepper
 ¼ teaspoon salt
  1 teaspoon margarine or butter
  2 firm, ripe pears
  1 tablespoon sugar
 ½ teaspoon dried rosemary, crushed
 ½ cup apple juice

1. Sprinkle both sides of pork with pepper and
salt. Melt margarine in a large nonstick skillet over
medium-high heat. Add pork; cook 3 minutes on
each side or until browned. Remove from skillet;
set aside.

2. While pork cooks, core pears, and cut into ½-
inch slices. Add pear slices to skillet; sprinkle with
sugar and rosemary. Cook over medium-low heat 3
minutes, stirring often.

3. Pour apple juice into skillet; return pork to skillet. Simmer 6 to 8 minutes or until pork is done.
Yield: 4 servings.

PINEAPPLE-GLAZED PORK CHOPS

To crush dried rosemary, chop it finely with a knife or use a mortar and pestle to crush it.

4   (4-ounce) lean boneless pork loin chops, trimmed
¼   teaspoon salt
¼   teaspoon pepper
     Cooking spray
1   (6-ounce) can pineapple juice
2   tablespoons dry sherry (optional)
2   tablespoons brown sugar
1   teaspoon dried rosemary, crushed
¼   teaspoon garlic powder

1. Press pork chops with palm of hand to flatten slightly; sprinkle with salt and pepper.

2. Coat a large nonstick skillet with cooking spray; place over high heat until hot. Add chops, and cook 1 minute on each side or until browned. Reduce heat to medium–high, and cook chops 4 additional minutes on each side or until done. Remove chops from skillet; set aside, and keep warm.

3. Add pineapple juice and remaining 4 ingredients to skillet, stirring well. Cook over high heat, stirring constantly, scraping particles that cling to bottom. Cook 5 minutes or until juice mixture is thickened. Return chops to skillet, turning to coat with glaze; serve immediately. **Yield:** 4 servings.

YIELD: 4 servings

EXCHANGES PER SERVING:
3 Lean Meat
1 Starch

PER SERVING:
Calories 226
(33% from fat)
Fat 8.3g
(saturated fat 2.8g)
Protein 25.2g
Carbohydrate 11g
Fiber 0.1g
Cholesterol 71mg
Sodium 224mg

PORK CHOPS WITH SPICED PEACH-RAISIN SAUCE

1 (16-ounce) can sliced peaches in extra-light syrup, undrained
1/2 cup raisins
3/4 cup orange juice
1/2 teaspoon ground nutmeg
1/4 teaspoon ground ginger
Cooking spray
6 (4-ounce) boneless center-cut pork loin chops
1/2 teaspoon salt
2 tablespoons cornstarch
1/4 cup water

1. Drain peaches, reserving syrup; set peaches aside. Combine syrup, raisins, and next 3 ingredients; set aside.

2. Coat a large nonstick skillet with cooking spray; place over medium-high heat until hot. Sprinkle pork with salt, and add to skillet; cook 4 minutes on each side or until browned. Reduce heat to medium. Add peaches and syrup mixture; cover and cook 5 minutes or until pork is done. Remove pork from skillet; set aside.

3. Combine cornstarch and water; add to skillet. Cook, stirring constantly, until mixture is thickened. Return pork to skillet, turning to coat with peach mixture. **Yield:** 6 servings.

SWEET-AND-SAVORY
PORK TENDERLOIN

*If you prefer not to butterfly the tenderloin, just grill it,
uncut, 10 minutes on each side or until done.*

2 (½-pound) pork tenderloins
2 teaspoons ground sage
1 tablespoon salt-free lemon-herb seasoning
¼ cup apricot spreadable fruit
2 tablespoons Dijon mustard
  Cooking spray

1. Slice pork lengthwise down center, cutting to,
but not through bottom. Press with hands to flatten
pork. Sprinkle sage and lemon–herb seasoning over
pork. Combine apricot spread and mustard. Spread
half of apricot mixture over pork.

2. Prepare grill.

3. Coat grill rack with cooking spray, and place on
grill over medium-hot coals (350° to 400°). Place
tenderloins on rack; grill, covered, 7 minutes. Turn
pork, and baste with remaining apricot mixture.
Cover and grill 7 additional minutes or until a meat
thermometer inserted into thickest part of tenderloin registers 160°. **Yield:** 4 servings.

YIELD: 4 servings

**EXCHANGES PER
SERVING:**
4 Very Lean Meat
1 Fruit

PER SERVING:
Calories 204
(23% from fat)
Fat 5.1g
(saturated fat 1.5g)
Protein 26g
Carbohydrate 11.8g
Fiber 0.5g
Cholesterol 83mg
Sodium 284mg

Make Ahead
PORK TENDERLOIN WITH MAPLE PAN JUICES

You can substitute dry white wine for the sake, which is a slightly sweet wine made from fermented rice.

⅓ cup diced onion
¼ cup fresh orange juice, divided
¼ cup maple syrup, divided
2 tablespoons sake (rice wine)
2 tablespoons low-sodium soy sauce
⅛ teaspoon black pepper
2 garlic cloves, minced
1 (1-pound) pork tenderloin
    Cooking spray
⅓ cup fat-free, less-sodium chicken broth

1. Combine onion, 2 tablespoons orange juice, 2 tablespoons syrup, sake, soy sauce, pepper, and garlic in a large zip-top plastic bag. Trim fat from pork. Add pork to syrup mixture; seal and marinate in refrigerator 2 hours.

2. Preheat oven to 400°.

3. Heat a 9-inch heavy ovenproof skillet coated with cooking spray over medium-high heat. Remove pork from bag, reserving marinade. Add pork to pan; cook 5 minutes, browning on all sides. Insert meat thermometer into thickest part of pork. Place pan in oven; bake at 400° for 30 minutes or until meat thermometer registers 160° (slightly pink). Remove pork from pan. Set aside, and keep warm.

4. Combine 2 tablespoons orange juice, 2 tablespoons syrup, reserved marinade, and broth in a small bowl. Add syrup mixture to pan, and place over medium-high heat, scraping pan to loosen browned bits. Bring to a boil; reduce heat, and simmer 5 minutes or until slightly thick. Serve sauce with pork. **Yield:** 4 servings (serving size: 3 ounces pork and 2 tablespoons sauce).

Super Quick
SWEET-HOT PORK MEDAILLONS

Sesame oil adds a rich, nutty flavor to this recipe, but you can use vegetable oil instead.

1   pound pork tenderloin
1/8 teaspoon dried crushed red pepper
1/8 teaspoon garlic powder
    Cooking spray
1   teaspoon sesame oil
2   tablespoons water
2   tablespoons reduced-sodium soy sauce
2   tablespoons brown sugar

1. Trim fat from pork. Cut pork into 1-inch-thick slices. Place slices between two sheets of heavy-duty plastic wrap, and flatten to ½-inch thickness, using a meat mallet or rolling pin. Sprinkle with pepper and garlic powder.

2. Coat a large nonstick skillet with cooking spray; add oil. Place skillet over medium-high heat until hot. Add half of pork medaillons, and cook 3 minutes on each side or until browned. Remove pork from skillet; set aside, and keep warm. Repeat procedure with remaining half of pork medaillons.

3. Add water, soy sauce, and brown sugar to skillet. Reduce heat to medium; cook, stirring constantly, 1 minute or until bubbly. Spoon sauce over pork. **Yield:** 4 servings.

YIELD: 4 servings

EXCHANGES PER SERVING:
3 Very Lean Meat
½ Starch

PER SERVING:
Calories 160
(23% from fat)
Fat 4.1g
(saturated fat 1.1g)
Protein 24.2g
Carbohydrate 5.1g
Fiber 0g
Cholesterol 74mg
Sodium 299mg

YIELD: 4 servings

EXCHANGES PER SERVING:
3 Very Lean Meat
2 Starch
1/2 Fat

PER SERVING:
Calories 303
(23% from fat)
Fat 7.9g
(saturated fat 1.9g)
Protein 27.1
Carbohydrate 29.1g
Fiber 1g
Cholesterol 79mg
Sodium 195mg

HOISIN PORK MEDAILLONS

1 tablespoon dark sesame oil
   Cooking spray
1/4 to 1/2 teaspoon dried crushed red pepper
3 garlic cloves, minced
1 (1-pound) pork tenderloin, cut into 1/2-inch slices
1/4 cup plus 2 tablespoons water
1/3 cup dry sherry
3 tablespoons hoisin sauce
3 tablespoons chopped fresh cilantro
2 cups hot cooked long-grain rice (cooked without salt or fat)
1/4 cup sliced green onions
   Fresh cilantro sprigs (optional)

1. Heat oil in a nonstick skillet coated with cooking spray over medium–high heat. Add pepper and garlic; cook, stirring constantly, 1 minute. Add pork; cook 4 minutes on each side or until browned. Remove pork. Wipe skillet with a paper towel.

2. Combine water and next 3 ingredients in skillet. Cook over medium heat, stirring constantly, 1 minute or until thickened. Return pork to skillet; turn to coat. Place rice on a serving platter. Spoon pork mixture over rice. Top with green onions; garnish with cilantro sprigs, if desired. **Yield:** 4 servings.

LEMON PORK SCALOPPINE

1 (1-pound) pork tenderloin
3 tablespoons all-purpose flour
¼ teaspoon salt
¼ teaspoon pepper
  Cooking spray
2 teaspoons olive oil, divided
3 tablespoons lemon juice
2 tablespoons water
1 teaspoon capers
¼ cup minced fresh parsley

1. Trim fat from tenderloin. Cut tenderloin into ½-inch-thick slices; place slices between 2 sheets of heavy-duty plastic wrap, and pound to ¼-inch thickness, using a meat mallet or rolling pin.

2. Combine flour, salt, and pepper in a large heavy-duty zip-top plastic bag; add pork slices. Seal bag, and shake until pork is coated.

3. Coat a large nonstick skillet with cooking spray; add 1 teaspoon oil, and place over medium-high heat until hot. Add half of pork slices; cook 2 minutes on each side or until browned. Transfer to a serving plate; keep warm. Repeat procedure with remaining 1 teaspoon oil and pork slices; remove skillet from heat.

4. Add lemon juice, water, and capers to skillet; bring just to a boil. Pour mixture over pork slices; sprinkle with parsley. **Yield:** 4 servings.

YIELD: 4 servings

EXCHANGES PER SERVING:
3 Very Lean Meat
½ Starch
½ Fat

PER SERVING:
Calories 171
(27% from fat)
Fat 5.2g
(saturated fat 1.3g)
Protein 24.4g
Carbohydrate 5.2g
Fiber 0.2g
Cholesterol 74mg
Sodium 258mg

YIELD: 4 servings

**EXCHANGES PER
SERVING:**
3 Very Lean Meat
2 Vegetable
1/2 Fat

PER SERVING:
Calories 182
(22% from fat)
Fat 4.5g
(saturated fat 1.3g)
Protein 24.8g
Carbohydrate 10.6g
Fiber 1.9g
Cholesterol 74mg
Sodium 207mg

PORK MEDAILLONS WITH GLAZED ONIONS

*Ask your butcher to trim the fat from the pork
tenderloin and cut it into slices.*

1   pound pork tenderloin
1/2   teaspoon dried thyme
1/4   teaspoon salt
1/4   teaspoon pepper
    Cooking spray
1   teaspoon olive oil
1   small red onion, thinly sliced and separated
        into rings
3   tablespoons balsamic vinegar
2   teaspoons honey

1. Trim fat from pork. Cut pork into 1-inch-thick
slices. Place slices between two sheets of heavy-
duty plastic wrap, and flatten to ½-inch thickness,
using a meat mallet or rolling pin. Sprinkle with
thyme, salt, and pepper.

2. Place a large nonstick skillet coated with cooking spray over medium heat until hot. Add pork;
cook 3 minutes on each side or until browned.
Remove from skillet, and keep warm.

3. Heat oil in skillet over medium heat; add onion.
Cook 8 to 10 minutes or until onion is tender, stirring often. Add vinegar and honey; cook, stirring
constantly, 1 minute or until onion is glazed. Spoon
onion over pork. **Yield:** 4 servings.

CRANBERRY PORK ROAST

You don't have to brown the roast before putting it in the slow cooker. However, browning the outside of the roast does add a rich caramelized flavor to the meat.

Cooking spray
1 (3-pound) boneless pork loin roast, trimmed
1 (16-ounce) can jellied whole-berry
   cranberry sauce
¼ cup steak sauce
1 tablespoon brown sugar
1 teaspoon prepared mustard
2 tablespoons water
2 tablespoons cornstarch

1. Coat a large nonstick skillet with cooking spray; place over medium-high heat. Add roast; cook until browned on all sides. Place roast in a 4- to 5-quart electric slow cooker coated with cooking spray.

2. Combine cranberry sauce and next 3 ingredients; pour over roast. Cover and cook on low-heat setting for 8 hours or on high-heat setting for 4 to 5 hours. Remove roast from sauce; cover roast, and keep warm.

3. Combine water and cornstarch, stirring until smooth. Stir cornstarch mixture into sauce in slow cooker. Pour mixture into a 1-quart microwave-safe glass measure. Microwave at HIGH 2 minutes, stirring after 1 minute. Serve roast with gravy. **Yield:** 12 servings.

YIELD: 12 servings

EXCHANGES PER SERVING:
3 Lean Meat
1 Starch

PER SERVING:
Calories 252
(33% from fat)
Fat 9.3g
(saturated fat 3g)
Protein 23.5g
Carbohydrate 17g
Fiber 0g
Cholesterol 68mg
Sodium 169mg

HAM STEAK WITH PINEAPPLE SALSA

YIELD: 4 servings

EXCHANGES PER SERVING:
2 Very Lean Meat
1¹/₂ Fruit

PER SERVING:
Calories 165
(19% from fat)
Fat 3.4g
(saturated fat 0g)
Protein 12.1g
Carbohydrate 23.3g
Fiber 0.5g
Cholesterol 31mg
Sodium 563mg

1 (15¹/₄-ounce) can pineapple tidbits in juice, undrained
¹/₃ cup chopped green onions
2 tablespoons brown sugar
1 tablespoon cider vinegar
2 teaspoons low-sodium soy sauce
2 garlic cloves, minced
   Cooking spray
³/₄ pound reduced-fat, lower-salt ham steak

1. Drain pineapple, reserving juice. Combine pineapple, 2 tablespoons pineapple juice, green onions, and next 4 ingredients in a bowl; stir well.

2. Prepare grill.

3. Coat grill rack with cooking spray; place on grill over medium–hot coals (350° to 400°). Place ham steak on rack, and grill, uncovered, about 4 minutes on each side, basting often with remaining pineapple juice. Serve ham steak with pineapple salsa. **Yield:** 4 servings.

♥ *The American Heart Association says it's okay to have up to 2,400 milligrams of sodium per day (unless your doctor has put you on a strict low-sodium diet). If you eat three meals a day, that works out to about 800 milligrams of sodium per meal. So you can have a serving of Ham Steak with Pineapple Salsa (563 milligrams sodium) and stay within the guidelines—just be sure to watch the sodium content of other foods you eat during the day.*

poultry

YIELD: 6 servings

EXCHANGES PER SERVING:
3 Very Lean Meat

PER SERVING:
Calories 105
(23% from fat)
Fat 2.7g
(saturated fat 0.7g)
Protein 17.6g
Carbohydrate 1.8g
Fiber 0.5g
Cholesterol 57mg
Sodium 161mg

LEMON-HERB ROASTED CHICKEN

Serve with steamed vegetables and hot cooked rice that has been tossed with lemon zest and chopped fresh herbs.

1   (3-pound) roasting chicken
3   sprigs fresh rosemary, thyme, or sage
2   tablespoons chopped fresh rosemary, thyme, or sage
1   teaspoon grated lemon rind
3   tablespoons fresh lemon juice
$1/4$ teaspoon salt
$1/4$ teaspoon pepper
2   garlic cloves, minced

1. Preheat oven to 400°.

2. Remove and discard giblets from chicken. Rinse chicken under cold water; pat dry. Trim excess fat. Starting at neck cavity, loosen skin from breast and drumsticks by inserting fingers, gently pushing between skin and meat.

3. Place fresh rosemary, thyme, or sage sprigs under loosened skin over breast. Combine chopped rosemary and remaining 5 ingredients; brush over chicken and in cavity of chicken.

4. Place chicken on a rack in roasting pan. Insert meat thermometer into meaty part of thigh, making sure not to touch bone. Bake, uncovered, at 400° for 1 hour or until thermometer registers 180°. Let stand 15 minutes before serving. **Yield:** 6 servings.

ROAST CHICKEN WITH CUMIN, HONEY, AND ORANGE

1 (3-pound) roasting chicken
¼ cup honey
1½ tablespoons grated orange rind
1 tablespoon ground cumin
¼ teaspoon salt
⅛ teaspoon black pepper
1 garlic clove, minced

1. Preheat oven to 400°.

2. Remove and discard giblets from chicken. Rinse chicken with cold water; pat dry. Trim excess fat. Starting at neck cavity, loosen skin from breast and drumsticks by inserting fingers, gently pushing between skin and meat.

3. Combine honey and remaining ingredients. Rub honey mixture under loosened skin and over breast and drumsticks. Lift wing tips up and over back; tuck under chicken.

4. Place chicken, breast side up, on a foil-lined broiler pan. Pierce skin several times with a meat fork. Insert meat thermometer into meaty part of thigh, making sure not to touch bone. Bake at 400° for 30 minutes; cover loosely with foil. Bake an additional 40 minutes or until thermometer registers 180°. Let stand 10 minutes before serving. Discard skin. **Yield:** 6 servings.

YIELD: 6 servings

EXCHANGES PER SERVING:
3 Very Lean Meat
1 Starch
½ Fat

PER SERVING:
Calories 182
(27% from fat)
Fat 5.5g
(saturated fat 1.5g)
Protein 20.8g
Carbohydrate 12.7g
Fiber 0.1g
Cholesterol 63mg
Sodium 161mg

EXCHANGES PER
SERVING:
4 Very Lean Meat
1/2 Starch
1 Fat

PER SERVING:
Calories 235
(28% from fat)
Fat 7.4g
(saturated fat 2g)
Protein 30.3g
Carbohydrate 6.9g
Fiber 0.2g
Cholesterol 87mg
Sodium 168mg

FORTY-CLOVES-OF-GARLIC CHICKEN

  4 garlic heads
     Olive oil-flavored cooking spray
  1 (3-pound) broiler-fryer, skinned
 1/2 cup dry white wine
 1/2 cup plus 2 tablespoons fat-free, less-sodium
     chicken broth, divided
 1/2 cup evaporated fat-free milk
  1 tablespoon cornstarch
 1/8 teaspoon pepper

1. Preheat oven to 375°.

2. Peel outer skin from garlic heads, and discard.
Cut off top one-third of each garlic head. Separate
garlic heads into 40 cloves. Reserve any remaining
cloves for another use. Place 35 cloves in center of
a piece of heavy-duty aluminum foil; coat garlic
with cooking spray. Fold foil over garlic, sealing
tightly. Set aside garlic packet and remaining 5
cloves.

3. Place chicken, breast side up, on a rack in a shallow roasting pan. Place 5 reserved garlic cloves in
cavity. Place garlic packet on rack in roasting pan.
Bake, uncovered, at 375° for 20 minutes. Pour
wine over chicken, and bake 40 minutes, basting
occasionally with pan juices.

4. Remove garlic from pan; let cool 10 minutes.
Bake chicken 30 minutes or until done. Remove
and discard papery skin from garlic. Squeeze pulp
from garlic cloves into container of a mini food
processor. Add 2 tablespoons broth; process until
smooth, stopping once to scrape down sides.

5. Combine remaining 1/2 cup broth, evaporated
milk, and cornstarch in a small saucepan, stirring
until smooth. Cook over medium-high heat 2 to 3
minutes, stirring occasionally. Stir garlic mixture
and pepper into broth mixture. Serve chicken with
garlic sauce. **Yield:** 6 servings.

LEMON AND ROSEMARY ROASTED CHICKEN WITH POTATOES

2 medium lemons
1 (3¼-pound) broiler-fryer
1½ tablespoons finely chopped fresh rosemary
6 garlic cloves, minced
1 teaspoon salt
¾ teaspoon pepper
2¼ pounds large red potatoes, cut into 2-inch pieces (about 5 cups)
3 tablespoons olive oil
Cooking spray

1. Preheat oven to 400°.

2. Remove yellow part of rind from lemons, using a vegetable peeler and leaving inner white skin on fruit; finely chop rind, and set aside. Squeeze juice from lemons; set juice aside. Reserve juiced lemon halves. Remove and discard giblets and neck from chicken. Rinse chicken with cold water; pat dry. Trim excess fat. Stuff body cavity with reserved juiced lemon halves.

3. Combine reserved lemon rind, rosemary, and next 3 ingredients in a small bowl; stir in 2 tablespoons reserved lemon juice. Discard remaining lemon juice. Combine potatoes and olive oil in a large bowl; toss well. Add 2 tablespoons lemon rind mixture to potatoes, tossing to coat; set aside.

4. Starting at neck cavity, loosen skin from breast and drumsticks by inserting fingers, gently pushing between skin and meat. Sprinkle remaining lemon rind mixture under loosened skin and rub over breast and drumstick meat. Place chicken, breast side up, on rack of a broiler pan coated with cooking spray. Arrange potatoes in a single layer around chicken. Bake at 400° for 1 hour or until meat thermometer inserted in meaty part of thigh registers 180°. Cover chicken loosely with foil; let stand 10 minutes. Discard skin. **Yield:** 6 servings.

YIELD: 6 servings

EXCHANGES PER SERVING:
3 Lean Meat
1½ Starch
½ Fat

PER SERVING:
Calories 301
(39% from fat)
Fat 13.2g
(saturated fat 2.7g)
Protein 26.2g
Carbohydrate 19.3g
Fiber 2.3g
Cholesterol 73mg
Sodium 469mg

YIELD: 6 servings

**EXCHANGES PER
SERVING:**
4 Very Lean Meat
1 Starch

PER SERVING:
Calories 220
(19% from fat)
Fat 4.6g
(saturated fat 1.1g)
Protein 30.9g
Carbohydrate 11.9g
Fiber 1.1g
Cholesterol 89mg
Sodium 255mg

CRISPY OVEN-FRIED CHICKEN

*Crispy "fried" chicken returns to the picnic basket with
this heart-healthy version of the traditional classic.*

$\frac{1}{3}$ cup egg substitute
1 tablespoon water
1 cup crispy rice cereal, crushed
$\frac{1}{3}$ cup toasted wheat germ
1 tablespoon instant minced onion
$\frac{1}{2}$ teaspoon salt-free herb-and-spice blend
$\frac{1}{4}$ teaspoon garlic powder
$\frac{1}{4}$ teaspoon salt
$\frac{1}{4}$ teaspoon pepper
1 (3-pound) broiler-fryer, cut up and skinned
$\frac{1}{4}$ cup all-purpose flour
   Cooking spray

1. Preheat oven to 350°.

2. Combine egg substitute and water in a small
shallow dish. Combine cereal and next 6 ingredients in a small shallow dish. Set aside.

3. Combine chicken and flour in a large heavy-
duty zip-top plastic bag; seal bag, and shake until
chicken is coated. Dip chicken in egg substitute
mixture; dredge in cereal mixture.

4. Place chicken on rack of a broiler pan coated
with cooking spray. Bake, uncovered, at 350° for 1
hour or until chicken is tender. **Yield:** 6 servings.

BRAISED LEMON CHICKEN

Braising is the technique of cooking meat and vegetables covered in liquid. It allows seasonings to seep into the food to keep it moist and flavorful. Just be sure to use a tight-fitting lid on your skillet.

Cooking spray
2 teaspoons margarine or butter
1 (3-pound) broiler-fryer, cut up and skinned
1 pound small round red potatoes, quartered
2 garlic cloves, crushed
1/2 cup fresh lemon juice
1/4 cup low-sodium chicken broth
2 medium zucchini, sliced
1 tablespoon minced fresh tarragon

1. Coat a large skillet with cooking spray; add margarine. Place over medium-high heat until hot. Add chicken, and cook 2 minutes on each side or until lightly browned.

2. Add potato and next 3 ingredients; bring to a boil. Cover, reduce heat, and simmer 15 minutes. Add zucchini and tarragon; cover and simmer 10 additional minutes. **Yield:** 6 servings.

YIELD: 6 servings

EXCHANGES PER SERVING:
3 Very Lean Meat
1 Starch
1/2 Fat

PER SERVING:
Calories 214
(21% from fat)
Fat 4.9g
(saturated fat 1.2g)
Protein 25.9g
Carbohydrate 16.4g
Fiber 1.7g
Cholesterol 76mg
Sodium 109mg

EXCHANGES PER SERVING:
4 Very Lean Meat
1 Fat

PER SERVING:
Calories 188
(35% from fat)
Fat 7.4g
(saturated fat 2g)
Protein 27.1g
Carbohydrate 2.1g
Fiber 0.5g
Cholesterol 85mg
Sodium 286mg

LEMON-GARLIC GRILLED CHICKEN

*For more flavor, rub herb mixture under chicken skin
and chill until ready to cook.*

> 3 (6-ounce) bone-in chicken breast halves
> 3 (5-ounce) chicken thighs
> 4 garlic cloves, peeled
> 1 cup fresh parsley sprigs
> 1 teaspoon grated lemon rind
> 3 tablespoons fresh lemon juice
> ½ teaspoon salt
> ¼ teaspoon pepper
>   Garlic-flavored cooking spray

1. Prepare grill.

2. Rinse chicken under cold water, and pat dry. Loosen skin from chicken by inserting fingers under skin and gently pushing fingers between skin and meat.

3. Drop garlic through food chute with food processor on; process until minced. Add parsley and next 4 ingredients; process until finely minced. Rub parsley mixture over chicken under loosened skin. Coat chicken with cooking spray.

4. Coat grill rack with cooking spray. Place chicken on grill rack; cover and grill 30 minutes or until chicken is done, turning occasionally. Remove skin before serving. **Yield:** 6 servings.

Make Ahead
GRILLED MAPLE-GLAZED CHICKEN

*Use pure maple syrup, not pancake syrup,
for this rich marinade.*

2 skinned, bone-in chicken breast halves
   (about 1 pound)
2 skinned chicken thighs (about ½ pound)
2 skinned chicken drumsticks (about ½
   pound)
1 cup maple syrup
⅓ cup bourbon
⅓ cup orange juice
2 tablespoons minced fresh sage
1 teaspoon coarsely ground black pepper
½ teaspoon salt
⅛ teaspoon ground red pepper
3 garlic cloves, crushed
   Cooking spray

1. Combine all ingredients except cooking spray in a large heavy-duty zip-top plastic bag; seal bag, and marinate in refrigerator at least 8 hours, turning bag occasionally.

2. Prepare grill.

3. Remove chicken from bag, reserving marinade. Place marinade in a saucepan. Bring to a boil; remove from heat. Coat grill rack with cooking spray; place chicken on rack over medium-hot coals (350° to 400°). Grill 6 to 8 minutes on each side or until done, basting frequently with reserved marinade. **Yield:** 4 servings.

YIELD: 4 servings

EXCHANGES PER SERVING:
3 Lean Meat
2 Starch

PER SERVING:
Calories 290
(17% from fat)
Fat 5.5g
(saturated fat 1.4g)
Protein 25.5g
Carbohydrate 34g
Fiber 0.1g
Cholesterol 74mg
Sodium 221mg

YIELD: 4 servings

**EXCHANGES PER
SERVING:**
4 Very Lean Meat
1½ Fruit
1 Fat

PER SERVING:
Calories 270
(25% from fat)
Fat 7.5g
(saturated fat 1.7g)
Protein 29.7g
Carbohydrate 21.2g
Fiber 2.5g
Cholesterol 118mg
Sodium 278mg

CURRIED CHICKEN WITH PLUMS AND GINGER

*If you don't have crystallized or candied ginger, you can
substitute 1 tablespoon minced fresh ginger and
1 teaspoon sugar. Serve with couscous or saffron
rice tossed with chopped fresh spinach.*

2 tablespoons all-purpose flour
1 teaspoon curry powder
1 teaspoon poultry seasoning
¼ teaspoon salt
¼ teaspoon black pepper
6 skinned, boned chicken thighs, each cut
    into 3 pieces
1 teaspoon vegetable oil
1 cup (1-inch) sliced green onions (about 4)
6 red plums, quartered (about 1½ pounds)
¾ cup dry white wine, divided
2 tablespoons minced crystallized ginger

1. Combine first 5 ingredients in a zip-top plastic
bag, and add chicken. Seal and shake to coat. Remove chicken from bag, shaking off excess flour.

2. Heat oil in a large skillet over medium–high
heat. Add chicken, and cook 3 minutes on each
side or until lightly browned. Remove chicken
from pan; keep warm.

3. Add onions to pan, and sauté 2 minutes. Add
onions to chicken, and keep warm. Add plums and
¼ cup wine to pan, scraping pan to loosen
browned bits; cook 4 minutes or until plums are
browned. Add ½ cup wine and ginger to pan;
bring to a boil. Add chicken mixture to pan; bring
to a boil. Reduce heat, and simmer 5 minutes or
until chicken is done. **Yield:** 4 servings.

INDONESIAN CORIANDER-HONEY CHICKEN

2   tablespoons peanuts
2   teaspoons bottled minced fresh ginger
3   garlic cloves, peeled
1/3 cup low-sodium soy sauce
1   tablespoon ground coriander
1   tablespoon honey
1/2 tablespoon Thai chili paste
12 skinned, boned chicken thighs (about 1 1/2
    pounds)

1. Place first 3 ingredients in a food processor; pulse 2 to 3 times or until minced. Add soy sauce, coriander, honey, and chili paste, and process until smooth. Place marinade in large bowl; add chicken, and toss to coat. Chill 10 minutes.

2. Preheat broiler.

3. Remove chicken from marinade; discard marinade. Place chicken on a foil-lined baking sheet; broil 6 minutes on each side or until done. **Yield:** 6 servings (serving size: 2 thighs).

YIELD: 6 servings

EXCHANGES PER SERVING:
3 Very Lean Meat
1 Fat

PER SERVING:
Calories 154
(30% from fat)
Fat 5.2g
(saturated fat 1.2g)
Protein 23.1g
Carbohydrate 2.8g
Fiber 0.2g
Cholesterol 94mg
Sodium 330mg

EASY BARBECUED CHICKEN

EXCHANGES PER SERVING:
4 Very Lean Meat
1 Starch

PER SERVING:
Calories 203
(16% from fat)
Fat 3.7g
(saturated fat 1g)
Protein 29.2g
Carbohydrate 16.3g
Fiber 0.8g
Cholesterol 78mg
Sodium 451mg

½ cup ketchup
2 tablespoons finely chopped onion
2 tablespoons peach or apricot jam
2 tablespoons white vinegar
1 teaspoon Worcestershire sauce
1½ teaspoons chili powder
⅛ teaspoon garlic powder
 Cooking spray
4 (6-ounce) skinned, bone-in chicken breast
 halves

1. Prepare grill.

2. Combine first 7 ingredients in a small saucepan; bring to a boil. Reduce heat, and simmer, uncovered, 5 minutes. Set aside ½ cup sauce; keep warm.

3. Coat grill rack with cooking spray; place on grill over medium–hot coals (350° to 400°). Place chicken, bone side up, on rack; grill, covered, 8 minutes on each side or until done, turning once and basting with remaining barbecue sauce. Serve with reserved ½ cup barbecue sauce. **Yield:** 4 servings (serving size: 1 chicken breast half and 2 tablespoons sauce).

Make Ahead
JALAPEÑO CHICKEN

Serve with grilled slices of zucchini, yellow squash, and red onion. For additional flavor, brush vegetables with remaining marinade before cooking.

⅓ cup steak sauce (such as Heinz 57)
⅓ cup jalapeño pepper jelly, melted
2 tablespoons low-sodium Worcestershire sauce
1 teaspoon garlic powder
4 (4-ounce) skinned, boned chicken breast halves
Cooking spray

1. Combine first 4 ingredients in a large heavy-duty zip-top plastic bag. Add chicken; seal bag, and shake until chicken is coated well. Marinate in refrigerator 8 hours or overnight, turning bag occasionally.

2. Prepare grill.

3. Remove chicken from marinade, discarding marinade. Coat grill rack with cooking spray, and place on grill over medium–hot coals (350° to 400°). Place chicken on rack; grill, covered, 5 minutes on each side or until done. **Yield:** 4 servings.

YIELD: 4 servings

EXCHANGES PER SERVING:
3 Very Lean Meat

PER SERVING:
Calories 109
(10% from fat)
Fat 1.2g
(saturated fat 0.3g)
Protein 19.2g
Carbohydrate 4.1g
Fiber 0g
Cholesterol 48mg
Sodium 140mg

EXCHANGES PER
SERVING:
4 Very Lean Meat

PER SERVING:
Calories 169
(18% from fat)
Fat 3.3g
(saturated fat 0.9g)
Protein 26.6g
Carbohydrate 2g
Fiber 0.2g
Cholesterol 72mg
Sodium 212mg

ROSEMARY-GRILLED CHICKEN

*For a 30-minute meal, begin with this easy two-step
dish. While the chicken marinates, make a green salad
and your favorite flavored couscous or rice.*

$1/2$ cup dry white wine
2 tablespoons lemon juice
$1\,1/2$ teaspoons dried rosemary, crushed
$1/2$ teaspoon pepper
$1/4$ teaspoon salt
2 garlic cloves, minced
4 (4-ounce) skinned, boned chicken breast
halves
Cooking spray

1. Combine first 7 ingredients in a large heavy-
duty zip-top plastic bag. Seal bag, and shake until
chicken is well coated. Marinate chicken in refrigerator at least 15 minutes.

2. Prepare grill.

3. Remove chicken from marinade, discarding
marinade. Coat grill rack with cooking spray, and
place on grill over medium-hot coals (350° to
400°). Place chicken on rack; grill, covered, 6 minutes on each side or until done. **Yield:** 4 servings.

GREEK CHICKEN WITH LEMON COUSCOUS

1   teaspoon dried oregano
¹/₂   teaspoon garlic powder
¹/₄   teaspoon salt
¹/₄   teaspoon pepper
4   (4-ounce) skinned, boned chicken breast
        halves
        Cooking spray
1¹/₄   cups fat-free, less-sodium chicken broth
1   tablespoon grated lemon rind
3   tablespoons fresh lemon juice (about 2
        lemons)
2   teaspoons reduced-calorie margarine
1   teaspoon dried parsley flakes
1   (10-ounce) package couscous, uncooked
        Lemon slices (optional)
        Fresh oregano sprigs (optional)

1. Prepare broiler.

2. Combine first 4 ingredients; sprinkle over both sides of chicken. Place chicken on rack of a broiler pan coated with cooking spray. Broil 5½ inches from heat 12 minutes or until done, turning once.

3. Meanwhile, combine broth and next 4 ingredients in a saucepan; bring to a boil. Remove from heat, and stir in couscous. Cover and let stand 5 minutes or until liquid is absorbed and couscous is tender.

4. Spoon couscous evenly onto 4 serving plates; top each serving with a chicken breast half. If desired, garnish with lemon slices and oregano sprigs. **Yield:** 4 servings.

YIELD: 4 servings

EXCHANGES PER SERVING:
4 Very Lean Meat
3½ Starch

PER SERVING:
Calories 401
(11% from fat)
Fat 5g
(saturated fat 1g)
Protein 36.3g
Carbohydrate 52.1g
Fiber 2.6g
Cholesterol 72mg
Sodium 385mg

EXCHANGES PER SERVING:
4 Very Lean Meat
$1/2$ Starch
$1/2$ Fat

PER SERVING:
Calories 213
(26% from fat)
Fat 6.1g
(saturated fat 0.9g)
Protein 27.4g
Carbohydrate 10.4g
Fiber 0.4g
Cholesterol 66mg
Sodium 456mg

CHICKEN PICCATA

Serve with parslied noodles and a spinach salad.

$1/2$ cup fat-free, less-sodium chicken broth
3 tablespoons fresh lemon juice
1 teaspoon cornstarch
$1/2$ teaspoon grated lemon rind
$1/2$ teaspoon sugar
$1/8$ teaspoon garlic powder
4 (4-ounce) skinned, boned chicken breast halves
$1/3$ cup all-purpose flour
$1/2$ teaspoon salt
$1/4$ teaspoon pepper
1 tablespoon olive oil
2 teaspoons reduced-calorie margarine
Chopped fresh parsley (optional)

1. Combine first 6 ingredients in a small bowl; set aside.

2. Place chicken between 2 sheets of heavy-duty plastic wrap; flatten to $1/4$-inch thickness, using a meat mallet or rolling pin. Cut each breast into 2-inch pieces.

3. Combine flour, salt, and pepper in a small bowl. Dredge chicken pieces in flour mixture. Heat oil in a large nonstick skillet over medium heat. Add chicken; cook 4 minutes on each side or until done. Remove chicken from skillet; keep warm.

4. Stir broth mixture, and add to skillet. Cook over medium heat until mixture is thickened and bubbly, stirring constantly. Stir in margarine. Spoon sauce over chicken; sprinkle with parsley, if desired. **Yield:** 4 servings.

Make Ahead
BASIL CHICKEN AND VEGETABLES

You can also grill the packets over medium-hot coals (350° to 400°) for 20 minutes.

Cooking spray
4 (4-ounce) skinned, boned chicken breast halves, cut into 1-inch strips
1 large red bell pepper, thinly sliced
1 small zucchini, sliced
²/3 cup thinly sliced carrot
¹/2 cup tightly packed shredded fresh basil
¹/2 teaspoon pepper
4 teaspoons olive oil
¹/4 cup (1 ounce) grated fresh Parmesan cheese

1. Preheat oven to 375°.

2. Tear off 4 (12-inch) lengths of heavy-duty aluminum foil; fold each piece of foil in half, shiny sides together. Place on a baking sheet, and open out flat, shiny side up. Coat with cooking spray.

3. Arrange one-fourth of chicken strips on half of each aluminum foil square near the crease. Spoon vegetables evenly over chicken; sprinkle with basil and ¹/2 teaspoon pepper. Drizzle 1 teaspoon olive oil over vegetables in each packet. Fold aluminum foil over chicken and vegetables, bringing edges together; fold edges over to seal securely. Pleat and crimp edges to make an airtight seal. Bake at 375° for 30 minutes.

4. Remove chicken mixture from packets, and transfer to individual serving plates. Or, if desired, place packets on individual serving plates; cut an opening in the top of each packet, and fold aluminum foil back. Sprinkle each serving with 1 tablespoon Parmesan cheese. Serve immediately. **Yield:** 4 servings.

Note: If desired, fill foil packets with chicken and vegetables the night before and chill. Bake at 375° for 35 minutes.

YIELD: 4 servings

EXCHANGES PER SERVING:
4 Very Lean Meat
1 Vegetable
1 Fat

PER SERVING:
Calories 219
(34% from fat)
Fat 8.3g
(saturated fat 2.2g)
Protein 29.7g
Carbohydrate 5.6g
Fiber 1.5g
Cholesterol 71mg
Sodium 196mg

YIELD: 2 servings

EXCHANGES PER SERVING:
4 Very Lean Meat
1 Vegetable
1 Fat

PER SERVING:
Calories 234
(28% from fat)
Fat 7.3g
(saturated fat 2.8g)
Protein 29.8g
Carbohydrate 8.2g
Fiber 1.3g
Cholesterol 78mg
Sodium 388mg

FETA CHICKEN AND VEGETABLES

1 tablespoon all-purpose flour
$^{1}/_{2}$ teaspoon dried marjoram or thyme
$^{1}/_{4}$ teaspoon black pepper
  Dash of salt
2 (4-ounce) skinned, boned chicken breast halves
1 teaspoon olive oil
  Cooking spray
$^{2}/_{3}$ cup red bell pepper strips
$^{1}/_{2}$ cup vertically sliced red onion
$^{1}/_{3}$ cup fat-free, less-sodium chicken broth
1 teaspoon white wine vinegar
$^{1}/_{4}$ cup (1 ounce) crumbled feta cheese, divided
  Oregano sprigs (optional)

1. Combine first 4 ingredients in a shallow dish. Dredge chicken in flour mixture. Heat oil in a nonstick skillet coated with cooking spray over medium–high heat. Add chicken, and cook 4 minutes on each side or until browned. Remove chicken from pan; keep warm.

2. Add bell pepper, onion, broth, and vinegar to pan; cook 5 minutes or until vegetables are soft, stirring frequently. Spoon bell pepper mixture into a bowl; stir in 2 tablespoons cheese.

3. Return chicken to pan, and sprinkle with 2 tablespoons cheese. Cover; cook over low heat 2 minutes or until cheese melts. Divide vegetable mixture evenly between 2 plates, and top each serving with a chicken breast half. Garnish with oregano sprigs, if desired. **Yield:** 2 servings.

SPINACH-STUFFED CHICKEN BREASTS

Pine nuts are expensive and sometimes hard to find, but you can get the same crunch and a comparable flavor if you substitute toasted slivered almonds.

4 (4-ounce) skinned, boned chicken breast
   halves
1 (10-ounce) bag fresh spinach
¼ cup water
¼ teaspoon salt
½ teaspoon pepper
2 garlic cloves, minced
2 tablespoons dried tomato bits
2 tablespoons pine nuts, toasted
½ teaspoon dried basil, divided
   Cooking spray
⅓ cup dry white wine

1. Place chicken breasts between 2 sheets of heavy-duty plastic wrap, and flatten to ¼-inch thickness, using a meat mallet or rolling pin. Set aside.

2. Trim and chop spinach; place in a large nonstick skillet over medium-high heat. Add water and next 3 ingredients; bring to a boil. Cook 7 minutes or until spinach wilts, stirring occasionally. Remove from heat; stir in tomato bits, pine nuts, and ¼ teaspoon basil.

3. Divide spinach mixture evenly among chicken breast halves, spooning mixture onto center of each half. Roll chicken up lengthwise, tucking ends under; secure chicken with wooden picks.

4. Coat skillet with cooking spray. Place over medium-high heat until hot. Add chicken, and cook 2 minutes on each side or until browned. Add wine and remaining ¼ teaspoon basil; bring to a boil. Cover, reduce heat, and simmer 20 minutes or until chicken is done. Transfer chicken to a serving platter, and remove wooden picks. Spoon pan drippings over chicken. **Yield:** 4 servings.

YIELD: 4 servings

EXCHANGES PER SERVING:
4 Very Lean Meat
1 Vegetable

PER SERVING:
Calories 175
(22% from fat)
Fat 4.3g
(saturated fat 0.8g)
Protein 29.6g
Carbohydrate 5.1g
Fiber 3.2g
Cholesterol 66mg
Sodium 322mg

EXCHANGES PER
SERVING:
3 Very Lean Meat
3 Starch
2 Vegetable
1/2 Fat

PER SERVING:
Calories 426
(13% from fat)
Fat 6.3g
(saturated fat 1.1g)
Protein 37.2g
Carbohydrate 54.9g
Fiber 2.6g
Cholesterol 66mg
Sodium 286mg

LEMON CHICKEN WITH ANGEL HAIR PASTA AND ARTICHOKES

*Start with 8 ounces uncooked angel hair pasta to yield
4 cups cooked pasta. Vermicelli or thin spaghetti
can be used as well.*

1/4 teaspoon salt
1/4 teaspoon pepper
4 (4-ounce) skinned, boned chicken breast
  halves
1 tablespoon olive oil
3 garlic cloves, minced
1 teaspoon grated lemon rind
2 (9-ounce) packages frozen artichoke hearts,
  thawed
3/4 cup fat-free, less-sodium chicken broth
1/4 cup fresh lemon juice
1/3 cup thinly sliced fresh basil leaves
4 cups hot cooked angel hair pasta (cooked
  without salt or fat)

1. Sprinkle salt and pepper over chicken. Heat oil
in a large nonstick skillet over medium–high heat.
Add chicken; cook 3 minutes on each side or until
browned. Remove chicken from skillet; set aside,
and keep warm.

2. Add garlic and lemon rind to skillet; cook 30
seconds. Add artichokes, and cook, stirring constantly, 30 seconds.

3. Add chicken broth and lemon juice to skillet.
Bring to a boil; return chicken to skillet. Cover, reduce heat, and simmer 8 minutes or until chicken
is done. Stir in basil. Serve immediately over pasta.
Yield: 4 servings (serving size: 1 chicken breast
half, 1 cup pasta, and 3/4 cup artichoke mixture).

CHICKEN CACCIATORE

Serve with a spinach salad and crusty French bread.

Cooking spray
1 ½ pounds skinned, boned chicken breast
halves, cut into large pieces
1 ½ cups sliced fresh mushrooms
1 cup chopped onion
2 (15-ounce) cans chunky tomato sauce (such
as Hunt's Ready Sauce with Onions,
Celery, and Green Bell Peppers)
½ cup dry white wine
1 ½ teaspoons dried Italian seasoning
⅛ teaspoon pepper
12 ounces uncooked spaghetti

1. Coat a large skillet with cooking spray; place over medium-high heat until hot. Add chicken; brown on all sides. Remove chicken from skillet.

2. Add mushrooms and onion to skillet; cook 2 minutes, stirring constantly. Add chicken, tomato sauce, and next 3 ingredients; bring to a boil. Cover, reduce heat, and simmer 15 minutes or until chicken is done.

3. Meanwhile, cook spaghetti according to package directions, omitting salt and fat. Drain. Serve chicken and sauce over spaghetti. **Yield:** 6 servings (serving size: 1 cup chicken mixture and 1 cup spaghetti).

YIELD: 6 servings

EXCHANGES PER SERVING:
3 Very Lean Meat
3 Starch
2 Vegetable

PER SERVING:
Calories 400
(9% from fat)
Fat 3.8g
(saturated fat 0.6g)
Protein 35.4g
Carbohydrate 55.4g
Fiber 3.9g
Cholesterol 66mg
Sodium 408mg

EXCHANGES PER
SERVING:
4 Very Lean Meat
2 Fruit

PER SERVING:
Calories 261
(14% from fat)
Fat 4.1g
(saturated fat 0.8g)
Protein 27.8g
Carbohydrate 28g
Fiber 3.7g
Cholesterol 66mg
Sodium 225mg

SAUCED CHICKEN BREASTS WITH APPLES AND ONIONS

2 tablespoons all-purpose flour
¼ teaspoon salt
¼ teaspoon black pepper
4 (4-ounce) skinned, boned chicken breast
    halves
2 teaspoons olive oil, divided
3 cups vertically sliced onion
2½ cups sliced peeled Granny Smith apple
    (about 3 apples)
1 teaspoon dried marjoram or ½ teaspoon
    dried rosemary
1 cup apple cider or apple juice

1. Place first 3 ingredients in a large zip-top plastic bag; add chicken. Seal and shake to coat. Heat 1 teaspoon oil in a large nonstick skillet over medium-high heat. Add chicken; sauté 2 minutes on each side. Remove from pan; keep warm.

2. Heat 1 teaspoon oil in skillet until hot. Add onion, and sauté 5 minutes or until lightly browned. Add apple and marjoram; sauté 5 minutes. Add chicken and cider; bring to a boil. Cover, reduce heat, and simmer 10 minutes or until chicken is done. **Yield:** 4 servings (serving size: 1 chicken breast half and ¾ cup sauce).

SAUTÉED CHICKEN BREASTS WITH CHERRY-PORT SAUCE

2 teaspoons olive oil
1/2 cup chopped red onion
1/2 teaspoon curry powder
1/4 teaspoon ground cinnamon
4 (4-ounce) skinned, boned chicken breast
   halves
1/4 teaspoon salt
1/4 teaspoon black pepper
1/3 cup ruby port or other sweet red wine
1/4 cup fat-free, less-sodium chicken broth
1/4 cup cherry preserves or seedless raspberry jam

1. Heat olive oil in a large nonstick skillet over medium-high heat. Add onion, curry, and cinnamon; sauté for 2 minutes. Sprinkle chicken with salt and pepper, and add to skillet. Sauté 2 minutes on each side. Add port, broth, and preserves, stirring until preserves melt. Cover, reduce heat, and simmer 10 minutes or until chicken is done. **Yield:** 4 servings (serving size: 1 chicken breast half and about 2 tablespoons sauce).

♥ *Cook with wines and other spirits to add flavor but not fat, saturated fat, or cholesterol. Most of the alcohol and its calories will evaporate during cooking, leaving only the flavor behind.*

YIELD: 4 servings

EXCHANGES PER SERVING:
3 1/2 Very Lean Meat
1 Starch

PER SERVING:
Calories 205
(17% from fat)
Fat 3.8g
(saturated fat 0.7g)
Protein 26.9
Carbohydrate 15.4g
Fiber 0.8g
Cholesterol 66mg
Sodium 261mg

YIELD: 4 servings

EXCHANGES PER SERVING:
4 Very Lean Meat
¹/₂ Starch

PER SERVING:
Calories 191
(20% from fat)
Fat 4.3g
(saturated fat 0.9g)
Protein 27.3g
Carbohydrate 8.6g
Fiber 0.2g
Cholesterol 66mg
Sodium 260mg

ORANGE-BALSAMIC CHICKEN

A wonderful rich glaze dresses up this chicken for company. Serve with couscous and steamed green beans.

  4 (4-ounce) skinned, boned chicken breast halves
¹/₄ teaspoon salt
¹/₄ teaspoon pepper
¹/₄ cup all-purpose flour
  1 tablespoon margarine or butter
²/₃ cup low-sodium chicken broth
1¹/₂ teaspoons cornstarch
¹/₂ cup low-sugar orange marmalade
1¹/₂ tablespoons balsamic vinegar
     Orange slices (optional)

1. Place chicken between two sheets of heavy-duty plastic wrap; flatten to ¹/₂-inch thickness, using a meat mallet or rolling pin. Spinkle with salt and pepper; dredge in flour.

2. Melt margarine in a large nonstick skillet over medium–high heat. Add chicken, and cook 8 to 10 minutes or until done, turning once. Remove chicken from skillet, and keep warm.

3. Combine broth and cornstarch; stir in marmalade. Stir broth mixture into skillet, and cook, stirring constantly, until mixture is thickened. Stir in vinegar. Reduce heat to medium; add chicken, turning to coat. Cook 1 to 2 additional minutes or until thoroughly heated. Garnish with orange slices, if desired. **Yield:** 4 servings.

CHICKEN WITH SPICED PEACH SAUCE

YIELD: 6 servings

1 (16-ounce) can sliced peaches in light
   syrup, undrained
¼ cup low-sugar orange marmalade
¼ teaspoon ground nutmeg
¼ teaspoon ground ginger
¼ teaspoon salt
⅛ teaspoon pepper
   Cooking spray
6 (4-ounce) skinned, boned chicken breast
   halves
1 teaspoon cornstarch
2 tablespoons water

1. Drain peaches, reserving ½ cup syrup. Set peaches aside. Combine ½ cup syrup, marmalade, and next 4 ingredients; set aside.

2. Coat a large nonstick skillet with cooking spray; place skillet over medium–high heat until hot. Add chicken, and cook 5 minutes or until browned on both sides, turning once. Add peaches and marmalade mixture to chicken; bring to a boil. Cover and cook 10 minutes or until chicken is done.

3. Remove chicken from skillet, and keep warm. Combine cornstarch and water; add to peach mixture. Bring to a boil; cook, stirring constantly, 1 minute or until sauce is thickened. Spoon sauce evenly over chicken. **Yield:** 6 servings.

EXCHANGES PER SERVING:
4 Very Lean Meat
½ Fruit

PER SERVING:
Calories 165
(9% from fat)
Fat 1.6g
(saturated fat 0.4g)
Protein 26.8g
Carbohydrate 8.4g
Fiber 0.6g
Cholesterol 66mg
Sodium 178mg

HAWAIIAN CHICKEN WITH PINEAPPLE SALSA

YIELD: 4 servings

EXCHANGES PER SERVING:
3 1/2 Very Lean Meat
2 Fruit

PER SERVING:
Calories 232
(7% from fat)
Fat 1.7g
(saturated fat 0.4g)
Protein 26.8g
Carbohydrate 27.7g
Fiber 0.6g
Cholesterol 66mg
Sodium 377mg

4   (4-ounce) skinned, boned chicken breast halves
1   teaspoon ground coriander
1/2   teaspoon salt
     Cooking spray
1/4   cup pineapple preserves, divided
1   (15 1/4-ounce) can pineapple tidbits in juice, drained
1/4   cup chopped fresh cilantro
1   tablespoon seasoned rice vinegar
2   teaspoons minced jalapeño pepper

1. Place chicken between two sheets of heavy-duty plastic wrap, and flatten to 1/4-inch thickness, using a meat mallet or rolling pin. Sprinkle chicken with coriander and salt; coat with cooking spray.

2. Coat a large skillet with cooking spray; place over medium heat until hot. Add chicken, and cook 5 to 6 minutes on each side or until chicken is done. Add 2 tablespoons preserves to skillet, and cook until chicken is glazed, turning once.

3. Combine remaining 2 tablespoons preserves, pineapple, and remaining 3 ingredients in a bowl; stir well. Serve with chicken. **Yield:** 4 servings.

CHUTNEY CHICKEN CURRY

Here's an easy skillet chicken dinner to put on the table in less than 30 minutes. Mango chutney is the base for the thick sweet-and-sour sauce that coats the chicken. Substitute another fruit chutney if mango isn't available.

- 2 teaspoons margarine or butter
- 1 cup chopped onion
- 2 teaspoons curry powder
- 1 (14½-ounce) can crushed tomatoes, undrained
- ⅓ cup mango chutney
- 3 tablespoons white wine vinegar
- 2 tablespoons honey
- ¾ pound skinned, boned chicken breast halves, cut into 1-inch pieces
- 3 cups hot cooked rice (cooked without salt or fat)

1. Add margarine to a large skillet; place skillet over medium-high heat until margarine melts. Add onion, and cook 3 minutes or until tender, stirring often. Stir in curry powder; cook, stirring constantly, 1 minute.

2. Stir in tomato and next 3 ingredients; bring to a boil. Reduce heat, and simmer 5 minutes.

3. Stir in chicken. Bring to a boil; reduce heat, and simmer 8 to 10 minutes or until chicken is done. Serve over rice. **Yield:** 4 servings.

YIELD: 4 servings

EXCHANGES PER SERVING:
2 Very Lean Meat
4 Starch
1 Vegetable

PER SERVING:
Calories 428
(7% from fat)
Fat 3.5g
(saturated fat 0.7g)
Protein 24.6g
Carbohydrate 72.4g
Fiber 2.2g
Cholesterol 49mg
Sodium 441mg

EXCHANGES PER
SERVING:
2 Very Lean Meat
1½ Starch
1 Fruit

PER SERVING:
Calories 246
(4% from fat)
Fat 1.2g
(saturated fat 0.3g)
Protein 19.7g
Carbohydrate 37.5g
Fiber 1.4g
Cholesterol 44mg
Sodium 315mg

SWEET-AND-SOUR CHICKEN

1   (8-ounce) can pineapple chunks in juice,
      undrained
2½   cups water, divided
⅓   cup cider vinegar
¼   cup packed brown sugar
1   tablespoon low-sodium soy sauce
½   teaspoon salt
     Cooking spray
4   (4-ounce) skinned, boned chicken breast
      halves, cut crosswise into thin strips
2   tablespoons cornstarch
1   cup thinly sliced onion (about 1 medium
      onion)
1   cup thinly sliced green bell pepper (about
      1 medium-size pepper)
1½   cups uncooked instant rice

1. Drain pineapple, reserving juice. Set pineapple
aside. Combine juice, ½ cup water, and next 4 ingredients; set aside.

2. Coat a large nonstick skillet with cooking spray;
place skillet over medium-high heat until hot. Add
chicken; cook, stirring constantly, until lightly
browned. Add juice mixture to skillet. Bring to a
boil. Reduce heat; simmer, uncovered, 10 minutes,
stirring occasionally.

3. Combine cornstarch and ½ cup water; add to
skillet. Cook, stirring constantly, 1 minute or until
sauce is slightly thickened. Add pineapple, onion,
and bell pepper. Cover; simmer 5 minutes or until
vegetables are crisp-tender, stirring occasionally.

4. Meanwhile, combine rice and remaining 1½
cups water in a saucepan. Bring to a boil. Cover,
remove from heat, and let stand 5 minutes or until
liquid is absorbed and rice is tender. Spoon ¾ cup
rice onto each individual serving plate. Top evenly
with chicken mixture. **Yield:** 6 servings.

SKEWERED SINGAPORE CHICKEN AND PINEAPPLE

YIELD: 4 servings

EXCHANGES PER SERVING:
3 Very Lean Meat
3 Starch
1 Fruit

PER SERVING:
Calories 419
(7% from fat)
Fat 3.4g
(saturated fat 0.6g)
Protein 31.3g
Carbohydrate 64g
Fiber 2.6g
Cholesterol 66mg
Sodium 332mg

  3 tablespoons brown sugar
  3 tablespoons low-sodium soy sauce
  2 tablespoons pineapple juice
  4 teaspoons fresh lime juice
  2 teaspoons grated peeled fresh ginger
  2 teaspoons vegetable oil
1 ½ teaspoons curry powder
  ¼ teaspoon salt
  3 garlic cloves, minced
  1 pound skinned, boned chicken breast, cut
       into 32 bite-size pieces
  1 cup (1-inch) pieces red bell pepper
1 ½ cups (1-inch) cubed fresh pineapple
       Cooking spray
  4 cups hot cooked rice (cooked without salt
       or fat)

1. Prepare grill or broiler.

2. Combine first 9 ingredients in a large bowl. Add chicken and bell pepper, tossing to coat. Thread chicken, pineapple, and bell pepper alternately onto each of 8 (12-inch) skewers. Discard marinade.

3. Place kabobs on grill rack or broiler pan coated with cooking spray; cook 10 minutes or until chicken is done, turning occasionally. Serve with rice. **Yield:** 4 servings (serving size: 2 skewers and 1 cup rice).

YIELD: 4 servings

EXCHANGES PER SERVING:
3 Very Lean Meat
3 Starch
2 Vegetable

PER SERVING:
Calories 396
(7% from fat)
Fat 3.1g
(saturated fat 0.6g)
Protein 32.1g
Carbohydrate 58g
Fiber 2g
Cholesterol 66mg
Sodium 388mg

Super Quick

GLAZED CHICKEN-BROCCOLI STIR-FRY

One family-size bag of boil-in-bag rice yields about 3 cups of cooked rice.

1   family-size bag quick-cooking boil-in-bag rice
    Cooking spray
1   teaspoon vegetable oil
1   pound skinned, boned chicken breasts, cut into 1-inch pieces
3   cups broccoli flowerets
4   green onions, sliced
¼   cup spicy honey barbecue sauce
¼   cup frozen orange juice concentrate, thawed
¼   teaspoon dried crushed red pepper
¼   teaspoon salt

1. Cook rice according to package directions, omitting salt and fat.

2. While rice cooks, coat a large nonstick skillet with cooking spray; add oil to skillet. Place over medium-high heat until hot. Add chicken, and stir-fry 3 minutes. Add broccoli and green onions, and stir-fry 4 minutes. Combine barbecue sauce and remaining 3 ingredients; add to broccoli mixture. Cook over medium heat 3 to 4 minutes. Serve warm over rice. **Yield:** 4 servings.

FIESTA CHICKEN AND RICE

Save cleanup time by chopping whole tomatoes while the tomatoes are still in the can, using kitchen scissors.

1 (14$\frac{1}{2}$-ounce) can no-salt-added whole tomatoes, undrained
1 (4.5-ounce) can chopped green chiles, undrained
Cooking spray
1 teaspoon olive oil
1 cup uncooked long-grain rice
$\frac{3}{4}$ cup chopped onion (about 1 small onion)
2 garlic cloves, minced
1 pound skinned, boned chicken breasts, cut into bite-size pieces
$\frac{1}{2}$ teaspoon salt
$\frac{1}{4}$ teaspoon pepper
$\frac{1}{4}$ teaspoon ground cumin

1. Drain tomatoes and green chiles, reserving liquid from each together in a 1–cup liquid measuring cup. Add water to reserved liquid to measure 1 cup; set aside. Chop tomatoes; set tomato and chiles aside.

2. Coat a large nonstick skillet with cooking spray; add oil. Place over medium heat until hot. Add rice, onion, and garlic; sauté 3 minutes or until rice is golden.

3. Stir tomato, green chiles, reserved 1 cup liquid, chicken, and remaining ingredients into rice mixture. Bring to a boil; cover, reduce heat, and simmer 20 minutes or until liquid is absorbed and rice is tender. **Yield:** 6 servings.

YIELD: 6 servings

EXCHANGES PER SERVING:
2 Very Lean Meat
1$\frac{1}{2}$ Starch
1 Vegetable

PER SERVING:
Calories 229
(8% from fat)
Fat 2g
(saturated fat 0.4g)
Protein 20.7g
Carbohydrate 30.8g
Fiber 2.1g
Cholesterol 44mg
Sodium 329mg

PER SERVING:
Calories 231
(23% from fat)
Fat 5.9g
(saturated fat 1.2g)
Protein 29.7g
Carbohydrate 13.2g
Fiber 4.3g
Cholesterol 72mg
Sodium 181mg

Make Ahead
STIR-FRIED CHICKEN
AND VEGETABLES

*Since this simple stir-fry isn't saucy, we suggest serving it
with sticky rice made from short-grain rice that "sticks"
together and is easy to eat with a fork.*

1 pound skinned, boned chicken breast
    halves, cut into 3/4-inch pieces
1 tablespoon low-sodium soy sauce
2 teaspoons sesame oil, divided
    Cooking spray
2 cups sliced fresh mushrooms
1 cup thinly sliced onion
1 cup thinly sliced carrot
1 garlic clove, minced
2 cups snow pea pods
1 (15-ounce) can whole baby corn, drained

1. Combine chicken, soy sauce, and 1 teaspoon
sesame oil in a large heavy-duty zip-top plastic
bag; seal and turn bag to coat chicken. Marinate in
refrigerator 1 hour.

2. Coat a wok or large nonstick skillet with cooking spray; heat at medium-high (375°) until hot.
Add chicken, and stir-fry 3 minutes or until
chicken is browned. Remove chicken from wok,
and drain; wipe drippings from wok with paper
towels.

3. Coat wok with cooking spray; drizzle remaining
1 teaspoon oil around top of wok, coating sides.
Add mushrooms, onion, carrot, and garlic to wok;
stir-fry 4 minutes or until carrot is tender. Return
chicken to wok; add snow peas and baby corn.
Stir-fry 3 minutes or until chicken is done and
vegetables are tender. **Yield:** 4 servings.

Super Quick
CURRY-ORANGE CHICKEN

YIELD: 4 servings

EXCHANGES PER SERVING:
2 Very Lean Meat
3 Starch

PER SERVING:
Calories 323
(9% from fat)
Fat 3.1g
(saturated fat 0.6g)
Protein 24.6g
Carbohydrate 47.1g
Fiber 1.7g
Cholesterol 49mg
Sodium 81mg

2 cups uncooked instant rice
¾ pound chicken breast tenders
2 tablespoons all-purpose flour
   Cooking spray
1 teaspoon vegetable oil
2 medium-size green bell peppers, cut into strips
1 tablespoon minced garlic
½ cup low-sodium chicken broth
⅓ cup low-sugar orange marmalade
1 teaspoon curry powder

1. Cook rice according to package directions, omitting salt and fat.

2. While rice cooks, combine chicken and flour in a zip-top plastic bag. Seal bag, and shake gently to coat chicken.

3. Coat a nonstick skillet with cooking spray; add oil. Place over medium-high heat until hot. Add pepper strips and garlic; cook, stirring constantly, 1 minute. Add chicken, and cook, stirring constantly, 6 minutes or until chicken is lightly browned. Add broth, marmalade, and curry powder; cook 5 minutes or until chicken is done, stirring often. Serve over rice. **Yield:** 4 servings.

EXCHANGES PER
SERVING:
2 Very Lean Meat
2 Vegetable
1 Starch
1 Fat

PER SERVING:
Calories 236
(23% from fat)
Fat 6.1g
(saturated fat 1.2g)
Protein 19.2g
Carbohydrate 25.9g
Fiber 2.4g
Cholesterol 30mg
Sodium 462mg

TURKEY VEGETABLE PIE

Cooking spray
1 tablespoon reduced-calorie margarine
1½ cups sliced fresh mushrooms
1½ cups broccoli flowerets
½ cup sliced carrot
½ cup chopped green onions
1½ tablespoons all-purpose flour
2 teaspoons dry mustard
¼ teaspoon dried thyme
1 (10½-ounce) can low-sodium chicken broth
1½ cups chopped cooked turkey breast (skinned before cooking and cooked without salt)
¾ cup reduced-fat biscuit and baking mix
1 large egg white, beaten
½ cup fat-free milk
2 teaspoons Dijon mustard

1. Preheat oven to 350°.

2. Coat a nonstick skillet with cooking spray; add margarine. Place over medium–high heat until margarine melts. Add mushrooms and next 3 ingredients; cook 5 minutes or until vegetables are tender, stirring often. Stir flour, dry mustard, and thyme into broth; add to vegetable mixture. Cook, stirring constantly, 2 to 3 minutes or until mixture is bubbly; stir in turkey. Spoon mixture into a 9-inch pie plate coated with cooking spray.

3. Place baking mix in a medium bowl. Combine egg white, milk, and Dijon mustard; add to baking mix, stirring just until baking mix is moistened. Pour over turkey mixture. Bake at 350° for 35 minutes or until golden. Serve immediately. **Yield:** 4 servings.

GINGERED TURKEY AND ASPARAGUS

1 pound turkey breast tenderloin
Cooking spray
16 asparagus spears
3/4 cup fat-free, less-sodium chicken broth
1/4 cup orange juice
3/4 teaspoon ground ginger
1/4 teaspoon pepper
1 tablespoon water
2 teaspoons cornstarch

1. Place turkey between two sheets of heavy-duty plastic wrap; flatten to ½-inch thickness, using a meat mallet or rolling pin. Coat a large nonstick skillet with cooking spray, and place over medium-high heat until hot. Add turkey, and cook 5 to 6 minutes on each side or until lightly browned. Add asparagus and next 4 ingredients. Bring to a boil; cover, reduce heat, and simmer 6 to 8 minutes or until turkey is done.

2. Combine water and cornstarch, stirring well. Add cornstarch mixture to turkey mixture in skillet; cook, stirring constantly, 1 minute or until sauce is thickened. Remove turkey and asparagus from skillet, and place on a serving platter. Spoon sauce over turkey and asparagus. **Yield:** 4 servings.

YIELD: 4 servings

EXCHANGES PER SERVING:
4 Very Lean Meat
1 Vegetable

PER SERVING:
Calories 162
(11% from fat)
Fat 2g
(saturated fat 0.6g)
Protein 28.7g
Carbohydrate 6g
Fiber 1.3g
Cholesterol 68mg
Sodium 163mg

SANTA FE TURKEY SKILLET

  2 (½-pound) turkey tenderloins, cut crosswise
     into ¼-inch-thick slices
1½ tablespoons chili powder
     Cooking spray
  8 green onions, cut into 1-inch pieces
  1 large garlic clove, minced
  1 (15-ounce) can no-salt-added black beans,
     rinsed and drained
  1 (10-ounce) package frozen whole-kernel
     corn, thawed
 ¼ cup water
  1 tablespoon fresh lime juice
 ¼ teaspoon salt
  8 cherry tomatoes, halved

1. Combine turkey and chili powder, tossing until turkey is coated. Coat a large nonstick skillet with cooking spray; place over medium–high heat until hot. Add turkey, and sauté 5 minutes or until done. Remove turkey from skillet; set aside.

2. Coat skillet with cooking spray; place over medium–high heat until hot. Add green onions and garlic to skillet; sauté 2 minutes. Add beans and next 4 ingredients; cook, stirring constantly, 3 minutes or until mixture is thoroughly heated.

3. Add turkey and tomatoes to skillet; cook, stirring constantly, until mixture is thoroughly heated. **Yield:** 4 servings.

Super Quick
LEMON TURKEY AND ASPARAGUS

Thaw the asparagus in the microwave oven while you combine the chicken broth mixture, chop the pepper, and cut the turkey.

½ cup fat-free, less-sodium chicken broth
2 tablespoons lemon juice
1 tablespoon reduced-sodium soy sauce
2 teaspoons cornstarch
¼ teaspoon pepper
Cooking spray
2 teaspoons vegetable oil, divided
1 (9-ounce) package frozen asparagus cuts, thawed
1 small red bell pepper, chopped
1 pound turkey breast tenderloin, cut into 1-inch pieces

1. Combine first 5 ingredients, stirring well; set aside. Place a large nonstick skillet coated with cooking spray over medium-high heat until hot; add 1 teaspoon oil. Add asparagus and red bell pepper; cook, stirring constantly, 2 minutes or until tender. Transfer to a bowl; set aside, and keep warm.

2. Add 1 teaspoon oil and turkey to skillet. Cook 3 minutes or until turkey is browned, stirring occasionally. Add broth mixture to skillet, and cook 2 minutes or until mixture is thickened and bubbly. Return asparagus mixture to skillet. Stir just until coated. **Yield:** 4 servings.

YIELD: 4 servings

EXCHANGES PER SERVING:
4 Very Lean Meat
1 Vegetable

PER SERVING:
Calories 190
(20% from fat)
Fat 4.2g
(saturated fat 1g)
Protein 28.8g
Carbohydrate 7.4g
Fiber 1.4g
Cholesterol 68mg
Sodium 318mg

EXCHANGES PER SERVING:
4 Very Lean Meat
1 ½ Starch
1 Vegetable

PER SERVING:
Calories 288
(8% from fat)
Fat 2.6g
(saturated fat 0.6g)
Protein 35.2g
Carbohydrate 28.7g
Fiber 8.7g
Cholesterol 68mg
Sodium 327mg

SPICY TURKEY SKILLET

1 (15-ounce) can no-salt-added black beans, drained
1 (10-ounce) can diced tomatoes and green chiles, undrained
1 (8¾-ounce) can no-salt-added whole-kernel corn, drained
2 tablespoons chopped fresh cilantro or parsley
1 teaspoon ground cumin
½ teaspoon hot sauce
  Cooking spray
1 pound turkey breast tenderloin, cut into 1-inch pieces
¾ cup chopped onion
½ teaspoon bottled minced garlic or 1 garlic clove, minced

1. Combine first 6 ingredients in a bowl; set aside.

2. Coat a large nonstick skillet with cooking spray; place over medium–high heat until hot. Add turkey, onion, and garlic; cook, stirring constantly, until turkey is browned. Stir in bean mixture; bring to a boil. Reduce heat, and simmer, uncovered, 5 to 7 minutes or until turkey is done and most of liquid is evaporated, stirring occasionally. **Yield:** 4 servings.

BALSAMIC TURKEY

YIELD: 3 servings

6 (2-ounce) turkey breast cutlets
¼ teaspoon salt
¼ teaspoon garlic powder
¼ teaspoon pepper
   Cooking spray
1 teaspoon olive oil
1 large red bell pepper, sliced into rings
¼ cup balsamic vinegar

1. Rub turkey with salt, garlic powder, and ¼ teaspoon pepper. Coat a large nonstick skillet with cooking spray. Add oil, and place skillet over medium-high heat until hot. Add turkey, and cook 2 minutes on each side or until lightly browned. Transfer cutlets to a serving platter; keep warm.

2. Add red bell pepper to skillet, and cook, stirring constantly, 3 minutes or until crisp-tender. Transfer bell pepper to serving platter. Add vinegar to skillet; cook 2 minutes or until slightly reduced. Spoon over cutlets. **Yield:** 3 servings.

♥ *Don't wait until the holidays to enjoy these heart-healthy benefits of turkey:*
• *Low-Calorie: A 3-ounce cooked portion of skinned turkey breast has only 115 calories.*
• *Low-Saturated Fat: Cooked turkey breast has only 0.2 grams of saturated fat in a 3-ounce serving.*
• *Low-Sodium: When roasted without salt, a 3-ounce portion of turkey breast has only 44 milligrams of sodium.*

EXCHANGES PER SERVING:
3½ Very Lean Meat
1 Vegetable

PER SERVING:
Calories 157
(21% from fat)
Fat 3.6g
(saturated fat 1g)
Protein 27.1g
Carbohydrate 2.5g
Fiber 0.7g
Cholesterol 68mg
Sodium 268mg

TURKEY CUTLETS WITH TARRAGON

Serve these cutlets with parslied noodles, a mixed green salad, and thin Italian breadsticks.

EXCHANGES PER SERVING:
4 Very Lean Meat
1/2 Fat

PER SERVING:
Calories 170
(28% from fat)
Fat 5.3g
(saturated fat 1.1g)
Protein 27g
Carbohydrate 2.3g
Fiber 0.2g
Cholesterol 68mg
Sodium 221mg

1	(1-pound) package turkey cutlets
2	garlic cloves, cut in half
3/4	teaspoon dried tarragon
1/4	teaspoon salt
1/4	teaspoon pepper
	Cooking spray
1	tablespoon extra-virgin olive oil
1/4	cup lemon juice
1/4	cup dry white wine
2	tablespoons chopped fresh parsley

1. Rub both sides of each turkey cutlet with garlic halves. Discard garlic halves.

2. Combine tarragon, salt, and pepper. Set aside.

3. Coat a large nonstick skillet with cooking spray; place over medium–high heat until hot. Add oil, tilting skillet to coat evenly. Add half of cutlets. Sprinkle half of tarragon mixture over cutlets. Cook 3 minutes on each side or until cutlets are done. Transfer cutlets to a serving platter; keep warm. Repeat procedure with remaining cutlets and tarragon mixture.

4. Add lemon juice and wine to skillet. Increase heat to high, and cook about 1 minute, stirring constantly. Spoon wine mixture over turkey cutlets. Sprinkle with parsley. **Yield:** 4 servings.

TURKEY, PEPPERS, AND BASIL WITH PASTA

8 ounces uncooked spaghetti
   Cooking spray
1 teaspoon olive oil
1 pound turkey cutlets, cut into 1-inch pieces
2 garlic cloves, minced
2 large green or red bell peppers, cut into thin
   strips
2 (14½-ounce) cans no-salt-added diced
   tomatoes, undrained
½ teaspoon salt
½ teaspoon pepper
½ cup sliced fresh basil
3 tablespoons grated Parmesan cheese
   Fresh basil sprigs (optional)

1. Cook pasta according to package directions, omitting salt and fat. Drain, and keep warm.

2. Meanwhile, coat a large nonstick skillet with cooking spray; add oil, and place over medium heat until hot. Add turkey and garlic; cook, stirring constantly, 3 minutes.

3. Add bell pepper strips; cook 5 minutes. Add tomato, salt, and ½ teaspoon pepper; cook over medium heat 5 minutes, stirring occasionally. Stir in sliced basil; cook until thoroughly heated.

4. Divide pasta evenly among 5 serving plates; top evenly with turkey mixture, and sprinkle with Parmesan cheese. Garnish with basil sprigs, if desired. **Yield:** 5 servings.

YIELD: 5 servings

EXCHANGES PER SERVING:
3 Very Lean Meat
2½ Starch
2 Vegetable

PER SERVING:
Calories 356
(11% from fat)
Fat 4.2g
(saturated fat 1.3g)
Protein 30.8g
Carbohydrate 48.1g
Fiber 1.9g
Cholesterol 57mg
Sodium 381mg

YIELD: 6 servings

**EXCHANGES PER
SERVING:**
4 Very Lean Meat
2 Fruit

PER SERVING:
Calories 253
(7% from fat)
Fat 2g
(saturated fat 0.6g)
Protein 26.9g
Carbohydrate 29.8g
Fiber 0.3g
Cholesterol 68mg
Sodium 290mg

TURKEY SAUTÉ WITH
CRANBERRY-PORT SAUCE

*This entrée has the flavors of holiday favorites. Serve the
turkey with mashed sweet potatoes and steamed broccoli.*

1½ pounds turkey breast slices
 1 teaspoon coarsely ground black pepper
 ½ teaspoon salt
   Cooking spray
 1 (16-ounce) can whole-berry cranberry sauce
 ¼ cup port wine
 3 tablespoons balsamic vinegar

1. Sprinkle turkey with pepper and salt. Coat a
large nonstick skillet with cooking spray; place over
medium-high heat until hot. Add half of turkey
slices; cook 5 minutes or until browned on both
sides, turning once. Remove from skillet, and keep
warm. Repeat procedure with remaining turkey.

2. Add cranberry sauce, wine, and vinegar to skillet; bring to a boil. Return turkey to skillet; reduce
heat, and simmer, uncovered, 3 minutes, basting
turkey with sauce. **Yield:** 6 servings.

Super Quick
TURKEY PATTIES WITH PIQUANT SAUCE

The thicker the patties, the longer it will take them to cook.

1 pound freshly ground raw turkey
1/2 cup chopped red onion (about 1 small)
1 tablespoon dried parsley flakes
2 tablespoons plain fat-free yogurt
   Cooking spray
2 tablespoons brown sugar
2 tablespoons reduced-calorie ketchup
1 teaspoon dry mustard

1. Combine first 4 ingredients in a large bowl, mixing well. Shape mixture into 4 patties.

2. Preheat broiler.

3. Place patties on rack of a broiler pan coated with cooking spray; broil 3 inches from heat 4 to 5 minutes on each side or until done.

4. While patties broil, combine sugar, ketchup, and dry mustard, stirring well. Spread mixture evenly over tops of patties; broil 30 additional seconds or just until ketchup mixture begins to bubble. **Yield:** 4 servings.

YIELD: 4 servings

EXCHANGES PER SERVING:
3 Very Lean Meat
1/2 Starch
1/2 Fat

PER SERVING:
Calories 177
(23% from fat)
Fat 4.5g
(saturated fat 1.4g)
Protein 25.4g
Carbohydrate 7g
Fiber 0.3g
Cholesterol 64mg
Sodium 69mg

SAUSAGE BREAKFAST CASSEROLE

YIELD: 6 servings

EXCHANGES PER SERVING:
1½ Lean Meat
1 Starch

PER SERVING:
Calories 156
(25% from fat)
Fat 4.4g
(saturated fat 1.9g)
Protein 13g
Carbohydrate 15.7g
Fiber 0.5g
Cholesterol 16mg
Sodium 450mg

3 cups (1-inch) cubed French bread
   Cooking spray
½ pound bulk turkey sausage (such as Louis Rich)
¼ cup chopped green onions (about 4 green onions)
¾ cup (3 ounces) shredded reduced-fat sharp Cheddar cheese
1 cup fat-free milk
1 cup egg substitute
½ teaspoon dry mustard
¼ teaspoon salt
¼ teaspoon pepper

1. Arrange bread cubes in an 11 x 7–inch baking dish coated with cooking spray.

2. Coat a large nonstick skillet with cooking spray; place skillet over medium–high heat until hot. Add sausage and green onions; cook until sausage is browned, stirring until it crumbles. Drain sausage mixture, if necessary. Layer sausage mixture and cheese over bread cubes.

3. Combine milk and remaining 4 ingredients; pour over bread mixture. Press down on bread mixture with a spatula to cover totally with milk mixture. Cover and chill 8 hours or overnight.

4. Preheat oven to 350°.

5. Bake casserole, uncovered, at 350° for 30 minutes or until set and lightly browned. Let stand 5 minutes before serving. **Yield:** 6 servings.

CORNISH HEN WITH CHUTNEY GLAZE

1 (1¼-pound) Cornish hen
   Cooking spray
2 tablespoons chopped mango chutney
2 teaspoons Dijon mustard

1. Preheat oven to 325°.

2. Remove and discard skin and giblets from hen. Rinse hen thoroughly with cold water; pat dry with paper towels. Split hen in half lengthwise, using an electric knife. Place hen halves, cut sides down, on a rack in a roasting pan coated with cooking spray. Combine chutney and mustard; brush one-third of chutney mixture over hen halves.

3. Bake, uncovered, at 325° for 50 to 55 minutes or until hen halves are done, basting twice with remaining chutney mixture. **Yield:** 2 servings.

♥ *Reduce your intake of saturated fat and cholesterol by removing the skin from chicken, turkey, and Cornish hens either before or after cooking.*

YIELD: 2 servings

EXCHANGES PER SERVING:
3½ Lean Meat
½ Starch

PER SERVING:
Calories 243
(30% from fat)
Fat 8.1g
(saturated fat 2.1g)
Protein 29.7g
Carbohydrate 10.8g
Fiber 0g
Cholesterol 91mg
Sodium 270mg

**EXCHANGES PER
SERVING:**
3½ Lean Meat
2 Fruit
½ Fat

PER SERVING:
Calories 344
(33% from fat)
Fat 12.6g
(saturated fat 5.8g)
Protein 24.7g
Carbohydrate 32.8g
Fiber 1.9g
Cholesterol 46mg
Sodium 371mg

ROASTED CORNISH HEN
AND PEACHES

Serve with herbed rice pilaf and steamed green beans.

1 (1¼-pound) Cornish hen
1 tablespoon lemon juice
¼ teaspoon salt
⅛ teaspoon pepper
1 (15-ounce) can peach halves in extra-light
    syrup (such as Del Monte Lite)
¼ teaspoon ground ginger
1 tablespoon brown sugar
1 teaspoon cornstarch

1. Preheat oven to 425°.

2. Remove and discard skin and giblets from hen.
Rinse hen under cold water, and pat dry. Split hen
in half lengthwise. Place hen halves, cut sides
down, in a shallow roasting pan. Brush with lemon
juice. Sprinkle with salt and pepper. Bake, uncovered, at 425° for 20 minutes.

3. Drain peaches, reserving syrup. Arrange peaches
around hen in roasting pan. Stir ginger into syrup;
pour syrup mixture into pan around hen. Bake, uncovered, 20 additional minutes or until hen halves
are done.

4. Combine brown sugar and cornstarch in a small
saucepan; stir well. Transfer hen and peaches to
serving platter. Pour juices from pan into a glass
measure. Add water to make ½ cup, and gradually
stir into sugar mixture in saucepan. Cook over
medium heat, stirring constantly, until mixture is
thickened and bubbly. Cook 1 additional minute.
Pour sauce over hen and peaches. Serve immediately. **Yield:** 2 servings (serving size: 1 hen half,
about 1 cup peach halves, and ¼ cup sauce).

salads

Super Quick
APPLE SALAD

*Omit the pecans and blue cheese for a more
kid-friendly fruit salad.*

 4 cups diced Red Delicious apple (about
   2 medium)
1 1/2 cups seedless green grapes, halved
 1/2 cup finely chopped celery
 1/2 cup finely shredded carrot (about
   1 medium)
 3 tablespoons fresh lemon juice
 1/4 cup plain fat-free yogurt
 3 tablespoons honey
 1/4 cup chopped pecans, toasted
 1/4 cup (1 ounce) crumbled blue cheese

1. Combine first 5 ingredients in a large bowl, and
toss well. Combine yogurt and honey in a small
bowl; stir with a whisk until well blended. Pour
over apple mixture; toss gently to coat. Sprinkle
with pecans and blue cheese. **Yield:** 6 servings
(serving size: about 1 cup).

Super Quick
WALDORF SALAD

1 1/2 cups coarsely chopped apple (about
   1 medium)
 1 cup coarsely chopped pear (about
   1 medium)
 1 cup red seedless grapes
 1/2 cup thinly sliced celery
 1/3 cup vanilla fat-free yogurt
 1 tablespoon apple juice
 1/4 teaspoon ground ginger

1. Combine first 4 ingredients in a medium bowl.
Combine yogurt, apple juice, and ginger; pour over
apple mixture, tossing to coat. **Yield:** 6 servings
(serving size: 2/3 cup).

Super Quick
CRISP APPLE AND CRANBERRY SALAD

Look for dried cranberries in the produce section or on the grocery shelf near the raisins. Check the label; some brands use more sugar than others, which increases the calories.

> 3   Red Delicious apples or firm ripe pears,
>   unpeeled and cored
> 1   (8-ounce) carton lemon low-fat yogurt
> 1/3 cup finely chopped celery (about 1 rib)
> 1/2 cup sweetened dried cranberries (such as
>   Craisins)
> 2   tablespoons chopped walnuts
> 1/8 teaspoon salt
> 1/4 teaspoon freshly ground black pepper

1. Cut each apple into 8 wedges; cut crosswise into chunks. Set aside.

2. Combine yogurt and remaining 5 ingredients, stirring well. Add apple, and toss to combine. **Yield:** 6 servings (serving size: about 1 cup).

♥ *Rather than depend on vitamin supplements to get the vitamins and minerals you need, it's best to eat a variety of foods each day. The recommended amounts include: 6 or more servings of breads, cereal, pasta, or rice; 5 servings of fruits or vegetables; 2 to 4 servings of fat-free milk or dairy products; and no more than 6 ounces of cooked lean meat, fish, or poultry.*

YIELD: 6 servings

EXCHANGES PER SERVING:
2 Fruit
1/2 Fat

PER SERVING:
Calories 159
(15% from fat)
Fat 2.6g
(saturated fat 0.2g)
Protein 2.5g
Carbohydrate 33.6g
Fiber 6.5g
Cholesterol 0mg
Sodium 80mg

YIELD: 12 servings

EXCHANGES PER
SERVING:
3 Fruit

PER SERVING:
Calories 178
(1% from fat)
Fat 0.2g
(saturated fat 0g)
Protein 2.3g
Carbohydrate 41.3g
Fiber 2g
Cholesterol 0mg
Sodium 63mg

Make Ahead
FRUITED PORT-CRANBERRY SALAD

- 1 envelope unflavored gelatin
- 1/2 cup port or other sweet red wine
- 2 (3-ounce) packages cranberry-flavored gelatin
- 1/4 teaspoon ground ginger
- 1/4 teaspoon ground allspice
- 2 cups boiling water
- 1 (16-ounce) can whole-berry cranberry sauce
- 1/2 cup ice water
- 1 1/2 cups finely chopped Granny Smith apple (about 1 large apple)
- 1 (14-ounce) package frozen unsweetened raspberries, thawed
- 1 (8 1/4-ounce) can crushed pineapple in juice, drained

1. Sprinkle unflavored gelatin over port; set aside. Combine cranberry gelatin, ginger, and allspice in a large bowl; stir well. Stir in boiling water and port mixture. Add cranberry sauce and ice water; stir well. Chill 30 minutes.

2. Combine apple, raspberries, and pineapple; stir into gelatin mixture. Pour into an 8–cup gelatin mold; chill 4 hours or until set. To unmold, dip mold into hot water for 5 seconds; invert onto serving platter. **Yield:** 12 servings.

MINTED MELON-CUCUMBER SALAD

2 cups cubed cantaloupe
2 cups cubed watermelon
1 cup thinly sliced cucumber (about 1 small
      cucumber)
2 tablespoons chopped fresh mint
2 tablespoons sugar
1 tablespoon minced onion
3 tablespoons raspberry-flavored vinegar

1. Combine first 4 ingredients in a large bowl.

2. Combine sugar, onion, and vinegar in a small jar. Cover tightly, and shake vigorously. Pour over melon mixture; toss gently.

3. Serve immediately, or cover and chill up to 2 hours. Serve with a slotted spoon. **Yield:** 6 servings (serving size: 1 cup).

YIELD: 6 servings

EXCHANGE PER SERVING:
1 Fruit

PER SERVING:
Calories 61
(7% from fat)
Fat 0.5g
(saturated fat 0.2g)
Protein 1.2g
Carbohydrate 14.6g
Fiber 1.4g
Cholesterol 0mg
Sodium 7mg

SLICED MELON WITH RASPBERRY SAUCE

1 (10-ounce) package frozen unsweetened
      raspberries, thawed
2 tablespoons raspberry vinegar
4 teaspoons honey
1 small cantaloupe
10 Boston lettuce leaves
2 tablespoons chopped fresh mint

1. Place first 3 ingredients in a food processor or electric blender; process until pureed. Pour through a wire mesh strainer to remove seeds.

2. Peel and slice cantaloupe. Place lettuce leaves and cantaloupe slices on 5 salad plates. Drizzle with raspberry sauce. Sprinkle with mint. **Yield:** 5 servings.

YIELD: 5 servings

EXCHANGES PER SERVING:
1 1/2 Fruit

PER SERVING:
Calories 99
(7% from fat)
Fat 0.8g
(saturated fat 0g)
Protein 2g
Carbohydrate 24.2g
Fiber 6g
Cholesterol 0mg
Sodium 22mg

YIELD: 8 servings

**EXCHANGES PER
SERVING:**
2 Fruit
1 Vegetable
1 Fat

PER SERVING:
Calories 201
(31% from fat)
Fat 6.9g
(saturated fat 0.9g)
Protein 3.6g
Carbohydrate 34.9g
Fiber 3.5g
Cholesterol 5mg
Sodium 121mg

WINTER FRUIT SALAD WITH POPPY SEED DRESSING

*Winter citrus—orange and grapefruit—star in this tender
lettuce salad. Drizzle it with poppy seed dressing, and
sprinkle toasted almond slices on top for crunch.*

> 4 oranges
> 4 pink grapefruit
> 2 cups purple or red seedless grapes
> 1 red onion
> 2 heads Bibb lettuce
> 1/4 cup sliced almonds, toasted
>   Poppy Seed Dressing

1. Peel and section oranges and grapefruit; cut
grapes in half. Cut onion into thin slices; separate
into rings.

2. Line individual serving plates with lettuce
leaves. Arrange fruit, sliced onion, and toasted almonds over lettuce. Drizzle each serving with
about 3 tablespoons Poppy Seed Dressing; serve
immediately. **Yield:** 8 servings.

Poppy Seed Dressing
> 1/2 cup sugar
> 1 teaspoon dry mustard
> 1/3 cup cider vinegar
> 2 tablespoons chopped onion
> 1/2 cup reduced-fat mayonnaise
> 1/2 cup fat-free sour cream
> 1 1/2 tablespoons poppy seeds

1. Combine all ingredients, stirring with a wire
whisk. Serve dressing immediately, or cover and
store in refrigerator. Allow to come to room temperature before serving. **Yield:** 1⅔ cups.

Make Ahead
RED AND GOLD FRUIT SALAD

2 tablespoons fresh lemon juice
1 tablespoon honey
¼ teaspoon ground ginger
⅛ teaspoon ground cardamom
2 cups fresh cantaloupe balls
2 nectarines, cut into very thin wedges (about 2 cups)
1 pint fresh raspberries

1. Combine first 4 ingredients in a bowl; stir well. Add melon balls, nectarine, and raspberries, tossing gently to coat. Cover and chill 1 hour. **Yield:** 6 servings (serving size: 1 cup).

YIELD: 6 servings

EXCHANGES PER SERVING:
1½ Fruit

PER SERVING:
Calories 84
(8% from fat)
Fat 0.7g
(saturated fat 0.1g)
Protein 1.4g
Carbohydrate 20.4g
Fiber 4.9g
Cholesterol 0mg
Sodium 5mg

TROPICAL FRUIT SALAD

1¼ cups cubed ripe mango (about 1 medium mango)
1 cup chopped ripe papaya (about 1 medium papaya)
1 cup chopped fresh pineapple
2 kiwifruit, peeled, cut in half lengthwise, and sliced
1 medium banana, sliced
1 tablespoon fresh lime juice, divided
½ cup vanilla low-fat yogurt
1 tablespoon honey

1. Combine first 4 ingredients in a large bowl. Toss banana with 2 teaspoons lime juice. Add banana mixture to mango mixture; toss gently.

2. Combine remaining 1 teaspoon lime juice, yogurt, and honey; stir well. Spoon fruit evenly onto individual salad plates. Drizzle yogurt mixture evenly over salads. **Yield:** 4 servings (serving size: 1 cup).

YIELD: 4 servings

EXCHANGES PER SERVING:
2 Fruit
½ Starch

PER SERVING:
Calories 161
(6% from fat)
Fat 1.1g
(saturated fat 0.4g)
Protein 2.9g
Carbohydrate 38.1g
Fiber 4.3g
Cholesterol 1mg
Sodium 22mg

CARROT-PINEAPPLE SALAD

YIELD: 7 servings

EXCHANGES PER SERVING:
1 ½ Fruit

PER SERVING:
Calories 103
(3% from fat)
Fat 0.4g
(saturated fat 0g)
Protein 2.2g
Carbohydrate 24.3g
Fiber 1.6g
Cholesterol 0mg
Sodium 10mg

Colorful bits of pineapple, carrot, and golden raisins float throughout this tangy-sweet gelatin salad.

1	envelope unflavored gelatin
1	cup cold water
1	(6-ounce) can frozen orange juice concentrate, thawed and undiluted
½	teaspoon grated orange rind
1	cup finely shredded carrot
½	cup golden raisins
1	(8-ounce) can crushed pineapple in juice, undrained
	Cooking spray
7	green leaf lettuce leaves

1. Sprinkle gelatin over cold water in a small saucepan; let stand 1 minute. Cook over low heat, stirring until gelatin dissolves, about 2 minutes. Stir in orange juice concentrate and rind. Chill until the consistency of unbeaten egg white.

2. Fold carrot, raisins, and pineapple into gelatin mixture. Spoon mixture evenly into 7 (½-cup) molds coated with cooking spray. Cover and chill until firm. Unmold onto individual lettuce-lined salad plates. **Yield:** 7 servings.

Make Ahead
CRIMSON GREENS

*In this salad, ruby raspberry vinaigrette blankets
light and dark greens flecked with orange
sections and sliced almonds.*

1 cup water
3/4 cup fresh raspberries
3 tablespoons sugar
1 tablespoon cornstarch
2 tablespoons lemon juice
2 tablespoons rice vinegar
2 tablespoons dry white wine
1 tablespoon vegetable oil
5 cups loosely packed Boston lettuce leaves
  (about 1/2 pound)
3 cups loosely packed watercress sprigs
2 cups fresh orange sections
4 teaspoons sliced almonds, toasted

1. Combine first 8 ingredients in a small saucepan.
Bring mixture to a boil over medium-high heat,
stirring constantly; boil 1 minute. Pour mixture
through a wire-mesh strainer into a small bowl or
jar, pressing mixture against sides of strainer with
back of spoon; discard seeds and pulp. Cover and
chill.

2. Arrange lettuce leaves evenly on 6 salad plates;
arrange watercress sprigs and orange sections evenly
over lettuce. Drizzle 1/4 cup raspberry mixture over
each salad; sprinkle evenly with almonds. **Yield:** 6
servings.

YIELD: 6 servings

**EXCHANGES PER
SERVING:**
1 Fruit
1 Vegetable
1/2 Fat

PER SERVING:
Calories 111
(26% from fat)
Fat 3.2g
(saturated fat 0.5g)
Protein 1.9g
Carbohydrate 19.9g
Fiber 5.2g
Cholesterol 0mg
Sodium 8mg

EXCHANGES PER
SERVING:
1 Fruit
1 Vegetable

PER SERVING:
Calories 77
(7% from fat)
Fat 0.6g
(saturated fat 0g)
Protein 1.9g
Carbohydrate 17.7g
Fiber 3.4g
Cholesterol 0mg
Sodium 60mg

FRUITED GREENS WITH ORANGE VINAIGRETTE

5 small oranges
1 tablespoon honey
2 teaspoons sherry vinegar
2 teaspoons coarse-grained mustard
1½ cups loosely packed watercress leaves
1½ cups arugula
1 cup thinly sliced Belgian endive
2 cups fresh strawberries, sliced

1. Grate 1 teaspoon rind from oranges; set grated rind aside. Peel and section 3 oranges; set sections aside. Squeeze enough juice from remaining 2 oranges to measure ½ cup juice. Combine juice and honey in a small saucepan; bring to a boil. Reduce heat; simmer, uncovered, 8 minutes or until mixture is reduced to ⅓ cup, stirring occasionally. Cool juice mixture.

2. Combine cooled juice mixture, grated orange rind, vinegar, and mustard in a jar. Cover tightly, and shake vigorously.

3. Combine watercress, arugula, and endive in a salad bowl; add juice mixture, and toss gently to coat. Arrange greens mixture evenly on 4 salad plates; top with orange sections and strawberry slices. **Yield:** 4 servings.

FIELD SALAD WITH CITRUS VINAIGRETTE AND SUGARED PECANS

Cooking spray
1/4 cup chopped pecans
2 teaspoons sugar
1/8 teaspoon ground red pepper
10 cups gourmet salad greens
3/4 cup Citrus Vinaigrette
2 navel oranges, peeled and sectioned
1/4 cup sweetened dried cranberries (such as Craisins)

1. Heat a small nonstick skillet coated with cooking spray over medium–low heat. Add pecans; cook 6 minutes or until lightly toasted, stirring frequently. Sprinkle with sugar and red pepper, and cook 1 minute, stirring constantly. Remove pecans from skillet. Cool on wax paper.

2. Combine greens, Citrus Vinaigrette, and orange sections in a large bowl; toss well. Place 1 cup greens mixture on each of 8 plates; top each serving with 1½ teaspoons pecans and 1½ teaspoons cranberries. Serve immediately. **Yield:** 8 servings.

Citrus Vinaigrette:
1/2 cup fresh orange juice (about 1 orange)
1/3 cup fresh grapefruit juice
2 tablespoons fresh lemon juice
1 tablespoon extra-virgin olive oil
1 tablespoon honey
1 tablespoon Dijon mustard
1 tablespoon low-sodium soy sauce
2 teaspoons minced peeled fresh ginger

1. Combine all ingredients in a blender; process until smooth. Pour into a bowl; cover and chill. **Yield:** 1⅓ cups.

Note: Store vinaigrette in an airtight container in the refrigerator for up to 1 week.

YIELD: 8 servings

EXCHANGES PER SERVING:
1 Fruit
1 Fat

PER SERVING:
Calories 90
(38% from fat)
Fat 3.8g
(saturated fat 0.4g)
Protein 1.9g
Carbohydrate 13.5g
Fiber 3.1g
Cholesterol 0mg
Sodium 72mg

ASIAN FLAVORS SALAD

YIELD: 4 servings

EXCHANGES PER
SERVING:
2 Vegetable
1/2 Fruit

PER SERVING:
Calories 84
(14% from fat)
Fat 1.3g
(saturated fat 0.2g)
Protein 1.2g
Carbohydrate 16.2g
Fiber 1.1g
Cholesterol 0mg
Sodium 13mg

 6 cups torn romaine lettuce
 1 (8-ounce) can sliced water chestnuts,
    drained
 1 (11-ounce) can mandarin oranges, drained
 1/4 cup rice wine vinegar
 1 teaspoon dark sesame oil

1. Combine lettuce, water chestnuts, and oranges in a large bowl; set aside.

2. Combine vinegar and oil in a small bowl, stirring well with a wire whisk. Pour vinegar mixture over salad mixture, tossing well. Serve immediately, or cover and chill up to 1 hour, if desired. **Yield:** 4 servings.

SPINACH-KIWIFRUIT SALAD

YIELD: 2 servings

EXCHANGES PER
SERVING:
2 Vegetable
1/2 Fruit
1/2 Fat

PER SERVING:
Calories 93
(28% from fat)
Fat 2.9g
(saturated fat 0.5g)
Protein 1.8g
Carbohydrate 15.4g
Fiber 3.2g
Cholesterol 0mg
Sodium 49mg

 3 tablespoons water
 2 tablespoons rice vinegar
 2 teaspoons honey
 1 teaspoon prepared mustard
 1 teaspoon vegetable oil
 1/2 teaspoon lemon juice
 1/8 teaspoon onion powder
 8 fresh spinach leaves
 8 Boston lettuce leaves
 2 kiwifruit, peeled and sliced
   Lemon rind curls (optional)

1. Combine first 7 ingredients in a jar. Cover tightly, and shake vigorously. Chill.

2. Arrange spinach and lettuce evenly on 2 salad plates; top evenly with kiwifruit. Garnish with lemon rind curls, if desired. Serve with dressing mixture. **Yield:** 2 servings.

Super Quick
LEMONY STRAWBERRY-SPINACH SALAD

A light, lemony vinaigrette adds a refreshing twist to this traditional strawberry-spinach salad.

  1 (10-ounce) package trimmed fresh
       spinach, torn
  2 cups sliced fresh strawberries
  ½ cup thinly sliced red onion
  ⅓ cup fresh lemon juice
  3 tablespoons sugar
  1 tablespoon vegetable oil
  2 teaspoons grated lemon rind
     Freshly ground black pepper

1. Combine first 3 ingredients in a large bowl.

2. Combine lemon juice, sugar, and oil in a small bowl; stir with a whisk until blended. Stir in lemon rind. Pour over spinach mixture; toss. Sprinkle with pepper. **Yield:** 6 servings (serving size: 2 cups).

YIELD: 6 servings

EXCHANGES PER SERVING:
2 Vegetable
½ Fat

PER SERVING:
Calories 75
(31% from fat)
Fat 2.6g
(saturated fat 0.5g)
Protein 1.8g
Carbohydrate 12.9g
Fiber 3.1g
Cholesterol 0mg
Sodium 38mg

**EXCHANGES PER
SERVING:**
1 Vegetable
$^1/_2$ Fat

PER SERVING:
Calories 49
(59% from fat)
Fat 3.2g
(saturated fat 0.6g)
Protein 1.3g
Carbohydrate 3.2g
Fiber 0.7g
Cholesterol 1mg
Sodium 119mg

Super Quick
CAESAR SALAD

*Buy 2 (10-ounce) packages torn romaine lettuce,
available in the produce section of your grocery store,
to keep preparation time to a minimum.*

$^1/_4$ cup water
   3 tablespoons white wine vinegar
   2 tablespoons olive oil
   1 tablespoon Dijon mustard
   1 teaspoon Worcestershire sauce
$^1/_2$ teaspoon garlic pepper seasoning (such as
      Lawry's)
   2 garlic cloves, crushed
  10 cups torn romaine lettuce
   1 cup fat-free Caesar croutons
   2 tablespoons shredded fresh Parmesan
      cheese
      Freshly ground black pepper

1. Combine first 7 ingredients in a small bowl; stir
well with a whisk.

2. Combine lettuce and dressing in a large bowl;
toss well. Add croutons and cheese; toss well.
Sprinkle with pepper. **Yield:** 10 servings (serving
size: 1 cup).

♥ *Olive oil is high in monounsaturated fat, the type of fat
that lowers "bad" cholesterol and raises "good" cholesterol. Avocados, peanuts, and canola oil are also good
sources of monounsaturated fat.*

SALAD OF VEGETABLES

YIELD: 6 servings

EXCHANGES PER SERVING:
2 Vegetable
½ Fat

PER SERVING:
Calories 53
(34% from fat)
Fat 2g
(saturated fat 0.3g)
Protein 1.7g
Carbohydrate 8.5g
Fiber 2.3g
Cholesterol 0mg
Sodium 107mg

 9 cups torn red leaf lettuce (about 1 head)
1¾ cups sliced peeled cucumber
1¼ cups yellow or red bell pepper strips
 1 cup sliced red onion
1½ cups chopped tomato, divided
 ¼ cup red wine vinegar
 2 teaspoons extra-virgin olive oil
 1 teaspoon dried oregano
 ½ teaspoon garlic powder
 ¼ teaspoon salt
 ¼ teaspoon freshly ground black pepper

1. Combine first 4 ingredients in a large bowl; toss gently.

2. Place ¾ cup chopped tomato in a blender; process until smooth. Press pureed tomato through a sieve over a bowl, using back of a spoon; reserve tomato juice, and discard solids. Add remaining ¾ cup chopped tomato, vinegar, and remaining 5 ingredients to reserved tomato juice in bowl; stir until well blended. Pour dressing over salad, tossing gently to coat. **Yield:** 6 servings (serving size: 2 cups).

**EXCHANGE PER
SERVING:**
1 Starch

PER SERVING:
Calories 82
(5% from fat)
Fat 0.5g
(saturated fat 0.1g)
Protein 3.9g
Carbohydrate 17.3g
Fiber 2.6g
Cholesterol 0mg
Sodium 164mg

Make Ahead
BLACK BEAN-AND-CORN SALAD

This crisp, slightly sweet combination is great as a salad anytime or at parties as an appetizer served with tortilla chips. As simple as it is, this recipe gets the most ardent compliments, even if it accompanies an entrée whose production was much more time-consuming.

¼ cup balsamic vinegar
¼ cup cider vinegar
2 tablespoons brown sugar
1½ teaspoons fresh lime juice
½ teaspoon ground cumin
¼ teaspoon salt
1 garlic clove, minced
1 cup fresh or frozen whole-kernel corn, thawed
1 cup chopped red bell pepper
¾ cup chopped onion
⅓ cup minced fresh cilantro
1 (15-ounce) can black beans, rinsed and drained

1. Bring first 7 ingredients to a boil in a small saucepan. Reduce heat, and simmer 2 minutes or until sugar dissolves. Combine vinegar mixture, corn, and remaining ingredients in a large bowl; cover and chill. **Yield:** 8 servings (serving size: ½ cup).

ROASTED BEETS-AND-MANGO SALAD

2 large beets (about ¾ pound), trimmed
¼ cup orange juice, divided
2 tablespoons lime juice, divided
¼ teaspoon black pepper, divided
1 tablespoon honey mustard
2 teaspoons olive oil
⅛ teaspoon salt
6 cups gourmet salad greens
1 cup diced peeled ripe mango (about
    ½ pound)

1. Preheat oven to 425°.

2. Place beets in a baking dish, and bake at 425° for 1 hour and 10 minutes or until tender. Cool beets. Combine 2 tablespoons orange juice, 1 tablespoon lime juice, and ⅛ teaspoon pepper. Peel beets; cut each into 8 wedges. Toss beets with orange juice mixture.

3. Combine 2 tablespoons orange juice, 1 tablespoon lime juice, ⅛ teaspoon pepper, mustard, oil, and salt. Combine salad greens and diced mango. Drizzle with mustard mixture, and toss well to coat. Divide salad evenly among 4 plates, and top with beet wedges. **Yield:** 4 servings (serving size: 1½ cups salad and 4 beet wedges).

YIELD: 4 servings

EXCHANGES PER SERVING:
1 Fruit
1 Vegetable
½ Fat

PER SERVING:
Calories 109
(24% from fat)
Fat 2.9g
(saturated fat 0.4g)
Protein 3.3g
Carbohydrate 19.8g
Fiber 2.8g
Cholesterol 0mg
Sodium 193mg

YIELD: 7 servings

EXCHANGES PER
SERVING:
2 Vegetable
1/2 Starch

PER SERVING:
Calories 78
(2% from fat)
Fat 0.2g
(saturated fat 0g)
Protein 0.9g
Carbohydrate 19.4g
Fiber 1.7g
Cholesterol 0mg
Sodium 54mg

Make Ahead
PEPPER SLAW

3 cups thinly sliced green cabbage
3 cups thinly sliced red cabbage
1/2 cup grated carrot
1/3 cup chopped green bell pepper
1/2 cup sugar
1/2 cup red wine vinegar
1/4 cup water
1/8 teaspoon salt

1. Combine first 4 ingredients in a large bowl. Combine sugar, vinegar, water, and salt; stir well with a whisk. Pour over cabbage mixture, tossing to coat. Cover and chill 1 hour. **Yield:** 7 servings (serving size: 1 cup).

YIELD: 6 servings

EXCHANGES PER
SERVING:
2 Vegetable
1/2 Fat

PER SERVING:
Calories 71
(37% from fat)
Fat 2.9g
(saturated fat 1.8g)
Protein 3.7g
Carbohydrate 8.1g
Fiber 1.9g
Cholesterol 7mg
Sodium 202mg

Make Ahead
BLUE CHEESE COLESLAW

3 tablespoons apple cider vinegar
2 tablespoons finely chopped onion
1 tablespoon sugar
3/4 teaspoon celery seeds
1/8 teaspoon salt
1/8 teaspoon dry mustard
1/4 teaspoon pepper
1 garlic clove, minced
1/4 cup fat-free sour cream
1 pound cabbage, finely shredded
1/2 cup (2 ounces) crumbled blue cheese

1. Combine first 8 ingredients in a bowl; gradually add sour cream, stirring with a wire whisk until blended. Cover and chill at least 1 hour. Combine cabbage and cheese; chill 1 hour.

2. Pour vinegar mixture over cabbage mixture; toss gently. Serve immediately. **Yield:** 6 servings (serving size: about 2/3 cup).

Make Ahead
CABBAGE-PINEAPPLE SLAW

1 (8-ounce) can pineapple tidbits in juice,
   undrained
3 cups finely shredded cabbage
1½ cups chopped Red Delicious apple
½ cup chopped celery
¼ cup golden raisins
¼ cup reduced-calorie mayonnaise
   Cabbage leaves (optional)
   Red Delicious apple slices (optional)

1. Drain pineapple, reserving 3 tablespoons juice. Combine drained pineapple, shredded cabbage, and next 3 ingredients in a large bowl.

2. Combine reserved pineapple juice and mayonnaise; add to cabbage mixture, tossing gently. Spoon mixture into a cabbage leaf–lined bowl, if desired. Cover and chill. Garnish with apple slices, if desired. **Yield:** 5 servings (serving size: 1 cup).

♥ *All foods contain calories—some more than others. The number of calories a food contains depends on the amount of fat, protein, carbohydrates, and alcohol present in the food. Fat contains 9 calories per gram, protein and carbohydrates each contain 4 calories per gram, and alcohol contains 7 calories per gram. Because fat provides so many calories per gram, foods high in fat are also high in calories. But even if a food is low-fat, its calories still count and can contribute to weight gain.*

YIELD: 5 servings

EXCHANGES PER SERVING:
1 Fruit
1 Vegetable
½ Fat

PER SERVING:
Calories 108
(29% from fat)
Fat 3.5g
(saturated fat 0.3g)
Protein 1.2g
Carbohydrate 20.2g
Fiber 2.9g
Cholesterol 4mg
Sodium 109mg

Super Quick
CHUNKY ASIAN SLAW

  4 cups coarsely shredded napa cabbage
  1 cup fresh Sugar Snap peas, cut in half
  1/3 cup thinly sliced red bell pepper
  1/4 cup diagonally sliced green onions (about
       2 green onions)
  2 tablespoons rice vinegar
  1 tablespoon hoisin sauce
  1/2 teaspoon dark sesame oil
  2 tablespoons chopped unsalted peanuts

1. Combine first 4 ingredients in a large bowl.

2. Combine vinegar, hoisin sauce, and oil, stirring well. Pour vinegar mixture over cabbage mixture; toss well.

3. Serve immediately, or cover and chill. Sprinkle with peanuts just before serving. **Yield:** 5 servings (serving size: 1 cup).

Make Ahead
CORN SALAD

  4 cups fresh or frozen whole-kernel corn
  1 cup chopped green bell pepper
  1/2 cup chopped red onion
  1/4 cup chopped fresh parsley
  1/4 cup balsamic vinegar
  4 teaspoons honey mustard
  2 teaspoons olive oil
  1/2 teaspoon salt
  1/2 teaspoon black pepper

1. Cook corn in boiling water 1 minute; drain. Combine corn, bell pepper, onion, and parsley in a large bowl.

2. Combine vinegar and remaining 4 ingredients in a jar; cover tightly, and shake vigorously. Pour over corn mixture, and toss gently. Cover and chill 1 hour. **Yield:** 10 servings (serving size: 1/2 cup).

Make Ahead
GARDEN POTATO SALAD

Serve with Easy Barbecued Chicken (page 330) or Crispy Oven-Fried Chicken (page 324).

   3 medium-size round red potatoes (about
       1 pound)
   1 cup frozen cut green beans
   1 cup frozen whole-kernel corn
   ⅓ cup chopped red bell pepper
   ⅓ cup thinly sliced green onions
   ½ cup fat-free sour cream
   2 tablespoons light mayonnaise
   ½ teaspoon salt
   ½ teaspoon pepper
   ½ teaspoon dried oregano
   ¼ teaspoon ground cumin

1. Peel potatoes, and cut into cubes. Place potato in saucepan; add water to cover. Bring to a boil; cover, reduce heat, and simmer 15 minutes or until tender. Drain and let cool.

2. Place green beans and corn in a saucepan; add water to cover. Bring to a boil; cover, reduce heat, and simmer 5 minutes or until beans are crisp-tender. Drain and let cool.

3. Combine potato, green beans and corn, red bell pepper, and green onions in a bowl. Combine sour cream and remaining 5 ingredients; stir well. Pour sour cream mixture over potato mixture, and toss well. Cover and chill 2 hours. **Yield:** 6 servings (serving size: ⅔ cup).

YIELD: 6 servings

EXCHANGES PER SERVING:
1 Starch
1 Vegetable

PER SERVING:
Calories 111
(13% from fat)
Fat 1.6g
(saturated fat 0.3g)
Protein 4g
Carbohydrate 21.1g
Fiber 2.7g
Cholesterol 2mg
Sodium 255mg

MARINATED TOMATO SLICES

Thick slices of red or yellow tomatoes add bold color to this simple salad.

EXCHANGE PER SERVING:
1 Vegetable

PER SERVING:
Calories 25
(11% from fat)
Fat 0.3g
(saturated fat 0g)
Protein 1g
Carbohydrate 5.9g
Fiber 1.4g
Cholesterol 0mg
Sodium 9mg

4 large red or yellow tomatoes, cut into ¼-inch slices
¼ cup lemon juice
2 tablespoons minced red onion
2 tablespoons red wine vinegar
1 tablespoon chopped fresh basil or 1 teaspoon dried basil
¼ teaspoon freshly ground black pepper
1 garlic clove, minced
Green leaf lettuce leaves (optional)

1. Arrange tomato slices in a large shallow dish. Combine lemon juice and next 5 ingredients; pour over tomato slices, turning to coat. Cover and marinate in refrigerator at least 2 hours.

2. Arrange tomato slices evenly on 8 individual lettuce-lined salad plates, if desired. Spoon marinade evenly over tomato slices. **Yield:** 8 servings.

Make Ahead
TABBOULEH

This tabbouleh has a crunchier texture than most because it calls for uncooked bulgur, which softens over time as it absorbs the marinade.

4 cups fresh parsley sprigs
¼ cup fresh mint leaves
2 cups diced seeded cucumber
2 cups diced seeded tomato
1 cup uncooked bulgur or cracked wheat
¾ cup diced onion
⅓ cup fresh lemon juice
2 tablespoons extra-virgin olive oil
½ teaspoon salt
1 garlic clove, minced

1. Place parsley and mint in a food processor; process until finely minced. Combine parsley mixture, cucumber, and remaining ingredients in a large bowl; toss well. Cover and marinate in refrigerator at least 4 hours. **Yield:** 6 servings (serving size: 1 cup).

YIELD: 6 servings

EXCHANGES PER SERVING:
2 Vegetable
1 Starch
1 Fat

PER SERVING:
Calories 164
(30% from fat)
Fat 5.4g
(saturated fat 0.8g)
Protein 5.2g
Carbohydrate 27.3g
Fiber 7.5g
Cholesterol 0mg
Sodium 229mg

YIELD: 6 servings

EXCHANGES PER SERVING:
1½ Starch
1 Vegetable

PER SERVING:
Calories 140
(21% from fat)
Fat 3.2g
(saturated fat 0.7g)
Protein 5.2g
Carbohydrate 24g
Fiber 1.8g
Cholesterol 1mg
Sodium 221mg

COUSCOUS-AND-CUCUMBER SALAD WITH BUTTERMILK-DILL DRESSING

Instead of coleslaw, try this with barbecued chicken or grilled salmon.

1¼ cups water
  1 cup uncooked couscous
  ½ cup low-fat or nonfat buttermilk
  ¼ cup plain low-fat yogurt
  2 tablespoons chopped fresh dill
  2 tablespoons white vinegar
  1 tablespoon olive oil
  ½ teaspoon salt
  ¼ teaspoon black pepper
  1 cup chopped red bell pepper
  ¼ cup thinly sliced green onions
  2 cucumbers, peeled, quartered lengthwise, and sliced (about ¾ pound)

1. Bring water to a boil in a medium saucepan; gradually stir in couscous. Remove from heat; cover and let stand 5 minutes. Fluff couscous with a fork; cool.

2. Combine buttermilk and next 6 ingredients in a large bowl; stir well with a whisk. Add couscous, bell pepper, onions, and cucumbers; toss gently. **Yield:** 6 servings (serving size: 1 cup).

Make Ahead

VEGETABLE-COUSCOUS SALAD WITH CITRUS VINAIGRETTE

1¼ cups water
1 cup uncooked couscous
1 cup chopped carrot
1 cup chopped broccoli
1 cup chopped cauliflower
½ cup chopped green onions
¼ cup minced fresh parsley
1 medium tomato, seeded and chopped
¾ cup orange juice
2 tablespoons white wine vinegar
1 tablespoon olive oil
1 tablespoon Dijon mustard

1. Bring water to a boil in a small saucepan; stir in couscous. Cover, remove from heat, and let stand 5 minutes. Transfer couscous to a large bowl. Add carrot and next 5 ingredients; stir well.

2. Combine orange juice and remaining 3 ingredients; stir well. Pour over couscous mixture; toss well. Cover and chill at least 1 hour. **Yield:** 7 servings (serving size: 1 cup).

YIELD: 7 servings

EXCHANGE PER SERVING:
1 Starch

PER SERVING:
Calories 90
(24% from fat)
Fat 2.4g
(saturated fat 0.3g)
Protein 2.6g
Carbohydrate 15.3g
Fiber 2.2g
Cholesterol 0mg
Sodium 83mg

YIELD: 5 servings

EXCHANGES PER SERVING:
2 Starch
1 Vegetable

PER SERVING:
Calories 207
(14% from fat)
Fat 3.3g
(saturated fat 0.6g)
Protein 8.1g
Carbohydrate 36.8g
Fiber 2.3g
Cholesterol 0mg
Sodium 181mg

1 (7-ounce) package spaghetti or 6 ounces Chinese noodles, uncooked
2 cups small fresh broccoli flowerets
1/4 cup sliced green onions
1 small red bell pepper, thinly sliced
2 tablespoons white wine vinegar
2 tablespoons water
2 tablespoons crunchy reduced-fat peanut butter
2 teaspoons grated peeled fresh ginger
1/4 teaspoon salt
1/4 teaspoon dried crushed red pepper

1. Cook pasta according to package directions, omitting salt and fat. Add broccoli to cooking water 1 minute before pasta is done. Drain pasta and broccoli well; transfer to a large bowl, and add green onions and red bell pepper. Set aside, and cool slightly.

2. Combine vinegar and remaining 5 ingredients; stir well. Add vinegar mixture to pasta mixture, stirring well. Serve at room temperature. **Yield:** 5 servings (serving size: 1 cup).

Make Ahead
ARTICHOKE-AND-PASTA SALAD

Radiatore is short, fat, rippled pasta that is shaped like little radiators. Start with 5 ounces dry pasta to yield 3 cups cooked.

1   (14-ounce) can artichoke hearts, drained and divided
1   tablespoon olive oil
1   tablespoon water
1   tablespoon lemon juice
1/2 teaspoon dried basil
1/4 teaspoon dried oregano
1/4 teaspoon black pepper
1   garlic clove, minced
3   cups cooked radiatore (cooked without salt or fat)
2   cups thinly sliced spinach
1   cup chopped seeded tomato
1/4 cup (1 ounce) crumbled feta cheese

1. Combine 2 artichoke hearts, olive oil, and next 6 ingredients in a blender or food processor, and process until mixture is smooth.

2. Chop remaining artichoke hearts. Combine chopped artichokes, pasta, spinach, and chopped tomato in a large bowl. Pour pureed artichoke mixture over pasta mixture, and toss well to coat. Cover and chill 2 hours. Sprinkle with feta cheese. **Yield:** 6 servings (serving size: 1 cup).

YIELD: 6 servings

EXCHANGES PER SERVING:
2 Vegetables
1 Starch
1/2 Fat

PER SERVING:
Calories 153
(23% from fat)
Fat 3.9g
(saturated fat 1.1g)
Protein 5.9g
Carbohydrate 24.9g
Fiber 1.8g
Cholesterol 4mg
Sodium 137mg

EXCHANGES PER
SERVING:
5 Lean Meat
1 Vegetable

PER SERVING:
Calories 317
(41% from fat)
Fat 14.6g
(saturated fat 2.6g)
Protein 37g
Carbohydrate 8.1g
Fiber 2g
Cholesterol 112mg
Sodium 392mg

GRILLED-SALMON SALAD

¾ cup chopped seeded peeled cucumber
3 tablespoons plain low-fat yogurt
2 tablespoons lemon juice
1½ teaspoons chopped fresh parsley
1½ teaspoons chopped fresh chives
1¼ teaspoons grated lemon rind
¼ teaspoon black pepper
1 garlic clove, sliced
4 (6-ounce) salmon fillets (about 1 inch thick)
1 teaspoon black pepper
½ teaspoon salt
Cooking spray
4 cups gourmet salad greens (about 4 ounces)
¾ cup fresh basil leaves
½ cup cubed peeled ripe mango

1. Prepare grill.

2. Place first 8 ingredients in a blender or food processor; process until almost smooth.

3. Sprinkle fish with 1 teaspoon pepper and salt. Place fish, skin sides up, on a grill rack coated with cooking spray; grill 5 minutes on each side or until fish flakes easily when tested with a fork. Remove skin from fillets; discard skin. Break fish into chunks.

4. Place greens and basil in a large bowl; add ¼ cup cucumber dressing, tossing well. Arrange salad on individual plates. Divide salmon chunks evenly among salads; top each serving with 2 tablespoons cucumber dressing and 2 tablespoons mango. **Yield:** 4 servings.

Make Ahead
LEMONY BEAN AND TUNA SALAD

Serve with soft breadsticks and a fruit sorbet.

¼ cup chopped green onions
1 teaspoon grated lemon rind
1 tablespoon dried basil
2 tablespoons fresh lemon juice
1 tablespoon white wine vinegar
1 teaspoon olive oil
1 cup cherry tomatoes, quartered
1 (15-ounce) can cannellini beans, rinsed and
   drained
1 (6-ounce) can chunk white tuna in water,
   drained and flaked

1. Combine first 6 ingredients in a large bowl, stirring well. Add tomatoes, beans, and tuna; toss gently. Cover and chill at least 1 hour. **Yield:** 3 servings (serving size: 1 cup).

♥ *Beans like cannellini beans are low in fat, high in fiber and protein, and packed with vitamins and minerals—all good reasons to include them often in a heart-healthy diet.*

YIELD: 3 servings

EXCHANGES PER SERVING:
2 Very Lean Meat
1 Starch

PER SERVING:
Calories 144
(15% from fat)
Fat 2.4g
(saturated fat 0.3g)
Protein 14.7g
Carbohydrate 15.5g
Fiber 0.8g
Cholesterol 12mg
Sodium 355mg

SALAD NIÇOISE

**EXCHANGES PER
SERVING:**
4 Very Lean Meat
1½ Starch
1 Vegetable

PER SERVING:
Calories 279
(20% from fat)
Fat 6.2g
(saturated fat 1.5g)
Protein 30.5g
Carbohydrate 26.5g
Fiber 3.8g
Cholesterol 43mg
Sodium 173mg

3 small round red potatoes, sliced
¼ pound fresh green beans, trimmed
1 (8-ounce) tuna steak (¾ inch thick)
⅓ cup white wine vinegar
1½ tablespoons lemon juice
1½ teaspoons Dijon mustard
2 cups torn Bibb lettuce or leaf lettuce
1 medium tomato, cut into 8 wedges
¼ teaspoon freshly ground black pepper

1. Arrange potato and green beans on one side of a steamer basket over boiling water in a Dutch oven. Place tuna on opposite side of basket. Cover and steam 8 to 10 minutes or until fish flakes easily when tested with a fork. Set tuna aside to cool. Plunge steamed potato and green beans into ice water to cool.

2. While tuna and vegetables steam, combine vinegar, lemon juice, and mustard in a jar; cover tightly, and shake vigorously.

3. Place lettuce on a serving platter. Drain potato and beans; arrange over lettuce. Flake tuna, and place on salad; add tomato wedges. Drizzle with vinegar mixture. Sprinkle with freshly ground black pepper. **Yield:** 2 servings.

Make Ahead
GRILLED ORANGE SCALLOPS

18 sea scallops
 1 cup orange juice
 3 tablespoons chopped fresh basil
    Cooking spray
 4 cups mixed baby salad greens
 1 head Bibb lettuce, torn
    Cilantro-Lime Vinaigrette
30 pear-shaped yellow tomatoes
30 pear-shaped red tomatoes
 2 cucumbers, cut into thin strips

1. Place scallops in a large heavy-duty zip-top plastic bag. Combine orange juice and chopped basil; pour over scallops. Seal bag, and shake gently until scallops are coated. Marinate in refrigerator 1 hour, turning bag occasionally.

2. Prepare grill.

3. Remove scallops from marinade; discard marinade. Coat grill rack with cooking spray; place on grill over hot coals (400° to 500°). Place scallops on rack, and grill, covered, 3 to 5 minutes on each side or until done.

4. Combine mixed salad greens and torn lettuce, and toss with Cilantro-Lime Vinaigrette. Arrange mixture evenly on individual plates; top evenly with scallops, tomatoes, and cucumber. Serve immediately. **Yield:** 6 servings.

Cilantro-Lime Vinaigrette
  ¼ cup sugar
   3 tablespoons rice wine vinegar
   3 tablespoons fresh lime juice
   2 tablespoons olive oil
1½ teaspoons finely chopped fresh cilantro
   1 garlic clove, minced
   1 shallot, minced

1. Combine all ingredients in a small jar. Cover tightly, and shake vigorously. **Yield:** ¾ cup.

YIELD: 6 servings

EXCHANGES PER SERVING:
1 Very Lean Meat
2 Vegetables
1 Starch
1 Fat

PER SERVING:
Calories 211
(25% from fat)
Fat 5.9g
(saturated fat 0.8g)
Protein 14.6g
Carbohydrate 27.2g
Fiber 3.9g
Cholesterol 21mg
Sodium 145mg

ASIAN SHRIMP
AND CHICKPEA SALAD

YIELD: 6 servings

**EXCHANGES PER
SERVING:**
2 Lean Meat
2 Vegetable
1½ Starch

PER SERVING:
Calories 274
(18% from fat)
Fat 5.5g
(saturated fat 0.9g)
Protein 23g
Carbohydrate 33.8g
Fiber 4g
Cholesterol 115mg
Sodium 295mg

2　cups cooked instant brown rice (cooked
　　without salt or fat)
1½　cups fresh bean sprouts
⅓　cup diagonally sliced green onions
1　pound cooked, peeled medium-size fresh
　　shrimp
1　(15½-ounce) can chickpeas (garbanzo
　　beans), rinsed and drained
1　(6-ounce) package snow peas, thawed
¼　cup rice vinegar
1　tablespoon low-sodium soy sauce
1　tablespoon dark sesame oil
2　teaspoons water
1½　teaspoons grated peeled fresh ginger
½　teaspoon brown sugar
¼　teaspoon pepper

1. Combine first 6 ingredients in a large bowl;
toss well.

2. Combine vinegar and remaining 6 ingredients;
stir well with a wire whisk. Pour over rice mixture;
toss well. Cover and chill until ready to serve.
Yield: 6 servings (serving size: 1⅓ cups).

SESAME SHRIMP-AND-COUSCOUS SALAD

3 1/4 cups water, divided
1/2 pound medium shrimp, peeled and
　　　deveined
1 cup uncooked couscous
1/4 cup seasoned rice vinegar
2 teaspoons vegetable oil
1 1/2 teaspoons low-sodium soy sauce
1/2 teaspoon dark sesame oil
1 garlic clove, crushed
1 1/2 cups thinly sliced romaine lettuce
1 cup chopped red bell pepper
3/4 cup frozen green peas, thawed
1/4 cup chopped fresh cilantro
2 tablespoons finely chopped unsalted,
　　　dry-roasted peanuts

1. Bring 2 cups water to a boil in a medium saucepan. Add shrimp; cook 3 minutes or until done. Drain and rinse with cold water; cut each shrimp in half. Bring 1 1/4 cups water to a boil in saucepan; gradually stir in couscous. Remove from heat; cover and let stand 5 minutes. Fluff with a fork; cool.

2. Combine vinegar, vegetable oil, soy sauce, sesame oil, and garlic in a large bowl; stir well with a whisk. Add shrimp, couscous, lettuce, bell pepper, peas, and cilantro; toss well. Sprinkle with peanuts. **Yield:** 4 servings (serving size: 1 1/2 cups).

YIELD: 4 servings

EXCHANGES PER SERVING:
1 Very Lean Meat
2 Starch
1 Vegetable
1 Fat

PER SERVING:
Calories 276
(21% from fat)
Fat 6.5g
(saturated fat 1g)
Protein 16.8g
Carbohydrate 35.6g
Fiber 4.1g
Cholesterol 65mg
Sodium 164mg

YIELD: 4 servings

**EXCHANGES PER
SERVING:**
3 Very Lean Meat
1 Starch
1 Fruit
½ Fat

PER SERVING:
Calories 279
(21% from fat)
Fat 6.4g
(saturated fat 2.1g)
Protein 26.9g
Carbohydrate 28g
Fiber 8.3g
Cholesterol 54mg
Sodium 74mg

Super Quick
BLACK BEAN AND PORK SALAD

*Serve with wedges of cornbread. If you don't have
orange juice on hand, use ½ cup of the juice
from the jar of orange sections.*

   Cooking spray
¾ pound lean boneless pork loin, cut into thin
     strips
1 teaspoon minced garlic
½ cup orange juice
2 tablespoons red wine vinegar
¼ teaspoon ground red pepper
¼ teaspoon ground ginger
1 small head Bibb lettuce
1 (15-ounce) can no-salt-added black beans,
     drained
1 (26-ounce) jar orange sections, drained, or 4
     large navel oranges, peeled and sectioned
1 green onion, sliced

1. Coat a large nonstick skillet with cooking spray;
place over medium-high heat until hot. Add pork
and garlic; cook 3 minutes or until pork is done,
stirring often.

2. Combine orange juice and next 3 ingredients in
a small bowl, beating with a wire whisk until
blended.

3. Wash lettuce leaves; arrange on a serving platter.
Arrange beans, pork, and orange sections over lettuce leaves. Drizzle with orange juice mixture, and
sprinkle with green onions. **Yield:** 4 servings.

BULGUR CHICKEN SALAD

Use frozen cooked chicken to keep preparation time to only about 20 minutes. Serve the warm chicken mixture on a bed of lettuce leaves. Enjoy any leftovers as a chilled salad for lunch.

    2 cups water
    1 cup uncooked bulgur
    2 cups frozen diced cooked chicken, thawed
    1 cup chopped green onions (about 8)
    2 tablespoons lemon juice
    1 teaspoon olive oil
  ¼ teaspoon salt
    1 (8-ounce) can pineapple tidbits in juice, undrained
    1 red bell pepper, finely chopped
  ½ cup chopped fresh parsley (optional)
       Dash of hot sauce (optional)

1. Bring water to a boil in a medium saucepan. Stir in bulgur; cover and simmer 15 minutes or until water is absorbed. Remove from heat, and fluff with a fork.

2. While bulgar cooks, combine chicken and next 6 ingredients; if desired, add parsley and hot sauce. Add to cooked bulgur, stirring well. **Yield:** 4 servings.

YIELD: 4 servings

EXCHANGES PER SERVING:
2 Lean Meat
1 Starch
1 Vegetable
1 Fruit

PER SERVING:
Calories 262
(14% from fat)
Fat 4.2g
(saturated fat 1g)
Protein 19.4g
Carbohydrate 39.5g
Fiber 8g
Cholesterol 37mg
Sodium 262mg

**EXCHANGES PER
SERVING:**
2 Very Lean Meat
2½ Starch
2 Vegetable
1 Fat

PER SERVING:
Calories 381
(27% from fat)
Fat 11.5g
(saturated fat 2.1g)
Protein 22.3g
Carbohydrate 46.4g
Fiber 2.6g
Cholesterol 39mg
Sodium 289mg

Make Ahead
CHICKEN PASTA SALAD

    3 (4-ounce) skinned, boned chicken breast
         halves
 3½ cups cooked small pasta shells (cooked
         without salt or fat)
    3 cups fresh broccoli flowerets
    1 cup red bell pepper strips
  ¼ cup sliced green onions
    6 ounces fresh snow pea pods, trimmed
    5 tablespoons red wine vinegar
    3 tablespoons vegetable oil
    2 tablespoons honey
    2 teaspoons sesame seeds, toasted
    1 teaspoon hot sauce
  ½ teaspoon salt
  ½ teaspoon ground ginger
    3 garlic cloves, minced

1. Place chicken in a medium saucepan; add water
to cover. Bring to a boil; reduce heat to medium,
and cook, uncovered, 15 minutes or until done.
Drain; cool chicken slightly. Cut chicken into bite-
size pieces.

2. Combine chicken and pasta in a large bowl; add
broccoli and next 3 ingredients, tossing gently.
Combine vinegar and remaining 7 ingredients in a
jar; cover tightly, and shake vigorously. Pour dressing mixture over chicken mixture; toss gently.
Cover and chill 2 hours. **Yield:** 5 servings (serving
size: 2 cups).

GRILLED JERK CHICKEN SALAD

*Check in the ethnic section of your supermarket
for habanero pepper sauce.*

  5   green onions, sliced and divided
  3   tablespoons fresh lime juice
  2   tablespoons habanero pepper sauce
  1   tablespoon white vinegar
2½   tablespoons salt-free Jamaican jerk
      seasoning blend
  4   (4-ounce) skinned, boned chicken breast
      halves
      Cooking spray
  8   cups mixed salad greens
  2   ripe mangoes, peeled and cubed
¾   cup fat-free mango dressing

1. Combine 2 tablespoons green onions and next 4
ingredients in container of an electric blender; cover
and process until smooth. Brush both sides of
chicken breast halves with green onion mixture.

2. Prepare grill.

3. Coat grill rack with cooking spray; place over
medium-hot coals (350° to 400°). Place chicken on
rack, and grill, covered, 5 minutes on each side or
until done. Cut chicken crosswise into ¼-inch-
thick strips.

4. Place 2 cups salad greens on each individual
serving plate; top with mango and remaining green
onions. Arrange chicken over salads; top each serving with 3 tablespoons dressing. **Yield:** 4 servings.

YIELD: 4 servings

**EXCHANGES PER
SERVING:**
3 Very Lean Meat
2 Vegetable
1 Fruit
½ Fat

PER SERVING:
Calories 241
(13% from fat)
Fat 3.5g
(saturated fat 0.9g)
Protein 27.4g
Carbohydrate 25.3g
Fiber 2.6g
Cholesterol 70mg
Sodium 164mg

CURRY CHICKEN SALAD

YIELD: 6 servings

EXCHANGES PER SERVING:
3 Very Lean Meat
1 Fruit
1 Fat

PER SERVING:
Calories 220
(21% from fat)
Fat 5.2g
(saturated fat 0.9g)
Protein 25.8g
Carbohydrate 16.8g
Fiber 1.8g
Cholesterol 66mg
Sodium 301mg

1½ cups peeled, chopped apple
1 teaspoon lemon juice
3 cups chopped cooked chicken breast
¾ cup thinly sliced celery
¼ cup raisins
⅓ cup low-fat mayonnaise
⅓ cup fat-free sour cream
2 tablespoons minced fresh chives
2 teaspoons sugar
½ teaspoon curry powder
¼ teaspoon salt
2 tablespoons slivered almonds, toasted and chopped

1. Combine apple and lemon juice in a large bowl; toss well to coat apple. Add chicken, celery, and raisins; toss well.

2. Combine mayonnaise and next 5 ingredients in a small bowl; pour over chicken mixture, and toss well. Sprinkle with chopped almonds. Cover and chill at least 1 hour. **Yield:** 6 servings.

Note: If you don't have 3 cups of leftover chicken, cook 1 pound of skinned, boned chicken breast halves on a baking sheet in the oven at 450° for 12 to 14 minutes or until the juices run clear. Toast the almonds on the same baking sheet during the last 3 minutes of cooking.

sandwiches & soups

PER SERVING:
Calories 314
(24% from fat)
Fat 8.3g
(saturated fat 3.2g)
Protein 16g
Carbohydrate 43.4g
Fiber 1.6g
Cholesterol 20mg
Sodium 447mg

Super Quick
FRENCH ONION SANDWICHES

Shave thin slices from an onion with a very sharp chef's knife or cut the onion in half and push slowly through the slicing blade of a food processor.

    8 (1-ounce) slices French bread
       Cooking spray
    2 teaspoons reduced-calorie margarine
    1 large onion, very thinly sliced
 1½ tablespoons brown sugar
    1 cup (4 ounces) shredded reduced-fat Swiss
       cheese

1. Preheat oven to 375°.

2. Arrange bread slices on a baking sheet. Bake at 375° for 8 minutes or until lightly toasted. Remove from oven, and leave bread slices on baking sheet.

3. While bread toasts, coat a large heavy saucepan with cooking spray; add margarine, and place over high heat until margarine melts. Add onion, and cook, stirring constantly, 3 minutes or until onion is tender. Add brown sugar, and cook 5 additional minutes or until onion is tender and browned, stirring often.

4. Preheat broiler.

5. Spoon onion mixture evenly on bread slices; top with cheese. Broil 5½ inches from heat 2 minutes. Serve immediately. **Yield:** 4 servings.

TANGY GROUPER SANDWICHES

You'll think you're at the beach when you sink your teeth into this mammoth seafood sandwich. The homemade tartar sauce lends just the right amount of sweet and salty sensations to the tender grilled fish.

2   tablespoons lemon juice
1   teaspoon low-sodium Worcestershire sauce
1   teaspoon olive oil
$^1/_2$ teaspoon pepper
$^1/_8$ teaspoon paprika
3   tablespoons fat-free mayonnaise
1   tablespoon minced onion
2   teaspoons dill pickle relish
$^1/_2$ teaspoon prepared mustard
       Cooking spray
1   (1-pound) grouper fillet, cut into 4 pieces
4   green leaf lettuce leaves
12   ($^1/_4$-inch-thick) slices Roma tomato
4   hamburger buns, split and toasted

1. Prepare grill.

2. Combine first 5 ingredients; set aside. Combine mayonnaise and next 3 ingredients; set aside.

3. Coat grill rack with cooking spray; place on grill over medium–hot coals (350° to 400°). Place fish on rack; grill, covered, 5 minutes on each side or until fish flakes when tested with a fork, basting with lemon juice mixture.

4. Layer 1 lettuce leaf, 3 slices tomato, and 1 piece fish on bottom half of each bun. Spoon mayonnaise mixture evenly over fish, and cover with top halves of buns. Serve immediately. **Yield:** 4 servings.

YIELD: 4 servings

EXCHANGES PER SERVING:
3 Very Lean Meat
1 $^1/_2$ Starch
$^1/_2$ Fat

PER SERVING:
Calories 243
(20% from fat)
Fat 5.3g
(saturated fat 0.8g)
Protein 25g
Carbohydrate 22.6g
Fiber 1g
Cholesterol 52mg
Sodium 338mg

**EXCHANGES PER
SERVING:**
3 Very Lean Meat
1 1/2 Starch

PER SERVING:
Calories 213
(14% from fat)
Fat 3.3g
(saturated fat 0.6g)
Protein 24.1g
Carbohydrate 20.3g
Fiber 1.1g
Cholesterol 162mg
Sodium 488mg

Make Ahead
INDIAN-SPICED SHRIMP WRAP

> 1 tablespoon ground cumin
> 2 teaspoons ground coriander
> 2 teaspoons ground turmeric
> 1 teaspoon ground cardamom
> 1/2 teaspoon ground cloves
> 1/2 teaspoon black pepper
> 1/4 teaspoon ground cinnamon
> 1/8 to 1/4 teaspoon ground red pepper
> 1/4 teaspoon salt
> 2 1/2 pounds medium shrimp, peeled and
>   deveined
> 2 teaspoons vegetable oil
> 8 (6-inch) fat-free flour tortillas

1. Combine first 8 ingredients in a small skillet, and place over medium-high heat. Cook 2 minutes, stirring constantly; stir in salt. Cool. Combine spice mixture and shrimp in a large zip-top plastic bag. Seal and marinate in refrigerator 1 to 2 hours.

2. Heat oil in a large nonstick skillet over medium-high heat. Add shrimp mixture; sauté 7 minutes or until shrimp are done.

3. Warm tortillas according to package directions. Spoon about 1/2 cup shrimp mixture down center of each tortilla; roll up. **Yield:** 8 servings.

FIESTA BURGERS

Top grilled patties with this blend of feisty ingredients, and you've got burgers "for adults only."

1 1/3 cups seeded, chopped tomato
 1/4 cup finely chopped onion
 1/4 cup taco sauce
  1 (4.5-ounce) can chopped green chiles, drained
  2 pounds ground round
  2 tablespoons low-sodium Worcestershire sauce
 1/2 teaspoon ground cumin
 1/4 teaspoon onion powder
 1/4 teaspoon garlic powder
  8 green leaf lettuce leaves
  8 reduced-calorie hamburger buns, split and toasted

1. Combine first 4 ingredients; cover and chill 30 minutes.

2. Preheat broiler.

3. Combine ground round and next 4 ingredients; divide mixture into 8 equal portions, shaping each into a 4-inch patty. Broil 3 inches from heat 4 minutes on each side or until done.

4. Place a lettuce leaf on bottom half of each bun; top each with a patty. Top evenly with tomato mixture, and cover with bun tops. **Yield:** 8 servings.

YIELD: 8 servings

EXCHANGES PER SERVING:
3 Lean Meat
1 Starch
1 Vegetable

PER SERVING:
Calories 266
(27% from fat)
Fat 8g
(saturated fat 2.5g)
Protein 26.8g
Carbohydrate 19.7g
Fiber 2.6g
Cholesterol 70mg
Sodium 423mg

YIELD: 6 servings

EXCHANGES PER SERVING:
2 Lean Meat
2 Starch

PER SERVING:
Calories 277
(30% from fat)
Fat 9.3g
(saturated fat 3.3g)
Protein 20.1g
Carbohydrate 28.8g
Fiber 3.2g
Cholesterol 28mg
Sodium 345mg

BURGERS WITH RED ONION SALSA

Serve with sliced cucumbers and reduced-fat potato chips.

1 pound ground round
1 large red onion, finely chopped and
      divided (about 1 1/2 cups)
2 tablespoons chili powder
    Cooking spray
1 large tomato, chopped (about 1 3/4 cups)
1 teaspoon chili powder
2 tablespoons lime juice
6 hamburger buns, split and toasted

1. Combine ground round, 2 tablespoons onion, and 2 tablespoons chili powder; shape into 6 (1/2-inch-thick) patties.

2. Coat a large nonstick skillet with cooking spray; place over medium-high heat until hot. Add patties; cook 4 minutes on each side or until done.

3. While burgers cook, combine remaining onion, tomato, 1 teaspoon chili powder, and lime juice. Place patties on bottom halves of buns; spoon salsa over patties, and cover with bun tops. **Yield:** 6 servings.

SLIM SLOPPY JOES

1 pound lean ground round
1 cup chopped onion
¼ cup reduced-calorie ketchup
2 tablespoons unprocessed oat bran
1 tablespoon low-sodium Worcestershire sauce
1 tablespoon prepared mustard
1 tablespoon lemon juice
1 (8-ounce) can no-salt-added tomato sauce
6 reduced-calorie hamburger buns, split and toasted

1. Cook ground round and onion in a large non-stick skillet over medium–high heat until meat is browned, stirring until meat crumbles. Drain and return to skillet.

2. Stir ketchup and next 5 ingredients into meat mixture; bring to a boil. Cover, reduce heat, and simmer 10 minutes, stirring often. Spoon mixture evenly over bottom halves of buns; cover with bun tops. **Yield:** 6 servings.

♥ *How do you know if you're buying the kind of ground beef with the least amount of fat? First, look for the cut of meat on the label. Ground chuck is higher in fat; ground round and sirloin are leaner. Or look for the percent lean; for example, "95 percent lean ground beef." This means 95 percent lean and 5 percent fat and indicates the type of ground beef recommended for heart-healthy cooking.*

YIELD: 6 servings

EXCHANGES PER SERVING:
2 Lean Meat
1½ Starch

PER SERVING:
Calories 226
(21% from fat)
Fat 5.3g
(saturated fat 1.7g)
Protein 21.2g
Carbohydrate 27.3g
Fiber 5.6g
Cholesterol 46mg
Sodium 319mg

YIELD: 6 servings

EXCHANGES PER SERVING:
2 Lean Meat
2 Starch

PER SERVING:
Calories 284
(24% from fat)
Fat 7.5g
(saturated fat 1.9g)
Protein 20.8g
Carbohydrate 31.4g
Fiber 1.2g
Cholesterol 58mg
Sodium 357mg

Super Quick
MEXICO JOES

Mix the leftover taco seasoning with fat-free sour cream to serve with fajitas or stir the seasoning into crushed corn flakes to use as a coating for oven-fried chicken.

Cooking spray
1 pound ground round
½ cup frozen chopped onion
1 (4.5-ounce) can chopped green chiles, undrained
2 tablespoons 40%-less-sodium taco seasoning
1 (8-ounce) can no-salt-added tomato sauce
6 hamburger buns, warmed

1. Coat a large nonstick skillet with cooking spray; place over high heat until hot. Add ground round and onion; cook 5 minutes until meat is browned and onion is tender, stirring to crumble meat. Add chiles, taco seasoning, and tomato sauce, stirring well. Cook over medium heat 3 to 4 minutes or until thoroughly heated, stirring often.

2. Spoon meat mixture evenly over bottom halves of buns; top with remaining bun halves. **Yield:** 6 servings.

GREEK WRAPS

Roll up your favorite sandwich ingredients in a flour tortilla. Wrap in foil, wax paper, or a napkin, and you'll have today's version of the sandwich—a wrap.

Cooking spray
8 ounces lean ground round
½ cup chopped onion (about ½ medium onion)
2 cups hot cooked rice (cooked without salt or fat)
½ cup plain low-fat yogurt
¼ cup pine nuts, toasted
¼ cup (1 ounce) reduced-fat feta cheese
1 tablespoon lemon juice
½ teaspoon garlic salt
¼ teaspoon pepper
⅛ to ¼ teaspoon ground cinnamon
4 (8-inch) flour tortillas
16 fresh spinach leaves (about 1½ ounces)

1. Coat a large skillet with cooking spray; place over medium-high heat until hot. Add ground round and onion; sauté 5 minutes or until beef is browned and onion is tender, stirring until beef crumbles. Drain well.

2. Combine beef mixture, rice, and next 7 ingredients; stir well. Lay tortillas on a flat surface; line with spinach leaves. Spread beef mixture evenly over tortillas, and roll up tortillas, jelly-roll fashion. Wrap in aluminum foil; cut in half to serve. **Yield:** 8 servings (serving size: ½ wrap).

YIELD: 8 servings

EXCHANGES PER SERVING:
1 Lean Meat
1½ Starch
½ Fat

PER SERVING:
Calories 202
(29% from fat)
Fat 6.4g
(saturated fat 1.7g)
Protein 11.5g
Carbohydrate 25.1g
Fiber 6.2g
Cholesterol 20mg
Sodium 289mg

STEAK AND ONION SANDWICHES

YIELD: 4 servings

EXCHANGES PER SERVING:
3 Medium-Fat Meat
2 Starch

PER SERVING:
Calories 370
(36% from fat)
Fat 14.6g
(saturated fat 5.6g)
Protein 27.6g
Carbohydrate 30.6g
Fiber 1.3g
Cholesterol 61mg
Sodium 549mg

2 teaspoons bottled minced garlic
1/2 teaspoon dried thyme
1/2 teaspoon dried basil
1/2 teaspoon freshly ground black pepper
1 (1-pound) flank steak, trimmed
4 (1/4-inch) slices red onion
Cooking spray
3 tablespoons fat-free mayonnaise
2 1/2 teaspoons Dijon mustard
8 (1-ounce) slices sourdough bread, toasted

1. Combine first 4 ingredients; rub mixture over steak. Place a nonstick skillet over medium–high heat until hot. Coat steak and onion slices with cooking spray; add steak and onion to skillet. Cook 12 minutes or to desired degree of doneness, stirring onion often and turning steak once.

2. Combine mayonnaise and mustard, stirring well; spread over 1 side of each bread slice. Thinly slice steak across the grain. Arrange steak evenly on 4 bread slices; top evenly with onion. Top with remaining bread slices. **Yield:** 4 servings.

LAMB POCKETS WITH CUCUMBER TOPPING

1 cup grated cucumber
$\frac{1}{2}$ cup plain low-fat yogurt
$\frac{1}{4}$ teaspoon seasoned salt
$\frac{1}{4}$ teaspoon dried dill
1 pound ground lamb or ground round
$\frac{1}{4}$ cup chopped onion
1 garlic clove, minced
$\frac{1}{4}$ teaspoon salt
$\frac{1}{4}$ teaspoon pepper
$\frac{3}{4}$ cup chopped tomato
$\frac{1}{4}$ cup sliced green onions
4 (6-inch) whole wheat pita bread rounds, cut in half crosswise
8 green leaf lettuce leaves
Fresh dill sprigs (optional)

1. Press cucumber between layers of paper towels to remove excess moisture. Combine cucumber, yogurt, seasoned salt, and $\frac{1}{4}$ teaspoon dried dill; cover and chill.

2. Cook ground lamb, chopped onion, and garlic in a large nonstick skillet over medium-high heat until meat is browned, stirring until it crumbles; drain, if necessary. Stir in $\frac{1}{4}$ teaspoon salt and pepper. Set aside.

3. Combine tomato and green onions. Line each pita half with a lettuce leaf; top evenly with meat mixture, cucumber mixture, and tomato mixture. Garnish with dill sprigs, if desired. Serve immediately. **Yield:** 8 servings.

YIELD: 8 servings

EXCHANGES PER SERVING:
2 Lean Meat
1½ Starch

PER SERVING:
Calories 227
(37% from fat)
Fat 9.6g
(saturated fat 3.8g)
Protein 14.9g
Carbohydrate 21.1g
Fiber 3.1g
Cholesterol 42mg
Sodium 321mg

YIELD: 8 servings

EXCHANGES PER
SERVING:
3 Lean Meat
2 Starch

PER SERVING:
Calories 320
(28% from fat)
Fat 10g
(saturated fat 3.7g)
Protein 25.2g
Carbohydrate 32.6g
Fiber 2.7g
Cholesterol 74mg
Sodium 413mg

LAMB PICADILLO WRAP

4 pounds boned lamb shoulder
2 tablespoons finely chopped seeded jalapeño
   pepper
1 tablespoon dried oregano
1 tablespoon chili powder
1/8 teaspoon salt
3 garlic cloves, minced
1 (6-ounce) can tomato paste
2 cups water
1/2 cup golden raisins
1 tablespoon unsweetened cocoa
1/4 cup chopped pimiento-stuffed olives
2 tablespoons minced fresh cilantro
2 tablespoons fresh lime juice
8 (6-inch) fat-free flour tortillas

1. Trim fat from lamb. Cut lamb into 3 x 1/4-inch
strips. Place a skillet over medium–high heat until
hot. Add lamb; sauté 4 minutes or until browned.
Add jalapeño, oregano, chili powder, salt, and garlic,
and sauté 1 minute. Stir in tomato paste, and cook,
stirring frequently, 2 minutes. Stir in water, raisins,
and cocoa; bring to a boil. Reduce heat; simmer 20
minutes. Stir in olives, cilantro, and juice.

2. Warm tortillas according to package directions.
Spoon about 1/2 cup lamb mixture down center of
each tortilla; roll up. **Yield:** 8 servings.

Super Quick
DILLED CHICKEN SALAD SANDWICHES

½ cup plain fat-free yogurt
2 cups chopped cooked chicken
¼ cup chopped celery
¼ cup chopped green onions
1 tablespoon honey mustard
¼ teaspoon dried dill
¼ teaspoon ground white pepper
4 green leaf lettuce leaves
8 (1-ounce) slices whole wheat bread, lightly toasted
4 (¼-inch-thick) slices large tomato

1. Spoon yogurt onto several layers of heavy-duty paper towels, and spread to ½-inch thickness. Cover with additional paper towels; let stand 5 minutes. Scrape yogurt into a medium bowl, using a rubber spatula.

2. Add chicken and next 5 ingredients to yogurt; stir well. Place lettuce leaves over 4 bread slices; top with chicken mixture, tomato slices, and remaining bread slices. **Yield:** 4 servings.

YIELD: 4 servings

EXCHANGES PER SERVING:
3 Lean Meat
2 Starch

PER SERVING:
Calories 323
(22% from fat)
Fat 7.8g
(saturated fat 2g)
Protein 28.1g
Carbohydrate 34.5g
Fiber 3.5g
Cholesterol 64mg
Sodium 410mg

EXCHANGES PER SERVING:
2 Very Lean Meat
1 Starch
1/2 Fruit

PER SERVING:
Calories 208
(16% from fat)
Fat 3.8g
(saturated fat 0.7g)
Protein 18.5g
Carbohydrate 23g
Fiber 2.7g
Cholesterol 46mg
Sodium 399mg

Super Quick
FRUITED CHICKEN SALAD PITAS

Serve with fat-free pretzels.

1/3 cup fat-free mayonnaise
1/8 teaspoon salt
2 1/2 cups chopped cooked chicken breast
1 cup halved seedless red grapes
1 1/2 tablespoons chopped pecans, toasted
1 (11-ounce) can mandarin oranges, drained
6 small green leaf lettuce leaves
3 (6-inch) whole wheat pita bread rounds, cut in half crosswise

1. Combine first 5 ingredients in a medium bowl, stirring well. Gently stir in oranges.

2. Place 1 lettuce leaf in each pita pocket half. Spoon 3/4 cup chicken salad into each pita half. **Yield:** 6 servings.

♥ *Using fat-free mayonnaise instead of regular can help you keep your intake of fat grams down to a healthy level. But remember that even though the mayonnaise is fat-free, it still contains sodium and may need to be limited if you're on a low-sodium diet.*

ASIAN CHICKEN PITA

2 (4-ounce) skinned, boned chicken breast
   halves
1/2 cup bean sprouts
1/4 cup diced water chestnuts
1/4 cup sliced green onions
1 tablespoon rice vinegar
1 tablespoon low-sodium soy sauce
1 teaspoon sesame oil
1 (7-inch) whole wheat pita bread round, cut
   in half crosswise
2 leaf lettuce leaves

1. Place chicken in a medium saucepan; add water
to cover. Bring to a boil. Reduce heat to medium,
and cook, uncovered, 15 minutes or until chicken is
done; drain. Let chicken cool to touch. Chop
chicken into bite-size pieces.

2. Combine chicken, sprouts, water chestnuts, and
green onions. Combine vinegar, soy sauce, and oil;
pour over chicken mixture, tossing gently.

3. Line each pita half with 1 lettuce leaf; spoon
chicken mixture evenly into pita halves. **Yield:**
2 servings.

YIELD: 2 servings

**EXCHANGES PER
SERVING:**
3 1/2 Very Lean Meat
1 1/2 Starch
1/2 Fat

PER SERVING:
Calories 271
(20% from fat)
Fat 5.9g
(saturated fat 1.2g)
Protein 28.2g
Carbohydrate 22.4g
Fiber 3.4g
Cholesterol 70mg
Sodium 264mg

ITALIAN BALSAMIC CHICKEN WRAP

YIELD: 8 servings

EXCHANGES PER SERVING:
4 Very Lean Meat
1 Starch

PER SERVING:
Calories 225
(13% from fat)
Fat 3.2g
(saturated fat 0.6g)
Protein 28.5g
Carbohydrate 18.5g
Fiber 0.9g
Cholesterol 66mg
Sodium 329mg

¹/₄ cup minced fresh parsley
1 tablespoon dried Italian seasoning
2 tablespoons olive oil
2 tablespoons balsamic vinegar
¹/₂ teaspoon black pepper
2 garlic cloves, minced
8 (4-ounce) skinned, boned chicken breast
    halves
   Cooking spray
8 (6-inch) fat-free flour tortillas

1. Combine first 6 ingredients in a large zip-top plastic bag. Add chicken to bag; seal and marinate in refrigerator at least 2 hours.

2. Prepare grill.

3. Remove chicken from bag; discard marinade. Place chicken on a grill rack coated with cooking spray; grill 6 minutes on each side or until done. Cool; cut chicken into ¼-inch strips.

4. Warm tortillas according to package directions. Divide chicken evenly among tortillas; roll up. **Yield:** 8 servings.

TURKEY-BLACK BEAN SLOPPY JOES

YIELD: 8 servings

2 teaspoons olive oil
1½ pounds ground turkey or ground round
1½ cups finely chopped onion (about 1
    medium)
¾ cup finely chopped green bell pepper (about
    1 medium)
1 garlic clove, minced
2 (8-ounce) cans no-salt-added tomato sauce
1 (15-ounce) can black beans, rinsed and
    drained
1 tablespoon chili powder
1 tablespoon cider vinegar
1 tablespoon Dijon mustard
2 teaspoons Worcestershire sauce
2 teaspoons honey
    Pinch of ground red pepper
8 reduced-calorie whole wheat hamburger
    buns

EXCHANGES PER SERVING:
2 Lean Meat
2 Starch
1 Vegetable

PER SERVING:
Calories 301
(28% from fat)
Fat 9.2g
(saturated fat 2.2g)
Protein 22.6g
Carbohydrate 37.1g
Fiber 7.3g
Cholesterol 67mg
Sodium 460mg

1. Heat oil in a large nonstick skillet over medium-high heat. Add turkey and next 3 ingredients; cook 10 minutes or until turkey is done and vegetables are tender, stirring until turkey crumbles.

2. Stir in tomato sauce and next 7 ingredients; simmer, uncovered, 10 minutes. Spoon turkey mixture evenly onto bottom halves of hamburger buns; top with remaining halves of buns. **Yield:** 8 servings (serving size: ¾ cup turkey mixture and 1 bun).

COOL SUMMER-BERRY SOUP

YIELD: 4 servings

EXCHANGES PER SERVING:
2 Fruit
1 Starch

PER SERVING:
Calories 208
(6% from fat)
Fat 1.4g
(saturated fat 0.5g)
Protein 3.6g
Carbohydrate 48.4g
Fiber 7g
Cholesterol 2mg
Sodium 37mg

2 cups fresh raspberries
2 cups halved fresh strawberries
1/2 cup cranberry-raspberry juice drink
1/2 cup dry white wine
1/4 cup sugar
1/8 teaspoon ground cinnamon
1 (8-ounce) carton strawberry low-fat yogurt
1 cup fresh blueberries
2 teaspoons sugar
2 teaspoons cranberry-raspberry juice drink

1. To prepare soup, place first 3 ingredients in a blender, and process until smooth. Strain raspberry mixture through a sieve into a medium saucepan. Stir in wine, 1/4 cup sugar, and cinnamon. Bring to a boil over medium heat; cook 2 minutes. Remove from heat. Place in a large bowl; cover and chill 3 hours. Stir in yogurt.

2. To prepare garnish, place blueberries and remaining ingredients in a blender; process until smooth. Strain blueberry mixture through a sieve.

3. Spoon 1 cup soup into each of 4 bowls. Drizzle each serving with 1 tablespoon blueberry garnish. **Yield:** 4 servings.

Make Ahead
CHILLED CHERRY SOUP

4 cups pitted sweet cherries
2 tablespoons sugar
1 teaspoon grated lemon rind
¼ teaspoon ground ginger
⅛ teaspoon ground allspice
⅓ cup Riesling or other slightly sweet
   white wine
2 tablespoons low-fat sour cream
2 tablespoons fresh lemon juice
1 (8-ounce) carton vanilla low-fat yogurt

1. Combine first 5 ingredients in a blender or food processor, and process until cherries are finely chopped. Add wine, sour cream, and lemon juice, and process until smooth. Add yogurt, and pulse 3 to 4 times or until blended. Pour into a bowl, and cover surface of soup with plastic wrap. Chill thoroughly. **Yield:** 7 servings (serving size: ½ cup).

YIELD: 7 servings

EXCHANGES PER SERVING:
1 Fruit
½ Starch

PER SERVING:
Calories 116
(13% from fat)
Fat 1.7g
(saturated fat 0.8g)
Protein 2.8g
Carbohydrate 22.6g
Fiber 1.9g
Cholesterol 3mg
Sodium 24mg

Make Ahead
PEACH-APRICOT SOUP

You can omit the cognac and use a total of 2¼ cups orange juice, if desired.

¼ cup cognac
2 tablespoons dried cranberries (such as
   Craisins)
2 cups orange juice
3 medium peaches, peeled, halved, and pitted
3 medium apricots, peeled, halved, and pitted

1. Combine cognac and cranberries in a bowl; let stand 15 minutes, stirring occasionally. Place cognac mixture in a blender; process until cranberries are finely chopped. Add orange juice, peaches, and apricots; process until peach mixture is smooth and cranberries are minced. Cover and chill. **Yield:** 4 servings (serving size: 1¼ cups).

YIELD: 4 servings

EXCHANGES PER SERVING:
2 Fruit
½ Starch

PER SERVING:
Calories 157
(2% from fat)
Fat 0.3g
(saturated fat 0g)
Protein 1.8g
Carbohydrate 29.7g
Fiber 2.5g
Cholesterol 0mg
Sodium 2mg

CHILLED ORANGE-PEACH SOUP

YIELD: 10 servings

EXCHANGE PER SERVING:
1 Fruit

PER SERVING:
Calories 65
(1% from fat)
Fat 0.1g
(saturated fat 0g)
Protein 1.2g
Carbohydrate 15.3g
Fiber 0.7g
Cholesterol 1mg
Sodium 9mg

1 (16-ounce) package frozen sliced peaches, partially thawed
¼ cup water
1½ cups orange juice
½ cup peach nectar
½ cup vanilla fat-free yogurt
2 tablespoons honey
Fresh mint sprigs (optional)

1. Position knife blade in food processor bowl; add peaches and water. Process until smooth, stopping once to scrape down sides.

2. Pour peach mixture into a bowl. Add juice and next 3 ingredients; stir with a wire whisk until combined. Cover; chill until ready to serve. Garnish with mint, if desired. **Yield:** 10 servings (serving size: ½ cup).

Make Ahead
TROPICAL GAZPACHO

YIELD: 8 servings

EXCHANGES PER SERVING:
2 Fruit

PER SERVING:
Calories 124
(3% from fat)
Fat 0.4g
(saturated fat 0.1g)
Protein 0.9g
Carbohydrate 30.7g
Fiber 2.6g
Cholesterol 0mg
Sodium 3mg

This cool and colorful soup is so refreshing, we rated it as one of our favorites. If you'd like to turn it into dessert, top each serving with a small scoop of fruit-flavored sorbet.

2 teaspoons grated lime rind
3 tablespoons fresh lime juice
1 teaspoon vanilla extract
½ teaspoon ground cardamom
3 (8-ounce) bottles papaya nectar
2 papayas, peeled, seeded, and chopped
2 mangoes, peeled, seeded, and chopped
2 kiwifruit, peeled and chopped

1. Combine all ingredients; cover and chill. **Yield:** 8 servings (serving size: 1 cup).

FRESH ASPARAGUS SOUP

2 pounds fresh asparagus
  Cooking spray
1 tablespoon reduced-calorie margarine
1/4 cup minced onion
1/4 cup chopped fresh parsley
1 teaspoon ground coriander
1 tablespoon all-purpose flour
1/4 teaspoon salt
2 1/4 cups low-sodium chicken broth
1/2 cup fat-free milk
1 tablespoon lemon juice
1/8 teaspoon ground white pepper
  Lemon slices (optional)

YIELD: 7 servings

EXCHANGE PER SERVING:
1/2 Starch

PER SERVING:
Calories 49
(24% from fat)
Fat 1.3g
(saturated fat 0.2g)
Protein 2.9g
Carbohydrate 6.9g
Fiber 1.9g
Cholesterol 0mg
Sodium 113mg

1. Snap off tough ends of asparagus. Remove scales from stalks with a knife or vegetable peeler, if desired. Place asparagus in a large saucepan; add water to cover. Cover asparagus, and cook 10 minutes or until tender. Drain. Cut 2 inches from tip of each asparagus spear; set aside tips and bottoms of asparagus spears.

2. Coat saucepan with cooking spray; add margarine. Place over medium heat until margarine melts. Add onion, parsley, and coriander; cook, stirring constantly, until onion is tender. Add flour and salt; cook, stirring constantly, 1 minute. Gradually stir in chicken broth; cook, stirring constantly, 5 minutes.

3. Ladle broth mixture into container of an electric blender; add bottoms of asparagus spears. Cover and process until smooth. Return puree to saucepan, and stir in milk, lemon juice, and pepper. Gently stir in asparagus tips. Cook over medium heat until mixture is thoroughly heated, stirring occasionally. Ladle soup into individual bowls; garnish with lemon slices, if desired. **Yield:** 7 servings (serving size: 3/4 cup).

BUTTERNUT SQUASH BISQUE

*This golden soup makes the most of two fall favorites—
butternut squash and Rome apples. Cooked and pureed,
they make the bisque smooth and creamy.*

**EXCHANGES PER
SERVING:**
1 Fruit
1 Vegetable

PER SERVING:
Calories 90
(3% from fat)
Fat 0.3g
(saturated fat 0.1g)
Protein 2.2g
Carbohydrate 21.1g
Fiber 3.1g
Cholesterol 0mg
Sodium 19mg

　1　small butternut squash (about 1 pound)
　1　stalk celery, sliced
1³/₄　cups low-sodium chicken broth
　2　cups peeled, sliced Rome apple
³/₄　cup peeled, sliced potato
³/₄　cup sliced onion
¹/₃　cup sliced carrot
¹/₄　teaspoon dried oregano
¹/₄　teaspoon dried rosemary
¹/₄　cup fat-free milk

1. Peel squash; cut in half, and remove seeds. Slice each half crosswise. Combine squash, celery, and next 7 ingredients in a Dutch oven; bring to a boil. Cover, reduce heat, and simmer 20 to 30 minutes or until tender.

2. Process mixture, in batches, in container of an electric blender until smooth. Return puree to Dutch oven, and stir in milk. Cook over low heat, stirring constantly, until thoroughly heated. **Yield:** 6 servings (serving size: 1 cup).

♥ *The recipes in this book call for a variety of canned broths. You will see "low-sodium," "no-salt-added," or "fat-free, less-sodium," depending on the type used in testing. "Low-sodium" contains the lowest amount of sodium while "no-salt-added" is a little higher. "Fat-free, less-sodium" chicken broth contains from 390 milligrams to 570 milligrams sodium per cup compared to over 900 milligrams per cup for some brands of regular canned broth. You may substitute one type of broth for another— just realize the soup may taste more or less salty (and the sodium content will be different) if you do.*

MELANIE'S GARDEN-TOMATO SOUP

2 teaspoons olive oil
3/4 cup chopped onion
1 tablespoon chopped fresh oregano or basil
1 teaspoon chopped fresh or 1/4 teaspoon
   dried thyme
2 garlic cloves, chopped
5 cups diced tomato (about 2 pounds)
1 1/2 cups water
2 1/2 tablespoons tomato paste
2 teaspoons sugar
1/4 teaspoon salt
1/4 teaspoon black pepper
   Thinly sliced fresh basil (optional)

1. Heat olive oil in a large saucepan over medium heat. Add onion, oregano, thyme, and garlic; cook 4 minutes, stirring frequently. Stir in tomato and next 5 ingredients. Bring to a boil. Reduce heat; simmer 15 minutes.

2. Place half of soup in a blender or food processor; process until smooth, and pour into a bowl. Repeat procedure with remaining soup. Serve warm or chilled. Sprinkle with fresh basil, if desired. **Yield:** 5 servings (serving size: 1 cup).

YIELD: 5 servings

EXCHANGES PER SERVING:
2 Vegetable
1/2 Fat

PER SERVING:
Calories 81
(29% from fat)
Fat 2.6g
(saturated fat 0.4g)
Protein 2.3g
Carbohydrate 14.6g
Fiber 2.9g
Cholesterol 0mg
Sodium 140mg

YIELD: 9 servings

EXCHANGES PER
SERVING:
1 Very Lean Meat
2 Starch

PER SERVING:
Calories 185
(11% from fat)
Fat 2.3g
(saturated fat 0.3g)
Protein 12.9g
Carbohydrate 29.6g
Fiber 6.1g
Cholesterol 0mg
Sodium 289mg

SPANISH LENTIL SOUP

*Onions, bell peppers, garlic, and sherry vinegar
lend this soup a Spanish flair.*

  1 tablespoon olive oil
  1 cup diced onion
  4 garlic cloves, minced
  ³⁄₄ cup chopped red bell pepper
  ³⁄₄ cup chopped green bell pepper
  2 tablespoons sherry vinegar or red wine
      vinegar
1¹⁄₂ teaspoons ground cumin
  ¹⁄₄ teaspoon dried crushed red pepper
1¹⁄₂ cups chopped plum tomato (about
      ³⁄₄ pound)
  1 teaspoon salt
  6 cups water
  2 cups dried red lentils
  1 teaspoon Hungarian sweet paprika

1. Heat olive oil in a large saucepan over medium-high heat. Add onion and garlic; sauté 2 minutes. Add bell peppers, vinegar, cumin, and crushed red pepper, and sauté 3 minutes. Add chopped tomato and salt, and cook 2 minutes. Add water, lentils, and paprika; bring to a boil. Partially cover, reduce heat, and simmer 25 minutes or until lentils are tender. **Yield:** 9 servings (serving size: 1 cup).

ITALIAN TORTELLINI SOUP

*Escarole is a type of endive with crisp, curly green
leaves that taste slightly bitter—it may be
substituted for spinach in this recipe.*

1   medium fennel bulb
2   teaspoons olive oil
1   cup finely chopped carrot
2   garlic cloves, minced
4   (10½-ounce) cans low-sodium chicken
      broth
1   bay leaf
¼   teaspoon salt
      Black pepper
1   (9-ounce) package refrigerated cheese-filled
      tortellini, uncooked
2   cups shredded spinach or escarole
7   teaspoons grated Romano or Parmesan
      cheese

1. Trim outer stalks from fennel; cut bulb in half
lengthwise, and remove cores. Cut each half vertically into thin slices.

2. Heat oil in a large saucepan over medium heat
until hot. Add fennel, carrot, and garlic; cook 10
minutes or until tender, stirring often. Stir in broth
and next 3 ingredients. Bring to a boil; cover, reduce heat, and simmer 15 minutes.

3. Stir in pasta and spinach. Bring to a boil; reduce
heat, and simmer, uncovered, 5 minutes or until
pasta is tender. Remove and discard bay leaf. Ladle
soup into individual bowls; sprinkle each serving
with 1 teaspoon cheese. **Yield:** 7 servings.

YIELD: 7 servings

**EXCHANGES PER
SERVING:**
1 Lean Meat
1½ Starch

PER SERVING:
Calories 179
(29% from fat)
Fat 5.8g
(saturated fat 1.7g)
Protein 9.2g
Carbohydrate 22.9g
Fiber 1.3g
Cholesterol 19mg
Sodium 312mg

**EXCHANGES PER
SERVING:**
1 Medium-Fat Meat
1 Starch

PER SERVING:
Calories 144
(29% from fat)
Fat 4.6g
(saturated fat 1.8g)
Protein 8.9g
Carbohydrate 16.6g
Fiber 3.2g
Cholesterol 19mg
Sodium 346mg

ALPHABET VEGETABLE-BEEF SOUP

*After browning ground chuck, be sure to drain
it well and even pat it with paper towels to
remove as much fat as possible.*

1   pound ground chuck
2   cups low-sodium vegetable juice cocktail
2   (16-ounce) packages frozen vegetable soup
      mix with tomatoes
2   (14.25-ounce) cans no-salt-added beef broth
2   (14 1/2-ounce) cans no-salt-added diced
      tomatoes
1/2   cup uncooked alphabet-shaped pasta
1 1/2   teaspoons salt
1   teaspoon dried Italian seasoning
1/2   teaspoon pepper

1. Cook ground chuck in a Dutch oven over
medium heat until browned, stirring until it crumbles. Drain and pat dry with paper towels. Wipe
drippings from Dutch oven with a paper towel.

2. Return beef to Dutch oven. Add vegetable juice
cocktail and next 3 ingredients; bring mixture to a
boil. Cover, reduce heat, and simmer 10 minutes.
Add pasta and remaining ingredients to Dutch
oven; bring to a boil. Cover, reduce heat, and simmer 10 minutes or until pasta is done. **Yield:** 14
servings (serving size: 1 cup).

♥ *Health advisory groups recommend that at least 50
percent of our daily calories come from carbohydrates, so
you can feel free to round out most soup or stew meals
with bread. French or Italian bread, bagels, breadsticks,
toasted pita bread, or warm flour tortillas are good
choices because they are all naturally low in fat.*

BEEF AND BARLEY SOUP

1 pound ground round
5¼ cups water
½ cup chopped onion
⅓ cup uncooked medium barley
⅓ cup dried green split peas
1 tablespoon beef-flavored bouillon granules
¼ teaspoon pepper
¼ teaspoon dried basil
¼ teaspoon dried oregano
1 (14½-ounce) can no-salt-added stewed
   tomatoes
1 (5.5-ounce) can low-sodium vegetable juice
1 bay leaf
¾ cup chopped celery with leaves
½ cup sliced carrot

1. Cook ground round in a Dutch oven over medium-high heat until browned, stirring until it crumbles. Drain, if necessary.

2. Return meat to Dutch oven; add water and remaining ingredients, except celery and carrot. Bring to a boil; cover, reduce heat, and simmer 30 minutes. Add celery and carrot to Dutch oven; cover and cook 30 minutes. Remove and discard bay leaf. **Yield:** 6 servings (serving size: 1½ cups).

YIELD: 6 servings

EXCHANGES PER SERVING:
2 Lean Meat
1½ Starch

PER SERVING:
Calories 224
(20% from fat)
Fat 5g
(saturated fat 1.8g)
Protein 21.2g
Carbohydrate 23.3g
Fiber 7.3g
Cholesterol 46mg
Sodium 240mg

SPLIT PEA SOUP

*Top this soup with fat-free croutons and
serve with sliced apples.*

  1 tablespoon reduced-calorie margarine
1½ cups minced onion
  ⅔ cup diced carrots (about 2 medium)
  ½ cup diced celery (about 2 stalks)
  3 garlic cloves, minced
  8 cups water
  1 (16-ounce) package dried split green peas,
     rinsed and drained
  ¾ cup peeled, diced baking potato (about
     1 medium)
  ¼ cup minced fresh basil
  2 tablespoons minced fresh oregano
  ¾ teaspoon salt
  ½ teaspoon pepper
  2 slices reduced-fat, lower-salt ham, finely
     chopped

1. Heat margarine in a large Dutch oven over
medium heat until margarine is melted; add onion
and next 3 ingredients. Cook 10 minutes or until
vegetables are tender, stirring constantly. Add water,
split peas, and potato. Bring to a boil; cover, reduce
heat, and simmer 1 hour or until peas are tender.

2. Stir in basil and remaining ingredients. **Yield:**
8 servings (serving size: 1 cup).

HOT-AND-SOUR SOUP

Fresh ginger and hot sauce supply the heat, while rice vinegar lends a pucker to this Chinese classic.

  5 cups low-sodium chicken broth
 1/2 cup sliced fresh mushrooms
  1 teaspoon minced fresh ginger
  1 (4-ounce) skinned, boned chicken breast
     half, cut into thin strips
 1/3 cup canned bamboo shoots, cut into thin
     strips
 1/3 cup rice vinegar
 1/4 cup low-sodium soy sauce
 1/4 teaspoon hot sauce
 1/8 teaspoon pepper
  1 large egg white, lightly beaten
 1/4 cup sliced green onions
 1/4 cup fresh snow pea pods
  1 tablespoon cornstarch
 1/4 cup water

1. Combine first 3 ingredients in a 2–quart sauce-pan; bring to a boil. Add chicken, and simmer, uncovered, 10 minutes. Add bamboo shoots; simmer 5 minutes. Add vinegar and next 3 ingredients; bring to a boil. Drizzle egg white into soup, stirring constantly (lacy strands will form). Stir in green onions and snow peas.

2. Combine cornstarch and water; stir into soup mixture. Bring to a boil; boil 1 minute, stirring gently. Serve immediately. **Yield:** 8 servings (serving size: 3/4 cup).

YIELD: 8 servings

EXCHANGES PER SERVING:
1 Vegetable
1/2 Very Lean Meat

PER SERVING:
Calories 42
(4% from fat)
Fat 0.2g
(saturated fat 0.1g)
Protein 4.3g
Carbohydrate 3.1g
Fiber 0.3g
Cholesterol 8mg
Sodium 216mg

YIELD: 6 servings

EXCHANGES PER SERVING:
3 Lean Meat
1/2 Starch

PER SERVING:
Calories 204
(30% from fat)
Fat 6.9g
(saturated fat 1.9g)
Protein 25.4g
Carbohydrate 9.1g
Fiber 1g
Cholesterol 82mg
Sodium 358mg

CHUNKY CHICKEN NOODLE SOUP

Our chicken soup may not cure the common cold, but it will comfort you with down-home goodness. Tender chunks of chicken and lots of curly noodles swim in a well-seasoned broth that will warm you to your toes.

1   (3-pound) broiler-fryer, skinned
4   cups water
3/4 teaspoon poultry seasoning
1/4 teaspoon dried thyme
3   celery tops
2   cups water
1   cup uncooked medium egg noodles
1/2 cup sliced celery
1/2 cup sliced carrot
1/3 cup sliced green onions
2   tablespoons minced fresh parsley
2   teaspoons chicken-flavored bouillon
      granules
1/4 teaspoon coarsely ground black pepper
1   bay leaf
      Additional coarsely ground black pepper
      (optional)

1. Combine first 5 ingredients in a Dutch oven; bring to a boil. Cover, reduce heat, and simmer 45 minutes or until chicken is tender. Remove chicken from broth, reserving broth; set chicken aside to cool. Remove and discard celery tops from broth.

2. Skim fat from broth. Add 2 cups water and next 8 ingredients to broth; bring to a boil. Cover, reduce heat, and simmer 20 minutes.

3. Bone and coarsely chop chicken; add to broth mixture. Cook 5 minutes or until mixture is thoroughly heated. Remove and discard bay leaf. Ladle soup into individual bowls, and sprinkle with additional coarsely ground black pepper, if desired. **Yield:** 6 servings (serving size: 1 cup).

SOUTHWESTERN CHICKEN AND RICE SOUP

Two (4-ounce) skinned, boned chicken breast halves will yield enough cooked chicken for this flavorful soup.

2 (15.75-ounce) cans fat-free, less-sodium chicken broth
1 cup water
1 cup frozen chopped onion, celery, and pepper seasoning blend
1/2 cup uncooked long-grain rice
1/4 teaspoon ground cumin
1 1/2 cups chopped cooked chicken breast
1 cup peeled, seeded, and chopped tomato (about 1 large tomato)
1/2 cup frozen whole-kernel corn
1 (4.5-ounce) can chopped green chiles, undrained
1/4 cup lime juice
2 tablespoons chopped fresh cilantro
1/4 teaspoon salt

1. Bring broth and water to a boil in a large saucepan. Stir in seasoning blend, rice, and cumin. Return to a boil. Cover, reduce heat, and simmer 15 minutes or until rice is tender.

2. Stir chicken and next 3 ingredients into rice mixture; bring to a boil. Remove mixture from heat; stir in lime juice, cilantro, and salt. **Yield:** 8 servings (serving size: 1 cup).

YIELD: 8 servings

EXCHANGES PER SERVING:
1 1/2 Very Lean Meat
1 Vegetable
1/2 Starch

PER SERVING:
Calories 117
(9% from fat)
Fat 1.2g
(saturated fat 0.3g)
Protein 11.1g
Carbohydrate 14.6g
Fiber 0.7g
Cholesterol 23mg
Sodium 395mg

**EXCHANGES PER
SERVING:**
2 Very Lean Meat
1½ Starch

PER SERVING:
Calories 213
(16% from fat)
Fat 3.9g
(saturated fat 1.7g)
Protein 21.9g
Carbohydrate 20.7g
Fiber 3.2g
Cholesterol 40mg
Sodium 178mg

WHITE CHILI

You might think that cloves seem out of place among abundant Southwestern flavors, but just a tiny amount enhances the other spices and adds a hint of sweetness.

     1 cup dried navy beans
     4 (10½-ounce) cans low-sodium chicken
          broth
 1¼ cups chopped onion
     1 garlic clove, minced
     2 cups chopped cooked chicken breast
     1 teaspoon ground cumin
    ¾ teaspoon dried oregano
    ¼ teaspoon salt
    ¼ teaspoon ground red pepper
    ⅛ teaspoon ground cloves
     1 (4.5-ounce) can chopped green chiles,
          undrained
    ¾ cup (3 ounces) shredded reduced-fat
          Monterey Jack cheese

1. Sort and wash beans; place in a Dutch oven. Cover with water to a depth of 2 inches above beans. Cover and bring to a boil; boil 2 minutes. Remove from heat; let stand 1 hour.

2. Drain beans, and return to Dutch oven; add broth, onion, and garlic. Bring to a boil; cover, reduce heat, and simmer 2 hours.

3. Add chicken and next 6 ingredients; cover and cook 30 minutes. Ladle soup into individual bowls; sprinkle evenly with cheese. **Yield:** 8 servings (serving size: 1 cup chili and 1½ tablespoons cheese).

EASY WEEKNIGHT CHILI

YIELD: 6 servings

EXCHANGES PER SERVING:
3 Very Lean Meat
2 Starch
1 Vegetable

PER SERVING:
Calories 302
(20% from fat)
Fat 6.6g
(saturated fat 2.2g)
Protein 29g
Carbohydrate 34.7g
Fiber 9.5g
Cholesterol 52mg
Sodium 277mg

- 1 pound ground round
- 1¼ cups chopped onion
- 1¼ cups chopped green bell pepper
- 6 garlic cloves, pressed
  Cooking spray
- 2 (14½-ounce) cans no-salt-added stewed tomatoes, undrained and chopped
- 1 (15-ounce) can no-salt-added kidney beans, drained
- 1 (8-ounce) can no-salt-added tomato sauce
- 1 (1-ounce) envelope onion soup mix
- 1 cup water
- 3 tablespoons chili powder
- 1 tablespoon paprika
- 1¼ teaspoons hot sauce
- 6 tablespoons (1½ ounces) shredded reduced-fat sharp Cheddar cheese

1. Cook first 4 ingredients in a Dutch oven coated with cooking spray over medium–high heat until beef is browned, stirring until it crumbles. Drain.

2. Return mixture to Dutch oven; add tomato and next 7 ingredients. Bring to a boil; cover, reduce heat, and simmer 20 minutes, stirring occasionally. Ladle chili evenly into 6 bowls; top evenly with cheese. **Yield:** 6 servings (serving size: 1½ cups chili and 1 tablespoon cheese).

YIELD: 8 servings

**EXCHANGES PER
SERVING:**
2 Very Lean Meat
2½ Starch
1 Vegetable

PER SERVING:
Calories 295
(10% from fat)
Fat 3.2g
(saturated fat 1g)
Protein 22.9g
Carbohydrate 38.3g
Fiber 2.5g
Cholesterol 52mg
Sodium 345mg

CHILI VERDE

*Appease hearty appetites with this robust two-meat chili.
Red wine, salsa, green chiles, and fresh cilantro
flame the flavor.*

- ¾ pound lean boneless round steak, cut into
    1-inch cubes
- ¾ pound pork tenderloin, cut into 1-inch
    cubes
- 1 large onion, chopped
- 1 large green bell pepper, chopped
- 1 garlic clove, minced
  Cooking spray
- 2 (14½-ounce) cans no-salt-added whole
    tomatoes, undrained and chopped
- 2 (4½-ounce) cans chopped green chiles,
    undrained
- 1 cup dry red wine
- 1 cup no-salt-added salsa
- ¼ cup chopped fresh cilantro
- 2 beef bouillon cubes
- 1 tablespoon brown sugar
- 3 tablespoons lemon juice
- 4 cups hot cooked long-grain rice (cooked
    without salt or fat)
  Fresh cilantro sprigs (optional)

1. Combine first 5 ingredients in a Dutch oven
coated with cooking spray. Cook over medium-
high heat, stirring constantly, until meat is
browned.

2. Add tomatoes and next 7 ingredients. Bring to a
boil; cover, reduce heat, and simmer 1 hour or until
meat is tender, stirring occasionally. Serve over rice;
garnish with cilantro sprigs, if desired. **Yield:** 8
servings (serving size: 1 cup chili and ½ cup rice).

PORK-AND-BLACK BEAN CHILI

1 pound lean boned pork loin roast
1 (16-ounce) jar thick-and-chunky salsa
2 (15-ounce) cans no-salt-added black beans, undrained
1 cup chopped yellow bell pepper
³/₄ cup chopped onion
1 teaspoon ground cumin
1 teaspoon chili powder
1 teaspoon dried oregano
¹/₄ cup fat-free sour cream

1. Trim fat from pork; cut pork into 1-inch pieces. Combine pork and next 7 ingredients in a 4-quart electric slow cooker; stir well. Cover with lid; cook on low-heat setting 8 hours or until pork is tender. Ladle chili into bowls; top with sour cream. **Yield:** 4 servings (serving size: 2 cups chili and 1 tablespoon sour cream).

♥ *Dietary fiber is an important component of a healthy diet. And many high-fiber foods, like beans and bell pepper, are packed with beneficial vitamins and minerals. The above slow-cooker recipe is an easy way to get a good start on the daily recommended intake of 25 to 30 grams of fiber.*

YIELD: 4 servings

EXCHANGES PER SERVING:
4 Very Lean Meat
2¹/₂ Starch
1 Vegetable
¹/₂ Fat

PER SERVING:
Calories 379
(22% from fat)
Fat 9.4g
(saturated fat 2.8g)
Protein 36.7g
Carbohydrate 45.4g
Fiber 14.2g
Cholesterol 62mg
Sodium 405mg

YIELD: 7 servings

EXCHANGES PER SERVING:
2 Very Lean Meat
1 Vegetable
½ Starch

PER SERVING:
Calories 135
(7% from fat)
Fat 1g
(saturated fat 0.2g)
Protein 18.8g
Carbohydrate 10.3g
Fiber 0.1g
Cholesterol 34mg
Sodium 237mg

SPICY TOMATO-FISH CHOWDER

Serve with corn sticks and fat-free marinated coleslaw.

  Cooking spray
1 (10-ounce) package frozen chopped onion, celery, and pepper seasoning blend
1½ cups frozen cubed hash brown potatoes
½ teaspoon garlic powder
1 cup water
½ cup dry white wine
1 (10-ounce) can diced tomatoes and green chiles, undrained
1½ pounds grouper, skinned and cut into 1-inch pieces

1. Coat a Dutch oven with cooking spray; place over medium–high heat until hot. Add frozen seasoning blend, potatoes, and garlic powder; cook, stirring constantly, 5 minutes. Stir in water, wine, and tomatoes and green chiles. Bring to a boil. Cover, reduce heat, and simmer 8 minutes.

2. Add fish to potato mixture; cover and simmer 4 minutes or until fish flakes easily when tested with a fork. **Yield:** 7 servings (serving size: 1 cup).

RED POTATO-AND-SALMON CHOWDER

1 (14.5-ounce) can red salmon
2 cups diced red potatoes
2 bacon slices
2 cups diced onion
1 cup diced celery
¼ teaspoon salt
½ teaspoon bottled minced garlic
1 tablespoon all-purpose flour
3 cups 1% low-fat milk
2 tablespoons chopped fresh chives
2 tablespoons lemon juice
¼ teaspoon black pepper

1. Remove bones and skin from salmon.

2. Place potato in a saucepan. Cover with water; bring to a boil. Reduce heat. Simmer 12 minutes or until tender; drain.

3. While potato is cooking, sauté bacon in a large saucepan over medium heat until crisp. Remove bacon from saucepan; crumble. Add onion, celery, salt, and garlic to bacon drippings in saucepan; sauté 4 minutes. Stir in flour; cook 30 seconds. Gradually stir in milk, and cook 3 minutes or until mixture begins to thicken. Stir in salmon, potato, bacon, chives, juice, and pepper; cook 3 minutes or until thoroughly heated. **Yield:** 5 servings (serving size: 1⅓ cups).

YIELD: 5 servings

EXCHANGES PER SERVING:
2 Medium-Fat Meat
1½ Starch
1 Vegetable

PER SERVING:
Calories 299
(36% from fat)
Fat 11.8g
(saturated fat 4g)
Protein 21.5g
Carbohydrate 26.6g
Fiber 2.7g
Cholesterol 41mg
Sodium 333mg

YIELD: 9 servings

EXCHANGES PER
SERVING:
2 Very Lean Meat
1 Starch
1 Vegetable

PER SERVING:
Calories 165
(9% from fat)
Fat 1.7g
(saturated fat 0.4g)
Protein 17.2g
Carbohydrate 21.3g
Fiber 2.1g
Cholesterol 33mg
Sodium 240mg

TURKEY CHOWDER

An Idaho or russet baking potato works best for chowder because, when cooked, it mashes easily and makes the broth thick and creamy.

    2 teaspoons reduced-calorie margarine
    ³/₄ pound peeled, diced baking potato
    2 cups chopped onion
    1 cup finely chopped celery
    2 (10½-ounce) cans low-sodium chicken
         broth
    1 (10-ounce) package frozen whole-kernel
         corn, thawed
    1 teaspoon dried thyme
    ½ teaspoon salt
    ¼ teaspoon pepper
   2³/₄ cups chopped cooked turkey breast
    1 (12-ounce) can evaporated fat-free milk
    1 tablespoon all-purpose flour
    2 tablespoons water

1. Heat margarine in a Dutch oven over medium heat until melted. Add potato, onion, and celery to Dutch oven; cook, stirring constantly, 5 minutes. Add broth and next 4 ingredients; bring to a boil. Cover, reduce heat, and simmer 15 minutes.

2. Remove 2 cups vegetables from broth with a slotted spoon; partially mash vegetables with a fork or potato masher. Return vegetables to Dutch oven. Add turkey and milk; bring to a boil over medium heat, stirring constantly. Combine flour and water, stirring until smooth. Gradually add flour mixture to Dutch oven; cook over medium heat, stirring constantly, 4 to 5 minutes or until thickened and bubbly. **Yield:** 9 servings (serving size: 1 cup).

CIOPPINO

Cioppino (chuh-PEE-noh) is a tomato-flavored fish stew with an Italian accent. Traditionally, this stew features several types of fish, but you can use ¾ pound of any one type, if you prefer.

- 2 (14½-ounce) cans no-salt-added diced tomatoes, undrained
- 1 cup reduced-sodium vegetable juice
- ½ cup clam juice
- ½ cup water
- ½ cup chopped green bell pepper
- 3 garlic cloves, minced
- 1 teaspoon dried Italian seasoning
- ½ teaspoon black pepper
- ¼ teaspoon salt
- 6 ounces tilapia or other firm white fish fillets, cut into 2-inch pieces
- 6 ounces red snapper fillets, skinned and cut into 2-inch pieces
- ½ cup chopped fresh parsley
- ⅓ cup (1⅓ ounces) grated fresh Parmesan cheese

1. Combine first 9 ingredients in a large saucepan. Bring to a boil; cover, reduce heat, and simmer 10 minutes. Add fish and parsley. Bring to a boil; reduce heat, and simmer, uncovered, 10 minutes or until fish flakes easily when tested with a fork.

2. Ladle soup into individual bowls; sprinkle evenly with cheese. **Yield:** 7 servings (serving size: 1 cup).

YIELD: 7 servings

EXCHANGES PER SERVING:
1 Very Lean Meat
2 Vegetable
½ Fat

PER SERVING:
Calories 109
(20% from fat)
Fat 2.4g
(saturated fat 1.1g)
Protein 12.9g
Carbohydrate 9.1g
Fiber 2.6g
Cholesterol 30mg
Sodium 315mg

**EXCHANGES PER
SERVING:**
2 Lean Meat
4 Starch

PER SERVING:
Calories 436
(21% from fat)
Fat 10.3g
(saturated fat 2.9g)
Protein 24.9g
Carbohydrate 60.2g
Fiber 5.5g
Cholesterol 51mg
Sodium 328mg

MAPLE PORK-AND-VEGETABLE STEW

1 tablespoon olive oil
1 (1½-pound) boned pork loin roast, cut into
   1-inch cubes
2 cups diced onion
1 (8-ounce) package fresh mushrooms,
   quartered
1¾ cups (⅛-inch) diagonally sliced carrot
¾ cup diced red bell pepper
2 tablespoons maple syrup
1 teaspoon dried rubbed sage
¼ teaspoon salt
¼ teaspoon black pepper
1 (15.75-ounce) can fat-free, less-sodium
   chicken broth
1 (12-ounce) bottle beer
2 tablespoons cornstarch
1 tablespoon red wine vinegar
1 tablespoon country-style Dijon mustard
8 cups hot cooked brown rice (cooked
   without salt or fat)
  Sage sprigs (optional)

1. Heat oil in a large Dutch oven over medium-high heat. Add half of pork, and sauté 5 minutes or until browned. Remove from pan. Add remaining pork; sauté 5 minutes or until browned. Remove from pan. Add onion and mushrooms to pan; sauté 4 minutes. Return pork to pan; add carrot and next 7 ingredients. Bring to a boil; reduce heat, and simmer 1 hour or until pork is tender.

2. Combine cornstarch, vinegar, and mustard in a small bowl, and stir with a whisk. Add to pork mixture, and bring to a boil. Cook 3 minutes, stirring frequently. Serve with rice. Garnish with sage sprigs, if desired. **Yield:** 8 servings (serving size: 1 cup stew and 1 cup rice).

side dishes

Super Quick
SAUTÉED APPLES

3 tablespoons margarine or butter
6 cups sliced peeled Granny Smith apples
    (about 2 pounds)
1/2 cup packed brown sugar
1/8 teaspoon ground cinnamon

1. Melt margarine in a large skillet over medium-high heat. Add apples; sauté 6 minutes or until apples are just tender. Stir in sugar and cinnamon. Cook 1 minute or until sugar melts. **Yield:** 8 servings (serving size: 1/2 cup).

YIELD: 8 servings

EXCHANGES PER SERVING:
1 1/2 Fruit
1 Fat

PER SERVING:
Calories 137
(30% from fat)
Fat 4.6g
(saturated fat 0.7g)
Protein 0.2g
Carbohydrate 25.7g
Fiber 1.6g
Cholesterol 0mg
Sodium 49mg

GINGERED PEARS

Crystallized ginger is ginger that has been cooked in a sugar syrup and coated with coarse sugar.

2 teaspoons margarine or butter
1 large firm ripe red pear, cut into eighths
1 large firm ripe green pear, cut into eighths
1 teaspoon grated orange rind
1/4 cup orange juice
1 tablespoon honey
2 teaspoons finely chopped crystallized ginger

1. Melt margarine in a nonstick skillet over medium heat. Add pear pieces; cook 2 to 3 minutes. Remove pear with a slotted spoon. Set aside, and keep warm.

2. Add orange rind and remaining 3 ingredients to skillet. Bring to a boil; cook 3 minutes or until mixture is reduced by half. Return pear to skillet, and cook until pear is tender. **Yield:** 4 servings.

YIELD: 4 servings

EXCHANGES PER SERVING:
1 1/2 Fruit
1/2 Fat

PER SERVING:
Calories 106
(20% from fat)
Fat 2.3g
(saturated fat 0.4g)
Protein 0.6g
Carbohydrate 23g
Fiber 2.8g
Cholesterol 0mg
Sodium 23mg

Super Quick
CRANBERRY-GLAZED ORANGES

Serve with roasted turkey breast, steamed green beans, and whole wheat rolls.

2 tablespoons sliced almonds
4 medium-size navel oranges (about 2½ pounds)
1 (8-ounce) can jellied cranberry sauce
¼ cup orange juice
¼ teaspoon ground cinnamon

1. Place a large nonstick skillet over medium–high heat. Add almonds, and cook, stirring constantly, 5 minutes or until toasted. Remove from skillet, and set aside.

2. Peel oranges, and cut crosswise into ¼-inch-thick slices. Set aside.

3. Combine cranberry sauce, orange juice, and cinnamon in a bowl, stirring well with a wire whisk until smooth. Combine cranberry mixture and half of orange slices in skillet. Cook over medium heat 2 minutes or until oranges are thoroughly heated, stirring gently. Remove oranges from skillet, using a slotted spoon; set aside, and keep warm. Repeat procedure with remaining orange slices.

4. Place orange slices and any remaining cranberry mixture in a large serving bowl; sprinkle with toasted almonds. Serve immediately. **Yield:** 6 servings.

YIELD: 6 servings

EXCHANGES PER SERVING:
2 Fruit

PER SERVING:
Calories 135
(8% from fat)
Fat 1.2g
(saturated fat 0.1g)
Protein 1.9g
Carbohydrate 31g
Fiber 6.5g
Cholesterol 0mg
Sodium 19mg

Super Quick
CINNAMON-SPICED PEACHES

YIELD: 5 servings

EXCHANGE PER
SERVING:
1 Fruit

PER SERVING:
Calories 67
(1% from fat)
Fat 0.1g
(saturated fat 0g)
Protein 0.4g
Carbohydrate 17.2g
Fiber 1.1g
Cholesterol 0mg
Sodium 3mg

$\frac{1}{2}$ (16-ounce) package frozen sliced peaches,
    thawed (about 2 cups)
$\frac{1}{4}$ cup sweetened dried cranberries (such as
    Craisins)
$\frac{1}{4}$ cup peach nectar
 3 tablespoons dark brown sugar
$\frac{1}{2}$ teaspoon ground cinnamon

1. Combine all ingredients in a medium nonstick skillet; stir well. Cover and cook over medium heat 10 minutes or until peaches are tender. Serve as a fruit side dish with ham or roast pork, or as a sauce for fat-free pound cake, angel food cake, or vanilla ice cream. **Yield:** 5 servings (serving size: $\frac{1}{4}$ cup).

Super Quick
RUM-GLAZED PINEAPPLE

YIELD: 4 servings

EXCHANGES PER
SERVING:
2 Fruit
$\frac{1}{2}$ Fat

PER SERVING:
Calories 134
(21% from fat)
Fat 3.1g
(saturated fat 1.4g)
Protein 0.6g
Carbohydrate 27.5g
Fiber 0.5g
Cholesterol 0mg
Sodium 35mg

1 (20-ounce) can chunk pineapple in juice,
    undrained
2 teaspoons margarine or butter
3 tablespoons brown sugar
2 tablespoons dark rum
$\frac{1}{4}$ teaspoon cornstarch
2 tablespoons flaked coconut, toasted

1. Drain pineapple, reserving $\frac{1}{3}$ cup juice.

2. Melt margarine in a large nonstick skillet over medium-high heat. Stir in pineapple juice, brown sugar, and pineapple chunks. Bring to a boil, and reduce heat; simmer 2 to 3 minutes, stirring often. Combine rum and cornstarch, stirring well; add to skillet. Cook 1 minute or until slightly thickened.

3. Spoon pineapple mixture into serving dish; sprinkle with coconut. Serve warm. **Yield:** 4 servings (serving size: $\frac{1}{2}$ cup).

HONEY-CURRY GLAZED PINEAPPLE

1 pineapple, peeled and cut into 2-inch
   chunks
¼ cup honey
1 tablespoon curry powder
1 tablespoon vanilla extract
¼ cup packed light brown sugar
¼ cup Grand Marnier (orange-flavored liqueur)

1. Preheat oven to 500°.

2. Combine pineapple chunks, honey, curry, and vanilla in a bowl; toss well. Arrange on a baking sheet. Bake at 500° for 10 minutes. Sprinkle with brown sugar, and drizzle with Grand Marnier. Ignite pineapple with a long match, and let flames die down. **Yield:** 4 servings.

YIELD: 4 servings

EXCHANGES PER SERVING:
4 Fruit

PER SERVING:
Calories 227
(5% from fat)
Fat 1.2g
(saturated fat 0.1g)
Protein 1.1g
Carbohydrate 56.4g
Fiber 3.3g
Cholesterol 0mg
Sodium 8mg

CURRIED BAKED PINEAPPLE

2 (20-ounce) cans pineapple chunks in juice,
   drained
15 reduced-fat round buttery crackers, crushed
   (such as Ritz)
¼ cup packed brown sugar
¼ cup (1 ounce) shredded reduced-fat sharp
   Cheddar cheese
½ teaspoon curry powder
   Fat-free butter spray (such as I Can't Believe
   It's Not Butter)

1. Preheat oven to 450°.

2. Place pineapple chunks in an ungreased 11 x 7-inch baking dish; set aside.

3. Combine cracker crumbs and next 3 ingredients, stirring well. Sprinkle cracker mixture over pineapple. Coat cracker mixture with butter spray (about 5 sprays). Bake at 450° for 10 minutes or until lightly browned. **Yield:** 8 servings.

YIELD: 8 servings

EXCHANGES PER SERVING:
1 Fruit
½ Starch

PER SERVING:
Calories 118
(11% from fat)
Fat 1.4g
(saturated fat 0.4g)
Protein 1.4g
Carbohydrate 24.6g
Fiber 0g
Cholesterol 2mg
Sodium 82mg

SPICED WINTER FRUIT

YIELD: 8 servings

EXCHANGES PER SERVING:
3 Fruit
1 Fat

PER SERVING:
Calories 219
(15% from fat)
Fat 3.6g
(saturated fat 0.6g)
Protein 0.7g
Carbohydrate 50.1g
Fiber 4.5g
Cholesterol 0mg
Sodium 38mg

Topped with low-fat vanilla ice cream, this also makes a simple and elegant holiday dessert. Quince is a yellow-skinned fruit that looks and tastes like a cross between an apple and a pear but turns pink when cooked; cooking mellows its tartness. (If you can't find quince, just use 2 additional apples or pears cut into wedges.)

1 cup packed light brown sugar
1 teaspoon ground ginger
1 teaspoon ground cinnamon
½ teaspoon ground nutmeg
2 tablespoons margarine or butter
2 quinces, each cut into 8 wedges (about ¾ pound)
3 cups sliced peeled Bartlett or Anjou pear (about 1½ pounds)
2½ cups sliced peeled Granny Smith apple (about 1½ pounds)
¼ teaspoon freshly ground black pepper
Cinnamon sticks (optional)

1. Combine first 4 ingredients in a small bowl; set aside.

2. Melt margarine in a large nonstick skillet over medium heat. Add quince; cover and cook 6 minutes, stirring occasionally. Add sugar mixture, pear, and apple; cover and cook 12 minutes, stirring occasionally. Stir in pepper; garnish with cinnamon sticks, if desired. **Yield:** 8 servings (serving size: ¾ cup).

Note: This dish will hold up to 3 days if refrigerated in an airtight container. To serve, reheat over low heat.

WARM CURRIED FRUIT

*For more color, substitute Bing cherries for the
Royal Anne cherries.*

2 (15-ounce) cans peach halves in juice,
   drained
1 (15-ounce) can pear halves in juice, drained
1 (15.25-ounce) can pineapple chunks in
   juice, drained
1 (16.5-ounce) can pitted Royal Anne cherries
   in heavy syrup, drained
⅓ cup low-sugar orange marmalade
⅓ cup chutney
2 tablespoons reduced-calorie margarine
¾ teaspoon ground cinnamon
½ teaspoon curry powder

1. Preheat oven to 350°.

2. Combine fruit in a medium bowl.

3. Combine marmalade and remaining 4 ingredients in a small saucepan. Cook over medium heat
until margarine melts, stirring often. Bring to a boil,
stirring constantly; add to fruit, and toss gently.

4. Spoon fruit mixture into an 8-inch square baking dish. Cover and bake at 350° for 40 minutes or
until mixture is bubbly. **Yield:** 11 servings (serving
size: ½ cup).

YIELD: 11 servings

**EXCHANGES PER
SERVING:**
1½ Fruit

PER SERVING:
Calories 100
(13% from fat)
Fat 1.4g
(saturated fat 0.1g)
Protein 0.3g
Carbohydrate 22g
Fiber 2g
Cholesterol 0mg
Sodium 107mg

YIELD: 6 servings

**EXCHANGES PER
SERVING:**
1 Vegetable
½ Fat

PER SERVING:
Calories 49
(33% from fat)
Fat 1.8g
(saturated fat 0.3g)
Protein 2.4g
Carbohydrate 6.6g
Fiber 2g
Cholesterol 0mg
Sodium 132mg

Super Quick
ASPARAGUS STIR-FRY

1½ pounds fresh asparagus
     Cooking spray
  1 teaspoon peanut oil
 ½ cup low-sodium chicken broth, divided
  1 tablespoon cornstarch
  1 teaspoon sugar
  2 tablespoons low-sodium soy sauce
  1 tablespoon sesame seeds, toasted

1. Snap off tough ends of asparagus; remove scales from stalks with a vegetable peeler, if desired. Diagonally cut into 2-inch pieces.

2. Coat a nonstick skillet with cooking spray; add oil, and place over medium–high heat until hot. Add asparagus; cook 2 minutes, stirring constantly. Add ¼ cup broth; cover and cook 4 minutes or until asparagus is crisp–tender.

3. Combine remaining ¼ cup broth, cornstarch, sugar, and soy sauce; stir until smooth. Add to asparagus mixture, stirring constantly. Bring to a boil; boil 1 minute, stirring constantly. Sprinkle with seeds. **Yield:** 6 servings.

♥ *Be aware that many Asian sauces and condiments are high in sodium. If you are trying to control the sodium in your diet, use low-sodium soy sauce instead of the regular version and omit other high-sodium ingredients such as salt and monosodium glutamate (MSG).*

Super Quick
SESAME ASPARAGUS AND MUSHROOMS

Use the heaviest jelly-roll pan or roasting pan available for roasting the vegetables.

 2 tablespoons rice wine vinegar
 1 teaspoon dark sesame oil
 1/4 teaspoon salt
 1/8 teaspoon garlic powder
 1/8 teaspoon black pepper
 1 pound fresh asparagus spears
 8 ounces whole fresh mushrooms
 1/2 teaspoon sesame seeds (optional)

1. Preheat oven to 500°.

2. Combine first 5 ingredients in a heavy-duty zip-top plastic bag. Snap off tough ends of asparagus. Remove scales with a vegetable peeler, if desired. Cut asparagus spears in half. Cut mushrooms into quarters (or in half, if small). Add asparagus, mushrooms, and, if desired, sesame seeds to vinegar mixture; seal bag, and turn to coat vegetables well.

3. Place vegetables in a single layer on a 15 x 10-inch jelly-roll pan. Bake at 500° for 10 minutes or until tender, stirring after 5 minutes. **Yield:** 6 servings.

YIELD: 6 servings

EXCHANGE PER SERVING:
1 Vegetable

PER SERVING:
Calories 31
(38% from fat)
Fat 1.3g
(saturated fat 0.2g)
Protein 2g
Carbohydrate 4.1g
Fiber 1.5g
Cholesterol 0mg
Sodium 101mg

YIELD: 4 servings

EXCHANGES PER SERVING:
3 Vegetable
$\frac{1}{2}$ Fat

PER SERVING:
Calories 91
(24% from fat)
Fat 2.4g
(saturated fat 1.3g)
Protein 3.5g
Carbohydrate 16.7g
Fiber 6.5g
Cholesterol 5mg
Sodium 28mg

ARTICHOKES WITH BROWNED GARLIC AND LEMON DIPPING SAUCE

4 large artichokes
2 teaspoons butter or margarine
1 garlic clove, minced
2 tablespoons lemon juice
1 tablespoon white wine Worcestershire sauce
$\frac{1}{4}$ cup water
1 tablespoon Dijon mustard
   Dash of ground white pepper

1. Wash artichokes by plunging up and down in cold water. Cut off stem to within 1 inch of base. Remove bottom leaves and tough outer leaves of artichokes. Place artichokes, stem ends down, in an 11 x 7-inch baking dish; add water to depth of 1 inch. Cover with heavy-duty plastic wrap, and vent. Microwave at HIGH 10 minutes or until a leaf near the center of each artichoke pulls out easily. Drain. Remove fuzzy choke from center of each artichoke with a spoon.

2. Melt butter in a small saucepan; stir in garlic. Cook over medium heat, stirring constantly, until garlic is lightly browned. Add lemon juice and remaining 4 ingredients; heat just until hot. Serve as a dipping sauce with whole artichokes. **Yield:** 4 servings (serving size: 1 artichoke and 2 tablespoons sauce).

GLAZED GREEN BEANS

1 tablespoon vegetable oil
2 1/2 cups vertically sliced red onion
2 pounds green beans, trimmed
1/2 cup water
1/4 cup low-sodium soy sauce
1 1/2 tablespoons sugar
3 tablespoons sake (rice wine) or rice vinegar

1. Heat oil in a large nonstick skillet over medium heat. Add onion, and stir-fry 1 minute. Increase heat to medium-high. Add beans; stir-fry 1 minute. Stir in water and remaining ingredients; bring to a boil. Cover, reduce heat, and simmer 12 minutes or until tender. Uncover and bring to a boil; cook 10 minutes or until liquid almost evaporates. Toss gently to combine. **Yield:** 10 servings (serving size: 1/2 cup).

YIELD: 10 servings

EXCHANGES PER SERVING:
2 Vegetable

PER SERVING:
Calories 62
(22% from fat)
Fat 1.5g
(saturated fat 0.3g)
Protein 2.3g
Carbohydrate 11.4g
Fiber 2.4g
Cholesterol 0mg
Sodium 200mg

GREEN BEANS WITH CARAMELIZED ONIONS

Here's a low-fat, high-flavor alternative to the familiar green bean and French fried onion casserole.

1 pound fresh green beans
1 1/2 cups frozen pearl onions, thawed
1 tablespoon reduced-calorie margarine
2 tablespoons brown sugar

1. Arrange beans in a steamer basket over boiling water. Cover and steam 15 minutes; set aside. Place onions in boiling water 3 minutes; drain.

2. Melt margarine in a large heavy skillet over medium heat; add sugar, and cook, stirring constantly, until bubbly. Add onions; cook 3 minutes, stirring constantly. Add beans; cook, stirring constantly, until heated. **Yield:** 4 servings (serving size: 2/3 cup).

YIELD: 4 servings

EXCHANGES PER SERVING:
3 Vegetable

PER SERVING:
Calories 87
(21% from fat)
Fat 2g
(saturated fat 0.5g)
Protein 2.6g
Carbohydrate 17.5g
Fiber 2.7g
Cholesterol 0mg
Sodium 41mg

GREEN BEANS AND PAN-ROASTED RED ONIONS

Leave beans whole, or cut into small pieces if you prefer.

5 cups water
1 pound green beans, trimmed
1 tablespoon olive oil
3 red onions, each cut into 8 wedges
½ cup fat-free, less-sodium chicken broth
1 tablespoon balsamic vinegar
2 teaspoons brown sugar
¼ teaspoon salt
¼ teaspoon black pepper

1. Bring water to a boil in a large saucepan; add beans. Cook 6 minutes or until crisp-tender. Drain; keep warm.

2. Heat oil in a large nonstick skillet over medium-high heat. Add onions; sauté 8 minutes or until browned. Add broth; cook 3 minutes, stirring occasionally. Stir in vinegar and remaining ingredients. Stir in beans; cover and cook 2 minutes. **Yield:** 7 servings (serving size: 1 cup).

PEPPERY GREEN BEAN MEDLEY

Strips of red and green bell pepper and rings of red onion streak these garlic-scented green beans with color.

  1 pound fresh green beans
  $2/3$ cup fat-free, less-sodium chicken broth
  $1/4$ teaspoon ground red pepper
  2 garlic cloves, minced
  1 small red bell pepper, seeded and cut into
     thin strips
  1 small green bell pepper, seeded and cut into
     thin strips
  1 red onion, sliced and separated into rings
  $1/4$ teaspoon black pepper
  $1/8$ teaspoon salt

1. Wash beans; trim ends, and remove strings. Cut beans into 1-inch pieces, and set aside.

2. Combine broth, ground red pepper, and garlic in a large nonstick skillet; bring to a boil over medium heat. Stir in beans; cover and cook 5 minutes. Add bell pepper strips and onion; cook, uncovered, 5 to 7 minutes or until crisp-tender, stirring often. Gently stir in black pepper and salt. Serve immediately. **Yield:** 5 servings (serving size: 1 cup).

YIELD: 5 servings

EXCHANGES PER SERVING:
3 Vegetable

PER SERVING:
Calories 63
(9% from fat)
Fat 0.6g
(saturated fat 0.1g)
Protein 2.9g
Carbohydrate 13.6g
Fiber 3.5g
Cholesterol 0mg
Sodium 77mg

EXCHANGES PER
SERVING:
2 Vegetable

PER SERVING:
Calories 57
(3% from fat)
Fat 0.2g
(saturated fat 0g)
Protein 1.9g
Carbohydrate 13.1g
Fiber 0.9g
Cholesterol 0mg
Sodium 91mg

GINGER-MARMALADE GLAZED BEETS

*Sweet orange marmalade kissed with crystallized ginger
envelops these beets in a syrupy glaze.*

3/4 pound fresh beets
3 tablespoons reduced-calorie orange
marmalade
1 tablespoon lemon juice
1 tablespoon apple juice
1 teaspoon minced crystallized ginger

1. Leave roots and 1 inch of stems on beets; scrub
beets with a vegetable brush. Cook beets in boiling
water to cover 30 minutes or until tender. Drain.
Pour cold water over beets, and drain. Trim off
roots and stems, and rub off skins. Cut beets into
¼-inch-thick slices.

2. Combine marmalade and remaining 3 ingredients in a saucepan; add beets, stirring to coat.
Cook, uncovered, over low heat until mixture is
thoroughly heated, stirring occasionally. **Yield:** 3
servings (serving size: ½ cup).

BROCCOLI WITH CARAWAY-CHEESE SAUCE

Caraway seeds have a distinct nutty flavor. Store the seeds in an airtight container in a cool, dark place up to six months to maintain this flavor.

     2   pounds fresh broccoli
     2   teaspoons margarine or butter
    ³/₄ cup fat-free milk
  1¹/₂ tablespoons all-purpose flour
    ¹/₄ teaspoon salt
    ¹/₈ teaspoon pepper
    ¹/₄ cup (1 ounce) shredded Gruyère or Swiss
         cheese
    ¹/₂ teaspoon caraway seeds
     1   (2-ounce) jar diced pimiento, drained

1. Remove and discard broccoli leaves; cut off and discard tough ends of stalks. Wash broccoli; cut into spears. Arrange spears in a steamer basket over boiling water. Cover and steam 8 minutes or until spears are crisp-tender. Drain and place on a serving platter; set aside, and keep warm.

2. Melt margarine in a saucepan over medium heat. Add milk and next 3 ingredients; cook, stirring constantly with a wire whisk, until smooth. Add cheese and caraway seeds; cook, stirring constantly, until cheese melts and mixture is thickened and bubbly.

3. Pour sauce over broccoli. Sprinkle with pimiento, and serve immediately. **Yield:** 8 servings.

YIELD: 8 servings

EXCHANGES PER SERVING:
1 Vegetable
¹/₂ Fat

PER SERVING:
Calories 58
(37% from fat)
Fat 2.4g
(saturated fat 0.9g)
Protein 4.2g
Carbohydrate 6.3g
Fiber 2.3g
Cholesterol 4mg
Sodium 128mg

GLAZED BRUSSELS SPROUTS AND BABY CARROTS

Make sure your Brussels sprouts cook evenly by cutting an "x" in the stem end of each sprout.

4 cups trimmed Brussels sprouts (about $3/4$ pound)
1 (16-ounce) package fresh baby carrots
1 cup orange marmalade
$1/2$ teaspoon ground ginger
$1/4$ teaspoon salt

1. Steam Brussels sprouts and carrots, covered, 10 minutes or until crisp–tender. Place vegetables in a serving bowl.

2. Combine marmalade, ginger, and salt; pour over vegetables, tossing to coat. Serve immediately. **Yield:** 8 servings.

♥ *Brussels sprouts, broccoli, cabbage, and cauliflower are all members of the same food family—cruciferous vegetables. Eat these crunchy veggies often; they contain nutrients that help your heart's health and may reduce the risk of cancer.*

BRAISED RED CABBAGE

*Thin slices of red cabbage are simmered in
tangy red wine vinegar until crisp-tender, then
mixed with aromatic bits of onion and garlic.*

Olive oil-flavored cooking spray
1 teaspoon olive oil
1 small onion, chopped
1 garlic clove, minced
½ teaspoon dried thyme
½ teaspoon celery seeds
¼ teaspoon salt
¼ teaspoon ground white pepper
2 bay leaves
1½ quarts water
1 cup red wine vinegar
1 small red cabbage, thinly sliced (8 cups)
2 tablespoons red wine vinegar
¼ cup fat-free, less-sodium chicken broth

1. Coat a large nonstick skillet with cooking spray;
add oil. Place over medium–high heat until hot. Add
onion and garlic; cook, stirring constantly, until
onion is tender. Stir in thyme and next 4 ingredients; cook 30 seconds. Remove from heat, and set
aside.

2. Combine water and 1 cup vinegar in a large
Dutch oven; bring to a boil. Add cabbage, and cook
10 seconds, stirring constantly; drain. Add cabbage,
2 tablespoons vinegar, and chicken broth to onion
mixture; bring to a boil. Cover, reduce heat, and
simmer 15 minutes or until cabbage is crisp-tender.
Remove and discard bay leaves. **Yield:** 8 servings
(serving size: ½ cup).

YIELD: 8 servings

**EXCHANGE PER
SERVING:**
1 Vegetable

PER SERVING:
Calories 32
(25% from fat)
Fat 0.9g
(saturated fat 0.1g)
Protein 1.1g
Carbohydrate 5.9g
Fiber 1.5g
Cholesterol 0mg
Sodium 98mg

BALSAMIC CARROTS

EXCHANGES PER
SERVING:
2 Vegetable

PER SERVING:
Calories 62
(20% from fat)
Fat 1.4g
(saturated fat 0.2g)
Protein 1g
Carbohydrate 12.5g
Fiber 3g
Cholesterol 0mg
Sodium 51mg

1 pound carrots (about 5 small), scraped and
   sliced diagonally
1 cup water
2 tablespoons balsamic vinegar
2 teaspoons honey
1 teaspoon olive oil
1/2 teaspoon Dijon mustard
1 teaspoon dried basil
1/8 teaspoon black pepper

1. Place carrot in a large saucepan; add water, and bring to a boil. Cover, reduce heat, and simmer 10 minutes or until tender. Drain; return carrot to saucepan.

2. Combine vinegar and remaining 5 ingredients in a small bowl, stirring well with a wire whisk; add to carrot. Cook over medium heat 2 minutes, stirring often. Serve warm. **Yield:** 4 servings (serving size: 1/2 cup).

ORANGE-SPICED CARROTS

EXCHANGE PER
SERVING:
1 Starch

PER SERVING:
Calories 80
(24% from fat)
Fat 2.1g
(saturated fat 0.3g)
Protein 1.2g
Carbohydrate 15.1g
Fiber 3.5g
Cholesterol 0mg
Sodium 67mg

3 cups sliced carrot
1 teaspoon coarsely grated orange rind
1/4 cup fresh orange juice
1 tablespoon brown sugar
1 tablespoon reduced-calorie margarine
1/4 teaspoon ground nutmeg
1/2 teaspoon vanilla extract

1. Arrange sliced carrot in a steamer basket over boiling water. Cover and steam 8 minutes or until crisp-tender. Combine orange rind and next 4 ingredients in a saucepan; stir in carrot. Bring to a boil; cook, stirring constantly, 5 minutes. Remove from heat, and stir in vanilla. Serve immediately. **Yield:** 4 servings (serving size: 3/4 cup).

SOUTHERN-STYLE CREAMED CORN

Thick slices of onion simmered with milky kernels of corn give this creamy side dish its fresh-from-the-farm taste.

 6 ears fresh corn
 1 cup 1% low-fat milk, divided
 2 teaspoons cornstarch
 2 (¹/₂-inch-thick) onion slices
 ¹/₄ teaspoon salt
 ¹/₄ teaspoon pepper

1. Remove and discard husks and silks from corn. Cut corn from cobs, scraping cobs well to remove all milk. Set corn aside.

2. Combine ¼ cup milk and cornstarch; set aside. Combine remaining ¾ cup milk and onion in a large saucepan; bring to a boil over medium heat. Cover, reduce heat, and simmer 5 minutes; remove and discard onion.

3. Add corn to hot milk, and bring to a boil. Reduce heat, and cook 5 minutes, stirring often. Add cornstarch mixture, salt, and pepper; cook, stirring constantly, 3 minutes or until thickened and bubbly. **Yield:** 4 servings (serving size: ½ cup).

YIELD: 4 servings

EXCHANGES PER SERVING:
2 Starch

PER SERVING:
Calories 141
(13% from fat)
Fat 2g
(saturated fat 0.6g)
Protein 5.3g
Carbohydrate 29.9g
Fiber 3.8g
Cholesterol 2mg
Sodium 194mg

EXCHANGES PER SERVING:
3 Vegetable
½ Fat

PER SERVING:
Calories 85
(24% from fat)
Fat 2.3g
(saturated fat 0.3g)
Protein 2.7g
Carbohydrate 15.4g
Fiber 3.3g
Cholesterol 0mg
Sodium 208mg

RATATOUILLE

*Serve on a bed of couscous or angel hair pasta
as a side dish to grilled chicken or pork.*

2 teaspoons olive oil
1 small onion, sliced
1 small eggplant, cut into ¾-inch cubes
1 (14-ounce) can stewed tomatoes, undrained
1 small yellow squash, cut in half lengthwise
   and thinly sliced
1 medium zucchini, cut in half lengthwise
   and thinly sliced
1 small green bell pepper, thinly sliced
4 garlic cloves, minced
1 teaspoon dried thyme
1 teaspoon dried basil
¼ teaspoon freshly ground black pepper

1. Heat oil in a large nonstick skillet over medium heat until hot. Add onion, and cook 5 minutes or until tender, stirring constantly. Add eggplant; cook 5 additional minutes, stirring constantly.

2. Add stewed tomatoes and next 5 ingredients; stir well. Cover, reduce heat, and simmer 15 minutes or until vegetables are tender. Add basil and black pepper; cook 2 additional minutes. **Yield:** 5 servings (serving size: 1 cup).

COLLARD GREENS

Collard greens seasoned with bacon drippings are a Southern classic, but we found that liquid smoke flavors the greens in similar fashion without adding fat.

2 (2-pound) packages washed fresh collard greens
Cooking spray
2 teaspoons vegetable oil
1/2 cup chopped onion
1 (15.75-ounce) can fat-free, less-sodium chicken broth
1/4 cup water
1/2 teaspoon seasoned salt
1/2 teaspoon sugar
1/2 teaspoon freshly ground black pepper
1/4 teaspoon liquid smoke

1. Remove coarse stems and discolored spots from greens; coarsely chop greens, and set aside.

2. Coat a large Dutch oven with cooking spray. Add oil, and place over medium–high heat until hot. Add onion; cook, stirring constantly, until tender. Add greens, broth, and remaining ingredients. Bring to a boil over medium–high heat. Cover and reduce heat; simmer 1 hour or until tender. **Yield:** 6 servings.

YIELD: 6 servings

EXCHANGE PER SERVING:
1 Vegetable

PER SERVING:
Calories 35
(44% from fat)
Fat 1.7g
(saturated fat 0.3g)
Protein 1.6g
Carbohydrate 3.4g
Fiber 0.7g
Cholesterol 0mg
Sodium 206mg

GREENS WITH GARLIC AND LEMON

YIELD: 4 servings

**EXCHANGES PER
SERVING:**
2 Vegetable
½ Fat

PER SERVING:
Calories 63
(31% from fat)
Fat 2.2g
(saturated fat 0.3g)
Protein 2.6g
Carbohydrate 10.3g
Fiber 4g
Cholesterol 0mg
Sodium 140mg

     4 quarts water
     6 cups torn turnip greens
     6 cups torn collard greens
  1 ½ teaspoons olive oil
     2 garlic cloves, finely chopped
    ⅛ teaspoon salt
     4 lemon wedges

1. Bring 4 quarts water to a boil in an 8-quart stock-pot. Add greens; cover and cook 20 minutes. Drain well. Heat oil in a small skillet over medium-high heat. Add garlic; sauté 30 seconds or until lightly browned. Combine greens, garlic mixture, and salt in a medium bowl; toss well. Serve with lemon wedges. **Yield:** 4 servings (serving size: ½ cup).

Super Quick
MUSHROOM AND PEPPER SKILLET

YIELD: 2 servings

**EXCHANGES PER
SERVING:**
2 Vegetable

PER SERVING:
Calories 48
(21% from fat)
Fat 1.1g
(saturated fat 0.1g)
Protein 2.8g
Carbohydrate 7.9g
Fiber 2.3g
Cholesterol 0mg
Sodium 271mg

     1 large red bell pepper
        Cooking spray
     1 (8-ounce) package sliced fresh mushrooms
    ¼ teaspoon dried rosemary
     1 tablespoon low-sodium soy sauce

1. Slice bell pepper into strips. Coat a nonstick skillet with cooking spray; place over medium-high heat until hot. Add bell pepper, mushrooms, rosemary, and soy sauce. Cover and cook 4 minutes. Stir well; cover and cook 3 minutes or until crisp-tender. **Yield:** 2 servings (serving size: ⅔ cup).

BRAISED LEEKS AND MUSHROOMS

6 leeks (about 3 pounds)
1 cup fat-free beef broth
1 tablespoon tomato paste
1/4 teaspoon salt
1/4 teaspoon dried thyme
1/8 teaspoon black pepper
1 1/2 teaspoons margarine or butter
2 cups quartered mushrooms (about 5 ounces)

1. Remove roots, outer leaves, and tops from leeks, leaving 6 inches of each leek. Cut each diagonally into thirds, then diagonally in half to form 6 triangular pieces from each leek. Rinse under cold water; drain well.

2. Combine beef broth, tomato paste, salt, thyme, and pepper in a bowl, and stir with a whisk.

3. Melt margarine in a large nonstick skillet over medium-high heat. Add leeks and mushrooms, and sauté 6 minutes or until vegetables are lightly browned. Add broth mixture. Cover, reduce heat, and simmer 15 minutes or until leeks are tender. Uncover; simmer 7 minutes or until liquid almost evaporates, stirring occasionally. **Yield:** 4 servings (serving size: 1/2 cup).

YIELD: 4 servings

EXCHANGES PER SERVING:
2 Starch

PER SERVING:
Calories 144
(14% from fat)
Fat 2.2g
(saturated fat 0.3g)
Protein 3.8g
Carbohydrate 29.3g
Fiber 2.9g
Cholesterol 0mg
Sodium 204mg

OKRA-PEPPER SAUTÉ

YIELD: 4 servings

EXCHANGES PER
SERVING:
1 Vegetable
½ Fat

PER SERVING:
Calories 52
(38% from fat)
Fat 2.2g
(saturated fat 0.4g)
Protein 1.6g
Carbohydrate 7.2g
Fiber 1.4g
Cholesterol 0mg
Sodium 173mg

2 teaspoons margarine or butter
1 cup yellow bell pepper strips
1 cup red bell pepper strips
3 cups okra pods, cut in half diagonally (about
      ½ pound)
2 tablespoons chopped fresh cilantro
¼ teaspoon salt
¼ teaspoon black pepper

1. Heat margarine in a large nonstick skillet over medium heat. Add bell peppers; sauté 4 minutes. Add okra; cover, reduce heat, and cook 15 minutes or until okra is tender. Stir in cilantro, salt, and black pepper. **Yield:** 4 servings (serving size: ¾ cup).

OKRA STEWED WITH TOMATOES

YIELD: 8 servings

EXCHANGES PER
SERVING:
2 Vegetable

PER SERVING:
Calories 50
(23% from fat)
Fat 1.3g
(saturated fat 0.2g)
Protein 1.8g
Carbohydrate 8.5g
Fiber 1.5g
Cholesterol 0mg
Sodium 82mg

1   pound small okra pods
1½ tablespoons white vinegar
¼   teaspoon salt, divided
2   teaspoons olive oil
1½ cups chopped onion
1   cup chopped tomato
⅛   teaspoon sugar
⅛   teaspoon black pepper
¼   cup chopped fresh parsley

1. Combine okra, vinegar, and ⅛ teaspoon salt in a bowl. Let stand 1 hour, stirring occasionally.

2. Heat oil in a medium nonstick skillet over medium–high heat. Add onion, and sauté 7 minutes or until tender. Stir in ⅛ teaspoon salt, tomato, sugar, and pepper. Reduce heat; simmer 15 minutes. Add okra mixture; cook 40 minutes or until tender, stirring occasionally. Stir in parsley. **Yield:** 8 servings (serving size: ¾ cup).

HONEY-ROASTED ONIONS

*Use these golden-colored onions as a side dish
for meat loaf, pork, or chicken.*

2 large Vidalias or other sweet onions (about
     1¼ pounds)
1 tablespoon water
¼ cup honey
1 tablespoon margarine or butter, melted
1 teaspoon paprika
¼ teaspoon salt
½ teaspoon curry powder
⅛ to ¼ teaspoon ground red pepper

1. Preheat oven to 350°.

2. Peel onions, and cut in half crosswise. Place
onions, cut sides down, in an 8-inch square baking
dish; drizzle with water. Cover with foil; bake at
350° for 30 minutes.

3. Combine honey and remaining ingredients. Turn
onions over; brush half of honey mixture over
onions. Bake, uncovered, an additional 30 minutes
or until tender, basting with remaining honey mixture after 15 minutes. **Yield:** 4 servings (serving
size: 1 onion half).

YIELD: 4 servings

**EXCHANGES PER
SERVING:**
1½ Starch

PER SERVING:
Calories 126
(22% from fat)
Fat 3.1g
(saturated fat 0.6g)
Protein 1.2g
Carbohydrate 25.6g
Fiber 1.8g
Cholesterol 0mg
Sodium 184mg

ROSEMARY-GLAZED VIDALIA ONIONS

EXCHANGES PER SERVING:
1 Starch
$1/2$ Fat

PER SERVING:
Calories 105
(23% from fat)
Fat 2.7g
(saturated fat 0.4g)
Protein 1.8g
Carbohydrate 19.9g
Fiber 2.8g
Cholesterol 0mg
Sodium 9mg

1　cup dry red wine
2　tablespoons sugar
1　tablespoon chopped fresh or 1 teaspoon
　　　dried rosemary
1　tablespoon fresh lemon juice
$1/8$　teaspoon ground cloves
$1/8$　teaspoon black pepper
2　medium Vidalia or other sweet onions,
　　　peeled (about 1$1/4$ pounds)
　　Cooking spray
2　teaspoons olive oil

1. Preheat oven to 400°.

2. Combine first 6 ingredients in a small saucepan; bring to a boil. Reduce heat to medium, and cook, uncovered, until reduced to ½ cup (about 10 minutes). Set aside.

3. Cut onions lengthwise in half. Place onions, cut sides down, in a small baking dish coated with cooking spray. Drizzle olive oil over onions. Cover and bake at 400° for 25 minutes. Uncover and bake 20 minutes.

4. Remove onions from oven. Turn onions over; pour wine mixture over onions. Bake an additional 20 minutes or until onions are tender, basting every 5 minutes. Serve onions with wine mixture. **Yield:** 4 servings (serving size: 1 onion half and about 1 tablespoon glaze).

Super Quick
HERBED ENGLISH PEAS
WITH MUSHROOMS

If you don't have tarragon, use the same amount of any savory herb such as oregano or basil. And if fresh herbs are in season, substitute 1 tablespoon of a minced fresh herb for each teaspoon of any dried herb.

1   teaspoon vegetable oil
1/2 cup thinly sliced onion
1 1/2 cups sliced fresh mushrooms
1 1/2 cups frozen English peas, thawed
2   tablespoons water
1/4 teaspoon salt
1   teaspoon dried tarragon
1/8 teaspoon black pepper

1. Heat oil in a large nonstick skillet over medium heat until hot. Add onion; cook 4 minutes or until tender, stirring often.

2. Add mushrooms to skillet; cook 4 minutes or until tender, stirring often. Stir in peas and remaining ingredients; cover and cook 4 minutes or just until peas are tender. Serve immediately. **Yield:** 4 servings (serving size: 1/2 cup).

YIELD: 4 servings

EXCHANGES PER SERVING:
2 Vegetable

PER SERVING:
Calories 69
(17% from fat)
Fat 1.3g
(saturated fat 0.2g)
Protein 3.6g
Carbohydrate 10g
Fiber 2.5g
Cholesterol 0mg
Sodium 212mg

STIR-FRIED SNOW PEAS AND PEPPERS

*Fresh snow peas, red bell pepper, and water chestnuts add
color and crunch to this Asian-inspired accompaniment.*

    Cooking spray
  1 teaspoon vegetable oil
  1/2 pound fresh snow pea pods
1 1/2 cups julienne-sliced red bell pepper
  1 (8-ounce) can sliced water chestnuts,
     drained
  1/4 cup water
  1 tablespoon low-sodium soy sauce
  1 teaspoon sugar
  1/2 teaspoon cornstarch
  1/4 teaspoon chicken-flavored bouillon granules
     Dash of pepper
  1 teaspoon sesame seeds, toasted

1. Coat a wok or large nonstick skillet with cooking spray; add oil. Heat at medium–high (375°) for
2 minutes. Add peas, bell pepper, and water chestnuts; stir-fry 3 to 5 minutes or until crisp-tender.

2. Combine water and next 5 ingredients; pour
over vegetable mixture. Cook, stirring constantly,
1 minute or until thickened. Transfer to a bowl;
sprinkle with sesame seeds. Serve immediately.
Yield: 4 servings (serving size: ¾ cup).

Super Quick
SUGAR SNAP PEAS WITH BASIL AND LEMON

Fresh basil and grated lemon rind mingle with sweet Sugar Snaps in this simple side dish.

1 teaspoon olive oil
3/4 pound fresh Sugar Snap peas, trimmed
1/4 cup coarsely chopped fresh basil
1/2 teaspoon grated lemon rind
1/4 teaspoon salt
1/4 teaspoon ground white pepper

1. Heat oil in a large nonstick skillet over medium heat until hot. Add peas; cook, stirring constantly, 3 minutes or until crisp-tender. Sprinkle peas with chopped basil and next 3 ingredients; cook, stirring constantly, 1 minute. Serve immediately. **Yield:** 5 servings (serving size: 1/2 cup).

YIELD: 5 servings

EXCHANGE PER SERVING:
1 Vegetable

PER SERVING:
Calories 37
(24% from fat)
Fat 1g
(saturated fat 0.2g)
Protein 1.9g
Carbohydrate 5.3g
Fiber 1.8g
Cholesterol 0mg
Sodium 120mg

Super Quick
MINTED SUGAR SNAPS

Cooking spray
1 (8-ounce) package fresh Sugar Snap peas, trimmed
2 green onions, chopped
1 large garlic clove, minced
2 tablespoons minced fresh mint
1/8 teaspoon salt
1/4 teaspoon black pepper

1. Coat a large nonstick skillet with cooking spray, and place over medium heat until hot. Add peas, green onions, and garlic; cook 3 minutes or until peas are crisp-tender, stirring often. Remove from heat; stir in mint, salt, and pepper. **Yield:** 3 servings (serving size: 1/2 cup).

YIELD: 3 servings

EXCHANGE PER SERVING:
1 Vegetable

PER SERVING:
Calories 30
(12% from fat)
Fat 0.4g
(saturated fat 0g)
Protein 1.7g
Carbohydrate 5.2g
Fiber 1.7g
Cholesterol 0mg
Sodium 97mg

YIELD: 4 servings

EXCHANGES PER
SERVING:
1½ Starch
1 Vegetable

PER SERVING:
Calories 158
(7% from fat)
Fat 1.3g
(saturated fat 0.3g)
Protein 10.4g
Carbohydrate 27.5g
Fiber 3.4g
Cholesterol 0mg
Sodium 120mg

SPICY-HOT BLACK-EYED PEAS

*A splash of liquid smoke gives these peas
a slow-simmered meaty flavor.*

    Cooking spray
½ cup chopped onion
½ cup chopped green bell pepper
1 (15.8-ounce) can black-eyed peas,
    undrained
1 (14½-ounce) can no-salt-added stewed
    tomatoes, undrained
1 tablespoon low-sodium soy sauce
1 teaspoon dry mustard
1 teaspoon liquid smoke
½ teaspoon chili powder
½ teaspoon black pepper
⅛ teaspoon ground red pepper
1 tablespoon minced fresh parsley

1. Coat a large nonstick skillet with cooking spray;
place over medium heat until hot. Add onion and
bell pepper; cook, stirring constantly, until crisp-
tender. Add peas and next 7 ingredients; bring to a
boil. Reduce heat; simmer, uncovered, 20 minutes.
Sprinkle with parsley. **Yield:** 4 servings (serving
size: ¾ cup).

BRAISED BELL PEPPERS

Serve these peppers as a side dish, or use them in other recipes. Although the aniseed is optional, it adds a subtle sweetness to the peppers. For a more robust flavor, try using 2½ teaspoons of finely chopped fresh rosemary in place of the anise, and omit the basil.

Olive oil-flavored cooking spray
4 cups red bell pepper strips (about 1¼ pounds)
4 cups yellow bell pepper strips (about 1¼ pounds)
2½ cups vertically sliced onion
¼ teaspoon salt
¼ teaspoon aniseed, crushed (optional)
2 garlic cloves, minced
2 cups water
2 tablespoons tomato paste
1 tablespoon chopped fresh basil
1 tablespoon red wine vinegar
¼ teaspoon black pepper

1. Place a large nonstick skillet coated with cooking spray over medium-high heat. Add bell peppers, onion, salt, aniseed, and garlic; sauté 15 minutes, stirring occasionally. Stir in water and tomato paste. Bring mixture to a boil; reduce heat, and simmer 30 minutes or until bell peppers are soft. Stir in basil, vinegar, and black pepper. **Yield:** 8 servings (serving size: ½ cup).

YIELD: 8 servings

EXCHANGES PER SERVING:
2 Vegetable

PER SERVING:
Calories 45
(12% from fat)
Fat 0.6g
(saturated fat 0.1g)
Protein 1.5g
Carbohydrate 9.6g
Fiber 2.5g
Cholesterol 0mg
Sodium 80mg

CHEESE FRIES

1½ pounds baking potatoes, unpeeled and cut
       into thin strips (about 3 potatoes)
       Cooking spray
¼ cup grated Parmesan cheese
¼ teaspoon salt
¼ teaspoon pepper
¼ teaspoon paprika

1. Preheat oven to 450°.

2. Coat potato strips with cooking spray, and place
in a large heavy–duty zip-top plastic bag. Combine
cheese and remaining 3 ingredients; sprinkle over
potato strips in bag. Seal bag and turn to coat potatoes well.

3. Arrange potato strips in a single layer on a large
baking sheet pan coated with cooking spray. Bake
at 450° for 15 minutes, turning once. Serve immediately. **Yield:** 6 servings.

♥ *Most of us know it's not what's **in** a potato but what's
on it that gets us into trouble. The innocent spud, which
has 220 calories and only 0.2 grams of fat, often takes the
rap for its toppings. Just 1 tablespoon of butter or margarine provides 102 calories and 11.5 grams of fat. One
tablespoon of reduced-fat margarine provides half the
amount of calories and fat, and low-fat sour cream has
only 21 calories and 1.9 grams of fat for the same
amount. To really keep the fat and calories low, try topping that potato with reduced-sodium salsa (it's fat free),
fat-free yogurt, or fat-free sour cream.*

GARLIC ROASTED POTATOES

1 1/2 pounds small round red potatoes, quartered
  Olive oil-flavored cooking spray
 1 tablespoon olive oil
 3 garlic cloves, minced
 1 tablespoon dried rosemary, crushed
 1/4 teaspoon salt
 1/4 teaspoon pepper

1. Preheat oven to 400°.

2. Place potatoes in a 13 x 9-inch baking dish coated with cooking spray; coat potatoes with cooking spray. Add olive oil; toss gently. Sprinkle with garlic and remaining ingredients; toss. Bake, uncovered, at 400° for 40 minutes or until tender, stirring once. **Yield:** 4 servings.

YIELD: 4 servings

EXCHANGES PER SERVING:
1 1/2 Starch
1/2 Fat

PER SERVING:
Calories 155
(27% from fat)
Fat 4.7g
(saturated fat 0.7g)
Protein 3.5g
Carbohydrate 25.8g
Fiber 2.8g
Cholesterol 0mg
Sodium 158mg

ROASTED NEW POTATOES

 24 new potatoes (about 2 1/3 pounds)
  Olive oil-flavored cooking spray
 1/4 cup Italian-seasoned breadcrumbs
 1/4 cup (1 ounce) grated fresh Parmesan cheese
 3/4 teaspoon paprika

1. Cook potatoes in a Dutch oven in boiling water to cover 15 minutes or until tender; drain and cool slightly.

2. Preheat oven to 450°.

3. Quarter potatoes; coat cut sides of wedges with cooking spray. Combine breadcrumbs, cheese, and paprika; dredge cut sides of wedges in breadcrumb mixture. Arrange wedges in a single layer on a baking sheet coated with cooking spray. Bake at 450° for 15 to 17 minutes. Serve immediately. **Yield:** 8 servings.

YIELD: 8 servings

EXCHANGES PER SERVING:
1 1/2 Starch

PER SERVING:
Calories 117
(10% from fat)
Fat 1.3g
(saturated fat 0.7g)
Protein 4.3g
Carbohydrate 22.8g
Fiber 2.4g
Cholesterol 2mg
Sodium 91mg

**EXCHANGES PER
SERVING:**
1½ Starch

PER SERVING:
Calories 116
(4% from fat)
Fat 0.5g
(saturated fat 0.1g)
Protein 2.9g
Carbohydrate 25g
Fiber 1.7g
Cholesterol 0mg
Sodium 189mg

DIJON SCALLOPED POTATOES

3/4 cup fat-free, less-sodium chicken broth
½ cup sliced leeks
½ cup fat-free milk
 2 tablespoons all-purpose flour
 1 tablespoon Dijon mustard
¼ teaspoon dried dill
¼ teaspoon salt
⅛ to ¼ teaspoon pepper
 4 cups peeled, thinly sliced baking potato
    (about 1½ pounds)
   Cooking spray

1. Preheat oven to 350°.

2. Combine broth and sliced leeks in a medium
saucepan; bring to a boil. Cover, reduce heat, and
simmer 5 minutes. Combine milk and next 5 ingredients, stirring with a whisk until smooth. Add
to broth mixture, stirring well. Cook 3 minutes or
until mixture is thickened and bubbly, stirring constantly. Remove from heat.

3. Layer half of potato in a 1½-quart oval au gratin
or baking dish coated with cooking spray; pour
half of leek mixture over potato. Repeat layers with
remaining potato and leek mixture. Cover and
bake at 350° for 55 minutes. Uncover and bake 15
minutes or until potato is tender and lightly
browned. **Yield:** 6 servings (serving size: ⅔ cup).

COLCANNON

Potatoes are a likely complement to an Irish seafood meal. The addition of onions, kale, or cabbage to mashed potatoes is traditional in this peasant dish.

  5 cups cubed peeled baking potato (about
        2½ pounds)
  1 tablespoon margarine or butter
  1 cup chopped onion
  2 cups chopped kale
  ½ cup 2% reduced-fat milk
  ⅓ cup low-fat sour cream
  ½ teaspoon salt
  ¼ teaspoon freshly ground black pepper

1. Place potatoes in a medium saucepan, and cover with water; bring to a boil. Reduce heat, and simmer potatoes 15 minutes or until tender; drain. Keep potatoes warm.

2. Melt margarine in a large skillet over medium heat. Add chopped onion; cook 5 minutes, stirring occasionally. Stir in kale, and cook 5 minutes. Remove from heat. Mash potatoes with a masher. Stir in kale mixture, milk, sour cream, salt, and pepper. **Yield:** 8 servings (serving size: ⅔ cup).

YIELD: 8 servings

EXCHANGES PER SERVING:
2 Starch
1 Vegetable

PER SERVING:
Calories 187
(16% from fat)
Fat 3.3g
(saturated fat 1.2g)
Protein 4.4g
Carbohydrate 35.3g
Fiber 2.8g
Cholesterol 5mg
Sodium 188mg

YIELD: 8 servings

EXCHANGES PER SERVING:
3 Starch

PER SERVING:
Calories 206
(13% from fat)
Fat 2.9g
(saturated fat 0.4g)
Protein 3.3g
Carbohydrate 42.5g
Fiber 4.3g
Cholesterol 0mg
Sodium 168mg

TWO-TONE ROASTED POTATOES

We like this recipe with a mixture of sweet potatoes and baking potatoes, but you can make it with just one or the other.

    1   teaspoon chili powder
    ½   teaspoon salt
    ¼   teaspoon ground cinnamon
    ¼   teaspoon ground red pepper
    ¼   teaspoon black pepper
 1½   tablespoons olive oil
    1   garlic clove, minced, or ½ teaspoon bottled
         minced garlic
    3   small sweet potatoes (about 1½ pounds),
         each cut lengthwise into 8 wedges
    3   small baking potatoes (about 1½ pounds),
         each cut lengthwise into 8 wedges

1. Preheat oven to 450°.

2. Combine first 7 ingredients in a large zip-top plastic bag. Add potatoes; seal and shake to coat potatoes with spice mixture. Place potatoes on a baking sheet. Bake at 450° for 35 minutes or until tender. **Yield:** 8 servings (serving size: 6 wedges).

MAPLE-GLAZED SWEET POTATOES

You'll need to peel and section a lemon for this dish. Take care to use only the flesh by removing the skinlike white membrane from each section.

- 8 cups (1-inch) cubed peeled sweet potato (about 3 pounds)
- 4 cups water
- ¼ cup lemon sections (about 1 large lemon)
- ¼ cup packed dark brown sugar
- 3 tablespoons maple syrup
- 2 tablespoons margarine or butter
- ½ teaspoon ground cinnamon
- ⅛ teaspoon ground red pepper
  Dash of salt

1. Combine first 3 ingredients in a large saucepan; bring to a boil. Cook 20 minutes or until tender, stirring occasionally. Remove sweet potatoes from pan with a slotted spoon, reserving cooking liquid.

2. Bring cooking liquid to a boil; cook until reduced to ⅓ cup (about 12 minutes). Stir in sugar and remaining ingredients. Stir in sweet potatoes; cook 2 minutes or until thoroughly heated. **Yield:** 12 servings (serving size: ½ cup).

♥ *When it comes to nutritious veggies, the sweet potato is one of the best. It's rich in vitamins A and C and provides a healthy dose of fiber, yet is low in both fat and sodium. Store sweet potatoes in a cool, dark place, not in the refrigerator.*

YIELD: 12 servings

EXCHANGES PER SERVING:
2 Starch

PER SERVING:
Calories 142
(14% from fat)
Fat 2.2g
(saturated fat 0.4g)
Protein 1.5g
Carbohydrate 29.8g
Fiber 2.7g
Cholesterol 0mg
Sodium 46mg

HARVEST STUFFED SWEETS

EXCHANGES PER SERVING:
3 Starch
1 Vegetable

PER SERVING:
Calories 234
(4% from fat)
Fat 1g
(saturated fat 0.3g)
Protein 4.5g
Carbohydrate 53.5g
Fiber 7g
Cholesterol 0mg
Sodium 145mg

6 (8-ounce) sweet potatoes
2 cups diced peeled rutabaga or turnips
1 cup diced peeled carrot
1 cup diced peeled parsnip
1/3 cup low-fat or nonfat buttermilk
1 tablespoon lemon juice
1/4 teaspoon salt
1/2 teaspoon dried thyme
1/4 teaspoon black pepper
3 garlic cloves, minced

1. Preheat oven to 375°.

2. Wrap potatoes in foil; bake at 375° for 1 hour or until tender.

3. Place rutabaga in a large saucepan; cover with water. Bring to a boil. Cook 5 minutes. Add carrot; cook 5 minutes. Add parsnip; cook 5 minutes or until rutabaga is tender. Drain; mash vegetables to desired consistency. Stir in buttermilk and remaining ingredients.

4. Unwrap potatoes; cut a 1/4-inch slice from the top of each potato; scoop out pulp, leaving a 1/4-inch-thick shell. Add pulp to rutabaga mixture; stir well. Stuff shells with potato mixture, and place on a baking sheet. Bake at 375° for 10 minutes or until thoroughly heated. **Yield:** 6 servings (serving size: 1 stuffed potato).

CRANBERRY-AND-SWEET POTATO BAKE

2 (15-ounce) cans sweet potatoes, drained
1 (8-ounce) can crushed pineapple in juice,
   drained
2 tablespoons margarine or butter, melted
1/4 teaspoon salt
1/8 teaspoon ground nutmeg
   Dash of black pepper
1 large egg
1 (16-ounce) can whole-berry cranberry
   sauce, divided
   Cooking spray

1. Preheat oven to 350°.

2. Combine sweet potatoes and pineapple in a large bowl; mash with a potato masher. Stir in margarine, salt, nutmeg, pepper, and egg. Swirl in 1 cup cranberry sauce. Spoon 1/3 cup sweet potato mixture into each of 8 (4-ounce) ramekins coated with cooking spray. Top each with about 1 tablespoon cranberry sauce. Bake at 350° for 40 minutes.
Yield: 8 servings.

Note: A 1-quart casserole may be substituted for ramekins. Bake at 350° for 40 minutes.

YIELD: 8 servings

EXCHANGES PER SERVING:
2 Starch
1 Fruit

PER SERVING:
Calories 212
(17% from fat)
Fat 3.9g
(saturated fat 0.7g)
Protein 2.6g
Carbohydrate 43.2g
Fiber 1.7g
Cholesterol 27mg
Sodium 186mg

TROPICAL SWEET POTATO CASSEROLE

EXCHANGES PER
SERVING:
2 Starch
1/2 Fruit

PER SERVING:
Calories 180
(9% from fat)
Fat 1.8g
(saturated fat 0.4g)
Protein 1.7g
Carbohydrate 42.5g
Fiber 3.3g
Cholesterol 0mg
Sodium 42mg

4 pounds sweet potatoes, peeled and cubed
1 cup mashed banana
1 cup packed brown sugar
1/2 cup canned light coconut milk
1 (8-ounce) can crushed pineapple in juice,
    drained
1/8 teaspoon salt
    Cooking spray
1 1/2 tablespoons flaked coconut

1. Place sweet potato in a large saucepan; cover with water. Bring to a boil; cook 20 minutes or until tender. Drain well; return sweet potato to pan. Beat at medium speed of an electric mixer until smooth; add banana and next 4 ingredients, beating well.

2. Preheat oven to 350°.

3. Pour sweet potato mixture into an 11 x 7-inch baking dish coated with cooking spray. Sprinkle mixture with flaked coconut. Bake at 350° for 30 minutes or until thoroughly heated. **Yield:** 16 servings (serving size: 1/2 cup).

♥ *Coconut milk is high in saturated fat and should be limited in heart-healthy eating. You can use light coconut milk instead—it contains 75 percent less fat than regular coconut milk.*

FRUITED ACORN SQUASH

The tender flesh of the squash absorbs the brown sugared sweetness of pineapple and orange as the squash bakes.

      2 medium acorn squash (about 1 pound each)
         Cooking spray
    ⅓ cup drained canned pineapple tidbits in
         juice
    ⅓ cup peeled, chopped orange
      3 tablespoons brown sugar
      2 tablespoons chopped pecans
    ¼ teaspoon salt

1. Preheat oven to 350°.

2. Cut each squash in half crosswise; remove and discard seeds. Place squash halves, cut sides down, in a 15 x 10-inch jelly-roll pan coated with cooking spray. Bake, uncovered, at 350° for 35 minutes or until squash is tender.

3. Combine pineapple and remaining 4 ingredients; spoon mixture evenly into squash halves. Bake, uncovered, 10 minutes or until thoroughly heated. **Yield:** 4 servings (serving size: 1 squash half).

YIELD: 4 servings

EXCHANGES PER SERVING:
1 Starch
1 Fruit

PER SERVING:
Calories 140
(18% from fat)
Fat 2.8g
(saturated fat 0.2g)
Protein 1.9g
Carbohydrate 30.2g
Fiber 3.1g
Cholesterol 0mg
Sodium 155mg

YIELD: 4 servings

EXCHANGES PER SERVING:
2 Vegetable

PER SERVING:
Calories 50
(18% from fat)
Fat 1g
(saturated fat 0.1g)
Protein 2.5g
Carbohydrate 10.1g
Fiber 3g
Cholesterol 0mg
Sodium 153mg

ROASTED SQUASH AND PEPPERS

Roasting fruits and vegetables is a simple, low-fat method of cooking. It locks in flavor while caramelizing the outer layers.

3 small yellow squash
3 small zucchini
2 medium-size red bell peppers
   Olive oil-flavored cooking spray
1 teaspoon dried oregano
¼ teaspoon salt
¼ teaspoon pepper
1 tablespoon balsamic vinegar

1. Preheat oven to 500°.

2. Cut squash and zucchini in half crosswise. Cut halves lengthwise into ½-inch-thick wedges. Cut bell peppers into 2-inch-long strips. Set pepper strips aside.

3. Coat a large baking sheet with cooking spray. Place squash and zucchini in a single layer on baking sheet, and coat vegetables with cooking spray. Sprinkle with oregano, salt, and pepper.

4. Bake at 500° for 5 minutes. Turn squash and zucchini gently; add pepper strips. Bake 8 additional minutes or to desired degree of doneness. Transfer vegetables to a serving bowl. Add vinegar to vegetables, and toss gently. **Yield:** 4 servings (serving size: 1 cup).

ITALIAN STUFFED ZUCCHINI

*It's easier to scoop out the pulp of the zucchini halves
if you use an ice cream scoop or a melon baller.*

4   large zucchini
1/4 teaspoon salt
    Cooking spray
1   teaspoon olive oil
1   cup finely chopped onion
3   garlic cloves, minced
1/2 cup finely chopped plum tomato
1/3 cup fine, dry breadcrumbs
1/4 cup chopped fresh parsley
3   tablespoons grated Parmesan cheese
1   tablespoon pine nuts, toasted
1/2 teaspoon black pepper

1. Cut zucchini in half lengthwise; scoop out pulp,
leaving 1/4-inch-thick shells. Sprinkle shells with
salt; set shells aside. Coarsely chop pulp.

2. Preheat oven to 375°.

3. Coat a medium nonstick skillet with cooking
spray, and add oil; place over medium-high heat until hot. Add chopped zucchini and onion; cook 10
minutes or until vegetables are tender, stirring occasionally. Add garlic and tomato; cook 2 minutes or
until mixture is thickened, stirring occasionally. Remove from heat; stir in breadcrumbs and remaining
4 ingredients.

4. Spoon vegetable mixture evenly into zucchini
shells. Place in a 13 x 9-inch baking dish coated
with cooking spray. Cover and bake at 375° for 20
minutes. Uncover and bake 20 additional minutes
or until zucchini shells are fork-tender and stuffing
is lightly browned. **Yield:** 8 servings (serving size:
1 zucchini half).

YIELD: 8 servings

**EXCHANGES PER
SERVING:**
2 Vegetable
1/2 Fat

PER SERVING:
Calories 69
(34% from fat)
Fat 2.6g
(saturated fat 0.8g)
Protein 3.6g
Carbohydrate 9.4g
Fiber 1.4g
Cholesterol 2mg
Sodium 164mg

YIELD: 8 servings

EXCHANGES PER SERVING:
2 Vegetable
1/2 Fat

PER SERVING:
Calories 72
(35% from fat)
Fat 2.8g
(saturated fat 1.5g)
Protein 4.6g
Carbohydrate 9.1g
Fiber 1.5g
Cholesterol 7mg
Sodium 126mg

BREADED BROILED TOMATOES

This familiar side dish is a popular companion to all types of meat. Any fresh herb can be substituted for cilantro—try oregano with beef, rosemary with lamb, or tarragon with chicken. We've updated it with a surprise: buttermilk in place of melted butter.

 1 (1-ounce) slice white bread
 4 large tomatoes (about 2 1/2 pounds)
 1/2 cup low-fat or nonfat buttermilk
 1/2 cup (2 ounces) grated fresh Romano or
      Parmesan cheese
 1 teaspoon freshly ground black pepper
 1 large egg white, lightly beaten
    Cooking spray
 8 teaspoons chopped fresh cilantro

1. Preheat oven to 400°.

2. Place bread in a food processor, and process until finely ground to measure 1/2 cup. Set aside.

3. Core tomatoes; cut each tomato in half crosswise. Push seeds out of tomato halves with thumbs. Spoon 1 tablespoon buttermilk into each tomato half. Combine breadcrumbs, cheese, pepper, and egg white in a small bowl. Divide breadcrumb mixture evenly among tomato halves. Place tomato halves on a baking sheet coated with cooking spray. Bake at 400° for 17 minutes.

4. Prepare broiler.

5. Broil tomato halves 2 minutes or until lightly browned. Sprinkle each tomato half with 1 teaspoon cilantro. **Yield:** 8 servings (serving size: 1 tomato half).

index

Alcohol, about, 12, 341, 383
American Heart Association, recommen-
   dations of, 7, 9, 12, 271, 280, 318
Appetizers. *See also* Snacks.
   Cheese Tartlets, 32
   Crostini, Roasted Garlic and
      Portobello, 34
   Dips
      Black Bean Dip, 21
      Blue Cheese-Bean Dip, 22
      Gazpacho Dip, 20
      Guacamole, Mock Pea, 26
      Hummus Dip, White-Bean, 24
      Hummus with Raspberry
         Vinegar, 23
      Onion Dip, Classic, 24
      Roasted Red Pepper and Onion
         Dip, 25
      Salsa, Fiesta Onion, 30
      Salsa, Fresh Tomato, 29
      Salsa, One-Minute, 29
      Salsa, Roasted Corn, 31
      Toffee Dip with Apples, 18
      White Bean Dip, 21
   Fruit Kabobs with Coconut
      Dressing, 19
   Mousse, Curried Chicken, 28
   Mushrooms, Spinach-Stuffed, 33
   Nachos, Mediterranean, 35
   Nacho Wedges, Chicken, 36
   Spread, Vegetable-Cheese, 26
   Tostadas, Miniature Chicken, 37
   Tuna Salad Bites, 27
Apples
   Cake, Cinnamon-Apple, 121
   Chews, Caramel Apple, 154
   Chews, Crispy Caramel Apple, 154
   Crisp, Cranberry-Orange Apple, 113
   Crumble, Apple, 117
   Dip with Apples, Toffee, 18
   Salads
      Apple Salad, 366
      Crisp Apple and Cranberry Salad, 367
      Waldorf Salad, 366
   Sautéed Apples, 444
Apricot Scones, 62
Apricot Soup, Peach-, 421
Artichokes with Browned Garlic and
   Lemon Dipping Sauce, 452
Asparagus
   Sesame Asparagus and
      Mushrooms, 451
   Soup, Fresh Asparagus, 423
   Stir-Fry, Asparagus, 450

Avocado
   about, 9, 20, 30, 378
   Gazpacho Dip, 20

Bananas. *See also* Beverages, Breads.
   Galette, Easy Caramel-Banana, 120
   Orange Bananas, Caramelized, 109
   Pudding, Old-Fashioned Banana, 135
   Shake, Peanut Butter-Chocolate-
      Banana, 51
   Smoothie, Banana-Berry, 49
Barley, Mushroom, 212
Barley Soup, Beef and, 429
Beans. *See also* Chili, Hummus, Lentils,
   Salads.
   about, 245, 247, 393
   Black
      Caribbean Black Beans and Rice,
         Spicy, 245
      Chili, Pork-and-Black Bean, 437
      Dip, Black Bean, 21
      Salad, Black Bean-and-Corn, 380
      Sloppy Joes, Turkey-Black Bean, 419
      Tacos, Rice and Bean Soft, 244
   Dip, Blue Cheese-Bean, 22
   Green
      Caramelized Onions, Green Beans
         with, 453
      Glazed Green Beans, 453
      Medley, Peppery Green Bean, 455
      Onions, Green Beans and Pan-
         Roasted Red, 454
      Salsa, Corn-Bean, 283
   White
      Dip, White Bean, 21
      Dip, White-Bean Hummus, 24
      Garlicky Stewed White Beans with
         Mixed Peppers, 246
Beef. *See also* Beef, Ground.
   about, 280, 409
   Pot Roast, Slow-Cooked Beef, 289
   Pot Roast, Sunday, 290
   Steaks
      au Poivre, Steak, 280
      Chili Verde, 436
      Filets with Vegetables, Beef, 285
      Flank Steaks, Marinated, 277
      Hoisin Beef with Shiitake
         Mushroom Sauce, 286
      Marinated Steaks, Port, 282
      Sandwiches, Steak and Onion, 412
      Savory Steaks with Mushroom
         Sauce, 287
      Sirloin Steak with Garlic Sauce, 281

487

Beef, steak *(continued)*

    Sirloin with Corn-Bean Salsa, Chili-
      Rubbed, 283
    Stir-Fry, Gingered Beef, 284
    Stir-Fry with Ginger Sauce, Beef,
      Pineapple, and Red Onion, 278
    Stroganoff, Skillet Beef, 279
    Swiss Steak, 276
    Tenderloin with Horseradish Cream
      Sauce, Beef, 288
Beef, Ground. *See also* Soups.
  Burgers, Fiesta, 407
  Burgers with Red Onion Salsa, 408
  Chili, Easy Weeknight, 435
  Joes, Mexico, 410
  Lasagna, Lazy, 237
  Meat Loaf, Favorite, 275
  Peppers, Picadillo-Stuffed, 274
  Sloppy Joes, Slim, 409
  Spaghetti, Casserole, 239
  Spaghetti with Beef, Tomatoes, and
    Zucchini, 238
  Wraps, Greek, 411
Beets-and-Mango Salad, Roasted, 381
Beets, Ginger-Marmalade Glazed, 456
Beverages
  Cocktail, Hot Cranberry, 53
  Crush, Five-Fruit, 47
  Freeze, Iced Coffee, 52
  Lemonade, Ginger, 42
  Lemonade, Old-Fashioned, 42
  Limeade, Key West Minted, 43
  Margaritas, Mock, 43
  Potion, Passion, 46
  Punch
    Citrus Punch, 56
    Fruit Punch, Holiday Hot, 54
    Mocha Punch, 55
  Shake, Frosty Coffee, 52
  Shake, Peanut Butter-Chocolate-
    Banana, 51
  Slush, Pineapple-Rum, 49
  Slush, Strawberry-Cherry, 48
  Slush, Sunrise, 48
  Smoothie, Banana-Berry, 49
  Smoothie, Strawberry, 50
  Smoothie, Tropical Tofu, 51
  Spritzers, Bellini, 46
  Tea, Cranberry-Apple Iced, 44
  Tea, Mint Limeade, 45
  Tea, Raspberry-Lemon, 45
  Tropical Wave, 47
Biscuits
  Buttermilk Biscuits, 59
  Herbed Biscuits, 61
  Honey Angel Biscuits, 60
  Light Biscuits, 58
Blackberry Cobbler, 111

Blood pressure, about, 6, 12, 15
Blueberries
  Crisp à la Mode, Blueberry, 114
  Muffins, Lemon-Blueberry, 64
  Pancakes, Blueberry, 77
  Syrup, Waffles with Two-Berry, 78
Body Mass Index (B.M.I.), about, 13
Bran
  Cookies, Raisin-Bran, 155
  Muffins, Apple Butter-Bran, 65
  Muffins, Molasses-Bran, 66
Breads. *See also* specific types.
  Banana Bread, Fruity, 80
  Banana-Oatmeal Bread, 79
  Coffeecake, Cranberry-Orange, 84
  Coffeecake with Streusel Topping,
    Orange, 85
  Corn Sticks, 71
  Hush Puppies, Baked, 72
  Popovers, Easy, 73
  Poppy Seed Quick Bread, 81
  Pumpkin-Pecan Bread, 82
  Scones, Apricot, 62
  Scones, Buttermilk-Cherry, 63
  Strawberry Bread, 83
  Yeast
    Cornmeal Yeast Bread, 97
    Cornmeal Yeast Muffins, 92
    English Muffin Bread, 98
    English Muffins, 93
    Focaccia, Rosemary, 104
    French Bread, 102
    French Bread, Rosemary-Herb, 103
    Monkey Bread, 95
    Oatmeal-Molasses Bread, 99
    Onion-Herb Bread, 100
    Pizza Dough, All-Purpose, 267
    Roasted Red Bell Pepper
      Bread, 101
    White Bread, Classic, 96
Broccoli with Caraway-Cheese
  Sauce, 457
Broth, sodium in, 424
Brussels Sprouts and Baby Carrots,
  Glazed, 458
Bulgur
  Pilaf, Bulgur, 213
  Pilaf, Mediterranean Bulgur, 250
  Tabbouleh, 387
Butter, about, 9-11, 147, 223

Cabbage. *See also* Salads/Slaws.
  Red Cabbage, Braised, 459
Cakes
  Angel Food Cake, Cinnamon-
    Swirl, 123
  Carrot Cake, 127
  Cheesecake, Chocolate-Almond, 128
  Cheesecake, Lemon, 129

Cinnamon-Apple Cake, 121
Coffeecake, Cranberry Orange, 84
Coffeecake with Streusel Topping,
   Orange, 85
Frosting, Lemon-Cream Cheese, 127
Gingerbread with Citrus Sauce, 126
Pound Cake, Brown Sugar, 124
Pound Cake, Lemon-Buttermilk, 125
Pudding Cake, Lemon, 122
Calcium, recommedations for, 11, 130
Calories, about, 8, 14, 15, 115, 383
Carbohydrate, about, 15, 65, 106, 113,
   213, 247, 383, 428
Carrots
   Baby Carrots, Glazed Brussels Sprouts
     and, 458
   Balsamic Carrots, 460
   Cake, Carrot, 127
   Orange-Spiced Carrots, 460
   Salad, Carrot-Pineapple, 372
Cherries
   Clafouti, Cherry, 119
   Crisp, Double Cherry, 115
   Scones, Buttermilk-Cherry, 63
   Slush, Strawberry-Cherry, 48
   Soup, Chilled Cherry, 421
Chicken. *See also* Salads/Chicken;
   Sandwiches; Soups.
   Barbecued Chicken, Easy, 330
   Basil Chicken and Vegetables, 335
   Braised Lemon Chicken, 325
   Cacciatore, Chicken, 339
   Chili, White, 434
   Cornish Hen and Peaches,
     Roasted, 364
   Cornish Hen with Chutney Glaze, 363
   Curried Chicken with Plums and
     Ginger, 328
   Curry, Chutney Chicken, 345
   Curry-Orange Chicken, 351
   Feta Chicken and Vegetables, 336
   Fettuccine, Dijon Chicken, 241
   Garlic Chicken, Forty-Cloves-of-, 322
   Greek Chicken with Lemon
     Couscous, 333
   Grilled Chicken, Lemon-Garlic, 326
   Grilled Chicken, Rosemary-, 332
   Grilled Maple-Glazed Chicken, 327
   Hawaiian Chicken with Pineapple
     Salsa, 344
   Indonesian Coriander-Honey
     Chicken, 329
   Jalapeño Chicken, 331
   Lemon Chicken with Angel Hair Pasta
     and Artichokes, 338
   Mousse, Curried Chicken, 28
   Nacho Wedges, Chicken, 36
   Orange-Balsamic Chicken, 342
   Oven-Fried Chicken, Crispy, 324

Pasta, Creole Chicken, 240
Piccata, Chicken, 334
Rice, Fiesta Chicken and, 349
Roast Chicken with Cumin, Honey,
   and Orange, 321
Roasted Chicken, Lemon-Herb, 320
Roasted Chicken with Potatoes, Lemon
   and Rosemary, 323
Sauced Chicken Breasts with Apples
   and Onions, 340
Sautéed Chicken Breasts with Cherry-
   Port Sauce, 341
Skewered Singapore Chicken and
   Pineapple, 347
Spiced Peach Sauce, Chicken with, 343
Stir-Fried Chicken and Vegetables, 350
Stir-Fry, Glazed Chicken-Broccoli, 348
Stuffed Chicken Breasts, Spinach-, 337
Sweet-and-Sour Chicken, 346
Tetrazzini, Chicken, 242
Tostadas, Miniature Chicken, 37
Chili
   Pork-and-Black Bean Chili, 437
   Verde, Chili, 436
   Weeknight Chili, Easy, 435
   White Chili, 434
Chocolate. *See also* Cookies.
   Cheesecake, Chocolate-Almond, 128
   fat in, 150
   Fondue, Chocolate-Almond, 107
   Mocha Fudge Pudding, 136
   Mocha Punch, 55
   Pie, Chocolate Cream, 138
   Pie, Frozen Chocolate Brownie, 141
   Shake, Peanut Butter-Chocolate-
     Banana, 51
Cholesterol, about, 6-11, 14-16, 207, 363
Chowders
   Red Potato-and-Salmon
     Chowder, 439
   Tomato-Fish Chowder, Spicy, 438
   Turkey Chowder, 440
Clams, Angel Hair Pasta with Fresh, 201
Clam Sauce, Linguine with Red, 234
Cobblers. *See* Pies.
Cocoa, about powdered, 150
Coconut and coconut milk,
   about, 19, 132, 482
   Crème Brûlée, Rum and
     Coconut, 132
   Dressing, Fruit Kabobs with
     Coconut, 19
Coconut oil, about, 9
Colcannon, 477
Cookies
   Bars and Squares
     Brownies, Butter Pecan-Toffee, 149
     Brownies, Fudgy, 150
     Brownies, Fudgy-Mint Pan, 151

Cookies, Bars and Squares *(continued)*
    Butterscotch Bars, 147
    Lemon Squares, Easy, 148
  Biscotti, Cranberry-Chocolate
    Chip, 152
  Biscotti, Snickerdoodle, 153
  Brownie Bites, Fudgy-Mint, 151
  Caramel Apple Chews, Crispy, 154
  Date Swirl Cookies, 156
  Drop
    Caramel Apple Chews, 154
    Fruitcake Cookies, Brandied, 157
    Meringue Cookies, Chocolate-
      Chip, 158
    Oatmeal-Raisin Cookies, 159
    Raisin-Bran Cookies, 155
  Peanut Butter-and-Jelly Cookies, 160
Corn
  Creamed Corn, Southern-Style, 461
  Relish, Peppered Pork with Corn, 307
  Salad, Black Bean-and-Corn, 380
  Salad, Corn, 384
  Salsa, Corn-Bean, 283
  Salsa, Roasted Corn, 31
Corn Breads. *See also* Breads/Yeast,
  Muffins.
  Hush Puppies, Baked, 72
  Sticks, Corn, 71
Cornish Hen and Peaches, Roasted, 364
Cornish Hen with Chutney
  Glaze, 363
Couscous. *See also* Salads.
  about, 251, 252
  Calico Couscous, 214
  Fruit, Couscous with Mixed, 215
  Lemon Couscous, Greek Chicken
    with, 333
  Ragoût, Couscous with Italian
    Vegetable, 252
  Salads
    Couscous-and-Cucumber Salad with
      Buttermilk-Dill Dressing, 388
    Sesame Shrimp-and-Couscous
      Salad, 397
    Vegetable-Couscous Salad with
      Citrus Vinaigrette, 389
    Timbales, Orange-Scented
      Couscous, 216
    Vegetable Couscous, Curried, 251
Crab Cakes, Curried Corn-, 202
Cranberries
  about, 367
  Bake, Cranberry-and-Sweet
    Potato, 481
  Biscotti, Cranberry-Chocolate
    Chip, 152
  Cocktail, Hot Cranberry, 53
  Coffeecake, Cranberry-Orange, 84

  Crisp, Cranberry-Orange Apple, 113
  Oranges, Cranberry-Glazed, 445
  Pork Roast, Cranberry, 317
  Salad, Crisp Apple and Cranberry, 367
  Salad, Fruited Port-Cranberry, 368
  Sauce, Turkey Sauté with Cranberry-
    Port, 360
Custards
  Boiled Christmas Custard, 130
  Crème Brûlée, Rum and
    Coconut, 132
  Crème Caramel, 131
  Custard, Fresh Strawberries with
    Lime, 106
  Custard, Fresh Strawberries with
    Orange, 106
  Flan, Low-Fat, 133
  Flan, Sweet Potato, 134

Dairy products, recommendations
  for, 11, 130, 245
Desserts. *See also* specific types.
  Bananas, Caramelized Orange, 109
  Clafouti, Cherry, 119
  Compote, Very Berry Summer
    Fruit, 108
  Crisps
    Blueberry Crisp à la Mode, 114
    Cherry Crisp, Double, 115
    Cranberry-Orange Apple
      Crisp, 113
    Strawberry-Rhubarb Crisp, 116
  Crumble, Apple, 117
  Crumble, Pear-Almond, 118
  Flan, Low-Fat, 133
  Flan, Sweet Potato, 134
  Fondue, Chocolate-Almond, 107
  Frozen
    Ice Cream, Vanilla, 142
    Mango Freeze, 143
    Sherbet, Peach, 144
    Sorbet, Passionfruit, 145
    Yogurt, Pineapple-Brown Sugar
      Frozen, 146
    Yogurt, Raspberry-Orange, 146
  Gallette, Easy Caramel-Banana, 120
  Pears with Toasted Hazelnuts, Port-
    Glazed, 110
  Sauce, Citrus, 126
  Strawberries with Lime Custard,
    Fresh, 106
  Strawberries with Orange Custard,
    Fresh, 106
  Sundae, Apricot-Glazed Pineapple, 109
Diabetes and heart disease, about, 6
Diabetic exchanges, use of, 15

Eggs, about, 14, 271
Eggs, Mexican-Style Poached, 270

Egg substitute and egg whites
   about, 11, 14, 64, 77
   Frittata, Vegetable, 271
   Omelet, Cheese and Vegetable, 272
Exercise, benefits of, 6, 14, 16, 53, 69, 219

Fat, about dietary, 7-9, 15, 296, 383, 409
Fat, in baking, 61
Fats, about hydrogenated, 9, 11
Fettuccine
   Chicken Fettuccine, Dijon, 241
   Chicken Pasta, Creole, 240
   Sea Scallops on Fettuccine, 206
Fiber, about, 14, 15, 65, 218, 247, 437
Fish. *See also* specific types and Seafood.
   about, 162, 167, 180, 195, 197
   Amberjack, Blackened, 163
   Catfish, Crispy Pan-Fried, 167
   Catfish in Foil Packets, Baked, 168
   Catfish Nuggets with Tartar Sauce, 169
   Catfish, Oven-Fried, 166
   Chowder, Spicy Tomato Fish, 438
   Cioppino, 441
   Flounder in Foil Pouches, 173
   Flounder in Orange Sauce, 170
   Flounder with Peppers and Green
     Onions, 172
   Flounder with Pimiento, 171
   Grouper à la Mango, 176
   Grouper Sandwiches, Tangy, 405
   Grouper with Charmoula, 177
   Grouper with Honey Citrus Glaze, 174
   Grouper with Pineapple Salsa,
     Grilled, 175
   Halibut Provençale, 178
   Mahimahi with Tomato Vinaigrette,
     Grilled, 179
   Orange Roughy, Newport, 181
   Orange Roughy, Wine-Baked, 180
   Pollock, Lemon-Dill, 182
   Sea Bass, Lime-Marinated Grilled, 164
   Seasoned Fish and Tomatoes, 162
   Snapper, Curry-Chutney, 190
   Snapper, Spicy Lemon Red, 189
   Snapper, Veracruz Red, 192
   Snapper with Roasted Peppers, Grilled
     Lemon-Basil, 191
   Striped Bass, Korean-Style, 165
   Swordfish, Cheese-Stuffed, 193
   Swordfish, Grilled Rosemary, 195
   Swordfish, Herb-Grilled, 194
   Trout, Herb-Baked, 196
Food servings, recommended, 14, 367
Frosting, Lemon-Cream Cheese, 127
Fruit. *See also* specific types and Beverages,
   Desserts, Salads, Salsas, Soups.
   about, 106
   Curried Fruit, Warm, 449
   Kabobs with Coconut Dressing, Fruit, 19

Salads
   Fruited Port-Cranberry Salad, 368
   Greens with Orange Vinaigrette,
     Fruited, 374
   Red and Gold Fruit Salad, 371
   Tropical Fruit Salad, 371
   Winter Fruit Salad with Poppy Seed
     Dressing, 370
   Soup, Cool Summer-Berry, 420
   Winter Fruit, Spiced, 448

Gazpacho Dip, 20
Gazpacho, Tropical, 422
Ginger, about crystallized, 328, 444
Granola, Maple and Peanut Butter, 40
Greens, Collard, 463
Greens with Garlic and Lemon, 464
Guacamole, Mock Pea, 26

Ham Steak with Pineapple Salsa, 318
Heart disease, risk of developing, 6, 13
Herbs, about, 196, 469
Hummus Dip, White-Bean, 24
Hummus with Raspberry Vinegar, 23
Hush Puppies, Baked, 72
Hypertension. *See also* Blood pressure.
   about, 12

Ice cream, about, 9

Juice, about fruit, 145

Lamb
   Braised Lamb with Lemon and
     Rosemary Beans, 303
   Chops
     Grilled Lamb Chops, Mint-, 296
     Grilled Lamb Chops, Rosemary, 295
     Herbed Lamb Chops, 298
     Honey-Balsamic Glaze, Lamb Chops
       with, 299
     Mustard-Garlic Lamb Chops, 297
     Simmered Lamb and Peppers, 300
   Kabobs, Curried Lamb, 301
   Kabobs, Tangy Raspberry Lamb, 302
   Meat Loaf, Moroccan Lamb, 294
   Pockets with Cucumber Topping,
     Lamb, 413
   Wrap, Lamb Picadillo, 414
Lasagna, Lazy, 237
Lasagna, Vegetable, 255
Leeks and Mushrooms, Braised, 465
Legumes and lentils, about, 247
Lentils and Rice, Creamy Indian, 247
Lentil Soup, Spanish, 426
Linguine
   Garlic and Lemon Linguine, 227
   Red Clam Sauce, Linguine with, 234

Linguine *(continued)*

Red Pepper Sauce, Linguine with, 228
Verde, Linguine, 229
Lipoproteins, about, 8

Macaroni and Cheese, 256
Mango
about, 50
Freeze, Mango, 143
Salad, Roasted Beets-and-Mango, 381
Manicotti, Easy Cheesy, 257
Margarine, about, 9–11, 147, 223
Margarine, about diet, reduced-calorie,
and reduced-fat, 10, 11, 58, 61, 147
Mayonnaise, about, 416
Meatless meals, about, 245
Melon with Raspberry Sauce, Sliced, 369
Milk, about, 9, 11, 130
Monounsaturated fatty acids, about, 7, 9,
30, 378
Muffins. *See also* Breads/Yeast.
Apple Butter-Bran Muffins, 65
Citrus Mini-Muffins, Glazed, 67
Citrus Muffins, Glazed, 67
Corn-Oat Muffins, 70
Lemon-Blueberry Muffins, 64
Lemon-Poppy Seed Muffins, 68
Molasses-Bran Muffins, 66
Pumpkin-Raisin Muffins, 69
Mushrooms
Barley, Mushroom, 212
Leeks and Mushrooms, Braised, 465
Portobello Crostini, Roasted Garlic
and, 34
Risotto, Mushroom, 225
Skillet, Mushroom and Pepper, 464
Stuffed Mushrooms, Spinach-, 33
Mussels Medley, Shrimp and, 210
Mussels with Garlic and Shallots,
Steamed, 203

Nutrient information, about, 15, 16
Nuts, substitute for pine, 337

Oatmeal/Oats
Bread, Banana-Oatmeal, 79
Bread, Oatmeal-Molasses, 99
Cookies, Oatmeal-Raisin, 159
Granola, Maple and Peanut Butter, 40
Muffins, Corn-Oat, 70
Pancakes, Whole Wheat-Oat, 76
Obesity, risks of, 6, 13
Oils, recommended cooking, 9, 30, 378
Okra-Pepper Sauté, 466
Okra Stewed with Tomatoes, 466
Olives, about, 30, 178
Omega-3 fatty acid, about, 197
Omelet, Cheese and Vegetable, 272

Onions
Bread, Onion-Herb, 100
Dip, Classic Onion, 24
Dip, Roasted Red Pepper and
Onion, 25
Pan-Roasted Red Onions, Green Beans
and, 454
Roasted Onions, Honey-, 467
Salsa, Burgers with Red Onion, 408
Salsa, Fiesta Onion, 30
Sandwiches, French Onion, 404
Vidalia Onions, Rosemary-
Glazed, 468
Oranges, Cranberry-Glazed, 445
Orzo and Peas, Parmesan, 230

Pancakes
Blueberry Pancakes, 77
Buckwheat-Honey Pancakes, 75
Honey Pancakes, 74
Whole Wheat-Oat Pancakes, 76
Pastas. *See also* specific types.
about, 229, 258, 261
Alfredo Sauce over Pasta, Herbed, 254
Angel Hair Pasta and Artichokes,
Lemon Chicken with, 338
Angel Hair Pasta, Dilled Shrimp
with, 235
Angel Hair Pasta with Fresh
Clams, 201
Caponata, Pasta, 258
Cherry Tomatoes over Pasta,
Herbed, 227
Chicken Pasta, Creole, 240
Lemon Pasta, 231
Noodle Pilaf, Rice-and-, 226
Orzo and Peas, Parmesan, 230
Penne Primavera, Creamy, 259
Penne, Shrimp-and-Squash, 236
Rigatoni, Ratatouille, 261
Salads
Artichoke-and-Pasta Salad, 391
Asian-Flavored Pasta Salad, 390
Chicken Pasta Salad, 400
Tortellini Soup, Italian, 427
Turkey, Peppers, and Basil with
Pasta, 359
Vegetarian Peanut Pasta, 262
Vermicelli with Tomato-Basil Sauce, 233
Peaches. *See also* Salsas, Sauces, Soups.
Bellini Spritzers, 46
Sherbet, Peach, 144
Spiced Peaches, Cinnamon-, 446
Peanut Butter
Cookies, Peanut Butter-and-Jelly, 160
Granola, Maple and Peanut Butter, 40
Pasta, Vegetarian Peanut, 262
Shake, Peanut Butter-Chocolate-
Banana, 51